also by Margaret Webster

THE SAME ONLY DIFFERENT

SHAKESPEARE WITHOUT TEARS

ROYAL HIGHNESS

Don't Put Your Daughter on the Stage

Don't Put
Your Daughter
on the Stage

Margaret Webster

ALFRED A. KNOPF   NEW YORK, 1972

THIS IS A BORZOI BOOK
PUBLISHED BY ALFRED A. KNOPF, INC.

Library of Congress Cataloging in Publication Data

Webster, Margaret, 1905—

Don't put your daughter on the stage.

Autobiography. I. Title.
PN2287.W4555A3   792'.0233'0924 [B]   72–2135
ISBN 0–394–47603–4

Manufactured in the United States of America

FIRST EDITION

For
Sybil and Lewis

Don't put your daughter on the stage, Mrs. Worthington,
Don't put your daughter on the stage.
The profession is overcrowded, the struggle is pretty tough,
And admitting the fact
That she's burning to act,
That isn't quite enough. . . .

NOEL COWARD

From a letter to Johanne Luise Heiberg:

Some say that the art of the theatre, born for and bound to the moment, must, like a soap-bubble or nocturnal meteor, dazzle, then burst to leave no trace. Free yourself from this dark thought! The very fact that your art is a child of fragrance, of the spirit, of a mood, of personality and imagination, and not something of wood and stone, or even a thought fixed fast in black and white, but a sprite for ever swinging free on beauty's vine, the fact that it lacks tangible form, renders it immune to the gnawing of time's worm. And that is what life truly means: to live in memory . . . to rest in people's minds free of the mildew and rust of age . . . and this lot has been granted to you.

HENRIK IBSEN

Contents

CONTENTS

Illustrations

Acknowledgments

My thanks are due to Sir Noel Coward and to Chappell and Co. Inc. (copyright 1935; copyright renewed) for permission to use the first quotation on the dedication page of this book, including, of course, its title; to Mr. Michael Meyer for the second, from a "Rhyming letter to Johanne Luise Heiberg," translated by him in his biography *Henrik Ibsen* (Doubleday, 1971); to the Society of Authors and Prof. Dan H. Laurence for extracts from the letters of George Bernard Shaw; to the *New York Times* for various letters and articles.

To the following for quotations from their letters, writings or speeches: Catherine Drinker Bowen, Marlon Brando, Cheryl Crawford, Elizabeth Fetske, Fiona Fraser, Larry Gates, Sir Alec Guinness, Louisa Horton Hill, Eva Le Gallienne (*With a Quiet Heart,* Viking Press, 1953), Louis Nizer, Gina Shields, Dame Sybil Thorndike, Tennessee Williams; the estates of John D. Rockefeller, Jr., Joseph Kesselring, John Van Druten.

For assistance in research, checking, typing and other chores sometimes tedious for them but invaluable for me: Eloise Armen, Edward Choate, Lehman Engel, Freda Gaye, Monica McCall, Mary Payne, Theodore Tenley, Berenice Weiler, Helen Willard; and to many other friends, for their memories, their encouragement and help of many kinds.

Prologue

Unfinished Letter to a Young Actress . . .

Dear Miss Worthington:

Many thanks for your letter.

As you point out, Noel Coward's advice to your mother is, in some respects, no longer valid; in the United States there is really no stage to go onto; in other ways it remains truer than ever. However, I see, of course, that since she has taken it to heart and is strongly opposed to your pursuing a stage career, you are the more determined to do so. The questions you ask on this subject are very usual. It would take a book to answer them. I append one.

I'm afraid that it doesn't fulfill your purpose, because it doesn't really offer advice. It may set a perspective. It begins in the happy, lost days when it was possible—just barely possible, with a lot of talent and more than a little bit of luck—to earn a living in the theatre. (You will note that I am talking about the theatre, not the entertainment industries. Which are you talking about?) It describes how this came to be impossible and illustrates some of the transitional and causative pressures; it tells what happened to me, personally, along the way.

I think you will agree that I had all the luck. I had some fine times —oh, yes, and some tough ones too. I hope I can share with you some of the memories . . . "to live in memory, to rest in people's minds, free of the mildew and rust of age . . ." Yes, that is worth going on the stage for, isn't it, Miss Worthington? I am grateful for the people

I knew, the things I saw, the things I was enabled to do. I hope I can share with you some of the fun. As to the advice I may have to offer you, I shall try and dredge it up at the end, in a letter you may not want to show to your mother.

As to the book, it comes under the heading of "unfinished business." I wrote another one; and my kind friends have said to me: "Why don't you pick it up where you left off?" Anyway the intention is kind. Of course you can never do that. The picker-up is not the same as the leaver-off, even though a quite brief span of time has intervened. In this case a still greater gulf is fixed.

The "it" to which they refer is a book called *The Same Only Different*—a sort of history of the theatre since 1800 seen through the eyes of five generations of my own family, who lived in it. It is mainly concerned with the English theatre, though there were substantial American excursions and it finished in 1937 in New York. If I were to continue it against a British background I could probably keep the same title and call it simply "Vol. II." But the intervening years, both for my father and mother during their lifetimes and for me until this day, have been spent chiefly in America; so the title won't do. I could call it *Totally Different* or *Something Else Again*. But as the book and I glare at each other I realize more and more sharply that these thirty-five years have revolutionized theatre patterns completely, and in ways undreamed of before.

In England it would be true, I think, to say that much of the Sameness remains even though the Differences are wide; not so in America. There the old landmarks have vanished, the old assumptions look ridiculous. "Broadway," for example, is a piece of Aztec nomenclature of which the original meaning has been lost. Old, and even quite recently "new," conditions have changed utterly. The present is a cluttered confusion, but at least it is not barren. The landscape lacks perspective, but it teems with life.

A lot of things have happened to me in that hurly-burly, senseless, here-we-go-round-the-mulberry-bush way that is common in the theatre. I have encountered many people, "famous" in their day, a few of whom may have left just a little more than a footprint in the sand. I have had some experiences which were like an echo from the past; my bus-and-truck Shakespeare Company, for instance, was only a blown-up version of the old Ben Greet vagabondage, covering greater distances on larger wheels. Others, such as directing opera at the Met, were totally new to me and as I try to write them down I have to convince myself that they really did happen.

I have survived lecture tours and recital tours—I can't think how, since they are designed to slay the strongest. I have directed professional theatre, university theatre, community theatre in New York and London, Berkeley and Birmingham, Johannesburg and darkest Wisconsin. My father and mother, deeply embedded in the London theatre for the first seventy years of their lives, spent the remaining decade in Hollywood, where she gained a small measure of fame that is still remembered. And of course there have been loves and deaths, wars and strifes, persecutions and comradeships, shattered hopes which broke my bones and unexpected, glorious things which uplifted my spirit.

Since I am now of the grandmother generation, and opinionated with it, I shall take advantage of the opportunity to air my opinions, or, more accurately, how and why I arrived at them. Sometimes I feel as if I had climbed aboard a hijacked plane which is now in full flight toward a destination I never heard of and don't want to reach. The fact that I helped to build the plane does not console me. Sometimes I seem to be living in foreign countries where the manners and customs are strange to me, but the people are not. We have a common language. I have always enjoyed travel. I still do. Come with me on the voyage. If you are still with me at the end, I will finish this letter. . . .

Don't Put Your Daughter on the Stage

Chapter One

---⁂---

Transitional

1

1937 was the year of transition; for my family as well as for me, though not for the same reasons. We kept on crossing the Atlantic in opposite directions, having, all of us, resided undisturbed on the Eastern side of it for nearly thirty years. My mother and father went to New York to play in *Night Must Fall.* Immediately after it closed they came back to London, and I went to New York to direct *Richard II* with Maurice Evans. It scored an unexpected success so great that —though I had no such idea at the time—it was to deflect my whole life to the Western side of the ocean. My mother returned to London and then almost immediately set off for Hollywood. We waved hello to each other in New York and I came back to London again and directed a play there.

I still didn't realize this was only to be a temporary interlude. I still set my sights on being a leading actress in London. But the fates had decided I was to act only rarely and was to be a director in New York. They were aided and abetted in these hidden designs because I have dual nationality; though brought up in England of British parents, I was born in New York. Each nation, therefore, claimed me as a national; and demanded some tax money in exchange. It has sometimes been an expensive advantage, but always a great freedom.

Meanwhile, my mother, dauntless as ever, had begun an entirely new career at the age of seventy-one. DAME MAY WHITTY IN "NIGHTY MUST FALL," a newspaper grandly announced, when she arrived in

3

Los Angeles to beard the MGM lion. Like me, she thought of her American laurels as transient and transitory. She, too, had no idea she was leaving her London life for good.

Ben, of course, went with her; without him even her courage might have faltered. He had been a star in the films of the early silent days, while she had made only a few fleeting appearances on those primitive, murky screens. It should have been very easy for him to make the transition to talkies, but somehow it never worked out. He was too old for romantic leads and too romantic for character parts and the British film industry had not yet reached its days of glory. As for May, I don't suppose she ever gave a thought to "doing a film" and certainly she never imagined that the "old beast in a wheelchair," as she described her part in Emlyn Williams's play, would ever carry her from the tiny Duchess Theatre in London to the immensity of Culver City.

When she arrived in Los Angeles she displayed far less excitement, shock, astonishment or delight than most newcomers. Though she was not an ardent moviegoer and was wholly ignorant of the popular literature of the trade, such as *Pic, Click* and *Foto-Lovers' Fancy,* she could hardly have evaded the waves of publicity from the flood tides of Hollywood. It was a much-discovered country from whose bourn all travelers loquaciously returned. Throughout her life she had maintained a voluminous correspondence with a host of friends, ancient and modern, English and American. She Had Been Warned. Among the accounts of gorgeous palaces and gilded, glamorous goings-on she had kept one letter which must have impressed her and which proved prophetic. It said: "This strange village is the only place in the world except London where one can have a garden and at the same time friends around the corner who are purely cosmopolitan in their culture and attitude. The writers come out, the artists and the New York actors. I don't know the big moving picture stars unless I play with them. We have nothing in common. They seem pleasant enough people."

May took no one's views for granted. She had a penetrating faculty of observation and a mind which reached its own conclusions without regard to accepted yardsticks. At first the kaleidoscope of Hollywood made no design. Visually, even, the impressions were fragmentary and unrelated. "This enormous straggling place," she wrote, "they think nothing of driving fifty miles to go to lunch." Miles of beautiful coastline and "charming little houses and then glaring, hideous gas-stations and pieces of waste ground where second-hand cars are dumped, looking so ugly you don't know how to bear it . . . huge advertising boards for everything from food to funeral parlours"; climbing mountain roads where it is impossible to find the number of the house you are looking for; and the wonderful view from the hills at night, with the lights of the city spread out below you like an immense, jeweled carpet. This view never lost its magic for her.

When Ben and May first arrived, Los Angeles was having its usual "unusual" January weather alternating between pouring rain and "smog," even though the smog was a mere gauzy ghost of what it has since become. Soon, however, came the long, brown months when everybody struggled with hose and sprinkler to retain the pride of color in their gardens. "I've never seen so many happily married people," she wrote, "who work so hard and tend their gardens in their spare time. . . . There is much less 'wild life' here than in New York or London. Everyone gets up too early." She soon began to find her own rhythm within this curious, remote community.

She was not impressed by its more grandiose displays and she found its pomposities quaint. But she did not moan or deprecate or scoff, as so many superior-sounding exiles used to do, forever lamenting the fate which had banished them from the glorious poverty of Art and made them into wealthy, celluloid citizens. She fully realized what Hollywood had to offer her, and it was a great deal: professional opportunity, financial security for herself and Ben, a peaceful pattern of living and many valued friendships. But she never yielded to the atmosphere. She impressed herself upon it and fulfilled herself within it.

She approached the medium itself, the craft of movie-making, with more curiosity than apprehension. The achievements of the technical departments she regarded as plainly magical—"all the wonders of earth and sky instantly created as required as if by the waving of a wand." But she was quite honestly ignorant of the identity of all the world-famous faces which now surrounded her in the commissary of MGM. This was not arrogance on her part; she had quite simply never seen them before. She rose to the new challenge without being in the least intimidated. Ten years later an interviewer asked her whether she was "nervous" of trying the new medium of television. She answered "Afraid of it? Never! I count on its giving me an opportunity to learn something new about my profession." In this frame of mind she entered the MGM factory.

Obviously she was lucky in that her first part was the familiar "Mrs. Bramson" whom she had played for two years in London and New York, rather than a two-dimensional stranger. She found, as was to be expected, that Mrs. Bramson's surroundings had become somewhat grander. The commonplace little bungalow in the middle of the woods was now a spacious country house, standing in its own grounds. In the extensive gardens every flower bloomed simultaneously, from crocuses to chrysanthemums "and even a few cabbages dotted carelessly about." There must have been an improbable number of gardeners. Even the two village policemen, who functioned at the end as necessary rescuers, had become a troop. When the picture was later released the publicity department made much of this. "Disguise heralds as English Bobbies," ran their promotion instructions, "and send them round town frightening clients."

May had hoped that she might be lucky enough to retain the services of her most valued comrade from the stage production—the wheelchair in which she had to spend almost the entire action. Their association had had a stormy beginning. "I didn't know then that the chair had a will of its own and required much humouring and wheedling." In Edinburgh, where the original try-out took place, the stage had a perceptible slope, or rake, "down which the chair careered in unbounded glee and celerity. It had a brake on one wheel only, and when in my horror I applied this with much force, it turned completely round and insisted on my playing the whole scene with my back to the audience."

Finally, however, the chair and she "became great friends and it was really most obedient and lovable." It played in New York and she tried to get it a Hollywood contract. But this was not to be. At the close of the New York run the chair, along with all the other contents of Mrs. Bramson's bungalow, including her clothes, was taken away to be burned. "This," she wrote, "was not for witchcraft," but because of the regulations governing the importation of alien scenery into the United States. She and the MGM property master had to search long and hard for a successor which would be meek in temper, light to handle and didn't squeak at the mike. A tribute to their final choice was made by a "fan" letter: "As for the chair—you almost made it talk. I never saw an inanimate object so expressive."

She grew to feel quite at home in the guarded vastnesses of Culver City. She got used to the routine of early rising, long drives to the studio and scarcely shorter ones around the lot itself. A car would

6

arrive to take her, "usually in the pouring rain," to lunch in the star-studded commissary. In the adjoining half of it there would generally be a mob of "extras." She studied the changing proletariat with fascination. "Today," she wrote, "an epidemic of peasants." She even got used to being "made up" by other people—an unnerving experience for anyone who had done their own make-up for nearly sixty years; rather like being in hospital and having someone brush your teeth. On the set she submitted meekly to the ceaseless ministrations, dabbings and tidyings of the make-up men and hairdressers—"fine artists and wonderful people," she wrote. The thoroughness and efficiency of the wardrobe and prop departments amazed her. "There is nothing you want that is not provided for you like magic."

Rosalind Russell and Robert Montgomery were unfailingly kind to her. After she had shot her first scene with him, he refused to believe that she had had no previous movie experience. He said "You have been making movies all your life, in the bathroom." A few days later she wrote: "I've been in the Studio most days—very tiring, though I have a stand-in for lighting and a little screened-off room with a sofa to rest on . . . but we do long-shots, close-ups, close-ups of everyone in the scene and it's an interminable game. We spent the whole of Thursday shooting—I'd have liked to—a cat walking across the garden; but when the cat walked Miss Russell dried up, and when she almost said the lines, the cat fled into the bushes." This was not an easy discipline for an actress who had been reared to play twelve different classic parts in a two-week repertory.

Before long they reached the sequence in which Mrs. Bramson, left alone in her cottage, works herself up into a hysteria of fear—a long, solo sequence in which, for the first time, she leaves her wheelchair and walks about the room. Even in the theatre it was a considerable feat of self-sustained emotional pressure. The director and cameraman had broken up the shot into different "takes" so that she would move into different rooms in the bungalow rather than attempting the entire sequence undivided, as it had necessarily been in the theatre set. But it came out disjointed and unsatisfactory. Finally the director said, "What did you do on the stage?" Very diffidently, she showed him. He shook his head. "I don't think we can follow you like that." The cameraman came forward. "Let her go wherever she likes," he said, "we'll follow her."

They set up the lights, boom, cameras. "Take One." She played it straight through, a sequence lasting over two minutes. She waited for the succeeding retakes, close-ups and so forth. "OK," said the director, "that's it." And exactly so it appeared in the finished picture. It earned her the label of "One-take Whitty," of which she was jealously proud, and a round of spontaneous applause from her fellow craftsmen at the Gala Premiere in Grauman's Chinese Theatre—"which," she wrote mildly, "was considered extraordinary."

Night Must Fall won her an Oscar nomination, abstruse tributes from distinguished psychiatrists, crediting her with analytical penetration she had never even thought of, and simpler applause from a vast number of fans. Moreover it moved the studio to take up their option on her contract and cast her for the leading part in one of their next pictures, *The Thirteenth Chair*. She wrote: "The 13th Chair indeed! If it's not one sort of chair it's another." She thought it an old-fashioned story and a poor script and the part "enormous and terrifying." Even praise from Louis B. Mayer in person did not allay her fears.

> I've had to concoct a strange, polyglot, common sort of speech with a touch of Irish. So clever, they think, so accidental I know. I gave my opinion to Ben of the day's rushes—"Bar the fact that I looked older than God—that my nose was right across my face—and that I blinked a bit and lapsed into the purest English—I was very good!"

When she saw the preview she conceded that her work "was at least sincere" though she still thought *The Thirteenth Chair* "a creaking article of furniture."

She was also following the well-trodden Hollywood path to the dentist. Apart from the vaunted "gaieties" of Beverly Hills, she summed up her life as "work at the Studio, a permanent wave and the dentist. All painful." Her next assignment was on a picture called *I Met My Love Again,* for Walter Wanger,

> I am a very healthy woman; but apparently the shock of my niece's elopement with the wrong man has been too much for me and has caused me to take to my bed for ten years. While in bed I remain very strong and vigorous and extremely English of accent (by request). I live in an old-fashioned calico nightgown and have remarkably thick hair, very tidy. The bed is trying, as, even in the hottest of weather it has to have an eiderdown and a hot-water-bottle filled with boiling water. When, after ten years of this, my niece comes back and announces her return to her first love, I leap out of bed completely cured and we drink healths in my medicine, aloin, bella donna and cascara.

While she was still undergoing this ordeal by hot-water-bottle, she started work simultaneously as Napoleon's mother in *Marie Walewska,* with Greta Garbo and Charles Boyer. It would be hard to imagine a more improbable piece of casting than Dame May as the tough, ferocious, old Corsican peasant who was "Madame Mère." But throughout her movie career she was regarded as a suitable mother for famous characters of history, no matter what their status or nationality.

Of Garbo, May wrote: "She is very charming, very shy, very afraid of any intrusion on her privacy, very beautiful to look at, very easy to act with," except that she would eat large quantities of garlic and this was disconcerting in close-up shots. Rumor said that it was intended to discourage proximity. May was not happy with the director and once, when he had told her to do something she found hard to interpret, she said to Garbo "Would you do it for me?" ". . . and Garbo did," said May, "beautifully, and it helped me very much."

During this picture the waiting-about was even more wearisome and interminable than usual but Garbo never complained. "She looked like a lovely flower," May wrote, "but is quite completely remote and unreal like the set. . . . I'm miserable, and miserably bad. I feel like the merest, rottenest beginner; but it will be a nice corrective to my swollen head." The shooting dragged on with interminable rewrites and retakes; she had hurt her knee during one of the more acrobatic shots and was in a lot of pain; her supposed "big scene" at her Imperial son's coronation in Notre Dame turned out to involve endless costume fittings and one long shot over the back of her shoulder. She did not enjoy herself.

Nevertheless, she was beginning to make a life outside the studio. She had rented a small house in Westwood Village ("more unlike a village than a car to a coster's barrow") and acquired, with some alarm, a car, a chauffeur and a treasured housekeeper. She held her first Hollywood party, sixty-five guests in relays beginning at 4 p.m. and finishing—she never knew when, since she had gone to bed soon after midnight to be ready for a 6 a.m. morning call. The smaller gatherings which had been so strong a characteristic of her London life began again. The British colony included many old friends and there were American actors and writers equally loved and cherished. Her home began to exercise the same attraction which had made her London flat in Bedford Street the meeting place of many minds and the refuge of many hearts.

Old patterns repeated themselves. The Screen Actors Guild was having one of its recurrent crises. There was talk of a strike. May, a warrior from the frontier battles of British Equity, took a lively interest. Her chairman's sense of order was appalled by "the wildness and lack of control" of the meetings, but she was, of course, pro-Guild. She wrote that she had "managed to convert some of the moss-backs" at a large gathering of agitated Britishers, and that her hostess, who was coping with neuralgia as well as the British, suddenly said, "You've made me laugh so much, you've cured me." But despite the friendliness, the hospitality, the acclaim, and even the climate, May felt "remote," as she put it, cut off.

It was much worse for Ben. Her time and energies were fully absorbed, but he had nothing to do. He played in occasional pictures—small parts which displayed his still-beautiful profile and did not burden him with too many lines to learn. People loved him immediately for his gentleness, courtesy and unexpectedly shrewd wit; but he missed the familiar theatre talk of things and friends he knew, buses to get about in, the almost nightly "spot of bridge" at the Garrick Club and, of course, his accustomed job. He wrote dolefully:

> There is only one thing here, which is the talkies and the entirely unimportant doings of their exponents in their daily and nightly escapades. The papers here are the limit of vulgarity and inanity and all mention of important things in the world is barred.

Charles Brackett once cynically remarked that the banner headline on page one of any Hollywood paper was likely to be "L.A. DOG CHASES L.A. CAT OVER L.A. FENCE." For a war or an election or an international issue, turn to page 6. I hasten to add that times and papers have changed since; but Hollywood then was a world unto itself, with its own crises, its own interests, its own values, its own jokes and even its own murder cases, always the juiciest on record. In the days before television it was almost as remote as the then inviolate moon.

Back in London, in 1938, May did her only British picture, the one by which she is probably best remembered, *The Lady Vanishes*. She wrote:

> I have spent this last week in a continental train being shot at, secreted in a very small cupboard with my feet in a wash-basin and

being lifted out by Michael Redgrave, climbing out of a window assisted by this same charming young actor, clambering down and running away over very uneven ground under a heavy fusillade of shots —eventually throwing up my arms and disappearing from view. I have never been asked to do things like that in the theatre.

The Lady Vanishes is often revived, not only on TV but in movie houses; it is one of Hitchcock's best achievements. May's performance as "the Lady" had the great value of authenticity. You really believed her as the character she pretended to be. You were genuinely astonished by the ending. While regarding movie goings-on with amused detachment, she had the faculty of quite simply *being* the character she played—entering into it as calmly as you would put on a coat, buttoning it up and wearing it without fuss, as if it had belonged to her for years.

It was a strenuous ordeal, however, and it was pleasant to be working from her home on Bedford Street instead of having to travel several thousand miles for the exercise.

At this time also, the BBC was beginning to send out its first television programs. These early experiments were cut short by the war; but my mother had managed to get involved in them. My father reported that she seemed to be quite good on the rare occasions when the picture was clear enough to be recognizable; but he didn't think the medium would ever be suitable for plays or acting.

2

Meanwhile, I pursued a different set of transatlantic travels. *Richard II* would have run indefinitely had it been produced in the days of air-conditioning. But in 1937 no production, however successful, could face the heat of the New York summer. There was nobody in town. *Richard* was laid aside to be revived for a month in September, followed by a coast-to-coast tour, and I spent the summer months in London. On the strength of our first success, however, Maurice Evans and his associates were contemplating other things. Maurice wanted to do *Major Barbara* and I had suggested *Androcles and the*

Lion; I had been commissioned to find out from George Bernard Shaw whether the rights to either or both plays would be available.

My father had known Shaw well and played in several of the original productions of his plays; I had a lesser acquaintance with him, but he replied to my letter promptly and received me with great cordiality. Twinkling at me acutely from under his eyebrows, he inquired why I had taken up directing instead of acting, for which I "appeared to have every qualification." This being my view also, I was charmed, as he intended. He discouraged the idea of *Major Barbara* but was enthusiastic about *Androcles,* which he said ought to be revived regularly every year, like *Peter Pan.* He was pleased that I had approached him directly, in person. "The Americans," he said, "are a very lonely people." They generally seemed to find it necessary to creep up on him by attempting to bribe or charm his secretary, his typist, the doorman, the taxi driver or the policeman on the corner.

Blanche Patch came in and laid a card on his table. "You did give him an appointment," she murmured. Shaw waved his hand in slight irritation. "Show him in," he said, adding to me, "Might amuse you." The caller turned out to be Colonel Ralph Heyward Isham, the original discoverer of the Boswell papers at Malahide Castle. He had just come back from Ireland with a new chapter to add to this fascinating literary treasure hunt, involving the discovery of a new cache of papers stuffed away in a box of croquet balls. He even produced a small green leather account book recording the day-to-day expenditures of Samuel Johnson, entered in his own hand. I was spellbound. Not so Shaw. He half-listened, doodled on the blotting paper, grunted occasionally and saw Colonel Isham out with evident relief. We returned to the more congenial topic of *Androcles.*

The New York success of *Richard II* had prompted various American managers to offer me other productions, some of them wildly unsuited to my talents. I had been offered Paul Vincent Carroll's *Shadow and Substance* to direct, went to Dublin to see it, arranged for Cedric Hardwicke to star in it and bought it for Eddie Dowling —one of the *Richard II* management. (He eventually did it with enormous success and another director.) I resisted, easily, the blandishments of an outfit which wanted me to direct an "adaptation" of *Antony and Cleopatra* with Tallulah Bankhead. The adaptation was of a blood-curdling ineptitude, and the production, when it eventually appeared, gave rise to the classic comment that Tallulah barged down the Nile and sank. This was unfair to her. There was no barge.

I accepted an offer to direct a play in the West End of London, the first I had ever had. The compass needle of my life, veering westward across the Atlantic, swung sharply back again. "At last," I thought, "I'm beginning to get jobs in England." It was eighteen years before I got another. This was a slap-up affair, in the elegant English tradition; the play, *Old Music* by Keith Winter, an extremely successful dramatist of those years; a star-studded cast; scenery by Rex Whistler; the theatre, the St. James's, a white-and-gold and red-plush playhouse which had been an important part of my whole family's history and was, for many decades, one of London's most fashionable theatres. (*Richard II* had been playing at the "Saint James" in New York; I had to guard against the hideous solecism of mixing up the pronunciations.)

The manager was the formidable Gilbert Miller, a power on both sides of the Atlantic, whose expansive white shirt front was to be seen regularly in the exclusive "Grills" of ocean liners, and the hautest hotels of Paris, London and the Côte d'Azur. He gave lavish parties to high society (in limited numbers) and Royalty called his wife Kitty. He had a reputation for unpredictable bouts of ferocity in his theatres, which were, nevertheless, impeccably well run, backstage and front, by a staff of tremendous efficiency whom he paid highly and bullied frequently. I had been a small-part actress at the St. James's only a few years before and hadn't much enjoyed it. The change of status made me nervous. After the first play-reading, Gilbert went off to "take the waters" at some continental spa and left me on my own.

Ten days or so later I was walking up the red-carpeted stairs to the executive offices when I heard the voice of his production stage manager. "Of course," he was saying, "she's doing absolutely everything that Gilbert hates most." I paled, retreated half a flight, coughed loudly and stamped up again. Cunning research revealed that, supposedly, I was letting the actors take too much time to get settled; that I was not forcing the pace or dictating the surface style of the production. I thought this over. Gilbert was due back in a few days. Should I spend them imitating a drill sergeant, and so present him with a spurious example of directorial slickness, or should I stick to my own timetable, make the foundations solid and rely on the final week for the spit-and-polish? I decided to trust to my own convictions and his seeing eye; and he did see, quite clearly, what remained to be done but didn't appear at all disturbed because I had not yet done it.

His suggestions were often very much to the point; but he disconcerted me considerably by sitting beside me at rehearsals and starting to puff and groan and thump his knee with his fist and generally manifest disapproval; I could never find out of what, and concluded it must be indigestion or asthma. Also, he would insist on giving the actors inflections. Now, as an actor, there is nothing which throws me off balance more completely than a dictated tune imposed on me for some reason that I do not understand. *"What* is the meaning of this?" "What is the meaning of *this?"* "What is the *meaning* of this?" It ceases to have any. Gilbert's required readings rarely made any sense to me but there was never time to argue. I couldn't hand them on to the actors because my own ear rejected them; so I used to say "Yes, Gilbert" and hope he'd forget. I have to admit that he seldom did.

The play was laid in the period of the Crimean War and the sets were magnificent—"Grand but somber," Gilbert had commanded Rex Whistler, "like my house in Farm Street." The clothes were exquisite, the accessories and furnishings perfectly chosen, nothing skimped or done meanly. It was in the splendid tradition of "drawing-room comedy" in London's West End. Only I had a faint, cold fear that it was all rather overimpressive. It was completely authentic without, somehow, being real. I was afraid the simple, sentimental little play would not stand up to all this somber grandeur. We spent two weeks in Manchester and Glasgow of minor though diligent polishing. The dress rehearsals were complicated by a second-act thunderstorm in an exterior set with lightning and "livid" skies and all the tortures of realism in a proscenium set. While we waited for the electricians Gilbert sustained me with exhaustive dissertations on the technical equipment and working methods of every important theatre in Europe and America, together with brief outlines of the relevant personnel and their major achievements. I was so fascinated by his phenomenal memory and knowledge that I quite forgot to fuss about the thunderstorm.

Meanwhile, I was preparing to head westward again, dealing with the problems of my dual nationality and rival passports, packing up my London apartment. The opening night of *Old Music* was of the smartest possible West End variety, with white ties and titles and fashion reporters and crowds at the stage door. The cast played beautifully, there was much applause, the rank-and-fashion were most gracious, Gilbert thanked me handsomely, the notices were good to moderate and the following day I was on a boat again, waving farewell, though I didn't know it, to a lot of things, including the St. James's tradition.

Some years later there was a small epilogue. One of the stars was Greer Garson. She made a big and deserved success which led her directly into the orbit of MGM and on to top movie stardom. The next time I saw her was at a big Charity Ball in Hollywood where she was sitting at a table with Louis B. Mayer and other studio grandees. She greeted me with the utmost cordiality. She asked had I met Mr. Mayer and I modestly shook my head; whereupon she turned radiantly to the Great Man and said, "Oh, Mr. Mayer, I do want you to meet Margaret Webster, who directed that play you liked me in so much." It is a form of introduction which I have always treasured.

3

New York, in August 1937, was as different from London as could be imagined. The city was having one of its hot spells, the first I had experienced. All energy evaporated in the blinding blaze of the streets, and at rehearsals the actors wilted in thick airlessness. Your clothes stuck to you, and everything you touched, leaned or sat on stuck to them. The nights were a black blanket of moist, furry hotness. Moreover, the American Legion was having a Convention. All the shops round Times Square were boarded up, carrying on their wooden windows the legend "WELCOME LEGIONNAIRES." The hazards of getting to the "Saint James" Theatre by crosstown bus included running a gauntlet of toy cannon playfully fired through its open windows. Maurice melted inside the velvet robes of Richard II and had to place his remarks on the death of kings delicately between the explosions and screams outside on 44th Street. "Should I wait for them?" he asked distractedly; but I was afraid this might mean waiting till the end of the Convention. We survived, and presently Richard became himself again and took to the road. Soon afterwards I was baptized in this new field.

I was waiting for Hardwicke and Dowling to set a date for *Shadow and Substance*. Meanwhile I took another look at Broadway. My previous experience had been brief but intensive. I had grasped the fact that most of the plans and schemes so frenziedly hurled about were merely fantasies. Sam Zolotow, drama columnist of the *New York Times,* was always announcing them convincingly in print even before the participants had settled what they were supposed to be doing or when or with whom. A lot of people got very excited and upset, but that didn't matter very much because none of it was real anyway.

In those dear, dead days money was not "tight" and a show could get produced handsomely for a quarter of what a shoestring costs in the Nineteen-Seventies. A lot of reputable little managements were able to put on shows intermittently if not continuously. The only constant factor was the theatre-owning Shubert Brothers who took toll of failure and success alike. The public could still get tickets for what they wanted to see approximately when they wanted to see it without having to hock their diamond earrings. Nevertheless, to my English-trained mind costs and prices were already much too high, the gambles too risky for comfort, the operations of the Street a little frightening. Certainly it had vitality—and achievement. The season of 1937–38 included *Our Town, Of Mice and Men, Susan and God, Amphitryon 38, On Borrowed Time* and *Golden Boy.* It also included a couple of crashing flops in which all three Websters, by a feat of extraordinary dexterity, managed to get themselves included.

I had chosen, ill-advisedly, an innocuous little piece called *Young Mr. Disraeli,* which had had a success in London. The cast was talented but not box-office, the management amiable but not forceful. My mother and father were en route from Hollywood to London; May accepted a part in an equally harmless little affair with Florence and Frederic March, and there was a good little part for my father in *Young Mr. Disraeli,* which he played charmingly. Both shows opened out of town.

Ours was in Baltimore at an ancient, once pleasant, old theatre called the Maryland, now derelict and rat-infested. I began to find out about American "try-outs"; they were very different from the dignified tinkerings we had performed on *Old Music* during our pre-London weeks. There were nervous suggestions for recasting, feverish gropings for a new second-act curtain, frantic fumblings with cuts and transpositions. But I soon realized that the play suffered from a marrow-of-the-bones malady, not to be cured by skin-disease remedies. (The discussions, as I later learned, were stability itself compared with what the Theatre Guild could do in Boston.)

I also found out a bit more about unions, specifically the stage hands' all-powerful IATSE. There was a certain door which, at a certain moment, had to be slammed and stay slammed. It never did. The defect could have been put right by a new catch, a screwdriver and fifteen minutes of applied effort by the production carpenter—or even me. But. The door belonged to a piece of scenery used only in Act III which was hoisted up into the air at the end of each performance. To lower it for the purpose of mending the catch a crew of ten men would have to be called and paid for three hours. Mildly, I suggested that the piece of scenery be left on the floor, attended to the following day by our carpenter during his regular hours, and hoisted up into the air again in the evening when the regular crew came on. This could not be done either. Why not? Well, it just couldn't. There was a perceptible feeling that I was being unfair to organized labor, and the actor learned a neat trick of holding it shut with his shoulder, which did nothing to help him play the scene.

The play was mismanaged into opening in New York in competition with a more important show. The critics therefore came to the final dress rehearsal and printed their reviews (devastating) on the morning of the official first night. The actors played with enormous gallantry and spirit, having already seen their death sentences. Meanwhile, May had had the novel experience of being fired from her show in Pittsburgh and replaced by a well-known American character actress, who was then fired in Detroit and replaced by my mother again in, I think, Cleveland. Her play, like ours, lasted just till the end of its first Broadway week.

Not the same week, however. Even in this brief interlude we managed to get separated. I was back in Baltimore wrestling with some "try-out" matinees of *Henry IV Part I* for Maurice Evans. He had thought he'd like to play Falstaff. ("Are you fat and lusty?" I had asked. "I can act," he justly replied.) Since the play is a chronological sequel to *Richard II*, it seemed possible to use the same cast, costumes (except for Falstaff) and much of the scenery. He and I had been brought up on doing things for free and he had managed to work around the actors and Equity matters so as to make it possible. All the same, it cost him more than he liked and gave me less than I needed. May recorded that she came upon me poring over my prompt copy, vainly trying to contrive the Battle of Shrewsbury from the *Richard II* manpower. She said that I finally hurled it to the floor, exclaiming, "I *cannot* make two armies with eight people. Maurice will *have* to give me one more."

While I was thus entangled, the Messrs. Hardwicke and Dowling decided that this was the moment, the one and only moment, to put *Shadow and Substance* into rehearsal. It became one of the successes of the season (as I had been sure it would), and I learned to get things in writing. (As a matter of fact, I learned this lesson imperfectly and still have a tendency toward the words of gentlemen, or honor among thieves.) Anyway, May and Ben decided, very naturally, to make their way as soon as possible to the rural peace of London, and I thought it would be nice to cast aside all this directorial rock-and-roll and indulge in a little quiet therapy, like acting. The Lunts were playing in *Amphitryon 38,* and I read that they were about to start rehearsing a production of *The Seagull.* There was an irony to this. John Gielgud had recently done one in London, and I was so heartbroken because he did not cast me as Masha that it impelled me powerfully toward the United States. Anyhow, I wrote to the Lunts and asked if I might read for Masha. They agreed. I read it abominably and they hired me.

To anyone familiar with the American theatre from the early Twenties to the middle Fifties it must seem presumptuous, even absurd, to introduce the Lunts; and of course there have been opportunities of seeing one or both of them since then. But there are an increasing number of unfortunates who never did see them. I have heard a college student, in the theatre department too, ask the almost blasphemous question: "Who were the Lunts?"

Alfred Lunt and Lynn Fontanne were great actors. Individually, there were others as fine or finer; but as a team, especially in high comedy, they were unequaled. Their range was wider than they often elected to show, as witness their simple and deeply moving performances in Robert Sherwood's *There Shall Be No Night.* Their playing together was flawlessly, invisibly synchronized. It was like watching two beautiful tennis players, two beautiful dancers; like listening to piano and violin perfectly answering each other.

It became the fashion during the days of "Method" supremacy to derogate them a little. Yes, they were mannered; yes, they were, if you like, "artificial"—but oh! the brilliance of the artifice, the electric vitality unleashed to leap over the footlights in a glittering cascade, the precision and the sure dexterity of their craft! Yes, some of their plays were trivial, or had no social message, and they seldom played a classic. But do not think they couldn't have played *The Balcony* or *Endgame* to demolish all competition had such plays been of their era. They were, quite simply, superb.

The Lunts in Chekhov, though? This was quite a new departure. The rehearsals were immensely interesting. As a director, you get very few opportunities to watch others direct. I have always wanted passionately to find out how different people do it, whether they are the skilled craftsmen of the old guard or the momentary "innovators" of a new style. So I welcomed the experience of being directed again, and especially of watching the Lunts at work and perhaps finding out what lay behind their seemingly effortless performances. I had no temptation whatever to be a back-seat driver. I only wanted to sit still and listen. I did not know the official "director," Robert Milton. I suspected that the Lunts did most of it themselves. In essence this was probably true, at least so far as their own acting went. But it did not work out as crudely as that. Bob Milton set his own pace; and a very curious one it was. I wrote to my mother:

> We rehearsed all Sunday afternoon and evening. He fussed and worried over the first act till I thought I should go mad—took five days over it—tries every detail of movement or business over and over again till it has been elaborated in every possible variety of ways. And yet he leaves you curiously free "inside." To me it is cart-before-the-horse directing and it took me a little while to adjust myself; but it's not without value, since his sense of detail is perceptive and often illuminating. It is as if he made all the icing and then left you to fill in your own cake from underneath.

The London revival had had a very notable cast including Edith Evans, John Gielgud, Peggy Ashcroft and Stephen Haggard. I was struck by the contrast between the two methods of approach:

> The Arkadina-Trigorin scene in Act III is astonishing—flexible, various, funny, true and slightly horrible. The whole production will, in its contrast to the London one, be typical of the difference between the best examples of English and American theatre. John's—of course

with Komisarjevsky's direction—was more balanced, smoother, more polished, more exact, much more polite, rather more beautiful and not nearly so alive. Looking back, it has a slightly dead-ish dreary-ish air to me—except for Edith, of course—in spite of its great beauty. I think this will be cruder, rougher, not nearly so right in detail, but much more flexible, with dashes of grotesque comedy and some splashes of real, harsh ugliness that may well be nearer to the "all-out-ness" of the Russians.

But I could not pretend that I was happy. I was exasperated by the constant picking-away at bits without any coordination of collective feeling or tempo in a scene. I felt unreal. Mechanical hurdles loomed enormous, and the "freedom inside" which I had hoped would occur was no more than a floating vacuum of insecurity, a feeling of no-relation to anybody or anything else in the play.

I was puzzled by the Lunts. They were wonderful to play with. They gave out a sort of electricity with which you yourself inevitably became charged. They did not, however, appear at all disconcerted by the director's wholly external approach. Indeed, it seemed to be a reflection of their own methods. They could be stopped cold by a faulty piece of mechanics, a lack of cohesion in movement or business, a tiny snag as to who sat when or crossed where. But if they lit upon exactly the right "sit" or "cross," it was as if they were suddenly enfranchised, even for whole stretches of a subtle and difficult scene. Lynn was fascinated by the last-act sequence where Arkadina, Trigorin, Masha and the others sit over a game of Lotto, making conversation which appears to be desultory but is actually shafted and feathered like arrows. After the curtain fell on the last act of *Amphitryon 38,* we would sit on the darkened stage of the Shubert Theatre solemnly playing Lotto—sometimes for a couple of hours. We did not always run the lines; we just played Lotto; an exceedingly dull game. I cannot imagine how the stage hands were induced to allow us to indulge this fancy, but we did.

The greatest hurdle in the play appeared to be the first entrance of Arkadina and Trigorin, accompanied by Masha, Sorin, Medvedyenko and Shamrayeff. With this we tinkered endlessly, while Lynn and Alfred tried it sitting, standing, walking, crossing, lighting a cigarette, picking up a glass, sitting on a chair, with innumerable permutations and combinations of these things. Bob Milton suggested everything under the sun. Nothing "did." Finally they asked me if I had any ideas. Very gingerly I ventured the notion that it all depended, didn't it, on what had been going on at the dinner table from which we had all just come and consequently on the precise state of mind in which we all arrived in view of the audience. This kind of approach had not been tried before, at least not in my hearing. It was received with great courtesy but no response. We returned immediately to the vexed question of how far Lynn should walk and where she should stop. This went on all through the try-out weeks, when we would stay in the theatre after the show to work on it some more, and even after the New York opening. I don't think they were ever satisfied.

I can hear superior voices saying "Why, they just wanted to make sure of the entrance hand"; but this is not so; they got the applause without trying. Even more superior remarks might well come from the so-called "Method," or Stanislavsky, disciples. For me, it is only another illustration of the fact that, in the theatre, one actor's meat is another one's poison and that talent cannot be tucked away into pigeonholes of orthodoxy. The Lunts were a law unto themselves, and in their presence one could do nothing but rejoice.

Nevertheless, I thought they took a curiously outside-to-inside path. En route, however, there sprang instinctive, extraordinary jets of emotional feeling. Lynn came to me one day and talked of the scene at the end of the first act where Masha suddenly breaks down and pours out to Dr. Dorn all the bottled-up anguish of her heart. "I think," said Lynn, "it should start like this . . ." and she gave a cry of agony, like an animal in unbearable pain. I was taken entirely by surprise. It wasn't my cry or my pain; it wasn't anything I should ever have dreamed of for myself; it was grotesque, uninhibited, revealing, wholly right. I went home and worked very hard. I made it into my own pain and wrung from it my own cry—I mean, of course, Masha's cry. Afterwards I found it frighteningly difficult to bring myself, at every performance, to the pitch where the cry broke from me irrepressibly, inevitably, not forethought or manufactured. That, obviously, is where craft and discipline must come in—commodities which the Lunts had in abundance but which are generally in shorter supply than raw emotion or histrionic masturbation.

Nevertheless, I don't think the Lunts were entirely happy in Chekhov. They could neither free themselves in their own ways nor yield to the author and trust him to do the work in his. Only Sidney Greenstreet seemed able continuously to be what he was playing. During the long periods of silent listening with which my Masha-world was filled, I would constantly be aware of him, sitting on the other side of the stage, and always my thoughts went to "Uncle Sorin," never to Sidney Greenstreet. Yet I suppose I enjoyed my little scene with Trigorin as much as anything in the play. The temptation to enjoyment is insidious. The scene is full of "laughs" and got them. One additional flick of an eye and it goes over the borderline of truth and becomes what I used to call Cheating on Chekhov.

I used to watch the scenes which didn't concern me with equal concentration; but I have inherited—or so I think—stringent theatre discipline and good manners. I would blot myself under a seat or behind a piece of scenery so that no one should be disturbed by uninvited prying eyes. The privacy of actors in the process of creation should be absolute. One day, however, Alfred sought me out in the darkness of the back seats. Self-consciously, and with many softening preliminaries, he told me that Lynn had asked would I please not watch her scenes. I was appalled and stammered every kind of apology. He assured me that it was no fault of mine; but, he said, "Lynn is sure you must be thinking how much better Edith Evans was"; which, at that moment, was identically what I had been thinking.

Shortly before we were due to leave for our out-of-town opening, Alexander Woollcott came to watch a run-through. We all felt despondent and frustrated; but he was deeply moved. He made a little speech to the cast. He said that he believed this kind of theatre was like the monasteries in the Dark Ages; that it kept a torch alight; that it was beautiful and holy. He called it "a sanctuary for the spirit of man amid the bloody violence of a marching world." No wonder we set out for Baltimore (Baltimore again!) "with magic in our eyes."

The magic was dissipated, naturally, under the stresses of the dress rehearsals. Robert Edmond Jones had designed some beautiful sets, very difficult to light, and lit them beautifully—but it took time. I had thought his costumes a little on the grand side, and had begged my way out of a charming black lace evening dress for Act I into a plain shirtwaist and skirt. He was generous and humble about this, as he always was over any question which touched the sensitive integrity of his theatre mind. He and Stark Young (the translator) and some of the actors would sit up till the small hours in absorbed and fascinating discussions. Lynn was furious when she heard about it. She said, very properly, that we should have been conserving our energies for the work we had to do. To hoard and direct vitality is an important part of the business of acting. Of this, the Lunts were a living proof.

The New York notices were mixed for the production, good for me personally. Lynn immediately cabled my parents to tell them so; good also for the young seventeen-year-old who was making her New York debut as Nina—Uta Hagen. Over the weeks of the run we played ourselves into some sort of a team. Some of the play's quality came through brilliantly; but there was a lack of rhythm, of wholeness, possibly of a kind of trust. We never let ourselves be carried along by the flowing curent of the play. We breasted the waves strongly, gaily even; but we shouldn't have had to thrash around so much.

I enjoyed being in their theatre, which, as always, they made a happy one, and I very much enjoyed being responsible for nothing but myself. Shadows of other responsibilities, however, were beginning to close in on me. Maurice Evans had returned from the tour of *Richard II*. It had been enormously praised but it had not been altogether easy to "sell." Maurice was almost unknown outside of New York, and in the South, Bill Shakespeare was a football player. In one theatre the house manager was overheard saying to the operator of the candy concession, "Put away the Baby Ruths and the Love Nests—this is a class show."

We were already deep in preparations for our next season's work. They had to be completed before we both left New York. The project was already becoming pervasive and absorbing. It was a production of the uncut *Hamlet*.

The Seagull had only been put on for a limited run because the Lunts had a commitment to play *Amphitryon* in London. Early in the summer of 1938 I sailed with them for Europe on that most beautiful of all doomed ships, the *Normandie*.

Chapter Two

"Go, Bid the Soldiers Shoot"

1

During the six months from April to October my life was dominated by two figures, Hamlet and Hitler. Truth compels me to reverse the world-wide order of importance, even though my spirit
was well aware of this incongruity. All through the summer, wherever I went, in London, Paris, Genoa, Amsterdam, even the small
villages of Italy, Holland and England, I felt I could almost touch
the appalled sense of impending catastrophe. It was like sliding
down a precipice, trying to imagine that some obstacle would somehow intervene to stop you, grasping at air. The air at which I grasped
was *Hamlet.*

It had never before been professionally played in New York in
the full, uncut text and we had decided to open with that. But we
did not mean to play it at every performance; at least five times a
week we would give a more normal cut version for the weaker
brethren. Strangely, perhaps, I had never been an impassioned *Hamlet*
fan—that is to say, I would have ranked several of the other Shakespeare plays above it. By the time we were through I would have
cast my vote for *Hamlet* as the most priceless piece of literature in
the human heritage.

There are, and always will be, a hundred different ways of interpreting the play, all of them hotly arguable, none (or very few!)
totally "wrong," none definitively "right." We had to make decisive choices long before the play ever went into rehearsal. I had

24

seen it, played in it, read and studied it at length for months without discovering what two weeks of rehearsal later taught me. But that, I have since found, is always the case. Decisions have to be made, all the same. In what period should we do it? In the historically accurate eleventh century, the "Early Bathrobe" period? in the ruffs and farthingales of its author's lifetime? or in some other arbitrarily chosen style? Were the sets to be realistic? expressionist? stripped and nonlocalized? with what indications, if any, of sociology or geography? Above all, what personalities and characteristics did we want for the King, the Queen, Laertes, Polonius and the rest? Lastly, a problem which only belatedly crashed in on me: we had undertaken to do "the entirety *Hamlet*," in the full text. But just precisely which text?

I had seen, I suppose, at least a dozen Hamlets and read or heard about many more. I had made my first professional appearance with John Barrymore in London and later played with Gielgud at the Old Vic. But I was a little cautious of descriptions and memories. I did not want to reproduce other people's "effects" or business unless they sprang naturally and inevitably from prepared soil. On the other hand I saw no reason to avoid an illuminating piece of action just because it had been done before or to think that novelty was in itself a virtue. Eventually I began to shun the academic commentators also. They began to confuse me with complex theories about problems which seemed to me largely artificial. I thought: "If the play is really as difficult as they seem to believe, Maurice can't act it, I can't direct it, nobody can understand it and we better not do it." So I shut the books and went back to the text.

The productions with which I had hitherto been connected had used one or other of the standard published editions, making whatever cuts the director wished and solving the more obvious textual variations on the summary basis of "what sounded best." I could recall seeing one performance in London which specifically claimed to be an illustration of the theories and textual researches of Dr. Dover Wilson. I had written a little crossly: "I'd never realised it was such a *long* play . . . and what does it matter whether you say 'solid flesh' or 'sullied flesh' so long as you can act?" But now, with my new sense of directorial responsibility, I began to study the First Folio and the Second Quarto and, in particular, Dover Wilson's *The Manuscript of Shakespeare's Hamlet*. I found myself enmeshed in a kind of bibliographical whodunit with a number of villains, a labyrinth of conflicting clues and two protagonists, "F.1" and "Q.2," who became as vivid to me as Hamlet himself.

Inevitably I applied an actor's ear and a knowledge of stage practices to the arguable points. Sometimes the knotty problems of the printed page resolve themselves quite easily in this context. I began to be pretty much a partisan of "F.1" just because it does seem to be the playhouse version for playhouse reasons; but of course I included the passages which it omits. I even found some illumination in the First or "Bad" Quarto, the earliest printed version generally discredited for one reason or another. I was tempted by its transposition of scene sequence, which brings the "To be or not to be" soliloquy into a more logical position. I have since watched the effect in two major productions and wished I had been bold enough to use it. But I was overawed by F.1 and Q.2.

I read and reread the text (or texts). I let it grow inside my heart and head; I made a determined effort not to think up neat little notions or to pick up my ideas and look at them every five minutes. I tried to make myself a channel of communication through which something greater than I might speak. Maurice and I had long sessions with the designer, David Ffolkes. We had decided to set the play in Shakespeare's own period and we were in basic agreement as to the kind of production we wanted to give it. David made preliminary sketches and rough ground plans.

We had gathered together a satisfactory cast, with the rather alarming exception of the King and Queen. The day before I left New York I went to a matinee of Orson Welles's production of *Heartbreak House,* and found the Queen. Mady Christians was blonde, distinguished, opulent; she would never (to quote the "Bad" Quarto) "have known of this most horrid murder"; she would have been much distressed by her difficult son's inexplicable dislike of his stepfather; she had a slight German accent, quite suitable to the probably foreign princess whom the Danish King had married. The King himself still evaded us; I didn't want him sinister and I did want someone who could capably rule a kingdom and with whom the women in the audience, as well as the Queen, might reasonably fall in love. Eventually we found him in England, in the person of Henry Edwards.

Maurice had taken a summer lease of the lovely Castello which stands on the promontory overlooking Portofino harbor, and there I joined him. We swam, we fished, we snorkeled, we lay on the terrace, we walked the cliffs; Hamlet always accompanied us; often Hitler too. Our conversations did not dwell exclusively on the inner meaning of "To be or not to be" nor on the choice between "solid" and "sullied." Maurice was a manager as well as an actor, and he had to consider the intricate problems raised by the production of a play whose running time would be about four solid (or sullied) hours, not counting intermissions. He had a passion for schedules. Here is one he sent me soon after I had left Portofino:

NIGHT PERFORMANCES

6:15 p.m.	Half-hour.
30 minutes	dressing time
6:45	advertised curtain time
7 minutes	late-comers' allowance.
6:52	Curtain up
1:48 minutes	Act I duration
8:40	Act I down
30 minutes	Feed-bag intermission
9:10	Act II up
57 minutes	Act II duration
10:07	Act II down
8 minutes	intermission
10:15	Act III up
1:13 minutes	Act III duration
11:28	Final curtain.

From a crew point of view, therefore, we shall have to pay two hours' overtime as they will be in the theatre 5½ hours. If Equity insists upon overtime and at the same time admits that "normal playing-time" may be construed as 7:30 (half-hour) to 11:30 (finale), we must offer the players a little over one-sixth of their salaries extra for the four Eternity performances. . . .

(I should add that these estimated running times turned out to be pessimistic. The actual show, apart from intermissions, ran three hours and thirty-eight minutes. We ultimately rang up the curtain at 6:30, extended the "feed-bag" interval to an hour, rang down at 11:15 and got the stage hands safely out before the witching overtime hour of 11:30.)

Maurice also turned with zest to the organization of the setting-up, technical and dress rehearsals. It used to be possible, in those happy, far-off days, to "stagger the crew call." For example, you could call the carpenter and prop departments at 9 A.M. to put together a given set which you then wanted to light. If the lights had already been hung, there would be nothing for the electricians to do till the set was ready, so you called them at, say, 11 o'clock. At noon you gave the props and "grips" their lunch hour while you finished the lighting, and when they came back you gave "electrics" an hour while they set up the next scene. All crew calls were continuous once the boys were in the theatre, but you could avoid wasting costly time at the beginning, the end and in the dinner hours.

This kind of organizing delighted Maurice and he excelled at it. The rocks of Portofino were strewn with plotted schedules of rehearsal calls. They worked, too, when we put them into effect three months later, and saved everybody a great deal of exhausting sitting around and waiting. Of course you can't do that sort of thing any more. Crew calls are all or nothing. Everybody comes in together, whether they are needed or not, and when the clock strikes for the "penalty hour" beginning at noon, everybody goes to eat en masse. The director (if it's me) feeds his impatience on a carton of black coffee till the clock strikes one and up we come, hickory-dickory-dock. Half the crew then start sitting around again until there's something for them to do. When these rulings were first introduced, they were considered a great advance; I did not know toward what. I now think it was toward theatre-in-the-round with as little scenery and as few stage hands as possible.

It will be seen from Maurice's schedule that the desirability of playing the uncut version was beginning to grow on us. There were to be four "Eternities" per week. All the same, I made a cut version, keeping as much as I decently could. I was arriving at some definition of what I would like to achieve: I wanted the play not to seem abstruse or obscure; to speak directly to its listeners in human terms. I wanted the characters to live, not only Hamlet and Ophelia but the small parts which the uncut text reveals with such brilliant clarity: Rosencrantz and Guildenstern, Fortinbras and Osric, even the tiny ones which vanish in the usual cut versions—Reynaldo, Voltemand, "a Sailor." I wanted them to be recognizable. I wanted to make it clear that there were bedrooms and kitchens at Elsinore as well as battlements. I wanted to capture the sheer excitement of the story itself, swift, cumulative, driven toward its ending by every word and action. Everything must lock into place for this purpose, every twist of chance or mischance in the plot, every trait of every character, strength or weakness, loyalty, courage, stupidity, hypocrisy —all of these must contribute to the central drive of the play itself. This integrated pattern comprises a wide catalogue of human beings and is also a magnificent melodrama.

Finally, I wanted to speak unaffectedly to the people "out front" and to make the play's life their life. It is certainly true that everyone gets from *Hamlet* what he himself brings to it—unless, of course, the production actively impedes his vision. Otherwise, the spectator will receive just as much as his own mind and spirit are equipped to receive. All (all!) I felt I could do was to place my craft at Shakespeare's service and leave the rest to him.

After I had left Maurice in Portofino I traveled back to England via Hitler-shadowed Europe. I spent some time in Holland, where my impressions were, of course, blurred because, though I could manage to read the newspapers and ask a few simple questions, I seldom understood a word of the answers. But the storm clouds across the Rhine seemed very distant as I walked through the villages of the Ijssel Meer, or sat in the marketplace at Delft, listening to the church bells and the bicycle bells and all the comfortable chatter, or steeped myself in the peace of Rembrandt's house at Amsterdam. Here at least, I thought, among these little people, Hitler will not come.

But England was filled with discussions and forebodings and the pressure of impossible choices. I tried hard to persuade May and Ben to come back with me to America. She said "I would, if I could get a job." But he looked miserable and said he thought he'd "drop round to the Garrick for a spot of bridge" and did so, and was late for dinner, and the consequent despair of our cook, Frances, momentarily dwarfed that of Czechoslovakia. I completed the plotting of *Hamlet.* It was all there in my prompt copy, laid out in parallel notes opposite the printed pages: business, music cues, effects, prop lists, scene plans, light plots, everything. My prompt copy became an irreplaceable object of quite alarming value.

For my last weekend I went to stay with a friend in Essex. A long-distance telephone call tracked me there. It was from Hamburg, Miss Mady Christians. Her voice sounded odd and a little breathless. She asked when was I sailing? On Thursday. Maurice too? Soon after. Was the rehearsal date the same? Yes. All our arrangements? nothing changed? I said, no. I was puzzled. I asked if there were any-thing I could do. "No," she said, with relief in her voice, "I just needed to know that you were there—that New York is there—that it really exists. I am in Germany, you see." On August 16 I sailed. By this time Hamlet and Hitler were practically neck and neck.

In New York the machinery went into gear. I visited the costume workrooms and the scene shops, chose the last spear-carrier, timed, with Lehman Engel, the last measures of the score. We had the first readings, then the first "blockings"; and it moved—this miracle happened—it began to work. Within four days the whole of my prompt copy was alive and in motion and transferred to other peo-ple's copies and could have been lost (God forbid!) with relative impunity. I hadn't been outrageously wrong anywhere; the frame-work held. I felt free and flexible and my nerve ends were alive to the vibrations I should receive and the discoveries I should make through the actors and of the actors. I had become a craftsman exer-cising his craft. There is no better feeling.

But we could not blot out the newspaper headlines or the almost hourly radio reports. We began to swing from the heights above Elsinore to the depths below Godesberg. We were suspended over the precipice. *Hamlet* began to take shape. Chamberlain flew to meet Hitler. We had a run-through of Act I. My mother to me from Lon-don:

> We are all bewildered—I feel we should do anything to keep out of war and yet I wonder if taking Hitler's orders will do that. But if the world is plunged into war, where is Czecho-Slovakia or any other country?

I to her:

> The reports tonight have been more than disturbing. At one time it was rumoured that Hitler had actually marched. . . . I cannot see that any good purpose would be served by your staying in London and adding some other medal to your D.B.E.

I add that *Hamlet* is "so far advanced that I get frightened." She to me:

> Yes, I would come to the U.S. if I could get any other job and we could let the flat. Frances [our devoted but intermittent cook-

housekeeper for over forty years] has arrived back, cat and all, and is prepared to caretake, war or no war.

May adds that she is starting to rehearse a television production of *Parnell* (the last play in which I had acted before I left London in 1936), and that after rehearsal she is going to fit on a gas mask.

The first crisis passes; but the second follows close on its heels. I to her:

> I don't know what to write to you. The prolonged strain, uncertainty and groping through the massed American rumor-services is destructive. I do know what you feel about "running away". Indeed I have a strong impulse to return myself. But it seems to me that every spare civilian will be a liability rather than an asset to the inadequate resources of the A.R.P. [Air Raid Precautions]. I do earnestly implore you to leave Bedford Street before and not after the bombs start dropping. . . . Daddy's letter today, written after the first Franco-British sell-out, indicates that we are all feeling much the same thing—that Hitler will have to be fought and that a surrender now will probably only postpone and worsen the inevitable time. "If it be not now etc." has acquired a new and grim significance. [The lines from *Hamlet:* "If it be now 'tis not to come; if it be not to come, it will be now; if it be not now, yet it will come: the readiness is all."]

> We were rehearsing both days during Hitler's and Chamberlain's speeches. The former was, I am told, "like raw meat being thrown to a pack of wolves"; the latter seems to have been well received here. But of course American isolationist feeling is hardening very strongly indeed. It would take a long war and a lot of passion to drag America into any kind of participation, despite the fine contempt for Chamberlain's "weakness".

> Yesterday was awful. Everyone expected that Hitler would make a terrible speech and that war might follow almost before it was over. The European *Hamlet* colony—Maurice and I with families in London, Rhys Williams whose wife is a Czech, George Graham [Polonius] with two brothers in the British army, "Tedwards" whose child is in a Belgian convent, and poor Mady Christians, an anti-Hitler German torn a million ways, were all very white and distracted as the scraps of news came drifting in . . . and oh, God! it's all so heart-breakingly unnecessary. . . .

> *Hamlet* plods along—shapes well, really. Mady will be excellent and is lovely to work with . . . the Ophelia has been hard work and

is a director-made performance . . . the Polonius very good in a slightly trivial way and Tedwards, tho' inclined to a little hearty pumping . . . has a fresh, bluff way of playing the King, so much better than the usual sinister hams. The small parts are of assorted goodness and badness. Maurice is better than in *Richard,* of great technical accomplishment and a sustained level of rhetoric and sense. . . . We have all our stuff in, mostly moved during the hurricane of which you may have read. . . .

The second Munich crisis coincided with our first technical run-through of *Hamlet.* I tried to place a transatlantic call from our offices above the theatre. Several thousand other people were trying to do the same thing for the same reason and it took many hours. I had to appoint relays of watchers to sit beside the telephone while I took notes on the rehearsal. The call came through during the closet scene and I rushed madly upstairs and hung over the telephone in the darkened office, listening to my mother, who sounded infinitely far away, and begging her to get out of London. "But darling," she answered patiently, "it's absolutely impossible, don't you understand? I'm rehearsing for television."

The second crisis passed in a confusion of horror, shame and relief. May wrote:

> Now that the first excitement of relief is over and we can begin to take stock, it looks pretty grim. Frances says "Well, it's a good thing. We didn't want a war just now anyway"; and someone has suggested we use our gas-masks for carnivals.

Hamlet began to overtop Hitler again. I wrote:

> I've been in the theatre fourteen hours a day. It's a heck of a show from the mechanical point of view . . . it's exciting, good—alive—patchy—bad—better than *Richard*—frightening—I don't know what it's like! . . . it's the sum of all I know and its lacks of invention, imagination, "greatness" are my own deficiencies or Maurice's too . . . but for all that, I think it's the most all-round satisfying *show* of *Hamlet* I've ever seen—so there!

The previews arrived. The technical difficulties of getting so long a show properly prepared had been immense; the lighting didn't satisfy me. I had a talk-back microphone installed behind the barrier at the back of the orchestra seats and here I crouched on the floor and hissed at "Kel," the electrician, whenever I saw a spotlight missing. It was usually the one marked "M" on the cue sheets. It was —it would be—the one for Maurice on his very first appearance; and Maurice noticed lights. "Kel!" I would whisper furiously into the mike, "M! No, not N, M! M for . . . Mississippi!" Walter Slezak, who was playing across the street in *I Married an Angel,* looked in for the first part of the preview and went backstage in the intermission to see Mady. He related to her the curious circumstance that there was a strange woman at the back of the orchestra sitting on the floor and swearing. He thought she must be drunk.

Time skids into the opening night, October 12, 1938, and we "put it to the touch" at last. All the usual agonies, magnified because we all care so much; and it holds, it moves, it catches fire. The first act is over, an hour and a half, and no shuffling or coughing, rapt attention throughout. They go out for the dinner break; they come back on time and don't talk in the aisles. The play scene looks splendid, the effect cues work as they should to bring down the curtain after the "How all occasions" soliloquy. Maurice is playing beautifully, a superb opening-nighter, always at the top of his powers and even an inch beyond them.

The second intermission—no snags yet and the audience look as if I had lit them too. Ophelia's mad scenes (how I hate them! but she does all right)—the graveyard—Osric—the fight—and at last the four captains lift Hamlet to their shoulders without so much as a tremor (thank Heaven!) and there is the voice of Fortinbras, steady and resolved:

> *. . . and for his passage*
> *The soldiers' music and the rites of war*
> *Speak loudly for him.*

(the lights are dimming to a single shaft, the music begins, very soft)

> *Take up the bodies: such a sight as this*
> *Becomes the field, but here shows much amiss.*
> *Go, bid the soldiers shoot.*

There is the heavy thunder of guns, the crash of the last chords, the four captains lift Hamlet high above their heads, the curtain slides

33

down to the floor and it is over. I feel infinitely thankful and un-speakably tired.

Four days later I wrote to May:

> Well, well. It's all been something quite special in my experi-ence. . . . It's exalting to find that rare combination in the theatre: first, an inexhaustibly great play. Secondly there was the company— not only they but the crew—backing us and working for us in the teeth of their union regulations—and everyone in the theatre . . . so that the whole thing swung along with a selfless, united devotion which has been something I hope I'll always remember in the black times: it has made all this theatre business, heartbreaks and shoddinesses and dirty work of all kinds, seem superbly worth while. Thirdly, and really quite a bad third, has been the reception and the notices—wonderful —and naturally we're all delighted to be told what geniuses we are. . . . But it's the work I shall remember. . . . Of course, con-sidered in cold blood—mine is cooling now—the show has many defects.

I proceeded to enumerate them analytically and, I think in retro-spect, quite soundly. I knew that I was matching the actors against a visionary performance which could never be realized in human terms. "The scope of the play is so tremendous," I said, "that almost as soon as the curtain had fallen, I felt a passionate urge to start again from the beginning and do it quite differently, stripped and bare, bony, undecorated, a *Hamlet* of the mind." But in any case the whole composition, virtues, faults, limitations and success had been keyed, of necessity, to Maurice Evans's performance, as a concerto is to the soloist. At the time, I wrote:

> Maurice gives a grand performance which dovetails into this kind of a production—I mean, with the emphasis on humanness, colour and truth. He lacks the final greatnesses, I think; is scared stiff of "To be or not to be", and makes nothing of it in consequence; misses his earlier Ghost scene too. But such sweep, power, honesty and, in all but the higher spiritual flights, understanding, that it's in a different class from his Richard. But so, in my opinion, is the whole show.

We abandoned our cut version performances after the first week, to everybody's great relief. The entirety version had been universally hailed. "No one has really seen *Hamlet* until he has sat enthralled be-fore the uncut version"; "Five hours race by, brief, exciting, unfor-gettable"; "The uncut version puts Hamlet into the play instead of on top of it"—such were the themes of the moment; and, not un-naturally, the public demand was for "the Eternities." It meant hard work for everybody—I was about to say especially for Maurice; but the Hamlets I have known who have played both versions have all testified to the fact that Hamlet is far less tiring uncut. The part as Shakespeare originally wrote it is very cunningly placed, constantly but unobtrusively rested between the stretches of great tension. The cut versions compel the actor to leap the high hurdles in relentless succession, with only one genuine rest—before the Graveyard scene —during the whole evening. For the time being we stuck to the "feed-bag" hour, but later we eliminated it, rang up at 7:30 and carried right on. The actors liked it better and the audience didn't seem to mind going hungry.

Hamlet became the talk of the town. *Life* spread it over four full pages. The *Times* carried an editorial which spoke of Hamlet as "the Great Individualist." He "speaks for us," it said, "as surely as Lincoln. . . . In the lands of the iron heel and the conscripted mind their words are distorted and meaningless." John Mason Brown wrote a whole series of informed and illuminating articles about the play. The review I appreciated most came (later) from William McDer-mott of the Cleveland *Plain Dealer:* "I have never seen a clearer *Hamlet* nor one which spoke more unaffectedly to the present times. . . . [It is] thoroughly alive and its life belongs to today." But I suppose our highest accolade came in the form of a lyric sung by Sophie Tucker which celebrated a Utopia "Where Maurice Evans' plays, Instead of running seven hours, Will last for days and days."

Thirty and more years later, my blood no longer "cooling" but quite cold, I am sometimes tempted to look back on all this as a rather highly-colored "success-story" and to denigrate our real accomplishments. Perhaps, indeed, it wasn't as good as I then thought—but it was pretty good all the same. It was of its period, in terms of decor; there was far too much scenery, too many props, "domestic" business which would be thought excessive today. Perhaps it was a *Hamlet* for the late Thirties, or early Forties. But it was exciting, it did succeed in freeing the play from a lot of stuffy and statuesque conventions and it did speak directly, as McDermott said, in living terms to its listeners. Above all, it succeeded in this without the slightest attempt at artificial analogies and spurious "relevance." It proved, I think, that you don't have to translate Shakespeare; you just have to let him be heard.

I could never be tempted to denigrate the wholehearted dedication that was put into it. It was an instance of that particular "mystique" which sometimes emerges among a group of actors, emotional and strangely innocent. In the midst of all the shams and vanities, the bickerings, jealousies, incompetence and general idiocy, we fall in love. On Broadway or Off-off-Broadway, in the West End, on campus, in a tent; no matter how much we are gaining or losing; often with little relation to the standard of the product, we still fall in love. It makes us disregard practical affairs. It makes us dreadfully vulnerable to criticism, or, more precisely, to the critics. This is not due simply to wounded vanity, as they generally suppose. They break in on a love affair and we hate them for it; not just because the show will close on Saturday, but because they have destroyed something which may have been an illusion but which, for us, was a "glory and a dream." When, as in *Hamlet,* we fall in love with something which isn't an illusion, we tend to get dedicated.

In this case the critics, far from destroying us, lavished praise upon us; but Maurice was too shrewd to be dazzled. He thought that the end of January would see the end of *Hamlet,* and so it proved. Shakespeare had never been "good for" more than three to four months on Broadway. John Barrymore's *Hamlet* had established a record of one hundred continuous performances on Broadway; *Richard II* played five more, *Hamlet* four less; and in each case they were revived the following season for three or four weeks. Later, the pattern was extended, though rarely. My own *Othello* with Paul Robeson in 1943–44 was the only Shakespeare revival to run through a full season. The Katharine Hepburn *As You Like It* in 1950 played 144 performances. No further attempts were ever made to run a single play on Broadway, except for the Richard Burton *Hamlet* in 1964. In my judgment, no more ever will be.

Maurice's good sense having been vindicated as usual, we picked up our *Henry IV,* refurbished it with some additional (and extremely unwieldy) scenery, retained most of our company and opened to a handsome press. Mr. Woolcott Gibbs, then feared if not revered on *The New Yorker,* described Mady Christians's witty and tender scenes as Lady Percy as "a really good study in manic depression": apart from this quaint conceit, we had no cause to grumble. Maurice's tour de force as Falstaff was justly praised; but as he had predicted (rightly again) the public wanted to see him in black silk tights rather than in a tour de force. The play closed after a run of some six weeks and *Hamlet* went off on a short, spring tour, the forerunner of a longer one the following season. They were both "all-Eternities" and we feared that audiences might be nervous of having to stay so long in the theatre. I begged Maurice to advertise "Shakespeare's *Hamlet* in its entirety. Eight minutes shorter than *Gone With the Wind.*"

2

The offices next to ours in the Saint James Theatre were occupied by Cheryl Crawford. We used to meet in elevators and passages. She had been one of the moving spirits of the Group Theatre and when it began to break up had started in management for herself. This was not easy for a woman, even then; but Cheryl has kept doing it even now, when it is quite impossible. No wonder I sensed in her a courage I respected as well as theatre ideals which I shared. There were talks, suggestions, discussions. Out of the usual Broadway welter of ideas inflated and deflated, promises made and broken, plans and counterplans, she managed to put together the production of a play called *Family Portrait.* It described some three or four years in the life of a humble little group of Judean peasants, the family of Jesus of Nazareth. It began just after he had left his home, and the final scene took place two or three years after his death.

It ran parallel to the Bible narratives, but never quite touched them. The closer it drew, of course, the more it was dwarfed by the towering shadow behind it. Perhaps there were moments of bathos; but there was a great deal that was charming and moving as well as some moments which sent the authentic chill down your spine. The curtain of the first act was one of the most chilling I have ever seen. It was written simply, within a framework which tried to be timeless. Accordingly, we dressed it in the homespun, full-skirted dresses and belted shirts of any western peasant community in almost any epoch.

Of all the new plays I have done, *Family Portrait* and *The Strong Are Lonely* (*Sur la Terre comme au Ciel*) are the two about which I have cared the most. Both of them were, in the widest sense, "religious," but neither was in the least "Jeezly"—a word coined by the authors of *Family Portrait* to denote artificial piety or reverence. Both had something to say to which the theatre too rarely lends itself—something about faith, something about God, not a specific God, far less a specific church, but God all the same. When plays like this are done, you become aware, even in these days, of the hunger in the audience, the grateful response. The problem is that unless the box-office attraction is very strong, people are apt to get scared and stay away. The Bible, especially, scares them; as it should. It is a scary book.

The leading character in *Family Portrait,* apart from Jesus of Nazareth who never appeared, was, of course, his mother. We asked Judith Anderson to play it. Eyebrows rose in astonished disbelief. The glamorous, sexy Judith of *Come of Age* and *As You Desire Me?* They rose still further when the first-nighters saw a little, contained, soft-spoken, mousy woman in a peasant dress walk onto the stage. Through her I learned two lessons—one of them by no means new, that you cannot pigeonhole fine acting within the rules of orthodoxy, neither traditional rules nor "Method" rules nor Grotowski rules nor any rules of thumb.

It used to be an accepted part of theatre discipline that after a reasonable number of performances a show arrives at an optimum "running time" and that it should not vary far from this except for accidents or special circumstance. If it does, or did, you looked for something wrong—the actors getting lazy, the "milked" laughs, the egotistical elaborations, the self-indulgent pauses. The director, or stage manager, then dealt with the offenders.

In *Family Portrait* there was a scene in which Mary describes to Mary Cleophas the birth of her eldest son. At a certain point she breaks off—pauses—and presently picks up the conversation on a quite different level. As Judith played the scene, the pause grew longer and longer and longer. The running time of the scene stretched out on the stage manager's time-sheet. Since I was playing Mary Magdalene myself, it was hard for me to see the rest of the performance; but I didn't appear until the last act so it was not impossible to watch the scene in question. He thought I should do so, and "speak to Judith." I went in front. The pause came. Judith didn't move. I counted, slowly and steadily, up to ninety-six before she spoke again; a minute and a half, an impossible length of silence. Not a soul in the audience stirred. They saw what Mary saw, remembered what she was remembering, felt what she had felt. They sat totally, absolutely still. When Judith resumed the scene a gentle breath passed over the house, like a light wind across a field of grass. I went backstage and told the stage manager to add one and a half minutes to the official time-sheet.

(The *Othello* stage management later preserved a notice which I had put up on the call board: "WATCH IT, PLEASE! Act I has run 92½–94 minutes during the last five shows, as against 89 and 90 when we began checking times. Don't you *want* to go home nights?")

The second lesson, or experience, concerned what happens when the author (two in this case) and the star really entrench themselves in opposition to each other; only I still don't know what you can do about it. Judith and our authors didn't get on. At one of the early rehearsals I was standing at the edge of the stage watching Judith run a scene. Mrs. Author walked down the aisle and said to me in a penetrating voice: "She isn't going to do it like *that,* is she?" Judith stopped and glared. Her expression was extremely un-Mary-like.

After a few more such incidents we posted spies at entrance doors to lure the authors away with cups of coffee or urgent press interviews or managed to get the rehearsal call mixed up. The Dramatists Guild contract wouldn't, very rightly, permit us to keep them out; it also gave them the final word in any script discussion; and it was the placement of the last word but four that nearly wrecked the production and did in fact cause the abandonment of the proposed subsequent tour. In the final scene a child has been born to Mary's youngest son. What shall he be called? Perhaps, Jesus? The authors' final line: MARY: "I'd like him not to be forgotten." Judith: "I can't say that. It's pedantic and artificial. 'I wouldn't like him to be forgotten.'" The authors: "No. 'Not.'" Judith: "No. 'Wouldn't.'" Cheryl and I both agreed with Judith; and anyway she and no one else had to bring down the final curtain. But no. "Wouldn't." "Not." I once got so exasperated that I threw my fur coat on the floor and stamped on it in helpless rage. On the opening night Judith, wouldn't you know, said "wouldn't"; and continued to do so throughout the run. But when it came to drawing up a touring contract the high contracting parties would not sign it. "Not."

A third lesson came my way, and I did learn and abide by it. The opening night was of the finest vintage. Even though I had to judge the final reception from behind the footlights instead of from the front, I knew it for the genuine article, not just the "Darling-darling-wonderful-marvelous-where-shall-we-go-for-supper" variety. The audience was genuinely moved and we were justifiably happy. We all went back to Lehman Engel's apartment to celebrate in that state of euphoric excitement which is induced by a successful first night. We were relaxed and vulnerable and Lehman had provided champagne. It was agreed that we should "sit up for the papers." About two o'clock in the morning our press agent telephoned. He read off the *Times* review; whoever had picked up the phone, Cheryl I think, repeated it to the rest of us: "casual . . ." "weak . . ." "diffuse . . ." were among the adjectives. The press agent hung up. Nobody spoke. The phone rang again. He read out the *Tribune.* It was repeated to us. He hung up. The happy warriors went into a state of shock. Judith wilted visibly, drooped while you watched. Everyone else just looked stunned.

They weren't bad notices; rereading them some years later I thought them not unreasonable. They were tepid, apparently untouched by what had so profoundly moved the rest of the audience; they concentrated on valid but minor defects. They were magnificent for Judith, pretty good for the production and death to the box office, on the familiar principle of damning with faint praise; but, considered in cold blood, quite defensible criticism. Only our blood was not cold but much overheated with excitement and expectation. The shock of disappointment was, literally, like a bucket of ice water. We couldn't even be indignant. We climbed miserably into our coats and went our several ways homeward through the damp night air, leaving Lehman with the dirty glasses and the ashtrays in a general air of stale sandwiches and desolation.

I swore then, and kept the oath, never again to sit up for the notices. Now, of course, you no longer have to. They assault your eyes and ears via television almost before you have taken your make-up off. Considered appraisals of your months of creative effort have been composed in about eight minutes and are passed on to the still-awake world just as soon as the commentators have got their make-up on. Whether or not this is better I do not know. It is certainly quicker; except that you still have to face the feared-but-not-revered critic of the *Times* next morning, and from him there is virtually no appeal. It is an absurd system from which there seems to be no escape.

3

While I was still playing in *Family Portrait* ("using my reddened hair and cello notes to slightly spurious effect" was my own summation), I plunged into an experience which, looking back, seems so extravagantly comic that it couldn't have happened; but it did. I undertook the direction of four "streamlined" Shakespeare plays, lasting forty minutes each, at the Merrie England concession of the New York World's Fair of 1939. A similar enterprise had proved extremely profitable in previous years at the Fairs of Chicago, Dallas and San Diego. A small-size replica of Shakespeare's Globe Theatre had been built, with the thoughtful addition of a roof, and here continuous performances were given throughout the afternoons and evenings. (The San Diego Globe stands to this day and is admirably, though differently, used.) It was thought that this cultural attraction would do equally well in New York. The fact that the whole Merrie England village, including the Globe, was nested away between Billy Rose's Aquacade and the Giant Racer was not considered a deterrent.

The Merrie England operators began, like almost all the World's Fair concessionaires, with lavish assurances of capital and visions of pie in the sky. Their success would be inevitable and everyone concerned would get a large slice of pie. They urged, further, that culture on the Midway must be of the highest quality. Like a fool, I fell for all this (that "Merrie" alone should have warned me), and decided that I could do the job even though I was still playing eight times a week on Broadway; it wouldn't be the first time, I thought. It was very nearly the last.

I made my own forty-minute adaptations of *The Taming of the Shrew*, *A Midsummer Night's Dream* and *As You Like It*; for *A Comedy of Errors* I used the Thomas Wood Stevens version. I saw literally hundreds of actors. Though the pay was poor, the work hard and the hours long, everyone wanted to jump on the World's Fair bandwagon. Also, young actors, to their honor, are always eager and willing do the classic plays since the opportunities are so pitifully few. My old collaborators, David Ffolkes and Lehman Engel, agreed to do the costumes and music.

We three were probably among the first to undergo the painful process of World's Fair disillusion. (It became a universal affliction.) There turned out to be almost no funds at all behind the Globe Theatre impresarios. Their backers apparently vanished. I had been assured that I would have all the facilities for doing things on a grand scale. I found myself with a small shoestring. My own contract turned out to be a piece of fiction so imaginative as to elude all legal redress. David had to have the clothes made out of mattress ticking and Lehman was compelled to orchestrate his music for one spinet and one recorder. There was no money to buy props and the very notion of electrical equipment was regarded as sheer fantasy. But this was minor. We had no theatre either; indeed there was no Village, Merrie or otherwise. There were only the swampy flats of Flushing, with inadequate piling sinking deeper and deeper into them and some unrelated planks lying about on top.

Rumors grew and multiplied about the whole World's Fair. It was said to be the most magnificent mixture of greed, graft, bullying, cheating, whitewash and wholesale inefficiency ever yet displayed. Committees, concessionaires, subconcessionaires, contractors and unions battled pell-mell together, and we poor performers struggled desperately for survival. The herald angels, however, continued to sing and I was summoned to several impressive ceremonials. They were generally canceled because of bad weather after causing everybody a long and useless journey. The only subway stations yet opened were a half-hour's walk away.

However, the dedication of the Globe Theatre did take place under the benevolent eye of the Great Impresario, the initiating genius of the Fair, the illustrious Mr. Grover Whalen himself. I found the movie cameras trained on me as I came up the muddy approach in a high wind, clutching at my hat, umbrella and briefcase, trying to look dignified and cultural. We stood for half an hour in the pouring rain on the scaffolding, waiting for the speech-making; on my right was Grover Whalen looking pleased and important, on my left a British Lord, identity uncertain, looking important but vague in a top hat. He had learned his speech by heart and impelled some noble platitudes into the wind, building up to a tribute to Grover Whalen. At this point he completely forgot who Mr. Whalen was or what he was supposed to have done and hastily proceeded to scatter a small box of earth from Stratford-on-Avon over the dripping boards. A phial of water from the River Avon was then emptied, redundantly, into the lake. (In fact, the original contents had been suspected of harboring typhoid germs and His Lordship was simply returning the lake to itself.) The ceremony completed, it was felt that the Globe Theatre could open its doors the very moment there were any.

Life became very difficult. There was no one in authority to do anything or get anything done, nothing with which to buy a shoe or a wig or a curtain. We spent one Sunday dragging apart crates of stuff from Chicago in the hopes of finding something usable. It all looked like the mildewing refuse of an abandoned amateur dramatic society. The winds blew bitterly over Flushing Meadows and the surrounding junk of the arising Midway looked unutterably tasteless and pointless. I found forty-minute Shakespeare "plain terrible" and was baffled by the pint-size "Elizabethan" stage which was neither fish, flesh nor good red minnow by modern standards of research. I described the basic results:

> Draw curtain across forestage, comedy scene in front of, while bench and stool set behind; pull back curtain, actors come on, sit on bench and stool, say lines, draw curtains and da capo.

Two days before the Fair's official opening, I wrote:

> . . . still chaos—theatre half ready, no equipment . . . I keep trying to hound *somebody* into doing *something* . . . and have named myself The Countercheck Quarrelsome. . . . I did succeed in acquiring two octogenarians from Brooklyn [who are] supposed to be "electrics" and "props"; they work in shifts receiving $15 per shift while the actors work for $40 a week. . . .

> The whole Fair, delayed by constant rain, is totally unready. There is no hope of our getting into our theatre till Sunday morning and we are supposed to do *The Shrew* and *The Dream* on Sunday afternoon. We dress rehearse and add *Comedy of Errors* on Monday and *As You Like It* Tuesday. . . . Roosevelt is opening the Fair at noon on Sunday and all traffic will be blocked.

I therefore stayed that night in Flushing. On Monday I wrote:

> On Saturday night at 10 o'clock there was still no electric current of any kind in the theatre, no track for the curtains to work on . . . and the clothes, props and minute allowance of lighting equipment etc. were all sitting on the trucks which had taken them out to the Fair vainly waiting for the checks to pay for them. . . . We did never-

theless manage to do one performance of the *Shrew* and one of *The Dream* on Sunday night! . . .

My stage staff of two nonagenarian nitwits does not even know the standard numbers of gelatines used in lamps so when I say I want a 62 I have to go and pick it out myself. The two electricians' unions are fighting jurisdictional squabbles; one lot works on putting in the wiring which my bright boys are not allowed to touch but have to take over without the smallest idea as to what is hooked up to which. So for about three hours on Sunday this sort of thing ensued:

ME: Give me the Number One circuit of Fronts. *Pause. Debate. Click.*
ME: No, that's a front-of-house bracket. *Pause. Debate. Click.*
ME: No, that's a ceiling strip. *Pause. Debate. Click. Many repeats. Finally they get it.*
ME: That's it! Now mark the switch, kill it, and then give it me on the dimmer. *Long pause. Several clicks.* No, dammit, that's another ceiling strip. . . . and so on ad inf.

At intervals this has been varied by the current's being cut off altogether because of some sort of strike. Today we could give no afternoon show at all because one of the workmen employed on building the far-from-finished Village had his tools stolen so everybody dropped everything and struck. There is no water and no toilets of any kind in the theatre as yet and the plumbers must not be hurried. The actors have to walk across to the "Lounge" on the other side of the Village, for which they pay a dime. I spent a large part of Sunday hammering, painting, crawling over the ceiling to fix a light . . . in fear and trembling lest my surreptitious activity should be discovered by a union delegate and the entire labour force of the Fair would down tools in consequence. . . .

Nobody is coming in and I can't see why they should as the rest of the Village is completely barren except for a band of juvenile females who play vigorously on the bagpipes whenever we are doing a quiet scene. During our first show there were bangs outside indicative of fireworks, and the entire audience of twenty or so rose and made for the doors looking onto the Lake. I flung myself across them in a "they shall not pass" attitude and forced them back! They escaped by other doors; but when the fireworks turned out to be a false alarm they all trooped back again!! The actors have been angels, as actors can be in a crisis, and have never grumbled or thrown temperament, which God knows they had every possible excuse for doing. The critics' visit has been postponed and I wish they wouldn't come at all for at best it can only be a village-hall entertainment.

They did come, however, and between blasts from the loudspeakers of the Aquacade which towered above us, we threw performances at them. They were courteous and gallant to us all. Indeed, when the chaos had subsided a little, the shows weren't so bad. David's mattress ticking looked very gay and cheerful and Lehman had managed to coax from his two-woman orchestra a little tinkling jollity which would have done credit to a band of grasshoppers. The *Shrew* had zest and the *Dream* was light and I flattered myself that I had been really inventive about *A Comedy of Errors*. I had thought my handling of *As You Like It* extremely dull and lacking in ideas. I was therefore chagrined to find that it turned out to be the most successful of the four, while the *Comedy of Errors* was probably the least. I was forced to conclude that this had something to do with Shakespeare.

Family Portrait tottered to a close, all Broadway business having been much damaged by the Fair, and Maurice came back from his *Hamlet* tour. But by this time Hitler was overshadowing everything. The certainty of war was very close. Danzig and Poland were the names in every newspaper. The World's Fair speeches proclaiming universal amity had a very hollow ring and the flags of all nations hung above the speakers in garish mockery. Shakespeare, as usual, kept pace with the times. Hamlet questions the Captain about the objective of Fortinbras's army. He replies:

> *Against some part of Poland. . . .*
>
> *Goes it against the main of Poland, sir,*
> *Or some frontier?*
>
> *Truly to speak, and with no addition,*
> *We go to gain a little patch of ground*
> *That hath in it no profit but the name.*
> *To pay five ducats, five, I would not farm it. . . .*
>
> *Why then the Polack never will defend it.*
>
> *Yes, it is already garrisoned.*
>
> > *. . . I see*
> *The imminent death of twenty thousand men*
> *That for a fantasy and trick of fame*
> *Go to their graves like beds, fight for a plot . . .*
> *Which is not tomb enough and continent*
> *To hide the slain. . . .*

My letters to May about the ludicrous World's Fair were layered with frantic plans to get her and Ben out of England. The agonized debates of only a few months before were repeated. Both her letters and mine moved closer to the total pacifist position (which I now believe to be the only tenable one), but were torn by the same unanswerable questions as before. She had been working hard, through British Equity, to rescue some of the German-Jewish actors imperiled by the Nazis, and was sickened to hear them spitefully referred to as "Equity's refugees." The inevitable jargon grew more pervasive. She quoted: "We can't help the damned foreigners," proclaimed one faction; and "All our boys must fight," announced the other. "Never dream of coming back," she said. "It makes me sick." She had lunch with three of England's most distinguished actresses, Sybil Thorndike, Edith Evans and Gwen Ffrangcon Davies, and "we talked treason loudly . . . and denounced National Service and vowed we would not take oaths to serve King and Country."

The next day she had to receive the King (George VI), the Queen and Princess Elizabeth at a charity matinee and have tea with them. He told her that "he loved *The Lady Vanishes* and was a fan . . . the Queen was most charming—Princess Elizabeth too, such nice manners, and the King so simple and shy—one's heart warms to them."

The inevitable crisis loomed closer. We all still assumed, as we had at the time of Munich, that a declaration of war would be followed, almost within minutes, by the bombing of London. No one imagined the months of the "cold war." May wrote: "I want to get out—and yet—what a fuss about one's life—why not just be finished off? if it were just that—but injuries past bearing to me and mine— and it's happening all the time to others." I knew that I would never get Ben and May to America without "a job." I kept trying to invent one. Faint trumpetings were heard from Hollywood and my hopes would rise; but they kept on fading away in gusty echoes from agents and dissonant chords.

At last I evolved a summer-stock "package": the play, Norman Ginsbury's *Viceroy Sarah;* the stars, Dame May Whitty and Mady Christians; the theatre, Deertrees, Maine; the manager, Bela Blau. It was a flimsy pretext. Fortunately Sam Goldwyn, from Hollywood, began a serious-sounding kind of approach. Equity was helpful about my mother's alien status. But everybody was in different parts of the world, and May vacillated in understandable torments of indecision. I went almost crazy.

To soothe myself, I bought a very ancient Ford and set off for two weeks' holiday on Martha's Vineyard. I do not know what happy stars, or guardian angel, led me there. Katharine Cornell had sounded the charms of her island and I had been attracted, for no particular reason, by the name "Menemsha" on a travel folder. Mady and I met there. For the first two days it poured with rain and we sat dismally at the Menemsha Inn in a little cabin the size and color of a cigar box. We put on mackintosh caps and raincoats and stood for considerable lengths of time gazing down at the sand dunes, the lobster pots and the tiered masts of small boats in Menemsha harbor. Mady pointed to a small cottage on the hill above it. "That's for rent," she said, "shall we take it?" I said "Yes." Thus began a love affair with Martha's Vineyard which, for Mady, ended only with her death and for me will probably only end with mine.

From the cottage in Menemsha, which had no telephone (or electricity or "mod. con.") I tried to maintain sensible but swift transatlantic communication with my mother. By now the outbreak of war had ceased to be a matter of "if" and become a question of "when." I remember that the planet Mars hung in the sky above the hill, larger and redder than I had ever seen it before. I drove almost hourly to Chilmark Post Office and stood in line to call Western Union. Lengthy and agonized telegrams came from Bela Blau in Deertrees as his deadline drew nearer and nearer. The Western Union operator, apparently surprised by their tone, had typed at the bottom of one of them "no love." At last May agreed to come. The Goldwyn contract was settled; she would come up to Maine to do *Viceroy Sarah* and then go on to the Coast. I sent reassuring messages to everybody with infinite relief and much love. Time was now very short; I had to go up to Maine before May and Ben landed in New York. One morning in August I drove the ancient Ford from Deertrees to Portland. The New York night express arrived and Ben and May got out of it. I think I have never been so glad to see anybody.

The try-out passed, in the usual summer-theatre mixture of rehearsals and beach picnics, scene-painting and barbecues, of strenuous endeavor alleviated by the sun and the crystal mountain air and the lack of strain. I took May and Ben back to New York and saw them off on a plane to Hollywood. They were both in their middle seventies and the flight, in those days, was quite an undertaking even for the younger and more experienced traveler. May described their arrival at La Guardia airport in the early evening and the ensuing delays— very usual, even then:

> Finally on to our plane—a luxurious affair where the stewardess welcomed me with joy and overwhelmed me with attention, and two men in the opposite section kept up a steady talk in their flat, toneless back-of-the-throat voices till after midnight. We were served a charming little dinner and all was very pleasant, some bad bumps and swoops at moments, but much nicer than a train. But then came the sleeper question. I was hoping to sit in our comfy seats—but Ben looked wistful and my fan stewardess loved me so, she made up the damned things about 9 and the heavy curtains were swung over and it was hell. . . . I couldn't sit up to see the most marvellous lightning storm from above it—could only raise up on an elbow—and eventually when we came down at Dallas I crawled out and got a corner of a seat just behind the control room where men came in and out and all was disturbance and discomfort and nearly twelve hours to go. . . . But I got out at Tucson and saw such a sunrise . . . and then we all had breakfast and I got into the control room and saw the thing being driven—and looked down at Arizona and then all the fruit groves and it was all very wonderful and exciting and we arrived half an hour early! . . .

to be greeted by a bevy of photographers wanting pictures of May and Ben holding gas masks.

Mady and I went back to the Vineyard for a few more days. It was indulging in one of its autumnal orgies of gale-force winds and torrential rain. We hung dismally over the radio, hypnotized, as the last vestiges of hope were extinguished one after the other. At last came the inevitable end—the invasion of Poland, the French and British declarations of war. We listened to King George's speech and stood for "God Save the King." We switched off the radio.

Chapter Three

Mountains of the Moon

Moving westward, far from the climate of war, May and Ben arrived in Hollywood with mixed sensations. This time it was all familiar, the friendly sunshine, the friendly people, the routines of studio life; they were no longer strangers. But the sense of distance and isolation was sharper than ever. "The old cut-off-from-life feeling returns," May wrote to me. It was not easy to be British in America during the months of the cold war. Everyone was torn by conflicting emotions, sentiment and loyalties on one hand, contracts and common sense on the other.

Everyone wanted to "do something." But the British authorities were very nervous about antagonizing American opinion by ill-advised propaganda, and maintained, in consequence, a clam-like silence as to the fact that Britain was at war. They urged their nationals to stay quietly in the United States, earning and sending home those nice dollars, lying low and saying nothing. The British writhed silently at the Neutrality Acts, combed the back pages of the Los Angeles *Times* for word of German submarines and dreaded the first air raids on London. There were decorous efforts at Allied War Relief. But it remained a very cold war.

From May 1940, in the midst of flame and disaster, it was still more difficult for an Englishman, or even an Englishwoman seventy-five years old, to be at peace with his heart among the swimming pools and the poinsettias, the abundant food markets and the hot, neutral sunshine of California. It was not easy to be enthusiastically grateful for America's very expensive "gift" of a few over-age destroyers or to watch with a polite smile the banners on Hollywood Boulevard proclaiming "THE YANKS ARE NOT COMING LET GOD SAVE THE KING." (I wrote: "I sympathize with their sentiments but I wish they'd put it better.") But to the question "Why not go back?" the answers, especially to the older generation, were insultingly obvious. Go back to that small beleaguered island, undersupplied, over-populated, besieged from the sea, attacked from the air, go back to do what? to get in the way of the air-raid wardens and be "another mouth to feed"? (Oh, that soothing, humiliating "another mouth to feed"!) Indeed, May had bitter arguments with her more jingoistic compatriots who were all for hounding home men younger than themselves; like the young and beautiful Richard Ainley, Harry's son, who did go back, did get himself into the army and was, in fact, smashed to pieces later in the war.

May worked for the war charities, including one called TABS, run by the women of the British colony to send food and clothing to England. She was an admirable public speaker with a ready, impromptu wit, and her talents in making "the appeal" were much in demand. The results were not as negligible as she sometimes feared. Lord Halifax later wrote to her: "Before I leave Washington as British Ambassador, I would like to tell you how highly your services to our country and its cause have been appreciated, and to thank you most warmly for all that you have done."

Nevertheless she felt miserable and impotent. When, in 1940, the bombings began, the dreadful fears grew worse and the self-reproaches too. No one in England uttered them, but Shakespeare had:

> *And gentlemen* [not] *in England, now a-bed,*
> *Shall think themselves accursed they were not here,*
> *And hold their manhoods cheap whiles any speaks*
> *That fought with us upon St. Crispin's Day.*

I went through all this too, of course, back in New York in the cold war months, what with my dual nationality and my transatlantic schizophrenia, even though I had begun to sink roots not only in New York, but the first of what were to become the strongest of all, on Martha's Vineyard. My way of life had changed by imperceptible degrees but steadily, becoming Americanized by interests, thought patterns and behavior. Even my accent had changed a little, though I still said "squir-rel," where my friends said "squirl." Fortunately for me, I was working too hard to have any choices of conscience. The *Hamlet* touring company had been partly disrupted by the outbreak of war. Tedwards was stranded in England, shipless, and we had to open without him. Several of the younger actors disappeared, as one of them mildly put it, "to trollop up to Canada and enlist." The journey to Canada, it seems, has been made for more reasons than one.

The Playwrights' Company asked me to direct Sydney Howard's last play, *Madam, Will You Walk?* He was to have done it himself, but he had been killed stupidly, wastefully, by a silly accident with a tractor on his Massachusetts farm. I felt a deep personal grief for his loss and an enhanced sense of responsibility for his play. I was honored that the Playwrights had chosen me to do it. From among their own members (including Maxwell Anderson and Elmer Rice) Robert Sherwood had agreed to act as the play's godfather, and Robert Edmond Jones had already designed the sets, wonderful good fortune for me. The casting had also been completed, and this provided me with a brief but dizzying contact with the great George M. Cohan.

Originally the part was to have been played by an English actor, who had left for home on the outbreak of war; someone had had the brainstorm of persuading Cohan into taking it over. I can't imagine why he consented. I don't think he understood what the play was meant to be about, or the part either, except that he was meant to be the Devil, albeit a jolly sort of Devil, and didn't altogether like that. He called me "Maggie"—the only person who ever has—was extremely amiable, and nobody seemed able to evoke from him any response whatever, neither I, the godfather-author nor the other actors. He always seemed to be thinking of something else; certainly not of his lines, which continued to elude him. He made a great parade of not being able to pronounce the word "Prometheus." *"What* is it, Maggie?" "Pro-*mee*-the-us, Uncle George." And I knew perfectly well that *he* knew perfectly well what it was.

Warning lights began to flash in my mind. I reminded myself about there being no rules for great actors; and since I myself had never seen him, maybe there was some glorious surprise in store. Bob Sherwood kept on telling me it would be all right on the night. This is a popular slogan which I have never yet found any evidence to support. Something which is basically wrong doesn't become suddenly right in a mystic moment when the lights go up.

It didn't in this case; and on the second night "Uncle George" gave in his notice. There was a farcical interlude (which included my having to fly to Chicago to rehearse a replacement for the Polonius in *Hamlet* and getting stuck there with tonsilitis), and finally the production was abandoned. Two young actors who had pinned their hopes of a stage career to the parts they were to play in it gave up the unequal struggle and left for Hollywood. They were Arthur Kennedy and Keenan Wynn. Nowadays, of course, nobody even imagines that they can make a living out of the "living" theatre. But in 1939 it still seemed possible, and the loss of talents such as theirs robbed the theatre of the life-blood it so badly needed.

I suppose it must have been this confused climate of emotions and events which induced me to accept a contract with Paramount Pictures. I had refused similar offers before. I knew perfectly well that no woman director had ever "made it" in Hollywood. I didn't really want to direct pictures; I'd rather have acted in them; I wasn't greedy for the money. Certainly I was keenly aware of the challenge and intrigued by it. I respected the medium—too deeply for my own good, I now think—and people kept reminding me of its tremendous possibilities and its vast potential audience, so much greater than the theatre could ever reach. Probably I also felt that if I wasn't going back to England largely because I had brought my parents to America, I might as well go in the opposite direction and join them. To all this was added the persuasive power of Richard Halliday, then head of Paramount's Story Department; and to this I yielded.

My contract ran to twenty-five pages of single-space typing and tiny print. I understood very little of it. *Variety* reported that I was to be a "femme Orson Welles" and that I was to "thesp scrib and collab." This was a bit obscure too. I did devise two safeguards; the first was that I was to spend six months on the lot "learning the business," and during that time I was to receive only a nominal salary. It has always seemed to me—ridiculously, I know—that to accept large sums of money from anybody, disproportionate to the work performed, involves a kind of indebtedness. I was determined not to feel obligated. At the end of six months either party could call the contract off. If not, it would go into full effect, spread over several years at increasingly munificent salaries. The second safeguard had meant a tigerish fight on my part. I had secured a definite period of three months in each year when I would be free to work on Broadway; there were specific dates to it, with no "yes, yes, later" or "after we've finished" or "when we're ready," widely used by movie companies to get themselves off this sort of hook. (I should have remembered about having your cake and eating it.)

Early in April I drove West in my little Chev, named "Charles, His Friend," to whom I was devoted. Nobody truly realizes the immensity and splendor of the North American continent until he has crossed it by road. Some of it goes on a bit too long; but most of it is magnificent—and perhaps it seemed even more so before eight-lane Thruways and Freeways existed to dull the eyes and blunt the mind. One morning very early I started from Salt Lake City with a long drive ahead of me across the desert and over the mountains beyond. The salt flats were pearly white, the sky a pale blue and the snow-capped peaks of the Sierra Nevada were touched with the rose-gold of the rising sun. Wreaths of mist hung in the air and the lake reflected back the colors of the hills and the sky; there was nothing solid but the road. It was a floating unreality, like being inside an opal. I turned on the car radio; and over it came the news that Hitler had invaded Norway. The cold war had exploded in flames.

As usual, my family and I missed connections. While I was driving West, May and Ben were en route East. She was to play the Nurse and my father Lord Montague in the stage production of *Romeo and Juliet* with Laurence Olivier and Vivien Leigh. I caught up with them for two days in San Francisco. They headed for Chicago and New York, and I drove on down the coast to enroll myself in my new factory. I was understandably terrified. Two days after my arrival, I wrote:

> I still feel like a puppy in the very middle of a pond who continues to swim, taking on faith the notion that somewhere there is a shore. . . .
> On Monday morning I drove to my agent's office, where I met him, my contracts and a raft of accumulated mail, and presently he, in a very grand Packard, preceded the humble Charles to Paramount. . . .
> [There] we accumulated Dick Halliday and proceeded on a round of visits to the Company Big Shots. I was inducted into my own office suite, whose closet alone is larger than that little toilet from which I have hitherto conducted my Broadway affairs, and was presently provided with an extremely efficient secretary who, by impressive telephonic activity and innumerable signatures on my part, summoned from the depths an array of notepaper, pencils, office memo pads, dictographs, files, note blocks and other such. What I am to do with all this, or with her, remains a mystery. . . .

Dick Halliday spent a lot of his valuable time initiating me into many matters connected with the personnel of the Studio, its present and future activities and the general outline of the political crises which are currently rocking it. After lunching with him in the Commissary, with a fresh introduction cropping up every five minutes, I decided that the only method was to empty my mind of anything but the concentrated effort to remember the various faces, their attendant names and functions in the hierarchy. . . .

Everybody seems enchanted to see me, is enthusiastic, cooperative, eager and hopeful; but hasn't the smallest idea what I am supposed to be doing. . . . Being conscientious, I arrive around 9 A.M. and stay till 5:30, but if I never turned up at all I don't believe anyone but Dick would be any the wiser. . . .

Later I added:

They all treat me with great deference, altho' none of the people on the sets have, of course, ever heard of me. But then they've never heard of anybody, from one bit of the lot to another. Sam Wood, working on Stage 5, is wraithlike to the De Mille outfit. Stanton Griffis, President of Paramount, now out here on a visit, is entirely unknown to any of them, and nearly everybody thinks Oscar Wilde is the name of that new actor who has just made such a hit. My position is very odd—not starting from the bottom of the ladder but climbing in through the attic window.

It turned out to be the scrib (or Story) department which aroused my first interests. Richard Halliday gave me a thorough briefing on the methods of the mills of God as they ground slowly through it, starting with the galley proofs of novels and stories yet unpublished and ending in the offices of the Writers' Building. In this rather scruffy edifice were confined a splendid, witty, iconoclastic and reckless bunch, Charles Brackett and Billy Wilder among them. We lunched together and laughed a lot. I was amazed by the encyclopedic knowledge of the Story Department. A vast amount of energy, including mine, was daily consumed in making "treatments" of every sort and kind of material, ancient and modern, from fossil to fetus, which might one day grow up and be a picture. Of course very little of it ever did. Numberless authors bought themselves some new shoes or a trip to Florida as a result of the department's quest for "options"; but in the vaults there accumulated mountains of discarded MSS, outlines, synopses, treatments, shooting scripts, "pinks," "blues" and "buffs" in every stage of composition and decomposition, all rotting peacefully underground. But once you grasped that you were simply playing one of those writing games, it was quite fun to join in.

My other activities were various. For several weeks I sat at the riding-booted feet of Cecil B. De Mille while he directed, with consummate skill, some very heavy traffic among the Northwest Mounted Police, Indians, Canadians and furry species, all in glorious technicolor. The use of color was still fairly new and involved endless technical complications, double sets of takes and retakes, interminable delays and general strain. Gary Cooper, aloof and quiet, managed to insert some remarkably assured and truthful acting. Paulette Goddard suffered and stormed as the inevitable half-caste tiger-cat and Walter Hampden suffered in another sense as Big Chief Bug-a-Boo by having to stand for hours in the blazing sun with a complete skin covering of latex and contact lenses to make his eyes look brown instead of blue. De Mille was fatherly and benevolent toward me, and the time I spent on his set was instructive.

I would sit for long, arduous hours in the cutting rooms, trying to get the hang of this delicate craft which can and does make or break a picture. Together with the studio heads, I attended the daily showings of "rushes" from all the pictures being made, and listened to the comments of the Top Brass, which were revealing in more ways than one. I spent many weeks on all the preparations for and shooting of *Victory,* with John Cromwell directing and Frederic March, Betty Field and Cedric Hardwicke as the stars. I directed some of the retakes when Cromwell had to leave. It was during the shooting of *Victory* that we began to hear the horrible series of broadcasts about the German invasion of France, culminating in Dunkirk. Cedric and I would sit in a far corner of the sound stage, incongruously huddled behind a clump of fake bamboo, with a portable radio which we only turned off when a shot was actually in progress.

The agonies multiplied. I couldn't imagine what I was doing in Hollywood, of all places, while France was going up in smoke. I got the president of the studio to agree to release me if I could get a job to do in France. I could drive well, speak near-perfect French, surely there must be something with the Quakers or the Red Cross units. I telephoned to friends in Washington and to Noel Coward, who was in New York fresh from Paris on some mysterious mission. I pulled strings and wrestled with red tape. All these problems, however, were swiftly and summarily resolved by the fall of France. May and Ben came back to Hollywood after the unexpected failure of *Romeo and Juliet* and begged me not to try and get to England and I didn't. But I knew that in making this decision I was making it for keeps. It was a choice I should not have again. England for love, for fun, for friends; rarely for work; America my home.

We all tried to bury ourselves in doing things. May began a series of pictures, I shot a series of tests with Paramount's embryo starlets, of whom they invariably picked the least talented. Susan Hayward was one they decided against; I tried to get her out and into a stage job, but they kept her hanging around and wasting her time and their money. She later vindicated my judgment and confounded theirs. I began to feel, as I later wrote: "I don't believe I should ever be more than a scrape-through director in Hollywood . . . but at least it has taught me to fuss in slower tempo than before."

Meanwhile, a real labor on behalf of the British war effort revealed itself. It turned into a laborious little war on its own. The Actors' Orphanage had existed in England for many years. The Committee, of whom May had been one, supported by voluntary contribution some fifty or sixty children whose fathers or mothers had been members of the theatrical professions. Its chief source of funds had always been the famous Theatrical Garden Party, one of the annual events of the London season, patronized by Royalty and attended by All. It was now bereft of this income and when the bombing of London began the Orphanage itself was seriously endangered. The Committee (president, Noel Coward) decided to try and transfer the entire Orphanage to America, preferably to California, where, it was thought, the British colony would be able to raise sufficient funds for its support. This little project was put into my mother's hands.

So began a saga which rebounded between London, Hollywood and New York for the next six years. Its protagonists became known in the Webster family as "The Awfuls." It started with burning enthusiasm all round. May called a meeting of representative British actors. They received the proposition with rapture. Of course the children must come, all of them, instantly, and be folded to the hospitable heart of the colony. Willing helpers rushed hither and thither questing for schools, houses, institutions, camps, ranches or any other locality where so large a band of refugees, big and small, male and female, could be housed, cared for and educated. Everybody fell in love with his own idea and poured cold water on everybody else's. This home would be too luxurious, that one too austere, this one too free, that one too regimented, this one too far away, that one too metropolitan. The children must obviously be kept together; they must necessarily be split up. The identity of the Orphanage must be preserved intact; the orphans must absolutely be divided so as not to be an alien group. Grandiose schemes were advanced and had to be tactfully discouraged as impracticable. My mother's patience and diplomacy as "Madam Chair" were strained to the utmost.

Means of transport for so large a party were scarce and dangerous; rules and regulations abounded in London, New York, Washington, Los Angeles and even, when a Canadian detour was suggested, Ottawa. Quantities of letters were exchanged, mostly written by May in longhand, endless forms filled out in triplicate and subsequently superseded. It became evident that each child would have to be separately sponsored by a specific individual, responsible to the U.S. government. At this point enthusiasm waned a little. Meanwhile, bombs were falling, time was passing and the London Committee was becoming clamorous. Once they cabled that the children had embarked on a certain ship. It was torpedoed in convoy. After a heart-stopping interval we found they hadn't.

Eventually the Californian project was abandoned for reasons of complication and expense, and a home was found for the entire contingent at the Edmund Gould Foundation, Pelham, New York. The Foundation administrators were generous and tactful, and the problems of adjustment were admirably met. It was an ideal solution.

The ardor of the Hollywood sponsors, however, cooled appreciably now that their protégés were so far away. May's enforced letter-writing continued unabated. Some of the guardian angels had to be nudged, chivied, bullied or plainly dynamited into the continued fulfillment of their pledges. Others had to be gently restrained from displays of ill-advised or too-lavish generosity toward their particular child. Christmas presents for instance; requests were invited. My little boy asked for a baby alligator; Gilbert Miller's, hopefully, for an automobile. The British authorities had forbidden a public appeal for funds since this might detract from more important charitable causes; so we managed to beg small slices for the orphans from the larger organizations to which we gave our services.

Once the children were established in the Bronx a New York Committee had to be established. It was, to say the least, flexible, depending on who happened to be in New York at the time. For considerable periods it seemed to consist of Maurice Evans and me.

There was one moment when all the orphans were threatened with adoption by Gertie Lawrence, not without attendant fanfares. May continued to be the sole liaison among London, Los Angeles, the Gould Foundation and the Washington authorities.

As time went on different complications arose. When the boys grew to be of National Service age they had to be got back to England. This began to apply to the older girls also. But by this time residence in the Bronx had become so agreeable to them that we met with spirited resistance. One meeting in New York was attended by May, Brian Aherne, Noel Coward and me. The Gould Administrator reported officially that one girl had refused to go back on the grounds that she was engaged to be married to an American citizen. "Is he," said Noel solemnly, "in a position to support her in the style to which she is accustomed?" It was revealed, with some hesitation, that the prospective bridegroom was a gravedigger. "With John Gielgud," asked Noel, "or Maurice Evans?"

When the war ended the remaining children of course went home; where they were faced, inevitably, with a further series of adjustments. The Orphanage was eventually closed in 1963 and reformed as part of the Actors' Charitable Trust, which still takes care of the children's individual needs, though no longer on an institutionalized basis. I don't know whether the American hegira promoted Anglo-American good will. It should have. It certainly saved lives.

During the early stage of The Awfuls saga I had left Hollywood. In September came my stipulated, dated period of leave; I was going to direct *Twelfth Night* for the Theatre Guild on Broadway. In October the first six months of my "apprenticeship" were up. Paramount and I had to decide about implementing my real contract. They wanted to keep me; but they wanted to strike out the leave-of-absence clause, or at least to leave it vague and undated. They thought this a trivial alteration; but I knew that it was crucial. I could see their point; as my employers they wanted first call on my services at all times. But if I gave it, my future in the theatre would become a matter of luck, secondary to their demands, a kind of bonus I could hope for but never count on. I would not concede the priority.

I had learned a profound respect for the camera medium and for the marvelous skills of its technicians. I thought I might have been able to write for the movies—certainly, to act in them. For a stage-trained actor the transition is not difficult; it requires concentration, economy, a slight shift of technique. But television has since amply proved, if proof were needed, that if you can act in a theatre you can act on a postage stamp. The reverse is not necessarily true. For a director, however, the change of medium is far more complex. Moreover, you are alarmingly dependent on a lot of experts who tell you what you can or can't do for technical reasons—let alone financial ones. Nobody can do this to me in the theatre without my knowing the answers. I did not think, however, that I was skilled enough to control the know-better-boys in Hollywood, let alone the Big Bosses. I didn't have the arrogance. Perhaps I didn't have the will either.

In those days people made movies in Hollywood or they didn't make them at all. The British film industry was largely paralyzed by the war; movie-making in Madrid, Rome and Ireland and on the sidewalks of New York had not yet threatened Hollywood's monopoly. Possibly I might have been tempted by the medium in other places or other circumstances. But a woman director in Hollywood had never managed to "make the grade"; even now, under more flexible circumstances and a variety of geographical and economic conditions, it is still very tough going for a woman.

Perhaps I had the sense to recognize this. But it is also worth noting that in 1940 you could still declare allegiance to the living theatre and stand a fair chance of earning enough to pay the bills. So I made this second decision, knowing that it was "for keeps." I climbed light-heartedly aboard that dream-train that is now a vanished glory, the Santa Fe Superchief, and headed East. Via Chicago and Boston I arrived on Martha's Vineyard in a near-hurricane and bought a house. It was a funny little affair with a high, steeply-pitched roof and it needed "doing things to." But it commanded beautiful views over the empty pastures of Gay Head and there were a couple of acres of land for me to call my very own—all for $1,200. Idiot that I was I could have bought a thousand feet of shore for not much more. But why should I? The beaches were empty and access to them was free. So I sank my little root on my hilltop and was very happy.

May and Ben remained in Hollywood, "living or partly living"— Ben, at least, might have echoed the T. S. Eliot phrase. May was working hard and the war activities increased, as did the anguish. The Bedford Street flat had to be cleared out and abandoned, since there seemed so little prospect of returning to it. Soon after came news that our faithful Frances had died, no longer dangerously "caretaking" in Bedford Street but "peacefully" in Brixton. May wrote: "She's been associated with us all our married lives and she goes at the same time as our home. One feels lost and stupefied." A documentary called *London Can Take It* was being shown. May said: ". . . the groups of people, the familiar streets—I couldn't bear it—just broke down and howled." Even Ben commented "One can't help feeling a bit anxious."

The United States was now going through the agonized dissensions of to fight or not to fight. After Pearl Harbor resolved the problem with horrible force, the position of the British "aliens" was at least alleviated by a feeling of unity. Hollywood got nervous about Japanese air raids. At Christmas, 1941, the shops took to closing early, despite the seasonal buying spree. There were some grim British smiles. On December 27, 1941, May wrote:

> The end of a horrible year, and we face more horrible things in the torture of men and nations, and at moments one stands aghast that such a thing should be and that this poor country has to go through it too . . . maybe to save her soul; tho' I suppose we must all bear our share of guilt for complacency . . . and for letting things slide . . . for suffering such things as the exploitation of labour, the tyranny of the financiers and their shameful marketing of their instruments of death —yet the innocent have to pay—the children in the slums—[she meant of London] there again our crime—the slums—those boys flying into such frightful dangers night and day . . .

"The Young" of today (that idiotic generalization) might sometimes pause to reflect that there have, in fact, been others in preceding generations who had a social conscience and who detested war.

In the Hollywood of the early Forties, however, neither sentiment was very much in evidence. The cameras rolled on. May confronted them in *Mrs. Miniver, The White Cliffs of Dover, Gaslight, Suspicion* and many other pictures. In one she put on a riding habit and rode a horse, which was a new experience. In another she was an "olde countye family ladye" lending a background of "class" to some air force training planes and Tyrone Power. In yet another she "supported" Lana Turner and was reported to have remarked mildly, "I don't know what Miss Turner has got that I haven't, only I've had it longer."

Her performance in *Mrs. Miniver* was one of her finest and very nearly won her an Oscar. She made the "ferocious old dowager with a heart of gold" stereotype into a human being. Among the very few fan letters she ever kept was one, which must have pleased her and was surely deserved. The writer spoke of her "good taste and discernment . . . sincerity and directness" and added:

> You appear to be so absolutely poised and at ease that you have all the time and energy to create your character, and to reveal to us what she is thinking and doing mentally. . . . One sometimes forgets how beautiful and polished our language can be until it is heard spoken as you speak it. I like the crispness, the clarity, the impeccable diction of your voice . . . the wonderful subtlety and suggestion that lie behind your reading of the lines. For you, like all great artists, know that one of the secrets of the profession is to leave enough to the imagination of the audience, to give wings to it. Intelligent acting is both flattering and a challenge to an audience.

In *The White Cliffs of Dover* she played a "Nanny" for a change. She didn't feel very good at it; and suffered especially from one sequence which involved Irene Dunne, C. Aubrey Smith and—the star —a three-months-old baby. The shooting was complicated by an unusual amount of camera, lights and mike trouble, together with missing props and other gremlins. At the end of a hot, exhausting day Aubrey Smith (then nearly eighty) remarked, "I don't know how that baby stands it. Look at it—fresh as paint—and I'm completely worn out." May, who had been holding the infant, looked at him in compassion. "Don't be silly," she said, "this is the fifteenth baby."

In *Lassie Come Home,* the first of that memorable, interminable sequence of Lassie pictures, May and Ben acted together for the first time in movies, stooging for Lassie, but enjoying themselves nonetheless. They found the star professional and disciplined, much easier to work with than others they had known. It restored Ben's spirits to be working. "He gets much praise for *Lassie,*" my mother wrote, "and it's lovely to have people praising his work again. He likes it and it compensates for all the anguish."

In fact, I think the anguish was dulling; but there wasn't much to interest him, though he never complained. He still played bridge, though not golf, which he had loved; I suppose because the courses were too distant and the fees too high. He wrote—not bitterly—"I am becoming a very efficient 'tweeny,' " meaning that humble maid-of-all-work who used to bear the domestic burdens of the household in bygone days. He became a familiar figure, walking up to the supermarket to do the shopping, with his felt hat rather jauntily on one side, his stick and his English-tailored suit, no longer new, the bones of the head and face still indestructibly beautiful; always courteous, with a smile and a joke for his fellow shoppers. They would look after him with affection and offer to help him across the road, which he didn't need and gently declined. Providence had sent the Websters a guardian angel in the shape of a Swedish woman named Gertrude who cooked, housekept, drove the car and adored "Uncle Ben." He began to "disremember."

He and May had established their home in a little house just below Sunset Boulevard, one of four or five grouped together haphazardly in a big, rather unkempt, garden which sloped down the hillside. To reach it you either had to climb up a long flight of steps from below or down a shorter one from above. But it commanded the view May loved so much, over the far-spangled lights of the city to the southern horizon. Here she began to recreate the kind of social focus which had made her Bedford Street home so widely known and loved. (I sometimes wonder how May's activities as a giver of parties, from intimate to enormous, over her whole married life, would have fared in these servantless days. She knew a very great deal about arranging and ordering meals, but nothing whatever about cooking them herself. So far as I know, she never, with her own hands, boiled an egg.)

The only drawback to the house on De Longpré Avenue was that the front door led directly into the living room and every visitor had the fullest opportunity to gaze in through the garden windows before knocking. It was therefore impossible to pretend to be "busy" or "out" to unwelcome guests. But then only a few of May's many guests ever were unwelcome, and with those she grappled bravely. On some evenings she "had a few people to dinner"; more frequently there were "two or three people for tea"; occasionally there was a full-fledged drinks affair with lethally strong cocktails concocted by May herself and entitled "the Dame's Downfall." But mostly the visitors "just dropped in"; sometimes on business about The Awfuls or some other activity, more often simply "to have a word with May and Ben."

These visits seldom tired my mother. "I am an old lady, I suppose," she wrote when she was eighty, "but I never feel it and I seem to be popular." For her, though never for Ben, Hollywood had grown to feel like home. In August 1942 they celebrated their Golden Wedding—an event conspicuous for its rarity in that city of divorces. Even the acid lady columnists, all spiteful two of them, purred in concert over Dame May and (a gratuitous ennoblement) Sir Ben. All in all, the Hollywood years brought them tranquillity, financial security and a great deal of loving-kindness; but fulfillment only to May.

Chapter Four

To Travel Hopefully

1

Once upon a time I was becalmed in a fog-bound train outside London. My companion and I were in the same play and we had to make the show. At last, in grim desperation, I asked, "Who was it said 'It is better to travel hopefully than to arrive'?" He answered, "Robert Louis Stevenson, the damn fool."

Two theatre events in the season of 1940–41 tended to vindicate Robert Louis in my eyes, and both deserve a tiny place in American stage history. One provided an unexpected and extremely inauspicious start for a young playwright with the improbable name of Tennessee Williams. The second may justifiably claim to have been the progenitor of Off-Broadway, Off-off-Broadway and other unlikely descendants. Both were complete failures at the time. But they both tried to break through the established formulae of Broadway, which, in those years, equated the entire American professional theatre.

Not that the record of contemporary accomplishment was a bad one—indeed, it seems effulgent in comparison with what has been happening on that little bit of territory thirty years later. The successes of the '39–'41 seasons included two major Sherwoods, *Abe Lincoln in Illinois* and *There Shall Be No Night,* two splendid Hellmans, *The Little Foxes* and *Watch on the Rhine,* the dawning of Saroyan's brief glory with *The Beautiful People* and *The Time of Your Life.* But the pattern of success can fairly be illustrated by such examples as *Charley's Aunt, The Philadelphia Story, Skylark, Ladies in Retirement, My Sister Eileen, Arsenic and Old Lace, Angel Street, The Corn Is Green, Blithe Spirit* and that sempiternal hold-over, *Life With Father.* There was the almost unfailing crop of musicals, including, most significantly, *Pal Joey.* Any recent season would have been highlighted by as many as two of these. But it will be noted that several were British (imported from a Britain at war) and that "the sweet smell of success" was just a little sugary. Young authors like T. Williams could and did regard it with dismay.

Secondly, as I had noted from the beginning of my life in the New York theatre, the costs of production and operation were far too high and were spiraling rapidly upward. And lastly, the supply of talent, authors and actors both, enormously exceeded the demand. Every train—trains in those days, not planes—brought a cargo of eager young men and women struggling to get into a consistently shrinking theatre. I sighed for the experimental theatre societies, the "do-it-yourself" clubs of my London upbringing in which my contemporaries, such as Gielgud, Olivier, Peggy Ashcroft and the rest had learned so much of their trade. But nobody in New York dared to face the prospect of actors acting for free—except, of course, the actors. Equity took the official stand that it would undo the fabric of society; producers (more accurately) figured that since only the actors would be free it would still cost them a lot of money, authors' agents shied away from no-royalty performances, and there was obviously no point whatever in trying to talk to the craft unions. So the prospects of experimental gambles were very remote indeed.

The Theatre Guild was trying bravely to live up to its high reputation. It even produced a classic, *Twelfth Night,* which I directed; and while we were still playing the try-out weeks Lawrence Langner brought me a script called *Battle of Angels* which he and Theresa Helburn had agreed to do. They had already got the star, Miriam Hopkins, and were to go into rehearsal soon after *Twelfth Night* opened.

Why they should have thought of engaging a young, English woman director who had never been farther south than Washington to direct this work, I cannot imagine. Perhaps it was because they thought (and so did I) that its emotional, almost mystic quality was more important than the local color and that the poetic prose in which it was written called for a director who was at ease in the medium of poetry. More probably it was just because I happened to be on the spot. I read the play, and thought that it wasn't, and never would be, a very good one, but that there was power in it and some splendid, multicolored words, and I believed the author would one day live up to his obvious potential talent and write a real dazzler. I also thought the Theatre Guild very brave to do it. So did they. In fact, Lawrence Langner's enthusiasm was the determining factor. Mrs. Langner had very little faith in it, and Terry Helburn held a wary watching brief.

These two productions, *Twelfth Night* and *Battle of Angels,* were the first of many I did for the Guild and only now, looking back, can I gain some sort of perspective. I must admit, to begin with, that although I liked them all personally I never once enjoyed working for them. But the peculiar circumstance is that I have never met anybody who did. They were almost certainly the most disliked, as they were also the most distinguished, management in New York and nobody quite knows why. The record of the Guild is unassailable; during the late Twenties they changed the whole character of the Broadway stage. They had high ideals, extensive knowledge, fine taste, vision—especially Lawrence Langner. It is no derogation to note that they were nearly all Jewish. The Jewish people have always been, and still are, more keenly alert to theatre than the average Anglo-Saxon. They introduced European authors to American audiences who had never heard of them and, from Eugene O'Neill onward, fostered unknown American playwrights. Langner managed to corner the Bernard Shaw market, which profited the Guild, amused Shaw and entertained the New York public. They attracted the finest actors, notably including the Lunts. It is not, however, coincidental that their best playwrights walked out collectively and formed their own Playwrights' Company, nor that many of their stars stormed out of that imposing building on 52nd Street in varying states of fury.

By the time I came to work for them, the original Theatre Guild group had recently dissolved, leaving effective control in the hands of Lawrence Langner and Theresa Helburn. There were occasional visits from Lee Simonson, the designer, and Maurice Wertheim gently and charmingly held a loose financial rein; but the legendary days of board meetings whose contending shouts rang through the building were gone. Confused mutterings had replaced them. The reputation of grandeur remained, and so did the endeavor; but there

66

was less vitality—and, of course, far more competition from other managements who had moved in to work the rich vein which the Guild had first discovered.

Terry and Lawrence, despite much personal kindliness, managed to antagonize and exasperate practically everybody. They seemed to be totally unaware of either the sensitivities of their authors and actors on the one hand, or of their professional skill and worth on the other. Splendid champagne parties on opening nights did not compensate for weeks of either neglect or niggling interference, combined with quite incredible tactlessness. They never knew why people got mad at them. It has been said, accurately I think, that throughout their careers at the top of the theatrical profession, they remained gifted amateurs. They were an extraordinary phenomenon.

The reign of Terry and Lawrence, augmented by the increasingly powerful influence of Lawrence's wife, Armina Marshall, was marked by their apparent inability to make up their collective mind or even their individual ones. They had a passion for rewriting, re-casting, changing and altering. You were forever receiving notes from one or other of them which were both self-contradictory and in conflict with each other. Terry's way of solving a problem was usually to vacillate until circumstances dictated a solution. Lawrence, if pressed—and if you had enough persistence to corner him alone— would take refuge in a protective vagueness; his speech would get slower and slower; his eyes would wander evasively away from you and he would take refuge in prolix stories about Bernard Shaw. If, like me, you were impatient and efficient, you went nearly mad.

One of the executives who worked with them during the Forties and Fifties has written this account of them with which I believe few in the same position would disagree:

> I *think* the basic problem was that neither Terry nor Lawrence could bear to have a free moment. They always had "projects" to deal with simultaneously with the problem actually at hand, so they never appeared to be giving any one thing their full attention. Meetings were always being interrupted by extraneous concerns. Their habit of arriv-ing late and talking to their secretaries and making phone calls [gave] the impression that they hadn't a clue as to what was being discussed because they had missed the operative phrase. So when they gave an opinion or made a decision it often appeared whimsical or arbi-trary. . . . They were incapable of delegating responsibility or differ-

entiating between matters of policy which were their true concern and idiotic details which could just as well have been handled by somebody else.

The result, of course, was total insecurity all round. Budgeting was a problem subject to violent swings of the pendulum. A production would be conceived in a spirit of lavish expenditure and subsequently, owing to the efforts of a succession of extremely able general managers, forced to undergo bursts of senseless economy which dislocated everything. Casting gave rise to fanatical controversy, complicated by Lawrence's total inability to remember anybody's name and trying to force into one production a well-known actor who was already playing for the Guild in another. (I am more sympathetic to his problems now than I was then.) Despite their desire to get the best actors they were masters of miscasting and their collective indecision made auditions a nightmare for director and actors alike.

In those days it was possible to fire an actor without penalty during the first five days, unless his contract carried specific safeguards against it. This was agony too. I hate rushing an actor; many of the best of them can't be rushed. You have to wait and coax them and have faith and pray you're right. Also I am thrown off balance when I have to go back and redo an old scene for the sake of a new actor, with the resultant waste of time and loss of rhythm and tempo. But the Guild batted actors to and fro like so many ping-pong balls.

In fairness I should add, however, that though I worked quite peaceably with Terry I was unreasonably exasperated by Lawrence. I think this was because he was one of the very few people in my theatre life who made me conscious that I was a woman doing what is more often a man's job. He would insist on patting me on the head (metaphorically) and saying "There, there!" A "wise old owl" who knew us both counseled me to take advantage of this "little woman" status by flinging myself on his manly chest and pleading for help; but I was stiff-necked and couldn't play it that way.

None of this detracts from the pre-eminent stature of the Theatre Guild in American stage history, though it may go a little way toward explaining the paradox I have described. Everyone who worked with them was aware of it; but it does not emerge in the statistics. Some of it I knew by hearsay—and a little by my previous

experience in *Twelfth Night;* but most of it was mercifully hidden
from me when we embarked together on *Battle of Angels.* I was also
confronting a star, Miriam Hopkins, whom I knew only from seeing
her on the screen, and an author, this Tennessee Williams character,
whom none of us had so much as set eyes on. It was arranged that
the three of us should meet in Miss Hopkins's extremely elegant
apartment at the Ambassador Hotel.

I arrived first and introduced myself. We began to discuss the
play. I found her lively, restless, stimulating. We speculated about
the author. It was three-quarters of an hour before he turned up, a
short, sturdy young man with crew-cut hair, pebble-thick glasses and
an even thicker Southern accent, dressed in a shabby corduroy
jacket and muddy riding boots. He greeted us amiably; Miriam said
she hoped he had enjoyed his ride; he replied that he never went
riding but that he liked the boots. He then sat down on the spotless
yellow satin chaise-longue and put them up on it. We started to talk
about the play; he didn't seem much interested; once, when Miriam
became a little vehement, he prefaced his reply with "As far as I can
gather from all this hysteria . . ." This is known in the language of
Variety as "a stoperoo."

Of course we should have realized that he was, in fact, stupefied by
the maelstrom of the Broadway theatre into which he had been
flung quite suddenly and unexpectedly. It eventually emerged that
he had regarded the MS which he had submitted to the Guild some
time before as no more than a first draft; he had been secretly appalled when, on his return from a vanishing trip to Mexico, he read
in the *New York Times* that the Guild was about to put it into
rehearsal. He knew, he afterwards declared, that he entirely lacked
the equipment and experience to make the write-as-you-go alterations they so often required of their playwrights and was dazed by
the "machine-like haste" of Broadway. We should have guessed
this. We were deceived by the maturity of the play into misjudging
the immaturity of the author. Tennessee concealed it, for a time
anyway, by getting increasingly vague, Southern and other-world;
and when confronted with really desperate demands for rewrites, he
would repeat his routine of lying down on the nearest suitable piece
of furniture, putting his feet up on the cushions and closing his eyes.

If Tennessee was dazed by theatrical New York, I was a little
dazed by the Deep South. I had stipulated that I should make a visit
to the author's home town, if only to "get the smell of it" and to

inform myself as to the appearance, atmosphere and contents of a General Store in the Delta country, where the play was laid. Tennessee and I flew down together. He introduced me to many of his friends. All of them assumed, first, that Tenn's play would certainly deal with the Negro question (on which it did not touch) and, second, that they would all simply love to see themselves and their surroundings as depicted by Tenn on the stage. I knew that in the unlikely event of their doing so a lynching would probably ensue and was accordingly a little embarrassed; but "Tenn" just grinned happily. When we got back to New York, I was exhausted from the effort to absorb and retain the impressions I had stretched my senses to receive, and I had grown very fond of this strange young man. Also I had acquired a perceptible Southern accent.

The auditions were just as bad as I had feared. We found the casting so difficult that we eventually settled for two actresses who had commitments on radio soap operas and would have to be replaced for one performance each week. One of them played the second lead. She and Miriam Hopkins took an instant dislike to each other and I thought she was miscast anyway; but for once Terry and Lawrence were in firm accord. The weight of the play really lay with the man, Val by name, and we plainly couldn't find him. One actor after another was tried and found wanting. Ten days before the Boston opening the Guild decided to use Wesley Addy, who was then playing Orsino, and I had the additional chore of discovering and rehearsing a replacement.

Moreover, the play was technically difficult. It called for endless sound effects, drums, guns, lightning and thunder, offstage pinball machines, wind, rain, guitars, songs, "hound-dawgs" and musical noises. It ended in an apocalyptic blaze of stage directions which really needed the resources of MGM, Wagner's fire music and Bernhardt to play the second (note, second) lead. Tennessee relates that I said from the beginning, "But how in the hell are we going to stage it?" It was a good question. But I allowed the Guild's technical staff to lull me into a false security, and Tennessee's poetic vision rose above such mundane matters.

So there we were, the classic Broadway setup: author, director, producers, star, all unknown quantities to each other; a delicate, intricate, physically complex play; a not very satisfactory cast; and no time flat in which to blend these elements together.

Things kept getting faster and furiouser. Miriam Hopkins became increasingly unsure about the play and herself in it. Her insecurity drove her madly round the "General Store," darting at the (substitute) props on the (substitute) counters, picking them up, waving them about and putting them down again in the wrong places. She would stand still only long enough to moan that the ending would never work and the other girl's long speech must be cut. Wesley Addy worried about his lines. The technicians and I worried about the fire which had to engulf the stage at the end of the last act. We all worried about an arty musical score which had somehow got tacked onto the script. Tennessee worried about all these things and his play and his draft status. (He kept on losing his draft card—theatre cleaners would pick it up from under seats. Obviously this was wasted worry. His eyesight was such that he couldn't have told an enemy soldier from a friendly tank.)

Later he described his feelings: "Oh, if only my head would clear up a little—if only I could find some lucid interval in this dervish frenzy that was driving us all to Boston and disaster!" At last he confessed to me "It is too late—I can't do anything any more. If I could get away from all of you for a month, I could return with a new script. But that's not possible." From being greatly irritated by his apparent obstinacy, I at once became soothing and maternal. I told him to stop worrying; the last speech would work, the store would burn down, we would throw out the musical score and all manner of things would be well. I didn't believe it. Only Lawrence and Terry remained calm, proffering no solutions to our problems but peacefully aloof from them.

The Boston dress rehearsals were pretty much what I had thought they would be. As a bonus, I jumped off the front of the stage, caught my ankle in a swing-seat in the front row and said "Ow!" Miriam fainted. We did throw out the score and scrambled around for substitute sound tracks. Lawrence began to pace the aisles and ask me where on earth I'd found this boy, Addy. We held post-mortems lasting into the small hours. The day before we opened Tennessee wrote a new last scene. Nobody had time to pay any attention. Above all the store would not, it absolutely would *not*, catch fire. After the final dress rehearsal the technical staff took solemn oaths on Bibles that it absolutely *should* catch fire, even if it meant self-immolation.

Came the opening night, complete with the Theatre Guild first-night Boston subscribers, a faithful body of supporters heartily detested by the entire theatrical profession for their stuffy, sit-on-your-hands, come-on-then-show-us superiority. This time they met their deserts. Several minutes before the final curtain, wisps of evil-smelling smoke began to drift onto the stage. The audience started to whisper, to shuffle, to cough. I thought, "They'll panic any minute now. . . ." Thank Heaven this disaster was averted by a sudden outburst of red spotlights, crashing breakaway beams and billows of sulphurous fumes, all far too theatrical to be true. The first six rows were asphyxiated, the rest fainted or fled.

The morning papers were less virulent than might have been expected, but they gave us no encouragement. Not one of them discerned the future playwright emerging from the clouds of smoke. We all decided to close after the Boston run. Everybody now started to behave calmly and sensibly, being too exhausted for recriminations. The Guild and Tennessee went back to New York and I took a night train to Minneapolis to fulfill a long-standing lecture date. There, over breakfast, I read the newspaper headline "MIRIAM HOPKINS SAYS BOSTON COUNCIL SHOULD BE THROWN IN HARBOR WITH TEA." It seemed they had condemned the play as immoral and had threatened to close it. This, oddly, was about the only thing none of us had thought of worrying about. Tennessee was completely taken by surprise and greatly shaken. "It seemed to me," he said, "that if *Battle of Angels* was nothing else it was certainly clean, it was certainly idealistic." But the City Council detected only that a middle-aged female religious hysteric painted a picture of Jesus with the face of "Val," and heard only that Miriam Hopkins said to him, "I can feel the weight of your body bearing me backwards." Merely *said* it, mind you; didn't *do* it; poor, cowardly Puritans that we were then. When I got back to Boston I found a castrated and largely incomprehensible edition of the play dying an inevitable death at the Wilbur Theatre.

Nothing whatever in this whole experience could have encouraged the author to go on writing for the stage; and it was that which troubled me most. But Tennessee loved this play and he had too much guts to abandon it. He rewrote it to some extent (not the major alterations which, many years afterwards, turned it into *Orpheus Descending*) and got it published. He had stuck to the theatre, though he had not yet succeeded in it. *The Glass Menagerie* was still just ahead of him; and I was still brooding over the possible loss of a playwright. Accordingly I wrote this footnote for the first published edition of *Battle of Angels:*

The American professional theatre is a hard racket. Some are born to it, some achieve it and some young poets from Mississippi have it thrust upon them; but it's hard, anyway. It isn't often art, but then it doesn't often pretend to be; it isn't "business" either, not as the efficiency experts understand the term. This confuses us all a good deal.

And yet, and yet . . . There are many people in [the theatre] with high hearts and great aspirations and a kind of bitter courage; and there are many to whom the art of the drama, the fine craft of acting, have something irreplaceable to say. Even now, most of all now, there must be a place for poetic drama by a dramatist more recent than Shakespeare, despite the fact that he may not be quite as good.

Tennessee Williams brings his gift of poetry, his love for words and images, his explorations of the deep-rooted mysteries of human behavior, to the service of a hard and unrewarding mistress. The muse of drama exacts laborious study, which is not difficult for the devoted to give, and much experience too, which is not easy to come by these days.

It is surely a sign of health that so many people, the most unexpected people too, were united in their feeling that *Battle of Angels* should be seen on the American stage: a commercial management, a film star ready to leave the lotuses of Hollywood, a number of distinguished actors with a living to earn and much easier ways of earning it available. Looking back, I think we made a mess of it between us, and that it was everybody's fault and nobody's fault. We did not capture the rainbow and translate it into the exacting terms of physical stage production, we did not bemuse the City Council of Boston, Mass. We probably should not have succeeded either in sending the Critics' Circle of New York out onto Broadway with stardust in their eyes. We had not made the alchemist's formula work, the ingredients were not right, or were not rightly blended.

I hope this does not matter. I believe it would only matter if any of us were deterred from trying again. For it is of the highest importance that we should. It is important to the future of our thinking as a race that we should not lose touch with each other, the poets, the theatre craftsmen, the audience, the people with ears and eyes.

Rereading the original typescript of my prompt copy I don't think we could have saved the play, no matter how good we had been.

The talent comes winging through—the hallmarks we all later came to know so well are there—but the weaknesses are too great and the ending has an almost endearing absurdity. It is touching to read the plain evidence of the young author's aims and ideals. There are no less than four explanatory or dedicatory quotations which, I think, were not afterwards reproduced. Under the title come the first two:

> I too am beginning to feel an immense need to become a savage and create a new world. (Strindberg)

and

> *While metals clashed,*
> > *a battle of angels above them*
> *And thunder and storm. . . .*

There follows a dedication:

> For D. H. Lawrence—who was, while he lived, the brilliant adversary of so many dark angels and who never fell, except in the treacherous flesh, the rest being flame that fought and prevailed over darkness
> > St. Louis, November, 1939

And lastly, to make everything quite clear, a further quotation of unacknowledged origin before the first stage direction under Act I, scene 1:

> There is only one true aristocracy—
> the aristocracy of passionate souls.

Tennessee Williams was later to get all the breaks even his great talent deserved—the shimmering, magical Laurette Taylor for his *Glass Menagerie,* an ideal director, Elia Kazan, for his *Streetcar,* a brilliantly imaginative designer in Jo Mielziner, and, too late, the actor who could have been born to play "Val," Marlon Brando. But all of them put together, plus a hundred dedicated firebugs, couldn't have won that battle of angels.

2

Nevertheless, I grieved and brooded. The young dramatist of talent but no experience necessarily writes imperfect plays. Where is he to learn better—to acquire some theatre skill before his stuff is catapulted out there onto the great spotlit arena before the rodent critics and the voracious crowd? Today, of course, no one would dream of doing *Battle of Angels* on Broadway. It would emerge quietly onto some tiny platform or squared circle south of 4th Street and everyone would just imagine the fire at the end. In 1941 there were no such solutions. There was no solution at all.

Once more it came back to the need for experimental theatres, producing for nothing, acting for free. I had already written about this, in the *New York Times,* the *Theatre Arts* magazine, anywhere I could get space. I had proseletyzed it in my lectures. Two years earlier I had talked about it at an Equity membership meeting. The actors had responded with enthusiasm. More unexpectedly, I had been invited to address the Council; and they, in turn, had appointed a Committee to investigate the possibilities of doing something. Its chairman was Antoinette Perry, she for whom the Tony Awards are named, she who was to become the organizing genius of the American Theatre Wing and the Stage Door Canteen; a shrewd and witty woman universally respected in the theatre for her knowledge and accomplishments.

Our meetings were often held at her house, where she hospitably eased our labors with champagne. Some of the members became a little uninhibited in consequence. I remember one of them waving his arms and proclaiming "Y'er stiflers! Y'er all stiflers!"; and another threw herself on the floor crying "I'm sick of being protected! I won't be protected! I want to act!" Certain stars shot madly from their spheres and talked a good deal of high-minded nonsense. The whole thing languished. In March 1940 I again wrote for the *Times* an article called "The Golden Eggs," on a text from its own critic, Mr. Brooks Atkinson, who had said: "The theatre is a failure as an industry. As a creative art it rests on the hollowest foundations it has had in my time." I supported the first phrase with statistics which prove a steady decline of 60% over a period of twelve years in the annual number of productions in New York City; the percentage of failures in the last few seasons varies from 68% to 83%; the average salary of a member of Actors' Equity (averaged, that is to say, over the total membership) is less than the prevailing relief scale, due, not to the small salaries paid to actors who are working, but to the staggering number who are more or less chronically unemployed. . . . We contrive to ignore this. We have a childlike faith that the theatre goose, starved though it may be, will somehow or other continue to hold golden eggs and not just lay eggs.

I argued the case for economic cooperation, which, of course, never came about, and went on to present one for "underpropping the theatre's artistic foundations" by the licensing of experimental theatres in one or other of many forms. I urged the proven value of the English examples, which had contributed greatly to young authors and actors without in the least degree weakening the position of British Equity or any other theatre union. "All last season," I continued,

> a committee consisting of delegates from the Council of American Equity and three co-opted members, worked on a scheme to evolve some kind of charter, or Joint Board, under whose aegis Sunday Societies could function, while all the participants were safeguarded from exploitation and assured of a share in the ownership of the enterprise and of the profits, if any. Finally, a scheme so heavily safeguarded that it looked to this member like the Man in the Iron Mask, was presented to the Equity Council; but they were not convinced; they asked for proof of co-operation from the Dramatists' Guild. For a year proposals have dragged inconclusively through the mails between representatives of these two organisations; and yet the whole thing could be put through in two weeks were it not for the apathy, mistrust and even hostility displayed towards it.

The sour and guarded report we had presented to Equity was eventually given a greenish light by the Dramatists Guild. Fears and scruples still shook everybody. But permissions and concessions were at last wrung from the stage hands; producers were wooed to lend us rehearsal space and theatres, while the most stringent prohibitions were devised to prevent them from taking any possible advantage of us or reaping any conceivable benefit. Under these meticulous rules and safeguards Equity gallantly offered to subsidize the venture; but it was understandably reluctant to spend anything substantial. The terms of the first "charter" precluded, for instance, any expenditure whatever on scenery or costumes. Nevertheless, toward the end of 1940, the first Experimental Theatre was born; in a strait jacket. We went to work on the first production.

Our choice—heavily influenced by me—was (I now think) courageous, justified and extremely stupid. It contrived to underline basic differences of principle which were to have disastrous results. We had repeatedly proclaimed that we didn't want to do only new plays, though we would search for them, but also examples of the classic repertory which had almost vanished from the professional theatre and were impossible to produce on Broadway. Second—and this was explicitly stated in the charter of the Experimental Theatre —we were to "enlist the finest forces active in our theatre"; in other words, known actors, even (sh!) stars, who would get a chance to play parts for which commercial managers would never cast them. This was, for me, part of my British theatre heritage which had paid such handsome artistic dividends. It was never our intention to do only plays by unproduced authors, with unknown actors and apprentice directors and all the inherent dangers of the blind leading the blind. We hoped judiciously to blend these elements. But before we could do this, we incurred the wrath and hostility of large numbers of our union members.

We read dozens of scripts, few of them with any particular merit. We chose two for our second and third productions; but the first was to be Euripides's *Trojan Women*. In 1971 the play was made into a movie, and it gets produced somewhere by someone every other week; but in 1941 it had been performed in the United States very rarely indeed. Granville Barker and an English company, under the auspices of Columbia University, had played it in 1915 for the opening of the Lewisohn Stadium; the Chicago Little Theatre had toured it, long ago, for the Women's Peace Movement; there had been only a small scattering of other isolated performances. At the end of 1940 it had acquired, obviously, a bitter contemporary significance. To emphasize this—but much more to placate the Dramatists Guild—we commissioned a one-act Prologue by Robert Turney. It was set on a road in Northern France, cluttered with refugees. It ended with smoke and the crash of bombs and Poseidon's voice rising through them and pronouncing the gods' curse on the victors:

How are ye blind, ye treaders down of cities,
Ye that cast temples to desolation . . .
Yourselves so soon to die!

Under the noise and smoke the other figures disappeared, except for one, a shapeless bundle of rags lying in the dark:

And she . . . would any eyes gaze now on Hecuba . . .

and so we blended into the play itself.

The device, though the emphasis was quite unnecessary, worked; the more smoothly because we were forbidden to spend any money on "costumes" and therefore had to do the play in a "sort of" modern dress. I was perfectly happy with this. But in any case, the Dramatists Guild was not placated by the Robert Turney Prologue. Euripides was a non-member and not a proper candidate for experiment. Much the same thing happened with Equity. Within the contemporary frame we cast Walter Slezak as a Teutonic Menelaus in a (borrowed) uniform and Tamara Geva as Helen with a teasing foreign (non-Trojan) accent and a mink coat (her own). For the "women" I borrowed some of the no-period clothes from *Family Portrait,* including my own black woolen robe worn by Mary Magdalene. The casting committee invited me to go on wearing it as Andromache. I agreed.

In the circumstances, this was extremely rash. I just plainly couldn't resist the temptation. I listened to lots of other Andromaches and thought I could play it better and still think I could and did. Why not? I had played in three or four Greek tragedies, schooled by a fine director, Lewis Casson, and I had the vocal equipment. Also the part is a gift. It was, I think, the only piece of professional self-indulgence of which I have ever been guilty and I have never regretted it. I knew the comments which would be forthcoming, and they forthcame. Worse was to follow.

Naturally there were hordes of would-be Trojan women applicants, as well as men for the Turney refugees and singers for the *a cappella* music (the only kind we could use) composed by Lehman Engel. I saw hundreds of them. At last I emerged with some forty actors none of whom had ever before had the opportunity of playing in this kind of stuff. We invited other managers and directors to some auditions in order to give the actors an opportunity of being more widely seen and heard. This idea was later systematized and extended. All that was fine. Only we didn't have a Hecuba. We approached (so my notes tell me) a dozen stars, including Jane Cowl, Margaret Anglin, Judith Anderson and others. They couldn't or wouldn't. We scoured many horizons. There were a lot of eager young women who were only too anxious to do it—one or two of unmistakable talent; but, rightly or wrongly, we were afraid of letting the burden of the play rest on such slender shoulders. We grew desperate.

At this juncture my mother wrote from Hollywood to the casting committee offering to do it, and prepared to pay her own fare East and the expense of three weeks' rehearsal in New York. Privately she wrote to me that she didn't think she could do more than "scuff about in Sybil Thorndike's shoes." The committee was deeply impressed, as well it might have been; the Equity Council (and membership) in much ferment, not because this Hecuba was the mother of the director and might have been selected for obviously "weighted" reasons, but because she was an alien. Privately I wrote to her:

> After . . . much deep thought I have come to the conclusion that the Hecuba thing would be too much of a risk for you, and the circumstances are such as to make it unwise. I am so angry at the Equity attitude; and I will not have it even faintly seem that you are asking a favour of them. It is just too silly. Apparently I am the subject of much bitter criticism from young actors and authors who think I am robbing them of their chances to "experiment" and doing myself some sort of favour and them some sort of harm.

Well, the reasons were obvious enough.

The Experimental Board made more motions to get true-blue Americans, some of whom I prayed would not accept. None did. The Board grew a bit annoyed. Antoinette Perry was not an aristocrat of the theatre for nothing. The Equity Council were softened. They finally accorded their permission; and in doing so showed themselves a good deal more liberal-minded, or more theatre-minded, than many of their successors. This matter of the "alien policy" of Equity runs like a long thread through my subsequent life, in London as well as in New York. Nobody in their senses would pretend that it is easy of solution; there are cogent arguments on both sides. But as a matter of demonstrable fact, and as applied to the narrow field of classical acting, one has only to take a quick glance at the achievements of Stratford, Ontario, which is "wide open," and those of Stratford, Connecticut, which is precluded from using British actors. It is not that British actors are naturally better; they are often not "naturally" nearly as good; but they have experience and a continuity of craft. The tradition of classical acting in America has ceased to exist.

To return, however, to Troy. The climax of a three months' obstacle race was the insertion of three performances of Euripides's play onto the stage of the Cort Theatre, kindly lent to us, but occupied by the set for *Charley's Aunt.* We had begged, borrowed and stolen to get that far. The Theatre Guild generously lent us rehearsal space in their theatre and some rostrums for the Cort. We managed to get some black velour "surrounds." How we contrived to banish Charley or his Aunt I no longer remember. It was a triumph of ingenuity and dedication. My mother got a dreadful feverish cold; I cut my hand to the bone wrestling with a radiator in her hotel room. Everyone worked like mad and we all enjoyed ourselves as people can only enjoy themselves when they are working for something they believe in and not getting paid for it.

Even now, I cannot really judge the results. My mother, thank Heaven, was to some extent rewarded. She wrote to Ben: "I was so nervous—my hands shook like castanets . . . but I've been spoiled with adulation . . . so many people came round, mostly in tears, and for a few surprised minutes I felt quite like a fine actress." I myself got wonderful notices—again, thank Heaven, and the part Euripides wrote, otherwise I would have had to shoot myself. Incidentally, *I* was so nervous that I practically dropped Astyanax, an enormous female child, weighing an even ton. But for the most part the critics condemned the approach, the direction, the translation (Gilbert Murray's) and most of the acting. They blamed Slezak and Geva because the Menelaus scene got laughs. We meant it to; and so, I haven't the least doubt, did Euripides. They also did us the honor of treating the production as if it had been a full-fledged, fully financed Broadway show. They couldn't have been accused of trying to give the Experimental Theatre a break, but they provided controversy, which was nearly as good.

We aroused interest. We got glowing support. I had a telegram from, of all unexpected people, Ina Claire, which I valued far above printed rubies because she was a lady who knew more about the theatre than the Critics Circle could begin to learn and because you would not think Greek tragedy was "her thing." It wasn't the critics' thing, at that time, either. Tony Perry, wise and farsighted lady, emphasized what the actors had learned, never mind what they had achieved. I wrote to one of the more virulent members of the press and said that it was nice, wasn't it, that he and I could disagree so totally about a play without our disagreement costing anybody $60,000. In fact, we paid our expenses and gave two performances for the benefit of the Stage Relief and the Actors' Fund. "Failure for Free" seemed to me a good slogan for the Experimental Theatre.

When the smoke cleared over Troy, the Board went on to its next two productions, both new plays. The press remained censorious and condemnatory. We struggled on. The charter was revised, supposedly to give the Experimental Board more freedom. But we were still in leading strings to our two parents, whose legal departments had devised the prohibitions and requirements. They had put a courageous toe into the cold waters of free enterprise, but they were never able to do more than that. Caution is not an inspiring watchword.

Fairly early on in these precarious proceedings, ANTA (the American National Theatre and Academy) entered the lists, impelled by Robert Breen, who bore a certain resemblance to Don Quixote— as did his starved, but impressive, steed. ANTA had managed to achieve a Congressional charter because it was headed by respectworthy people who were not in the professional theatre and didn't ask for a subsidy. It has never had any; and has consequently had to run on dedication and a certain amount of blissful ignorance. It enlisted the cooperation of the nonprofessional and educational theatres, but for some reason the professional theatre as a whole has always behaved very grudgingly toward it. Despite the unstinted efforts of individuals, Peggy Wood for example, amateurism always won out. Robert Breen, however, was determined to put his heavily letter-headed, penniless organization on the theatre map. He put the ANTA sticker onto a number of vehicles which had run out of gas and somehow made them go.

He was appointed Executive Secretary in 1946. By methods of prestidigitation best known to himself he managed to acquire offices in the Hudson Theatre; the Board, with vague ideas of an "Academy" to justify its title (and the Congressional interest aroused by this dreadful word), was about to lease the little, abandoned Princess Theatre, once graced by the WPA and Orson Welles. Breen didn't much want an academy but he did want an experimental theatre. There was no money or machinery with which to start one. He delved back into the history of the Experimental Theatre, found the patient in a deep coma and gave it the kiss of life. I once asked him who put up the money. His answer was: "There was *no* money—all the work was done by volunteers." Subscriptions were sold for the opening season. ANTA, being a charitable organization, could also accept contributions which could not have been made directly to the Experimental Theatre. Equity and the Dramatists Guild graciously permitted all this to happen. Brooks Atkinson in his bible of *Broadway* has stated that ANTA started the Experimental Theatre. This is not so. But it did resuscitate it.

I was already a member of the ANTA Board and of the Equity Council. I became a member of the Experimental Theatre Board jointly appointed by Equity and the Dramatists Guild. My life became a conflict not of interest but of meetings. Subcommittees were formed. The play-reading committee was snowed under with scripts, despite preliminary weeding-out by volunteer readers. Whatever plays we did choose were widely considered to be the wrong ones. This was not surprising. The Board generally differed violently among themselves and vocally dissident minorities opposed every vote. Nevertheless, the first two seasons' record was not a bad one. It included the first U.S. performance of Brecht's *Galileo* with Charles Laughton, some one-act plays including Richard Harrity's *Hope Is the Thing with Feathers,* Jan de Hartog's *Skipper Next to God,* with John Garfield, and John Latouche's pioneering musical, *Ballet Ballads.* I do not know what organization then or since could show a better list. Some of these productions were successful enough to transfer to Broadway. The labor unions then moved in to exact heavy compensation for having been done without; and they were all flops.

The casting committee held laborious auditions and invited other producers in order to provide talent showcases, which were afterwards formalized as such. They didn't succeed, need it be said, in pleasing the bulk of the Equity membership. The actors resented Charles Laughton and John Garfield. It was hard to find "star material" actors to carry an imperfect play and the authors resented inadequate casting. The blind started leading the blind again.

All the criticisms, many of them justified, could have been absorbed if the basic foundations of the Experimental Theatre had been sound. But the selection, casting and production of a play depend, ultimately, on personal judgment and individual responsibility. It is difficult enough for any single producer, or director, to be subject to a money-providing board. To please several thousand union or guild members is impossible; you cannot make decisions in terms of how bestest to satisfy the mostest.

It is also next to impossible to run an organization such as the ET on an entirely volunteer basis. Devotion and zeal we received in plenty from a swarm of secretaries, readers, press representatives, office boys and general dogsbodies, let alone the actors and stage managers. Producers like Cheryl Crawford gave generously of their administrative talents. But the necessity of earning our respective livings called us all off the job, sometimes at crucial moments. There was too much division of responsibility without final authority. The restrictions within which we were compelled to work were muddling and oppressive. The productions cost more than we could afford but less than we should have been able to spend. We became less Experimental, perhaps, when the corners of people's eyes began to turn toward Broadway transfers. The two seldom mix. At last, in 1949–50, the Experimental Theatre faded out in a confusion of incompatibilities and a certain degree of rather tired acrimony between its constituent elements; thus, says Brooks Atkinson, "effectively eliminating the threat of high-mindedness on Broadway."

But it had sequels. One of them was the ANTA Theatre Series which did ten productions in five months for special performances. Another was the Equity Library Theatre, dedicated to the unknown actor, but forbidden by its charter to do new plays. Another was the gradual emergence of the Off-Broadway theatres and all their off-offspring. I had been elected to the Equity Council in 1942, and for the next ten years I helped to fight the long battles to enfranchise Off-Broadway and to persuade the other unions to devise regulations which would permit it to function.

In the case of the IATSE and other labor unions the opposition was simple, basic and understandable; their members would get no jobs. It was pointed out that no jobs of that nature currently existed, and none ever would under their present rulings, so they had nothing to lose. They finally agreed to exempt minimal operations altogether, moving in gradually, and exacting compensation if or when "off" became "on" Broadway. Most fortunately, TV came along at about this time and eventually offered the IATSE more jobs than the members of their tightly restricted New York Local could fill. Off-Broadway's freedom was greatly enlarged by this unexpected redistribution of labor employment.

The Musicians Union, both in England and in the United States, has always been one of the most intransigent of the entertainment industry groups. In New York, under Mr. Petrillo's guidance, it decided to have no part whatever in contractual relations with Off-Broadway, except in the case of actual "musicals." On Broadway itself music in the intermissions, music in or with straight plays was rarely heard any more. Nobody could afford it. Now it is silenced; a loss all round.

The ATPAM (press agents, company managers, box-office treasurers, etc.) is comprised of extremely hard-working and able men—as well as a few who deal in "ice." The vagabond pioneers in their downtown hide-outs supposed (often quite wrongly) that they could do the jobs perfectly well themselves. The moving spirit of the ATPAM was Milton Weintraub, a fierce, dedicated man, ferociously well informed as to facts and statistics; and prominent in many enlightened, forward-looking theatre movements—ANTA for one. He led his union into a reasonable form of cooperation, and deserved more grateful remembrance than he probably ever got.

The designers' union presented other problems and had to be reassured and placated. The cagey Off-Broadway pioneers accordingly stuck, so far as they could, to a policy of no scenery at all. The spectacular rise of theatre-in-the-round, thrust stage (often just a bare platform), open-space stage and the like may be traced as clearly to economic necessity as to an advance in true theatre art. It became a cult, an artistic discovery, or rediscovery, a new means of communication, a theatre philosophy, an idol of the avant-garde. Freedom from expensive and complicated buildings of limited and uneconomic use; freedom from the proscenium and the second balcony, freedom from costly scenery and costly labor to move it around, freedom from obsolete and very difficult techniques of acting. Do your own thing. Heyday, Freedom.

Equity's problems were, of course, more subtle. It was right that they should be the pioneers since they were the principal beneficiaries. But they were afraid that allowing actors to play for far less than union minimum scales would end by undermining the standard contracts for which Equity had worked so hard; and that commercial managers would get free try-outs of productions for which they would otherwise have had to pay. The geographical definition which gave rise to the endearing term "Off-Broadway" was designed to protect the small enclave which then comprised all theatre employment in New York. The severely restrictive "ceilings" on theatre capacity and box-office grosses had the same, not unreasonable, object.

Although authors, unproduced authors especially, were passionate to get their plays done, however "experimentally," the Dramatists Guild was not as enthusiastic and agents were decidedly cool about the lack of proper royalties. Off-Broadway began with a predominance of revivals of classic, nonroyalty plays. Chekhov and even Ibsen raised their unfamiliar heads. It was a little while before the new playwrights began to take over the field and Off-Broadway began its distinguished advance to total nudity. A turning point in its history came when the Circle-in-the-Square acquired Tennessee Williams's Broadway flop, *Summer and Smoke,* and turned it into a long-running success. He had an enlightened agent. This could well have happened, had the time sequence been different, to *Battle of Angels.*

It should be remembered that the beginnings of this whole new manifestation in the American theatre arose not only in drafty downtown attics and crowded cellars, but in tough arguments and laborious union dickerings in smoke-filled office rooms. Also that God vouchsafed the movement an apostle and an evangelist in no less a form than the mighty critic of the *New York Times,* Brooks Atkinson himself. It has all paid off magnificently. What the present is doing to it or what the future may do has yet to be assessed, and may still lie in the smoke-filled rooms as well as in the converted dugouts. Off-Broadway has long outgrown the conceptions with which it originated; economically it is unrecognizable—dangerously so, most people think.

Certainly the tiny seeds from which the first Experimental Theatre began have been largely overgrown by more exotic plants—and perhaps a few weeds as well. Ironically, the British membership clubs and Sunday societies which were, in part, its models, have completely ceased to exist, though for other reasons and with different successors.

None of us on the stage of the Cort Theatre in April 1941 could have foreseen any of this when the lights dimmed down and the women of Troy went "forth to the long, Greek ships, and the seas' foaming." We never reached the shores of Greece, but we were among the vanished pioneers.

Chapter Five

Dear William

INTRODUCTORY

For nearly ten years, following the first production of *Richard II* in New York, I made a good part of my living and most of my reputation by directing the plays of Shakespeare; an astonishing piece of good fortune for me. There were a few disadvantages. I was trapped as a director and rarely got a chance to act, which I greatly preferred. Also I became irretrievably identified with "the classics." By the term "classic" I mean the international heritage of drama up to and including such playwrights as George Bernard Shaw (how he would have hated to be a classic!), Ibsen, Chekhov, Pirandello and the finest playwrights of either Europe or America who wrote in the first quarter of this century. To be so identified is a distinction but also a limitation. I am reminded of my father's aphorism when, after making a spectacular success as Hippolytus (in London, 1903), he wrote: "It's a bad thing to be an ancient Greek. It limits one's chances of employment." But the rewards were enormous.

I enjoyed Shakespeare. I had been brought up on him—in the theatre, not the schoolroom—as a normal diet. I had had wide and varied experience of acting his plays. But I never set out, as many people seemed to imagine, to devote my life to him. Indeed the "study" of Shakespeare was not at all my line until the production of the uncut *Hamlet* led me to serious book work. In one sense I was born to Shakespeare, but in another I had him thrust upon me. The unexpected successes of *Richard II* in 1937 and *Hamlet* in 1938 set

86

up a chain reaction. They were followed by *Henry IV Part I* (1939) and the World's Fair productions in the same year; *Twelfth Night* (1940), *Macbeth* (1941), *Othello* (1942 and again 1943–44), *The Tempest* (1945), *Henry VIII* (1946). I did many other productions of different plays in different places later on, but this was my New York decade. I also gave lectures and recitals about Shakespeare, and wrote a book called *Shakespeare Without Tears,* which involved me in a great deal of fascinating study and research from which I probably learned more than I was able to hand on.

Articles in national magazines dubbed me "The Bard's Girl Friend." One of them got annoyed with me for perpetually doing my thing and published a profile from which it appeared that I regarded myself as having superior qualifications and proprietary rights in Shakespeare—as being a kind of Supreme Authority. Apart from the factual inaccuracies involved, this was a total distortion of the truth. I have never approached a Shakespearean production except with respect and in trepidation. I was always totally committed and always gratefully surprised if and when it came out all right.

I received a lot of critical acclaim. It is mortifyingly easy for the director of Shakespeare, if he is not a complete bungler, to be hailed as a genius. The genius is nearly always Shakespeare's. The productions I have named happened to come at a fortunate moment in time. I believe they did make a contribution to the evolution of Shakespearean staging in the United States, and, moreover, they paid their way and didn't have to be subsidized. They did well on Broadway and, with one exception, went on tours of varying lengths. They were almost the last of their kind. This is as it should be. The plays were written to be performed in repertory and always have been, except for a brief period in the first half of the present century, when managers tried to get continuous runs out of single plays. This is a killing effort for the actor. No one should be asked to play Macbeth eight times a week. Laurence Olivier has told me that when he played Othello in the National Theatre repertory, he needed at least four and preferably ten other performances between Othellos. Trying to play such parts continuously is soul-destroying. As Eleonora Duse once said to Eva Le Gallienne, "Vous allez tuer votre âme."

To write about Shakespeare is very rewarding. You lay down rules, pronounce a "right" and a "wrong" interpretation, set up hypotheses and prove them by bibliographical, historical, philosophical or psychiatric computerization. You harness your own hobbyhorse and ride it to death. You put it all down in print, immutable, enduring. I have tried this exercise and found it extremely gratifying. I shall not do it here, for this is a book about the theatre and the theatre isn't a bit like that. It is flexible and transient and perishable; which is perhaps why stage people tend to find their academic counterparts either baffling or exasperating. Within the theatre context of this book I can only chronicle what I tried to do, and how and when and with whom, in a series of attempts to put theories into practice.

I keep on learning. Every production I did (or still do) involved new discoveries, even of plays I had seen twenty times and practically knew by heart. They reveal themselves when they move and sound and take on flesh as they never do in print. Even a ground-plan laid out on your desk with tiny puppet figures planted across it has something to teach. A two-inch Cleopatra once refused, point-blank, to go and sit down as I placed her; and I presently saw why. During rehearsals I have invariably gained new insights which prolonged study had never revealed. Sometimes they were provided by the actor's own vision, but not always. Often it was because the plays do not come totally alive without the human element of incarnation.

But that, obviously, is not all clear gain. In the theatre you have to be flexible, to adjust, to concede or sometimes to refuse. In the productions I did in New York the leading actor was often a part of the initial plan, occasionally, as in the case of Helen Hayes as Viola, settled even before I came into the picture at all. The Evans productions were done for Evans, *Othello* for Paul Robeson. The other stars and leading players were cast by mutual agreement, as and when we could obtain their services. I never could, or did, undertake a production which I thought seriously miscast. But the demands of the box office in the Broadway theatre of those days had to be considered and met. This could necessitate bending your ideas a little —not always disadvantageously.

If you are working under conditions which do not demand a star or a "name," if it is a fine repertory company, you must still have to have the actor sizable enough to act Macbeth, the actress sparkling enough for Rosalind. Without them the plays won't work—or many of them won't. And when you have actors of outstanding personality and talent, you cannot negate them or plow ahead on the theory that they should be quite different. Macbeth becomes Evans's Macbeth, Othello Robeson's Othello and you had better help them to fulfill themselves. Sometimes—very frequently these days—the director stars himself. I have always thought this a dangerously vainglorious procedure unless you are a puppeteer. But there are infinite variations of the priorities and sequence of casting. There is no answer to the question of the bird and the egg, nor should you try to enforce one.

In the theatre you have to take into account a hundred shifting factors. You must watch and weigh and balance, gratefully accepting the bonus of a good actor's contribution, however unforeseen, hastening to compensate for the weakness of a poor one, ready to adjust and counterbalance. Sometimes your fancy theories, to which you were so devoted, become plainly ineffective in practice. You had better let them go and write a program note.

This does not mean that you improvise as you go along or merely preside over a "happening." There are guidelines, principles by which a director is governed. Looking back over a dispassionate distance I can recognize some of mine. First and foremost, I never set out to impose myself on a play, but always to reveal it. Inevitably there were particular emphases and angles of approach. I have described those which led up to *Hamlet. Othello,* quite deliberately, emphasized the casting of a black actor as Othello. *The Tempest* came at the end of a bitter war and spoke of peace and pardon. But I never found it desirable to "gimmick" the plays in order to bring them up to date or make them what is hideously known as "relevant." You can only be contemporary for a year or so at a time. It is more difficult to achieve a universal "relevance"; but it is there, if you begin at the beginning, that is to say, with the author.

I used to try for the simple virtues; for instance, to make the plays march, to make them exciting. I found that you must believe the plot to make others believe it, trust the story and project it boldly. I seldom remember good reviews (only bad ones, which are sometimes indelible); but I cherished this, from Brooks Atkinson, because I hoped it was true: "She can see through the lines of a part into the fire of the spirit it represents, and she knows how to make a ripping good drama out of the material of the script." Sometimes I sacrificed introvert detail and the lingering caress in the cause of impetus, energy and tempo. Tempo is not the equivalent of haste. It is rhythm and variety, exactly as in a musical score. You must husband time so as to have it to spare when you need it, so that a silence can strike like a thunderclap, or hold the stage immobile for a full minute, if that is what you want.

I like to think that the Atkinson comment was true of the small parts especially. I took immense trouble with them. I saw them sharply and in depth, as they are written: the two Carriers in *Henry IV,* the "cream-faced loon" in *Macbeth,* Reynaldo in *Hamlet,* the Scrivener in *Richard III.* Shakespeare's little people are immensely important to his big ones. Even the bystanders, the "crowd," must be individually realized; even soldiers think. All the characters in the play are people, not chunks of the peerage or the proletariat.

Sometimes I was criticized for domesticating the plays and cluttering them with visual "business." This may well have been true. But I am sure that character can be revealed and situations clarified by visual action not specified in the author's exiguous stage directions. In the comedies I am quite certain that some of the "funny" lines, now obscure and meaningless, relied upon the "comic" business which accompanied them.

What I rarely succeeded in doing was to get the verse (or prose, for that matter) well enough spoken. No one was more keenly aware of it than I. It is the one supremely important factor in the playing of Shakespeare, no matter what the production style, no matter how "advanced" or outrageous to old-fashioned susceptibilities it may be. In England the National Theatre and Royal Shakespeare companies seem able to put on all-male *As You Like It*'s or play *A Midsummer Night's Dream* hanging from trapezes while they still use the words as the words were meant to be used. But American actors are not brought up on lyric poetry or Biblical prose and they seldom hear it spoken. They often have more vitality and guts than their English counterparts and they frequently delve deeper into the characters they play; but words confuse them and make them nervous, when set out in iambic pentameters. They find it hard to see imagery in visible form or to use the potency of sound and rhythm without loss of truth.

A great part of Maurice Evans's success lay in his ability to make melody—a dangerous one, of course. It was once said of an accomplished English comedienne that she wound up a part, started it off, and then left it to go on by itself. Occasionally I would reproach Maurice with sending his voice to the theatre while he stayed at home. But goodness! he knew what the words were about and how to convey their meaning. He had a fine vocal instrument, an exact musical ear as well as a precise understanding of what he was supposed to be saying. Audiences responded to Shakespeare thus revealed as they always have and will, whether or not they agree with the interpretation.

Every Shakespeare production I ever did taught me something and all of them are memorable to me because of particular incidents, exciting or funny or even disastrous. They always held some reward for me. In the context of their time, I think they were not without value.

HENRY IV PART I

One of the things they had in common was too much scenery. The late Thirties and Forties still belonged to the age of scenery, and a lot of ours was good. Nowadays we should use much less, which would be a considerable gain, though some loss also. But the more the scenery, the greater the hazards. Most of my disaster-memories are connected with scenery. On a thrust stage, even more in a theatre-in-the-round, you don't have to agonize about whether the stage hands will make the shift on time—the actors are doing it in front of your eyes. Tired as one may get of those busy little beetles who infest open-space stages, scurrying about as soldiers or servants or anonymous gremlins, nevertheless they are actors and you can choreograph them to a pattern. The chances of chaos are less than they used to be. On the other hand, there is no merciful curtain to slide down, in case of dire necessity, and obliterate everything.

Henry IV was heavily scenic; clumsily so, too, because we were trying to use as much as possible of our stuff from *Richard II* and it didn't all fit in. I use the term literally, because someone had made a six-inch error in plotting the depth of the St. James's stage and when we came to hang it we found that the Boar's Head wouldn't clear the Hotspur tent and the pillars got fouled up with the light pipes. I do not care to recall the night of the first dress rehearsal;

nor, I am sure, does Maurice. The overtime costs must have been phenomenal. How we managed to achieve a flawless opening night I shall never know, but we did.

The scenery wasn't all misguided effort. I believe it is important to preserve the splash and color of Shakespeare's historical plays. I sometimes wonder whether we do not risk impoverishment when we banish the visual glamour which good old scenery provided, and still does, when allowed. *Henry IV* is a turbulent, thrusting play, full of vitality and drive and panache. Heraldry is in order. The evidence indicates that the author and his colleagues cut a rich visual dash when they could.

Of course it is possible to take the opposite view, since Shakespeare himself took so many. A few years ago the Royal Shakespeare Company produced a series of the histories with the emphasis entirely on the brutality, sordidness, cruelty and animal suffering of those miserable medieval scrimmages called the Wars of the Roses. This is quite legitimate, though it works better with the crudenesses of the early *Henry VI* plays than it does with the *Henry IV*'s, when the writer was at the peak of his powers. One of his most brilliant achievements in Part I is to keep the balance between the Hotspur ideals of chivalry ("By heaven! Methinks it were an easy leap to pluck bright honour from the pale-faced moon . . .") and Falstaff's devastating mockery of ". . . honour? . . . Who hath it? he that died o' Wednesday. . . ." Hal, like the author, understands both. The play is poised on a high wire.

The RSC knocked it right off in the last two minutes by a piece of contrived sensationalism. "Bear Worcester to the death, and Vernon too. Other offenders we will pause upon." The two are led off; but not by the RSC, who staged a realistic hanging scene in full view. Shakespeare could be brutal when he wanted—as witness the putting-out of Gloucester's eyes. But surely in this case his summary is reserved for the end of the next play, Part II. It is bitter and shocking; but it is not a concession to the physical horrifics which the Jacobean dramatists were to bring into fashion and the theatre of cruelty revels in today. His views about war are more subtle than gratuitous onstage hangings.

Battles, however, are a perfectly dreadful stage problem. That little affair at Shrewsbury was the first I had ever tackled, and what I learned was never to do it again if I could help it. (After seeing that comic masterpiece in *Beyond the Fringe,* I swore off battles for good.) To disguise my lack of manpower I was forced to suggest that the fighting began long before dawn, over a lot of rocks and behind a series of gauzes. I relied on the convention that one man rushing across the stage with a very large banner would look like a lot more men, on the Birnam Wood principle laid down by Shakespeare himself. Indeed, he explicitly apologizes, in *Henry V,* for identically the same deficiencies from which we suffered:

> *Piece out our imperfections with your thoughts.*
> *Into a thousand parts divide one man,*
> *And make imaginary puissance.*

The massive rocks imperiled everybody's ankles as they dove behind them, and Arthur Kennedy almost had his eye put out by a spear. (He survived, however, to speak Vernon's dazzling speech "All furnished, all in arms . . ." with a golden effulgence I shall never forget.) The sun rose fairly rapidly, the gauzes were hoisted away (I listened for the sound of tearing as they disappeared into the flies), and the final duel, staged by Giorgio Santelli, was just as thrilling as it ought to be and far less dangerous than the rock-climbing.

I learned from this production also that armies are not to be trusted with battle cries. One night, coming late to the theatre, I heard the Hotspur cheerleader triggering the charge with a yell of "Esperanze! (Take it easy . . .)"; and the contending troops, all twelve of them, dashed at each other shouting "Art and Mrs. Bottle!" against "Susan and God!" I went home and wrote a lot of more appropriate slogans. By extension, this eventually led me to write practically every line for every member of the crowd scenes I was to direct from then on.

We had an excellent cast, stronger in the small parts than any I have had before or since. The fact that many of them had played with us in *Richard* or *Hamlet* or both showed up clearly. Maurice is the least greedy of actors, and he never tried to make his Falstaff overshadow the two young men, Wesley Addy and Edmond O'Brien, who were playing Hotspur and Hal. But it was an admirable performance, a reminder to the discerning eye that he was an extremely fine "character" actor, which he had proved as the Dauphin in *Saint Joan* and Napoleon in *St. Helena.*

For the first time, and at his suggestion, I had made a major textual alteration. I substituted the first Justice Shallow scene from Part II (Act III, scene 2), somewhat cut, for the scene about Falstaff and his recruits in Part I (Act IV, scene 1). I did it in fear and trembling—but few of the press or public even noticed. It is the kind of liberty which the U.S. still affords; in England it would be an extremely perilous venture. Perhaps it could be said that it threw the play off balance by underlining its warmth and humanity as against the harsh realities of war. But I think on the whole we gave it a fair deal, erring a little on the story-book side, but an exciting and entertaining show—what someone called (and I was content with the description) "a classical belly-laugh with cerebral overtones."

TWELFTH NIGHT

Twelfth Night has this in common with *Henry IV Part I:* it is a play of disparate elements which require accurate measurement and skillful blending. The component parts are, of course, more delicate and finer in texture. Both plays belong to Shakespeare's zenith, when his vision encompassed all humanity in affectionate mockery but in compassion also. *Twelfth Night* is, in Feste's phrase, "a very opal," elusive and glimmering. It is romantic, farcical, lyrical, satiric. It is deceptively pliant and bruises easily. I thought we bruised it rather badly.

The production started out with the Theatre Guild in its most lavish mood. Gilbert Miller was associated in the management, Helen Hayes was cast as Viola, Ruth Gordon as Olivia, Maurice as Malvolio, June Walker as Maria; Stewart Cheney was to do the sets, Paul Bowles the music, Karinska to make the costumes. All these ingredients were more or less established by the time I was invited to direct. The only one which worried me was Ruth Gordon, whom I admired very greatly but could not see as Olivia. Fortunately she couldn't either, and we were lucky in getting the best performance in the play from the least known of its principal players, Sophie Stewart, who managed to hold all its elements together and in focus.

In this list it will be noted that there are no "clowns." Sir Toby,

94

Sir Andrew and Feste were conspicuous by their absence. They remained so. We conducted an intensive Sir-Toby-search in vain. This was desperately important to me, since it is Sir Toby who must hold the "comic" half of the play together and lock it to the other half, as befits his "consanguinity" with Olivia. We couldn't get the actors we wanted and couldn't agree on the ones we could get. At last we arrived at a compromise; and as soon as we started to rehearse I knew it was fatal. Entrenched opponent of change as I am, I begged the management to replace him. With unheard-of unanimity they refused, then and thereafter.

On the other hand, they insisted on changing Orsino, Sir Andrew and (frequently) Feste. At one point they told me, starry-eyed, that there was a chance of our getting Bobby Clark for this part. I was sure that Bobby, a great genius of a clown, would rip through the fragile fabric of *Twelfth Night* as if he were leaping through a paper hoop. He couldn't have helped it. He was a dear and modest man. I went to talk with him and he considered the matter deeply and I shivered. At last he decided against it. I stopped shivering and felt guilty of cowardice.

Of Maurice I wrote to my mother after an early rehearsal: "He read like a dream—is pompous, with a slight touch of genteel Cockney, very much in earnest, very endearing and funny." It was a portrayal in the lighter vein. I expected criticism of the Cockney accent from those who think, justifiably, that the steward of Olivia's household should himself be very upper-crust. But Shakespeare's major characters are capable of widely different interpretations; I knew Maurice's would fit the letter scene perfectly, the prison scene less well. But it was a legitimate concept, most skilfully executed. Freed from the cares of management, he was unfailingly helpful when asked for advice or comment, though not always encouraging. Hankering in my own heart for some of the lovely, familiar settings to Feste's songs, I asked him what he thought of our distinguished composer's new score. "Wind and tinkle," he replied succinctly.

Of Helen I wrote in the same letter that "she has a kind of lost gallantry which will be touching." Her duel with Sir Andrew was a delight, innocently fresh and funny. When Malvolio leaves her with Olivia's ring, she looked at it, came forward and said to the audience quite simply and truthfully, "I left no ring with her. What means this lady?" They were immediately in the palm of her hand. How ridiculous it is to suppose that "audience participation" depends on proximity or can only be achieved by actors rushing up and down the aisles falling over people's feet or climbing onto their knees. It depends only on a quality of the spirit and a little stardust, and has nothing to do with buildings.

At the same time, I couldn't really imagine Miss Hayes making willow-cabins at people's gates and singing love songs in the middle of the night. Her damask cheek was not one, I thought, on which the worm of concealment would readily feed. Patience on a monument was not quite her line nor poetry her native element. But she was unassuming and charming to work with. She told someone later that she had not been happy at the prospect of working with a woman director. (It is often so—"women, beware women.") But she quickly gave me her confidence. It was no fault of hers that the problem of her clothes precipitated the worst crisis we encountered.

The question of how to dress the indistinguishable twins has always presented problems—at least until the present day, when they would be indistinguishable anyway. The first set of designs looked fine on paper, but no good on Helen. A second set was designed only a few days before we left for the New Haven dress rehearsals. Cheney's elegant, rococo costumes were being executed by the inimitable Karinska, of Russian ballet fame, whose flair and finesse were universally acknowledged. But she was equally famous for never, ever, having her things ready on time. I had already begun to make Cassandra-like noises to the management, who took no notice at all. The Viola-Sebastian complication toppled the Karinska schedule to its doom.

I wrote to May from New Haven:

The first dress rehearsal looked like charades at an old-fashioned house-party where the men had raided the hostess's wardrobe for appropriate clothes. There was a fairly complete supply of hats and gloves, a few pants, a cloak or so and one or two jackets. For the rest, the men made out with a selection of their own trousers, coats or dressing-gowns as the spirit moved them. Wes Addy (Orsino) ambled around in a brown towelling bathrobe patterned with white anchors, from beneath which his modern trousers and shoes emerged, a full make-up with beard and an enormous, plumed hat. Maurice displayed a most endearing ingenuity in securing props for these childish games, and made the cross-gartering from the girdle of his bathrobe on one leg and a couple of ties on the other. Clothes began to drift in during the evening and people kept popping up in some additional bit as the play progressed.

By the second dress rehearsal it was all a good deal less funny. Helen's breeches and tunic were among the last arrivals and when she finally did put them on, toward the end of the play, nothing fitted anywhere. Her fortitude and sweetness of temper, already much strained, collapsed. So did mine. Stemming the torrent of our fury, Stewart Cheney spoke meekly from behind me. "Do you suppose they're really meant to be Helen's clothes?" he said. We glared at him. Apologetically he added "There is Sebastian, you know." And sure enough, they were Sebastian's.

Miss Helburn, Mr. Langner and Mr. Miller remained calm, neither saying a word nor lifting a finger. I said I would organize a Bundles for Illyria drive and sent minions to New York who came back by each arriving train throughout the opening day. Orsino still had nothing but a hat. Finally, we pinned Wes Addy into the last bit of his costume as the orchestra started to play the overture and got him onto the stage just in time to murmur, rather breathlessly, "If music be the food of love, play on. . . ." I offered up a prayer of thanks to whoever invented safety-pins.

The production aroused mixed feelings in me and conflicting ones in other people. It was gay, decorative, witty in a slightly sophisticated way, but seldom funny from the heart; charming and even occasionally touching, but lacking in shadows or in depth. The critic of *Time* magazine thought Helen "wise to eschew the poetic side of Viola" because "this is difficult to express on the stage"; a remark which still seems to me totally bewildering. No wonder I wrote to May that I thought some of the weekly reviews "unutterably silly because they get hold of all the wrong reasons"; but that I knew they missed something that ought to have been there and wasn't; several things, in fact.

The so-called "comics" tried very hard but not very successfully, despite June Walker's lively, miniature Maria. With this half of the play, it is Sir Toby or nothing. I found myself cutting increasing numbers of incomprehensible jokes such as: "Are they like to take dust like Mistress Mall's picture?" or "Sowter will cry upon't . . . though it be as rank as a fox." These are what I call footnote jokes and are often irretrievable. Some were "actors' cuts"—lines I knew were good, but I couldn't get the actors to bring them alive. Some, I knew, needed visual business which I was sometimes, but not always, successful in devising. Occasionally I thought our mutual inventions were too elaborate and slowed down the tempo.

For the Malvolio letter scene I stole a piece of business from Michael Chekhov's production for the Habima Players, which I had seen many years before and never forgotten. The conspirators carried round with them little, toy, potted trees which they would plant down in front of themselves as a ludicrous sort of concealment. I was careful to have them really out of the way when the focus needed to be on Malvolio, with no distracting antics from the rest. This kind of stealing is, in fact, the perpetuation of good ideas. It finally amounts to "tradition." One piece of business in *A Midsummer Night's Dream* was described by a member of the audience in Shakespeare's own day and is still common practice. At one time I used to be angry when I came upon bits of my ideas copied in other people's subsequent productions; and I still think that a director's prompt book should be subject to copyright protection. But now I look upon it as a kind of compliment; and often, very naturally, the same sort of business occurs to different directors as illustrative of the lines and the situation concerned.

A lot of people liked that production of *Twelfth Night.* The Guild did, which was nice for them, and my mother (to my astonishment) thought it the best she had ever seen. But my verdict on myself was that I had "done an expert piece of figure-skating over thin ice" and that it was "a job I shall never look back on with pleasure or pride."

This was, I'm sure, unduly severe. It was because I loved *Twelfth Night* very much and the gap between my vision and the concrete result was wider than it had ever been before. There always is a gap of some sort, somewhere. You get used to it, but you never stop trying to narrow it down. In fact, I think *Twelfth Night* is one of the most difficult plays in the whole canon to do really well. Yet everybody does it; everybody thinks it's easy. And in a horrible sort of way it is nearly foolproof. I once saw an incredibly dreadful college performance which the audience appeared to enjoy immeasurably. Salute Mr. Shakespeare.

MACBETH

During the winter and spring of 1941, distant rumblings, as of an uncertain thunderstorm, began to be heard from *Macbeth*. Maurice decided to do it the following September, and we accordingly set up the production. Meanwhile, I had an interlude of assorted summer stock, acting as well as directing. Of this I wrote to my mother: "What is there to say about summer stock productions? The curtain goes up and eventually comes down and in between everybody does what the French call 'their possible.'" I made up an interleaved prompt script for *Macbeth* and went to Martha's Vineyard to work on it.

Macbeth is a play about the power of evil, and its ultimate defeat. The influence of evil is all-pervasive and contaminating, like dry rot, or smog or the pollution of a river. Unfortunately the two men, Macduff and Malcolm, who breathe free air, who stand and say "No," are rather dull characters. Even Shakespeare, at least in his tragedies, seems to have found it easier to write interesting "baddies" than "goodies"; which, put very baldly, is what distinguishes tragedies from Westerns. The two chief "baddies" in *Macbeth* are such magnificent parts and the story itself so headlong and dramatic that the play is presented, more often than not, as a splendid thriller with two actors of star quality and a trio of "witches" thrown in as a necessary device to get the plot going. It was in Maurice's temperament to approach the play somewhere along those lines; but I saw darkness and black magic in it. I would still approach it rather as if I were defusing a bomb.

I decided not to try any fancy tricks with the outward appearance of the "weird sisters," but to present them just as they are described by Macbeth and Banquo. Shakespeare's choice of the symbolic has lost, for a modern audience, the force it must have had for an Elizabethan one. Even so, I am not entirely convinced that his attempt to incarnate the powers of evil can have been wholly satisfying to him. His audiences would have accepted implicitly the potency of the Three Weird Sisters and would have hated and feared them accordingly. But the witches are the instruments of darkness, not its origin. They provided, in the framework of their times, an outlet for the fear, hatred and insecurity of ordinary people; for mankind's horrified impotence in the face of unexplained disaster, bloodshed, senseless violence. There is no modern equivalent; though I suppose that in certain communities you could try one witch as Chairman Mao, another as a Congolese tribesman and the third as a shaggy "student" of uncertain sex. But the transcendental operates unseen; evil, in this play, is invisible, twisting and echoing through all its patterns, not a series of conjuring tricks like a souped-up séance. It is best to keep things simple.

I suppose, equally, that it might be possible to represent Macbeth as merely having had "a bad trip." I cannot imagine that this interpretation had occurred to the Boston theatre authorities in 1941. Nevertheless, we found the following clauses in our theatre contract:

> All forms of muscle dancing by either sex is prohibited. The portrayal of a dope-fiend by either sex, wherein the act of taking a hypodermic injection, the inhaling or eating of dope, or the use of dope in any manner intended to show its effects upon the human being is forbidden.

I presume these clauses have now been removed; if not, the Boston censors must have been asleep for a nice, long time.

As all theatre people know, the stage history of *Macbeth* is loaded with disaster, documented by overwhelming evidence. It may be that if you do the play without ever setting a light to the fuse the bomb won't go off. It doesn't always; but it did this time. No one actually died of it, but a lot happened that was, to say the least, unfortunate, especially to me. (As a faintly macabre footnote, I might add that when in the first rough draft of this book, I had written the sentence, *"Macbeth* is a play about the power of evil," I glanced at my watch and saw that it was time to go off to my doctor for a minor routine check. He told me that I must go into hospital immediately to undergo a piece of major surgery. However . . .)

In the case of the Maurice Evans–Judith Anderson production, I was not very happy with the results. It was received with great favor by press and public; it had, I think, pace, drive, excitement, clarity of pattern. The verse was well spoken; it made sense. Too much sense, perhaps. There was little mystery. The scenery was again too heavy and too literal, and this matters more in *Macbeth* than in *Henry IV*. I did not have, none of us did, the forward-leaping imagination to transcend our period, except in rare sequences. The opening scene was one of them: bagpipes and drums (real, live music!), Duncan's army filing across the front of the stage; behind them a translucent backdrop of stormy sky, the clouds reforming into the shadows of the three witches, their couplets of doom (over an echo mike) whispering through the martial music, fading out as King Duncan spoke the opening line and the blood-spattered soldier reeled onto the stage and fell at his feet.

This, however, is a sufficient illustration of why the physical production turned out to be—in the stage manager's phrase—"a whistling bitch." Heavy scenery and rapid changes—live music in the orchestra pit—recorded "echo music" and sound effects backstage— live, "prop" sound (thunder-sheets and so on)—complicated lighting including Linnebach projections—no torturous hazard was omitted. Synchronization was everything, and it had to come from the stage manager's corner; and in New Haven, at the dress rehearsals, he became paralyzed with stage fright. I have known this to happen before and since to actors, but only once to the stage manager and this, understandably, had to be it. We were saved only by the arrival of my own ex-stage manager, Thelma Chandler, who had been acting as my personal assistant and who arrived in New Haven with her own prompt copy and a complete set of cue sheets which she had made up at rehearsals "just for fun." The Boston opening was appalling. The New York one got through by the skin of its teeth, one major disaster averted only by Thelma's seeing it about to happen and scrambling up the iron ladder to the fly gallery just in time.

The "power of evil" was, even so, more manifest in external circumstance than in events onstage. "External circumstance" included the bombing of Pearl Harbor a month after we opened. Inevitably New York audiences became rather less concerned about the goings-on at Glamis. But several lesser happenings had a faintly witch-like flavor. One of them concerned the sleepwalking scene.

Ever since *Family Portrait,* Judith Anderson and I had regarded each other with affection and respect; we worked well together. But in this case we were slightly inhibited by the fact that we had both already played Lady Macbeth—I at the Old Vic in 1932 and she, much later, for the same company with Laurence Olivier. (Both occasions were fraught with disaster; the presiding genius of the Old Vic, Lilian Baylis, died during the dress rehearsal of the Olivier-Anderson production.) During our early rehearsals, Judith and I treated each other with exaggerated respect and positively Oriental courtesy. At last, she broke down and asked me what I really and truly thought of the way she was playing the sleepwalking scene. "Really and truly?" said I, nervously. "Cross your heart." I said— as tactfully as I could—that her Lady M. seemed more than a trifle manic, but never for a moment asleep. She took this gallantly. "But how," she wailed, "do I learn to sleepwalk? I can't haunt the hos- pitals on the off chance that somebody may. . . ." I hazarded a few guarded suggestions as to how one sleepwalks; but the next day she came armed with a masterly scheme.

A doctor friend of hers knew another doctor who used hypnosis in his psychiatric work. He was currently in the army but still had some private patients. He would bring one of them to Dr. A's apart- ment and induce her, under hypnosis, to sleepwalk for Judith's bene- fit. I asked who the patient was to be; a seventeen-year-old girl from Pittsburgh. I said cautiously that seventeen-year-old girls from Pitts- burgh might not sleepwalk like Lady Macbeth. Judith agreed, but felt she could learn from the externals. I asked if I might come too, and did.

Dr. A greeted us in a spacious penthouse apartment. Dr. B arrived, in uniform, with his patient, a plump, pretty, rather vacant-looking girl. We were not introduced by name and she had been told nothing about the experiment. Dr. B asked her to sit down in an armchair and take off her shoes. He began talking to her quietly; within a few sentences she was "asleep." He told her to walk across the room. She did so. Her eyes were open, but blank. She moved as if she were blind, each foot feeling the floor, heel, instep, toe, before she put her weight on it. Dr. B told her to do various things—listen to a shout or cry—look toward another room—move to stop someone from coming in; her movements were all small, miniature indications of a waking action, like a sleeping dog which dreams of hunting. Her voice, when he told her to say something, was flat and toneless.

Presently Dr. B moved over to Judith and whispered into her ear so softly that I could only guess what he asked; but I could lip-read her answer. It was: "Wash her hands." Aloud, he said to the girl, "There's a bowl of water on that table" (it was an ashtray); "go over to it and wash your hands." She did so, beginning with the usual motions of hand-washing. After a moment her body tensed. She stared at the back of her right hand. The fingers stiffened. She began to rub it with her left hand, at first gently, then harder, then frantically, over and over, from the wrist to the fingertips. "What are you doing?" asked Dr. B. "What's that on your hand?" In a dull, flat voice she answered, "Blood."

The lessons of all this were not lost on Judith; but they began to acquire a slightly theatrical dimension. The scene is, Heaven knows, difficult at the best of times, but especially on Saturday matinees when the theatre is crowded with schoolchildren. In America, for some reason known perhaps only to high school teachers, the line "Out damnèd spot" is the second funniest in all dramatic literature, beaten only by "something is rotten in the state of Denmark." Judith, infuriated by a laugh at this point, would become more and more dramatic, which, bless their dear little hearts, they thought funnier than ever. (In fact, the only way is to wait—whisper as quietly as you dare—and cheat the rhythm so that the line is gone before they recognize it: "Out . . . . . damnèd spot out! I say . . .")

During the winter of the New York run we began to lose the Thanes of Scotland to the armed forces of the United States; and when we left for the tour, we also lost one or two actors who didn't want to leave New York, including Judith's understudy. I had managed to rehearse replacements between having my appendix out and then getting flu. When the company finally left for Buffalo one snowy Sunday morning, I retired back to bed. But the next day Maurice telephoned. Judith had laryngitis, her new understudy didn't know the lines, would I fly up and play that night? I got myself out of bed, scrambled together some clothes and make-up, telephoned Barris, the wig-maker, to contrive something for my short-cut hair, got to La Guardia Airport and boarded a plane, clutching my prompt copy, as the snow began to fall.

I could remember the lines all right—or rather, I knew they were inside my head really, and would come out of my mouth at the proper time so long as I didn't fuss. But I was frantically unsure of when I was supposed to do what—the stage moves and business of my own devising. The plane bucketed along in a near-blizzard and I shut my eyes and tried to visualize the scenes. Someone touched my arm; my neighbor was leaning toward me solicitously; he said "I have some air-sickness tablets if that would help. . . ." I thanked him kindly and feared it wouldn't.

Against the odds, the plane got down in Buffalo; still against them, I managed to get into Judith's clothes and come out with Shakespeare's words and not get a laugh on "Out damnèd spot" (nor did I at the kids' matinee the next day) and be in the right places and even act a little. The following morning a huge bunch of flowers was delivered to my hotel. The card said: "Never again will I mistake a rehearsal of the sleepwalking scene for air-sickness."

By the end of the tour there was hardly a Thane left unless he had asthma or flat feet. Before they finally disbanded, Maurice persuaded the U.S. Army authorities to let him present a *Macbeth* performance at the Fort Meade training camp. It was a guinea-pig affair, undertaken by the army to prove, I think, that the troops couldn't possibly be persuaded to like Shakespeare. Our production had to be stripped to the barest essentials for the available conditions and I set out to join the company in Baltimore. That morning my old enemy tonsilitis leaped upon me again; I managed to get as far as Newark, ten minutes from New York, and was then forced to get out of the train, cross the platform and come back again. I heard only at secondhand that the Fort Meade performance had a tumultuous reception from its GI audience, eighty percent of whom had never seen a Shakespearean play before.

This may or may not have had much effect on army policy and USO Camp Shows, but it must certainly have influenced Maurice. He enlisted in what was then known as the Army Specialist Corps with the rank of captain. The Pentagon presently reorganized this as a part of the regular army, to which it transferred those who were willing to go. I wrote to May: "Captain Evans has left for some God-forsaken camp in Missouri. He looked a little wistful and a little scared, and small blame to him; but determined to control the whole outfit before long, as no doubt he will." This he subsequently did in Hawaii, where, among other things, he presented a replica of our *Macbeth* with the assistance of an amiable Sergeant named George Schaefer. The so-called "GI *Hamlet*" followed and came to Broadway after Captain (by now Major) Evans and Sergeant Schaefer resumed their civilian status in 1945. Thus began the career of the man who became the most important director of television drama in the United States and might well have been known as Mr. Hallmark.

I worked with Maurice again a few times—at the City Center, where he was helping to try and establish seasons of drama between popular-price opera and ballet; we did *The Devil's Disciple* and a revival of *Richard II.* We were urged to bring *Richard* back to Broadway, but Maurice refused; it had become too expensive to run. A number of years later he played in *The Aspern Papers,* which

I directed, but it was not his own management and I don't think he enjoyed it very much.

I am often asked "How good an actor *was* Maurice Evans?" The past tense saddens me; and the answer can only be my personal estimate. He was always a critic's actor rather than an "actor's actor"; his enormous public success was interrupted by the war years; but he could easily have recaptured it—and in fact did so, but in a different way. *Dial M for Murder, Man and Superman* (in both of which he played), *Teahouse of the August Moon* and *No Time for Sergeants* were all big hits. He applied his admirable judgment, shrewdness and tough executive ability to the production field, whose problems, I think, had always fascinated him as much as, or more than, those of the actor. He was the last of the independent actor-managers on Broadway.

Perhaps these preoccupations stood in the way of his acting achievements. I do not believe that acting ever meant to him what it has meant to Gielgud or Olivier. It was not the breath of life. This may have been one of the reasons why he never, in my judgment, touched the heights or plumbed the depths of Hamlet or Macbeth. He was a "tragic" actor in voice, but not in spirit. He was always, from his youngest amateur days, a brilliant character actor, one of the finest I have ever seen. By the same token, he was a brilliant Shavian actor, whether as John Tanner or Captain Shotover. His clarity of thought and virtuosity of speech are admirably suited to Shaw's sparkling prose, which makes more demands on the intelligence than on the emotions. There was no reason whatever why he should not have gone on playing the finest available character parts as and when he chose.

But the Broadway theatre changed to a degree which forced out the independent manager. Maurice preferred to be his own boss and it was always a point of honor with him to repay his backers and show a profit; this became increasingly difficult and the gamble an increasing risk. Possibly in his heart he shared the general view that something which doesn't pay its way can't be very well worth doing; also, there is the small matter of earning a living. It became apparent a very long time ago (for myself, I would say about twenty-five years) that this was not a thing you could do just by working in the theatre field on Broadway. You had to plan the alternatives or the supplementary sources of supply. Movies and television are, of course, the most obvious; or there is the kind of life I have been able to work out for myself and shall later describe; there are many ways of living. To be dedicated to acting is not necessarily a virtue.

It is a loss that Maurice is no longer, at least for the time being, active in the theatre; but it is largely the theatre's fault. The options which were open to Gielgud and Olivier in England were never available to Maurice in America. Both British classical repertory theatres, the National and the Royal Shakespeare Companies, use star actors who appear for them from time to time, but not continuously. In between, they can do movies, television or sometimes even commercial plays. It is possible to have your theatre cake and eat it in the other media. As against this, only the United States could ever have given Maurice the enormous popular and financial success he at one time enjoyed and the ability to be his own master and "write his own ticket." This could no longer happen. But the art-theatre producers and managers of today might well ask themselves whether they could even have got started if, like Maurice, they had had to pay their own bills.

OTHELLO

Othello is a play I would like to do again. Its potential is inexhaustible; and although there is plenty about evil, it is not the imponderable, elusive black magic of *Macbeth*. I directed it, was part of the production management and played Emilia in it with Paul Robeson in New York in 1943; it had taken us four years to get there, in the teeth of every possible hostility and prediction of doom. As it turned out, the production and Robeson's performance made theatre and even social history; it was the first time the part had been played by a black man in the United States. It also broke all records in box-office terms.

Paradoxically, it wasn't an especially fine piece of acting. Robeson was never a born player and he had not acquired much acting skill. I had seen him play it in London in 1930 and thought him very bad. He later told me that he had been so overwhelmed by the thought of playing Shakespeare at all, particularly in London, with his unmistakable American accent, that he had never reached the point

I

May and Peggy, going over the script
of *Viceroy Sarah,* Deertrees, Maine, 1939

Ben in his seventies

May around 1946

Dame May Whitty, the wheelchair, Robert Montgomery, in *Night Must Fall,* 1937

Ben and May "stooging" for Lassie
in her debut performance. *Lassie Come Home,* 1942

Dame May with Margaret Lockwood in a famous scene
from Hitchcock's *The Lady Vanishes,* 1938

Maurice Evans

As Macbeth, with
Judith Anderson as
Lady Macbeth, 1941

As Hamlet, 1938

As Falstaff in *Henry IV
Part I,* 1939

Helen Hayes (Viola—
in the rejected costume),
Margaret Webster
(exuberant anyway),
Maurice Evans
(Malvolio—a perfect fit),
Twelfth Night, 1941

The Tempest set,
"gossamer lovely," 1945

Othello, 1943

Othello
(Paul Robeson)
kills Desdemona
(Uta Hagen)

Othello (Robeson)
and Iago
(José Ferrer)

Eva Le Gallienne as Ella Rentheim   Margaret Webster as Mrs. Borkman
in *John Gabriel Borkman,* 1946

Eva Le Gallienne as the White Queen, Bambi Lynn as Alice,
Margaret Webster as the Red Queen, in *Alice in Wonderland,* 1947

More A.R.T.

Top: The coronation of Anne Boleyn in Westminster Abbey. *Henry VIII*, 1946

Bottom: *Androcles and the Lion*, 1946. "Even the critics liked this one."

of looking Othello squarely in the eye. His study of the part began when the run ended. In 1959 at Stratford-on-Avon, he had grown too old and too fat and there had been no time to shape the production for him—or no one had realized how vitally necessary that was going to be. But in the production which opened at the Brattle Theatre, Cambridge, in August 1942, and at the Shubert in New York just over a year later, he matched the part and the hour. From the moment he walked onto the stage and said, very quietly, " 'Tis better as it is," he endowed the play with a stature and perspective which I have not seen before or since. I wrote to May: "Is it possible to be a great Othello without being a good Othello?" No. But the moment lent it greatness. The Robeson *Othello* became more than just a successful revival; it was a declaration and its success an event in which the performance itself was of less importance than the public response.

It was in 1938, after *Hamlet,* that Paul first came to talk with me about it. He thought the work he had done on the part had by now made him ready to play it and that audiences were ready to let him. I believed this. We wanted Maurice to play Iago. I offered all ten cents I had in the bank to prove my faith. But Maurice shook his head and said the public "would never go for it." Everybody else said the same. Stars wouldn't play Iago, nor, of course, Desdemona. It had been all right, they said, for Peggy Ashcroft to do it in London, but she was English and that was London. In America—a white girl play love scenes with a *black* man . . . they were appalled. If you pointed out that Othello and Desdemona are never alone on the stage together until the last scene when he kills her that didn't seem to make it any better. Everyone gave different reasons, but they were all plain scared.

The problems of the Negro in American society were being sharply highlighted by the war and the inevitable integration of Negroes into the armed forces and war industries. (I am aware that "Negro" has become, for the moment, a dirty word in America; I use it in this context because in the Forties "Black" was the dirty word. To be truly polite, "colored" was the term to use. These political semantics are confusing; "Negro" is of its period and in quotations is unavoidable.) When Paul and I realized the pressures we were up against, we determined that we would do *Othello* ourselves, on a street corner if necessary, like *The Cradle Will Rock.* In the spring of 1942 we canvassed all the summer-stock theatres. We would assemble the company and pay the freight if they would give it a try-out production. This wasn't easy since the draft was taking all the young men and gas rationing was depriving theatres of their audiences; many had gone out of business; and the ones who were left were as scared as their Broadway brethren. At last we found two who weren't: John Huntington of the Brattle Theatre, and the Messrs. Day Tuttle and Richard Skinner of the McCarter in Princeton. Both theatres could draw on university audiences and were close to metropolitan centers, and we would face the test of the first-string critics in Boston and probably some from New York. We started casting.

I owe to Eva Le Gallienne the inspired suggestion of José Ferrer for Iago, and his then wife, Uta Hagen, as Desdemona. She was comparatively inexperienced, but she had the strength and enough classical training to meet the demands of the part—no dewy-eyed lamb-to-the-slaughter for Uta. In the beginning she needed almost no help from me. Her performance was simple, direct and her own; Paul liked her and they played excellently together. I jumped at the idea of Joe for Iago because I had seen him in *Charley's Aunt.* This was not frivolous. Although he had never done Shakespeare, he had not merely virtuosity, but the power of persuasion. If he could fool people into thinking he was Charley's Aunt "from Brazil where the nuts come from," he might be the Iago who could really convince the inhabitants of Venice and Cyprus that he was not only the life and soul of the party, but "Honest, honest Iago." I had never seen this done.

I still haven't. Joe gave a brilliant, stimulating performance; but he was never, oh, never, honest. He compensated for this, however, in a way which I had sensed but hadn't fully realized. Robeson was heavy, simple, slow in thought and motion, a great, handsome bull of a man. Ferrer, a "theatre-ape" from his skull to his toenails, danced around him like a matador, flourishing the scarlet cloak, the sword-blade wicked and gleaming but too quick for the victim's eye.

Joe was rewarding to direct. His experience and training hadn't given him the instruments he needed, either in movement or the use of words; but if I laid them out for him, he would pick them up instantly. I once suggested to him that rehearsing in sneakers and shorts, with his hands in his pockets was going to do him no good when it came to doublets and thigh boots. The next day he had acquired boots and kept his hands (deft, febrile, expressive) free for a vivid use of gesture which people still remember. When he confronted an audience, his magnetism claimed them.

Iago, when he is possessed of this quality, is much easier to accept on the stage than in print. Perhaps people kept nagging the author to put in a few reasons for this "motiveless malignity" and he reluctantly pushed in a few which are notably unconvincing. He had simply imagined a man who was evil. It is worth noting that the audience knows a lot about Iago which the other characters never do. Quite early in the play he tells us, in perfect confidence, what he plans to do; he makes us, as it were, accessory to it. Even so, an unsophisticated audience can take quite a long time to get the message. I heard this illustrated by two senior citizens of Boston; after the stabbing of Roderigo, close to the end of the play, one turned to another and said in tones of shocked amazement, "Why he's nothing but an archfiend!"

In the past many Iagos have stolen the play from Othello, which is a somber and far more difficult part—Olivier thinks it the most difficult Shakespeare ever wrote. This didn't happen with Ferrer and Robeson, which it could very easily have done; partly because I wouldn't let it, but mostly because Robeson's personality, appearance, voice and race were overpowering. Yet, though he understood Othello, he could never play him.

His appreciation of the verse saved him from having the usual American actor's trouble with it. He told me that the study of Pushkin in Russian had taught him a feeling for words. Yet he spoke with the slight artificiality of an opera singer and was apt to get sonorous and preachy. He was at his best in the gentle passages. The description of the wooing of Desdemona was done with tenderness and loving humor. "I think this tale would win my daughter too" said the Duke and most people agreed. The arrival in Cyprus ("If it were now to die, 'Twere now to be most happy . . .") was disarming and beautiful; sometimes in the last scene he could be moving; but all too often he started as if it were a sermon and never got out of the pulpit; and the scenes of frenzy and rage, the so-called "jealousy" scenes, he never matched at all.

He was difficult to direct—not from any feeling of obstruction or lack of good will. Essie Robeson wrote to my mother: "Paul has never before enjoyed so much relaxation and confidence in work or in preparation for work. . . . He understands Shakespeare for the first time in his life. . . . Paul and I will always be grateful to Peggy for what she has done for him in *Othello*." At first, during the talking stage, I was delighted by the progress he made, and wrote that he would seize on an idea like lightning and it blossomed at once. Early in rehearsals I wrote: "He curiously lacks the quality of real rage." He had plenty of power but no flash. I tried to induce it by all sorts of "methods." He, of all people, must have experienced injustice, hatred, fury. He told me of his experience as an All-American footballer—one of the first Negroes to achieve this distinction. One of the opposing team yelled at him "You black bastard!" A few minutes later, said Paul, "I smashed his face into the ground." Apparently this incident had made a deep impression on him; he spoke of it to many people. But he could not bring it onto the stage with him; he could not recapture it for:

> *Villain, be sure thou prove my love a whore;*
> *Be sure of it, give me the ocular proof;*
> *Or, by the worth of man's immortal soul,*
> *Thou had'st better have been born a dog*
> *Than answer my waked wrath.*

It was much the same in the agony of the final scene. He worked hard at feeling it, but it never rose and engulfed him.

I wrote:

> Not only has he no technique, which *he* knows, but no conception of "impersonation". He can only do it if he can get a kind of electric motor going inside himself and this has to be started by some feeling—not Othello's feeling, but Robeson's. Fortunately his tremendous vocal resources protect him; my job is to jockey him into some approximation of Othello, and then make a kind of frame round him which will hold the play together. It's very difficult—like pushing a truck up-hill—yet sometimes when he catches fire (from me) he goes careening off at eighty miles an hour and leaves all the rest of us standing. But he's so undependable.

Perhaps I should have been better at this had I been more of a "Method" director—at least about releasing the pent-up emotions in Paul. But I doubt if I should have known any better about getting him inside Othello's skin, and almost certainly less able to lend him the skills he needed. I learned the tricks to help him—speed above everything; if he slowed down, he was lost. I learned to mask his heaviness of movement by having him stay still, while the other actors moved around him. I devised all sorts of detours round the difficult bits. But what I had called his undependability remained.

Later, during the New York run, I wrote:

Paul is a special problem [in keeping the show in shape]; the framework holds him pretty steadily. The craft of acting is not intrinsically his, nor do I think he can at present absorb any more of it than he already has. The effort, not, as he thinks, of energy, but of emotional and nervous concentration which Othello requires is still a foreign language to him—as it is to many other successful actors—and the sporadic way in which it works with him is what causes the immense variation in his performances. Sometimes they are filled with his own personal quality; sometimes they are an empty house with nobody home.

Brooks Atkinson described him as "a slack and ponderous Othello." All too often this was true; but, thank Heaven, not always, and not on either the opening night in Cambridge nor the final opening in New York.

The rehearsals for the summer-stock production were hard for me. Officially we had only two weeks, one in New York; but the Ferrers, Paul and I had worked on the play long before that. I had decided to play Emilia myself. At first this made things easier, since during the New York rehearsal week we were only allowed three other actors besides the Ferrers and Robeson. Later it confronted me with hazards, as I well knew it would. I have never been much in favor of the director acting in his own show. It used to be widely done; now much more rarely. I don't really like doing it myself, especially when the play is one of depth and stature. I don't believe my work as a director suffers; with a good technical staff and a reliable understudy, the rehearsal stages can be well covered; but my acting does. I find it very difficult to close my directorial eyes and ears and to become subjective, immersed, spontaneous. Whenever I have done it, the part has been compressed (Mary Magdalene appeared only once) and left me free for the big scenes. But when we got to Cambridge, with only one week in which to rehearse all the other members of the cast (drawn from the Brattle company), I began to feel hard-pressed. In addition I was doing a daily radio stint every morning at 9:15 a.m. reading *Jane Eyre*.

Above all, I was engaged in a task which today sounds ludicrously unnecessary: that of proving in print, on the air, through press interviews and by every known propaganda means, that Othello was really intended to be a black man from Africa, not a coffee-colored gentleman who has been spending the winter in Tunisia. I did this with conviction because I myself believe it. But I found that you could make a perfectly good case for anything you wanted to prove merely by selecting your favored commentator. "Tawny" says one scholar decisively; "black" snaps another without hesitation. "A half-caste" describes Fechter's famous rendering; "an animal, tropical black" decides a fourth. Edmund Kean broke away from the original "black" tradition by presenting a pale, café-au-lait Othello—"a most pleasing probability," said Coleridge; but Shakespeare's own Burbage, poor simple man, seems to have played just what the text says —"black"; "begrimed and black"; "sooty bosom"; "thick lips" and all. With this, of course, I made much play; also using as targets the more ludicrous of the coffee-colored brigade through such quotes as this, from Miss Mary Preston of Maryland in 1869: "We may regard, then, the daub of black upon Othello's visage as an EBULLITION of fancy, a FREAK of imagination—one of the few erroneous strokes of the great master's brush. Othello was a WHITE man."

Rehearsals proceeded. I got a terrible cough and cursed *Jane Eyre* every morning at 9 a.m. At the dress rehearsal a peculiar thing happened, proving that a great play can be brought to a complete standstill for lack of a prop. We had reached the scene where Desdemona, seeking to comfort Othello, offers him her handkerchief; he knocks it from her hand; they go off, leaving it lying on the ground; Emilia picks it up. But on this occasion Uta dropped the handkerchief close to her feet; when she walked off, it got caught up in the train of her dress and went off with her. I stood in the middle of the stage with nothing to pick up, and the whole plot-sequence flashed through my head: no handkerchief, no play. I couldn't give it to Iago, he couldn't plant it on Cassio, Othello couldn't see Cassio give it to Bianca, Iago couldn't use that to prove Desdemona's guilt—the whole play fell to pieces like a house of cards. Fortunately this was only the dress rehearsal; thereafter I never played the scene without an understudy handkerchief up my sleeve, prepared to duck behind a chair and "pick up" what wasn't there.

The opening night in Cambridge was about the hottest I ever remember. The small theatre had a corrugated-iron roof and was packed to its girders with sweating humanity. We sweated even more, from nerves and also because we were all encased in velvet gowns, heavy cloaks, leather thigh boots and so on. Paul's robes had to be wrung out between scenes. The tension added to the heat. But when the final curtain fell, the audience cheered and clapped and roared, accompanied by a steady, rhythmic stamping of feet. "What's that?" I asked the man beside me, one of the local actors. "Boy!" said he, "that's Harvard! that's the best you could get!" Within twenty-four hours the telephones were red-hot with all the New York managers who had turned us down asking for "a piece of the show."

It was a year before we were able to open there, however, because of Paul's intervening concert commitments. After much discussion it was agreed that the Theatre Guild should "present" the show, finance it and control all the "front of the house" part; but that the production itself should be in the hands of a trio consisting of Robeson, our production stage manager and myself. We got Bobby Jones to do the sets and costumes. He took infinite trouble to choose for Paul fabrics and colors which would suit him, and to have them cut to his best advantage. The sets were simple and swift to change, but they had the richness and line characteristic of Jones's best work.

The Ferrers stayed with us, Joe's performance improving all the time. Uta lost a little of her first, spontaneous simplicity—the hardest thing to retain or recapture. Paul grew in confidence through the rehearsals and try-out weeks; but he would keep fiddling around with an electronic gadget which was supposed to hang in the auditorium and echo back his voice so that he would "hear himself." This harassed the rest of us and took weeks to banish. The try-out dates were fine; but I knew very well that an out-of-town triumph doesn't at all preclude destruction by the New York press, and was not lulled into a false security. Came the opening at the Shubert, October 19, 1943.

I have never been so paralytic with fright. Director's nerves, which are the worst kind; actor's nerves—including the two minutes of pure agony just before you step on the stage; the accumulated pressure of the past four years; and the menacing awareness that the issues were larger than theatre-size. I didn't listen to the opening scenes; I tried to blot out everything but Emilia. Jauntily, I landed with Uta at Cyprus. I hadn't been on the stage two minutes before I knew for certain that it was going to be all right.

There is, perhaps, only one thing which totally distinguishes the stage from its mechanical competitors—the live communication between living actors and a living audience. When the electric spark leaps from the stage to the auditorium, when the pressure mounts till the needle almost runs off the gauge, the theatre could quite easily explode. Bobby Jones said of the *Othello* opening "If a cat had walked across the footlights it would have been electrocuted."

In cold blood, I think the performance that night could be ranked as "good." We gave others just as good or better; but that night "the spirit gave us utterance"—or maybe it rested on the audience: in either case, it was, I still think, the most exciting evening I have ever experienced in the theatre. When, as Emilia, I finally "died," I lay on the floor (back to the audience, of course) helpless to move a muscle, with the tears running down my face. Someone has rightly said that it isn't losing the race which makes you cry, it's winning it.

There followed an ovation worthy of one of today's Pop singers, lasting twenty minutes, all of us in a pool of tears, yells for a "speech," all of us speechless, a final choky "thank you" from me, and the next morning's adjectives: "unbelievably magnificent," "terrific," "consummate genius," "one of the great events of theatre history," and a line at the box office as soon as it opened. I wrote a note of congratulations and thanks and put it up on the call board. I added: "We have set ourselves a terrific standard . . . but . . . there's nothing about it we cannot retain and surpass. . . ." I hope we did.

An odd footnote: though the "consummate genius" basically concerned was undoubtedly the author, the press did not fling their bouquets that far. "Not one of the great tragedies," said the *Tribune* judicially; "A fair share of it in these days seems tedious" remarked the sophisticated *Times;* "Othello is Shakespeare's simplest hero and Iago his most shallow villain" opined the *Mirror,* with its flawless literary sense; George Jean Nathan's notice was distinguished, as always, by his extreme personal prejudices and pithy style. I quote it in full: "One of the very few virtues of Margaret Webster's production of *Othello* is that it contains no ballet." There was the usual flurry of success and we all beat each other on the back—except Paul. I wrote to May: "He's a funny fellow—has never said a word to me of good wishes, congratulations, or thanks—and never will! He's not ungrateful—just inarticulate. It frightens me when I look back on the razor-edge between triumph and disaster along which we have walked."

The audience reactions continued as vocal as ever. Two episodes remain with me. Once, as Emilia, I was waiting in the extreme downstage corner for my last entrance while Othello and Desdemona played out their scene. I heard a young girl's voice from the front row whispering over and over again, "Oh, God, don't let him kill her . . . don't let him kill her . . . don't let him kill her. . . ." The second was after I had left the cast and was watching the show from the front. After the first act, two elegantly dressed types passed me going up the aisle. She was saying to him, "Now, for Heaven's sake *don't* tell me what happens."

The audience tribute that I valued most of all came to me by letter from a boy in the U.S. Army who was stationed some distance from New York and came up with four buddies on a weekend leave. He wrote:

> Last Saturday night I saw *Othello*. It took a lot of coaxing to get four soldiers to spend a Saturday night of the first weekend leave in a month, in a theatre, watching something by Will Shakespeare. You didn't know what was at stake when the curtain went up—my life, practically. Well, what followed is only natural. We all of us, for those few brief hours, went into a trance; we were living every emotion of the play. (One was a First Sarge, and my dear Miss Webster, that which moves a First Sergeant is almost miraculous). . . . I'm not a critic, just a soldier when I say that each night when the curtain goes up at the Shubert, each and every one of you, from prop man to extra to star, is fighting a war against our common enemy. . . . In this production of a great classic you have given five soldiers reason enough to win this war. . . . Incidentally, going back on the troop train (it's a six-hour ride), for the first time in my army career I saw five soldiers sprawled over the seats, feet in the air, sleeves rolled up, shirts open, talking not about the babe they met at the Broadway Brewery, but of all things, a thing called *Othello*.

Naturally, it was not roses, roses all the way. Prejudice had not entirely ceased; there was an occasional scream of abuse and, undoubtedly, large numbers of people just plain stayed away. Still, enough of them came to ensure the play's running through the entire season, which is much more than any Shakespeare play had ever done before or has since. But a long run is also a test, and a severe one, for the actors, especially when they are constantly being told how good they are. I used to keep a constant check, using, for one thing, a coughing chart. The stage management kept it for several weeks. My theory was (is) that an audience coughs and shuffles more because it is bored or can't hear than because it has a cough. My chart always bore this out. "Much coughing" meant a slow, slack scene.

While I was still playing myself (I left the cast in the spring) it was difficult to keep track of the other actors. I asked Eva Le Gallienne to come and watch for me. Afterwards we discussed the performance in detail. At last I said, rather nervously, "Anything—er—about—er —Emilia?" "Well," she answered in a considering sort of way, "do you *mean* to play her like an efficiency expert?"

About halfway through the run, when we had established some sort of record, the *Herald Tribune* gave us an editorial:

> . . . the run of the play is a tribute to the art which transcends racial boundaries. The fact that it is considered noteworthy that a Negro should play Othello is a sufficient commentary on the raw edges of prejudice that are continually abraded afresh by the frictions of various groups within the U.S. . . . But it is surely a recognition of the essential folly of such group antagonisms—a sign of hope for the future —when a Negro actor of the quality of Mr. Robeson is so enthusiastically welcomed into the great tradition of the English-speaking stage in a part of such power and nobility as Othello. . . . Although Will Shakespeare would doubtless be extremely surprised to learn of the social significance his tragedy has acquired in a new world, it is, as it happens, uniquely adapted to serve as a vehicle for conveying mutual understanding and mutual respect.

It would be nice to record that we all lived happily together for ever after, but it wasn't exactly so. The "whirligig of time" brought round unforeseen happenings. Paul was, to use a modern phrase, "where the muscle lay," and if there was anything he wanted done, or not done, he flexed those muscles—more plainly, he just said he would not play the following performance, or any other, unless he got what he wanted. That he was only one of three on the production board meant nothing to him; neither did the views of the Theatre Guild, the advice of his own lawyers, the existence of written contracts. This sweet, unassuming, dear, big bear of a man could crush us all. I wrote to May: "It turns out I have not been playing Svengali to his Trilby, but Frankenstein to his monster."

What he demanded was seldom of great consequence, and was more often something for the Ferrers than for himself. But I was unwilling to accept responsibility without power, and I asked the Guild to take over my share of the managerial functions. This they did, and behaved with great firmness and dignity throughout. I continued, of course, as director but I left the cast. I may add that I also continued to draw my agreed percentage. *Othello* was the only show out of which I have ever made "real" money.

We were to send out a coast-to-coast tour the following fall. It presented obvious difficulties. We would not play in any theatre where there was discrimination in the seating of Negroes. This meant we could not, for instance, play Washington. We hoped to get Roosevelt to "command" a performance at the White House; but he had a few other things on his mind. However, it was not difficult to set up a coast-to-coast tour, and when we had organized and cast it, we all broke up for the summer. When I returned just before the rehearsals were to begin, I found out, by the merest chance, that Paul had had an entirely new set of costumes designed for himself by a friend of the Ferrers. I telephoned Bobby Jones, who telephoned the Theatre Guild, the designers' union and a couple of other people and the project was hastily abandoned. When I met Paul at rehearsal, he seemed amiably baffled. "Oh," he said, "I didn't think you'd mind."

Just before this rehearsal the stage manager had warned me that Emilia would not be there because she had to do a bit of rerecording. "Of what?" said I. "Why, of *Othello*—didn't you know?" I didn't. Neither did the Theatre Guild. Paul and Joe had made an entirely separate contract with a recording company and, using the same cast, made a complete recording of the play. The Guild and I decided it would be wisest to acquiesce rather than imperil the tour by a fight with Paul. The records were not good and I was sorry that they should be considered a fair representation of the production. And yet, with all this, it was hard to get—or to stay—angry with Paul. There was a kind of monolithic innocence about him; and you couldn't argue with him, because that takes two, and he would only contribute "Ugh." At all events the tour proceeded, causing astonishingly few racial tensions and doing all the things in the way of notices and box-office grosses that *Variety* likes to describe as "fab."

But time still had some whirligigs in hand relating to *Othello*. Only a few years later all those who had been prominently connected with it, and lauded for our contribution to "mutual understanding and respect in the U.S.," were subjected to the attention of the House or Senate Investigating Committees as either Communists or fellow travelers. Paul had never made any secret of his love for all things Russian, and the Ferrers and I—known "leftists" anyway—were guilty by association. In fact, I never discussed politics with Paul; except that I used to reproach him for dashing into the theatre straight from a meeting of some kind and hurl himself onto the stage in ten minutes flat. I told him Othello needed more concentration and deserved more respect than that. I also told him during one of his "big bear" spells that he didn't know anything about democracy and was only a dictator out of office. He said "Ugh" as usual. He certainly paid for his convictions, whatever they were—and I did not and do not believe they were predominantly political. But when Uta Hagen and I came together again a few years later in a production of *Saint Joan,* also for the Theatre Guild, many of its subscribers were quite disturbed. St. Joan, after all, was well known to have held extremely radical views.

Twenty years on, an even greater change has occurred. If it was difficult and dangerous in the United States in 1942 to do *Othello* with a black actor, it would be almost suicidal to do it in 1971 with a white one. Everyone told us then that we would be lynched; now I feel sure they would prophesy that a white Othello would cause the theatre to be attacked, the National Guard turned out and several people shot. Or possibly none of these things would happen, any more than they did in 1943. More people have more sense than is generally supposed.

The art of acting does, and must, transcend racial restrictions. A man with a black skin is not axiomatically able to get inside Othello's black skin. An actor with a white skin is not debarred from doing so, any more than Shakespeare was prevented by his whiteness from writing the play. Othello is as far from Harlem as from Westchester. Olivier has played the part recently both on stage and screen. I saw only the theatre production, and that, of course, in England. It happens that I disagreed totally with his interpretation of the man— not of the man's race, which he tried very hard to make as African as possible. But nobody could deny his histrionic brilliance or his right to play the part. He was invited to do it in New York; circumstances made it impossible, as well as his refusal to attempt playing it for a run. But one of these days a white actor will try. I hope he will be good enough to get a fair hearing.

Whatever has happened since, either to Robeson, to the theatre in the United States or to the structure of American society does not, I think, vitiate or invalidate what we managed to achieve through our production. I shall always be proud of my share in it.

THE TEMPEST

The Tempest, as compared with *Othello,* belied its name. Its storms were of teacup size, though they had a certain ferocity while they lasted. It is a play of white magic, as *Macbeth* is of black magic. But it is almost as difficult to put onto a stage, gossamer-lovely yet full of muscle, lyric and yet profound, rewarding to eye, ear and mind. It seizes on the imagination and lodges there. As I became known as a Shakespeare director, people began to write to me about plays they wanted to see, and a surprising number wanted *The Tempest.* These included actors, managers and faraway fans from Iowa or Texas. Cheryl Crawford and I used to talk about it, in the *Family Portrait* days. But no one ever actually produced it; commercial and economic reasons deterred them.

Eva Le Gallienne and I were forever planning schemes for repertory theatres—in Washington or Chicago or Podunk or on the moon. They never happened. But among our imagined repertoire *The Tempest* remained constant. Eva was intrigued by the unexpected affinity between Shakespeare and Ibsen; Prospero as compared to Solness, magic on the Norwegian mountains of *Peer Gynt,* magic in the "still-vexed Bermoothes," the dramatic skill of beginning a play almost at the end of a story and compressing it within the minds of its protagonists.

Eva, whose hands can make the things she imagines, began tinkering with bits of cardboard and balsa wood. Presently an Island emerged, set on a wooden revolving disk. A museum outside Detroit gave us the next idea; natural stone and rock are preserved there, glittering quartzite of brilliant colors, crystal webs of infinite delicacy and brutal, dark granite from the first cooling of the Earth. By no stretch of geological imagination could all these elements come together on the same Island—unless it were a magic one; Prospero's, for instance. We packed up the model and went to see Cheryl Crawford. She beetled at it, was abrupt as always; reread the play; telephoned and said "Yes."

There was a two-year interlude before we did it—quite brief as such lacunae go in the theatre world. I studied the play, layer beneath layer. Mark Van Doren once wrote: "Any set of symbols, moved close to this play, lights up as in an electric field." You can make it mystical, political, psychiatric; Prospero can be anything from God to Lyndon B. Johnson in a huff; Ariel and Caliban have been interpreted in staggeringly different ways according to the personal whims of designers and directors and the social background of their time. There is also the strong probability that it was Shakespeare's last play and that Prospero is making his farewells for him.

It is certainly not a play about which I would want to pontificate. If I did it now, I should undoubtedly find that the world of the Seventies dictated to me a different approach from the one I used in the Forties, but some of the things I wrote at that time seem to me still valid:

> The play deals with themes which are now and have been and will be of immediate significance to all of us. The use and abuse of power is one of them; the search for freedom is another—shadowed with the penetrating implication that freedom often turns out to be different from what we had imagined, involving responsibility and not merely license, and that each of us must find his own way to the resolution of the conflicting impulses within ourselves. . . . And finally the play is strong with the longing for peace and reconciliation; it leads from the story of old wrongs unresolved and violence unrequited to compassion and the promise of "a clear life ensuing". After twelve years of privation and discipline in the mastery of his powers, Prospero gains his victory and denies himself the fruits of it. "The rarer action is in virtue than in vengeance. . . . My charms I'll break, their senses I'll restore, and they shall be—themselves."

This was the first Shakespeare play I had done in which there was no pre-contracted "star"; also, it is not, or should not be, a star's play. But there was always the box office demand for ticket-selling names. We persuaded Vera Zorina (then Mrs. George Balanchine) to play Ariel. She was beautiful, charming, a star of ballet and musicals, with a very good speaking voice and an ear for poetry; it is a criticism of us, not of her, that the casting was too sugary. We tried, obviously, to get a "name" for Prospero; but there are few fine classical actors in America; the war had taken some of them and had also precluded the use of the British ones. Arnold Moss had everything Prospero needs, voice, appearance, intelligence, skill—everything except magnetism.

Determined not to let the Robeson-Othello precedent wither for lack of successors, we got the Negro actor, Canada Lee, for Caliban;

this was only the second time that a black actor had played in a classic play on Broadway. But at the last minute we almost lost him. Some of his friends had tried to persuade him that it would be derogatory to his race to play the enslaved and brutish Caliban; but the arguments against this type of racism eventually prevailed.

We were lucky in getting an ideal Stephano-Trinculo team, two brilliant Czechoslovakian actors, Jan Wierich and George Voscovec. They had been famous in Prague as actor-author-comedians, satirists and vaudevillians, running their own theatre and writing their own material. They had escaped a jump ahead of the Nazis and were doing broadcasts for the Voice of America. They had been reared in the same ancient and honorable tradition of "clowns" that Shakespeare's own men must have followed, with the same flexibility and invention plus that touch of fantasy that present-day comics too often lack. Canada Lee was delighted with them and was the perfect foil for them.

The Stephano-Trinculo scenes are much easier to direct than many subtler ones which depend on verbal jokes. Drink is a great promoter of good comedy, and certain business which the text clearly implies lies in stage tricks current to this day. Voscovec and Wierich were the type of actors who can transform your ideas instead of merely translating them, and I was very grateful. The rest of the play was well cast, I think, and included some small-part actors who were later to make names for themselves. The team was well balanced and in harmony. Two of the famous trio of designers known as "Motley" were in New York and agreed to do the set, based on our balsa-wood original, and they created some splendid costumes, full of color. David Diamond, young and full of talent, composed the music, delicate and intricate. And that became one of our problems.

It was scored for, I think, nine instruments, with Diamond himself conducting, and we duly engaged eight musicians, four more than the Alvin Theatre, as a "contract house," would have had to keep employed. But when Local 802 of the Musicians Union discovered that there was to be an overture to introduce and accompany the storm, a good deal of incidental music throughout the play, three or four song settings for Ariel and some odds and ends of unaccompanied ditties for the clowns, there was a great uproar. "This piece," they said, "is not a play at all. It is a musical; and as such it must have a minimum of twenty-two musicians in the pit, as provided in the union's contract for musicals."

This demand came to us very late in the day and almost stopped the production. It was all we could do to carry the salaries of eight men; the additional number would have wrecked the operating budget completely. Cheryl bravely challenged the ruling and ferocious argument ensued. Finally, the union was persuaded to evolve a wholly new category. *The Tempest* was pronounced to be neither a play nor a musical but a "play with music." Productions in this category were to employ a minimum of eight men in the pit; but the total length of the music played by them was not to exceed twenty minutes. We heaved huge sighs of relief and got out our stopwatches. We eliminated a few bits of incidental music and made one of the songs *"a cappella."* We were the pioneer guinea-pigs of this piece of enlightened union legislation.

Probably we wouldn't have got by even then had we not decided to cut the masque. I am forced to admit that the basic reasons for this were economic. The cost of a ballet of "nymphs and reapers," a choreographer and all the rest of it was more than Cheryl felt she could face. We were prepared for the songs of blessing; the three goddesses (I had played Ceres in my youth) were cast, rehearsed, scored for, and provided with exquisite and madly expensive costumes, together with a small, black page to carry Juno's golden sunshade. It turned out to be so heavy that it toppled him backward off the stairs behind her.

But it was no good. The masque is all or nothing and these "maimed rites" were insufficient. In the end we cut it, an expensive sacrifice, but worth five or six minutes of musicians' playing time. I do not really believe I would have let it go, no matter what the economics, had I not previously come to the conclusion that the masque was not in Shakespeare's original text at all, but was only inserted at a Royal Command Performance to celebrate the marriage of King James's daughter to the Elector Palatine.

Nor do I believe that Prospero's famous speech "Our revels now are ended . . ." was meant to stand where it now does, after the masque; I think it was intended to end the whole play. It says a farewell more subtle, profound and moving than the author's last-night speech which is the accepted epilogue. I later found scholarly support for my theory, but I had the courage of it anyway. "Please you, draw near" says Prospero (the last line of the play as it now stands) and steps forward a little, saying quietly to the audience, "Our revels now are ended. These our actors, As I foretold you, were all spirits and Are melted into air, into thin air. . . ." As he speaks the lights begin to dim and the other actors fade back imperceptibly into the shadows. Over the final words the light on Prospero dims too, and with "our little life is rounded with a sleep" there is an enfolding darkness. Staged that way it was very moving, or I found it so, and the total silence which always followed testified to its power over the audience.

But I was nervous. One takes liberties with Shakespeare at one's peril because almost all of the time he is so damnably right. However, few of the New York critics were very good at detecting textual changes, as had been demonstrated over the Justice Shallow scene in *Henry IV*. One of them, I remembered, had accused me of having "streamlined" *Othello,* when I had done nothing of the sort; and in *The Tempest* one perceptive scribe remarked that I had "cut Ariel's speeches and songs practically down to zero, and that is a very good thing." I had, in fact, cut about fifteen words of the entire part and not a single note of the songs. But they did notice the transposition of the "revels" speech and were approving. John Kieran, who was not a professional drama critic but whose opinion I valued, thought the production the best I had done, and the revels speech "a perfect ending . . . a stroke of genius." It did send the audience out of the theatre with a perceptible sense of awe, of mortality and immortality, a glimpse of mighty things.

We had our troubles, of course. The Island was mounted on a revolving stage which revolved visibly. After the shipwreck opening, the lights never dimmed or blacked out; the curtain never fell (except for the intermission); the scenes melted into each other as the Island revealed a different aspect of itself. This meant complications, especially during the pre-New York touring dates—a false stage for the revolve, a circular cyclorama, tricky lighting problems. Furthermore, we wanted Ariel, on Prospero's final "Be free, and fare thou well," to fly. This could easily have killed Zorina and almost did kill Le Gallienne.

Eva was a veteran flier from her *Peter Pan* days, when a German family named Schultz worked the mechanisms they had themselves invented, including the famous "audience fly" which took Peter right beyond the proscenium arch and up over the heads of the audience as far as the first balcony and back again. But alas! the Schultzes could not be traced and their skills had vanished with them. We didn't worry too much; all we needed was one simple operation which would lift Zorina from center stage and whisk her off into the wings. Master carpenters and stage managers assured us that it would be as simple as a song.

During our opening week in Philadelphia we didn't try it—we had too many other technical troubles on our hands; nor for the Boston opening, where the scenery got lost en route in a blizzard-tempest and I managed to be quite rude to the critics at a press cocktail party (exhaustion, exasperation, cold, fright and Dry Martinis being contributory causes). All the disasters common to Boston openings occurred; I used to think that was what the first-night subscribers subscribed for. Then we got down to the flying business. Eva had just finished the tour of *The Cherry Orchard* and she offered to come and help. I described the ensuing events as follows:

> The flying now has to be done very amateurishly with elderly stagehands pulling and hauling and yelling to each other. After I'd watched them heaving a sand-bag around, sometimes dumping it smack on the ground and sometimes rushing it thirty feet in the air and clear to the fly-rail, I was for forgetting the whole thing. But Eva insisted that you couldn't tell with a dead weight, and that she, as an experienced flyer, would try it out for Zorina. We were all scared stiff and looked on with white faces while Eva accomplished a few precarious journeys. [One of the stage-hands, having dumped her on the floor for the third time, remarked "Gee, that's a good-natured dame!"] But we all decided the margin of error was too great; and that even if we didn't smash up Zorina we might easily wreck the show by some absurd mishap in the last two minutes. So we have contrived a disappearing act which isn't as good but a lot safer.

To our astonishment, *The Tempest* recovered from its Boston opening and did better business during its second week than *Othello* ever had. The Boston matrons seemed to like it. I sat behind two of them, suitably be-hatted, at a matinee. They appeared absorbed by the long, explanatory opening scene between Prospero and Miranda. At the end of it, one turned to the other and said, "My dear, I can't quite make out—is he her father or isn't he?" "But my dear," replied the other in righteous tones, "haven't you been listening? she's just found out that he isn't."

This same long sequence, lasting nearly twenty minutes, was the cause of a narrow escape from disaster on the night of the Broadway opening. Caliban does not make his first entrance until the end of it;

but I wanted him to appear suddenly, over the top of a high rock, and he therefore had to be ensconced behind it before the curtain rose. There was nothing but open space between the "Island" and the masking side wings. He was quite used to this routine, naturally, but, just to make sure, the stage manager (Thelma Chandler again) peeked out a minute or two ahead of time to see that he was all right. He was. He was lying peacefully behind the rock, fast asleep. She could not reach him without being seen, and dared not hiss at him too loudly; she was frantic. At the last moment she caught sight of a long "stage brace" (a sort of pole for holding up scenery) which happened to be standing in a corner. Sliding it along the floor she succeeded in jabbing Canada Lee ferociously enough to wake him up. "What ho! Slave! Caliban! Thou earth, thou, speak!" called Prospero. "There's wood enough within," muttered Canada sleepily; pulled himself together, and five lines later clambered up his rock and appeared.

In doing so he almost caused heart failure to Cheryl, the Motleys and me. He was dressed—or rather undressed—in a costume none of us had ever seen before. The semi-fish-like headdress was much as it had been, but his facial make-up was entirely different and the rest of his body was stuck over with bits of fur, feather, spangles and so forth, which gradually came unstuck as the evening wore on. We later discovered that George Balanchine, attending the dress rehearsal at his wife's request, had had "some ideas"; so on the opening night he had very kindly put them into execution. We thanked him and asked Canada *never* to repeat them.

We had heart failure again a little later. We had fixed up a dandy device, involving a specially focused UV lamp, for Ariel's harpy speech so that she would seem to float in midair; and when the cue came, there was total blackness. After what seemed like a week, Zorina's voice came through the darkness, rather tremulously, and she spoke the whole of it in the dark. It transpired that the electrician (an extra man hired for this purpose and hidden inside the "cave") had forgotten to plug in the proper contact. I was in despair. But a woman in front of me whispered to her neighbor *"That's* a daring effect." So go the best-laid schemes. I wrote to May:

> The rest went like a charm and everyone played well. But the
> audience were beastly—hard and granite-faced, not wanting to like it;
> the play was expected to be dull, Canada inadequate, Zorina miscast,
> etc., etc. But the first act held beautifully and the intermission talk was

filled with surprised admiration. I didn't think the second act went so well, but the applause was fine. . . . But the spell hadn't worked as it did in Boston and I expected a bad press. To my surprise all the morning papers were fine and the evening ones were mixed, but so befuddled that they sounded quite good.

Well, now that we again have repertory companies in which Shakespeare is played, we are delivered from the torture of those life-or-death Broadway openings; which is a very excellent thing.

HENRY VIII

What might easily have been the most spectacular production of my "Shakespeare decade," and certainly under the most improbable auspices, never happened; at least, not until later and then in a wholly dissimilar context.

While I was still playing in *Othello,* I was sent for by Billy Rose. This was tantamount to a command from the Empress of China; I hastened to his Palace on Beekman Place. I knew him—who didn't? —as the Impresario of Everything, the Potentate of Diamond Horseshoes, the Pint-size King of Show Biz. My only personal contact, or rather collision, with him had been at the 1939 World's Fair when his stupendous Aquacade was neighbor to my mini-Shakespeare and totally overwhelmed it.

I arrived early; was shown his very lovely collection of paintings, salaamed a good deal, and we got down to Show Biz. It appeared that Jane Cowl and he had got together on an idea of producing *Much Ado About Nothing.* What enchanted Stork Club evening had given rise to this notion, I cannot imagine; but I did not think it a good one. I regarded Miss Cowl with the highest respect and some trepidation. She had once practically hypnotized me into doing a perfectly dreadful play for her; I had only extricated myself at the last minute, half out of "artistic integrity" and half out of fright. She was a very fine actress, beautiful, despotic, star of the era of stars; she had grown a trifle stately in her middle years, for she was considerably over fifty. I could not think that Beatrice was an ideal part for her return to Broadway.

But she was a persuasive lady, and if she started asking me to lunch with her again I wasn't too sure how long my negative answers would last.

Largely in order to get myself out gracefully, I suggested that we might do *Henry VIII* instead. It would have to be a splendiferous production needing lots of dough, which Billy had and liked to spend ostentatiously; it would be a showcase for a lavish impresario, which he believed himself to be; and it had a fine part for a not-so-young actress, which Miss Cowl liked to think she wasn't. She therefore withdrew. Not so Billy Rose, who assured me that he could manage the Met better than the Met (not difficult), the Dodgers better than the Dodgers (not easy), and could certainly produce Shakespeare as, poor man, he had never been produced before. There ensued a long, hot summer.

For some reason the Palazzo Billy Rose was not available to him. He inhabited a suite at the Hotel Astor on Times Square. He had installed a small air-conditioning unit—then a very great rarity—which iced the neck and shoulders of anyone (Billy) sitting in front of it, and left everyone else sweating away as before. In this setting, and in between long, long autobiographical accounts, all quite fascinating, he insisted on discussing everything, but everything, about the proposed production. I think I should have died of it had I not by then enlisted the cooperation of that darling, gentle, immensely gifted, humorous, selfless aristocrat of the theatre, Robert Edmond Jones.

We talked about the casting. With extraordinary originality, Billy suggested Charles Laughton, who, however, refused us. He then "tossed around" an idea for getting the famous Sherlock Holmes duo, Basil Rathbone and Nigel (Willie) Bruce, both good friends of mine. Basil wrote that he would be delighted to play Wolsey (he would have been excellent) but he must know the date, hour, locality etc. of Billy Rose's birth, to see whether their horoscopes were congenial. Willie, a most un-Shakespearean type, sent me a drawing of himself as Henry saying "Elementary, my dear Wolsey, elementary!" But if Rathbone and Rose were astrologically congenial, their ideas of finance were not, so the idea subsided. About twenty Katherines of Aragon were suggested by me and rejected by Billy.

Meanwhile, Bobby had made some superb, large-scale water-color sketches for the sets. Billy Rose's suggestions were often stimulating as well as startling and Bobby had a leaping imagination which would pick up any clue. The whole thing, said Billy, should be framed by the Tower of London. Bobby produced a magnificent drawing of a proscenium arch entirely rebuilt as Traitors' Gate. I advanced tentative reservations about its suitability to the play.

Billy had conceived a tremendous admiration for George Jean Nathan and kept trying to make me go to supper with him and ask his advice. When Nathan's annual book of collected criticisms was about to appear, Billy assured me that people were hanging themselves from lamp-posts rather than face annihilation. I assured him that the world was full of happy people who had never heard of George Jean Nathan, as well as people like me who would as soon ask the advice of a puff adder.

As we discussed the play, I stressed the significance of the final scene, the baptism of the baby who was to become Queen Elizabeth. Who, he asked, had ever heard of Queen Elizabeth? "Plenty," I replied, "she's always cropping up in movies, and Lynn Fontanne played her." He challenged me to walk ten blocks up Broadway, stopping any or every passer-by, and come up with three people who'd ever heard of Queen Elizabeth. (I should add that in those days there had only been one Queen Elizabeth; she would have been outraged, I'm sure, to be thought merely the first of two.)

Meanwhile, I worked on the script and evolved the version which I later used. Since the text is only partly Shakespeare's work I felt less afraid of messing about with it. I cut the Cranmer subplot at the end of the play, believing that once Wolsey and Katherine were dead we had to get Elizabeth baptized as soon as possible and go home. More importantly, I devised two Narrators, using the textual narrations ascribed to the two "Gentlemen," plus some brief linking passages from the Holinshed *Chronicles* which are the play's source material. I didn't think that American audiences were too familiar with the political history of Tudor England; and the Narrators put mortar between some rather loose bricks.

In one instance, I planned an effect which anticipated television technique before television arrived at it. As one Gentleman (in the text) describes to the other the scene in Westminster Abbey, I planned to dissolve through a scrim gauze to the Abbey itself where the Coronation would actually happen; Anne, as the lines describe her, would kneel at the altar and we should see the culminating ceremonial, when she

Cast her fair eyes to heaven and prayed devoutly,
Then rose again and bowed her to the people;
When by the Archbishop of Canterbury
She had all the royal makings of a Queen;
As holy oil, Edward Confessor's crown,
The rod, and bird of peace, and all such emblems
Laid nobly on her: which performed, the choir,
With all the choicest music in the kingdom,
Together sung Te Deum.

Not so many years later we were to see all this on our television screens at the Coronation of Elizabeth II, with precisely the same ritual.

I planned to follow this up in the next scene, where the dying Queen Katherine has a vision of a "blessed troop" who bring her palms and garlands (meticulously described in the textual stage directions). The ritual was to follow exactly the balletic pattern of the Abbey scene, making it a heavenly counterpart to the earthly Coronation.

But I stressed to Billy Rose that this double emphasis made it essential to have a really fine actress for Anne, one who could convey the tremendous moment of triumph as the crown was placed on her head. "But," said Billy, "she doesn't have anything to say, so what does it matter?" I explained once again. "Oh," he said, "you mean she makes faces."

Of course I knew "he only does it to annoy because he knows it teases." Bobby Jones laughed, but I was fresh out of a sense of humor. Finally the whole project slowed to a standstill. This was not because the costs of Bobby's production looked like rising to some $125,000 —enormous for a straight play in those days; Billy was not daunted by that. But he decided we couldn't get a good enough Henry. "As for instance?" I asked. "Monty Woolley." I lost heart. Bobby and I had put in months of work and work with Bobby was never wasted. Fortunately some of his sketches are still preserved. And so far as I was concerned, the labor I had expended on my "Rose with lots of thorns" blossomed a couple of years later. I went back to the Vineyard and bound up my wounds.

Chapter Six

Strange Interludes

1

My theatre life in the Forties wasn't all Shakespeare, by any manner of means. In 1942 there were two war plays in quick succession, *Flare Path* by Terence Rattigan, about the RAF, and *Counterattack,* adapted from the Russian by Janet and Phil Stevenson, about the Russian army. Both had been extremely popular in their respective countries; both were, I think, quite well done; but neither was a success in New York. The Russians had a slight edge over the British. But Broadway, understandably perhaps, was not interested in other people's soldiers.

We had a hard time casting the leading part of a young RAF officer; all the young Englishmen had gone home and most of the young Americans had other uniforms on. Through the influence of Gilbert Miller (the "management") we managed to borrow a fledgling British officer from the RNVR (the Royal Naval Volunteer Reserve) who was at the moment in New York waiting for his ship. This cockleshell, destined for North Africa and eventually for the Sicilian landings, was being built, improbably, in Cincinnati. The British Navy had stationed its becalmed members at the HMS Barbizon-Plaza Hotel on 58th Street. Every morning Sub-Lieutenant Alec Guinness reported to the senior officer on duty requesting permission to go ashore for rehearsals. This was frequently Lieutenant-Commander Robert Douglas, also a well-known member of British Equity, who regarded his junior with some envy. Fortunately for us, the building of Lieutenant Guinness's ship was delayed long enough to last out the run of *Flare Path.* Its author, now himself an officer in the RAF, had managed to get himself sent to his North African assignment via New York and gave us all the necessary authentication.

But the very authenticity of the "domestic scenes" was what made them unrecognizable to an American audience, which still thought of war in terms of sentimental heroics, such as those on view in *Mrs. Miniver,* and did not feel exalted by British jokes over glasses of beer. I was very happy to work with Alec Guinness. His successes in England had been made since I had left; I knew him only by reputation and from smallish, but beautifully played, parts. He viewed me—or so he told a dear friend of ours, Martita Hunt—with some apprehension; women directors are customarily expected to be strong-minded and rather head-mistressy. But he told her that he found me better than that; that I sensed what the actors were trying to do before they had arrived at doing it and that I had "the great gift of keeping the company happy." For the opening night, he wrote me a letter of which I am proud, even allowing for the rush of warmth and comradeship which comes over everyone on an opening night. He said: "I have always found you a constant source of help, resourcefulness, patience, tact, appreciation . . . in fact the very humble possessor of all the theatre's greatest qualities." From an actor of the unquestioned quality of Alec Guinness, you couldn't ask better, could you?

I was terrified that this young man might get destroyed in the war and not live to do the things he could do. I gave him a curved, metal liquor flask. "Wear it," I besought him, "in your *breast* pocket!" I don't know whether he ever did. But he took his little dinghy of a boat across the Atlantic and the Mediterranean and practically led the British Navy ashore in Sicily; and lived to do work for which my words would be, as I think they might be his, "laus Deo."

Counterattack, about another of our then Allies, later contributed to my troubles with Congressional Committees, as it did to those of the translators and several of the cast. The backing was provided by Warner Bros. under the aegis of Harry Cohen, improbable casting for Soviet agents. Three-quarters of the action was concentrated upon the efforts of two Russian soldiers to hold prisoner six or seven German ones in a cellar which, at the end of scene 1, was blocked up by a falling bomb. The only light supposedly came from one small lantern. A number of very small "baby spots" had to be hidden behind things and I had to shift the action around with the utmost ingenuity so as to preserve the lantern-illusion and yet see whoever must, at any given moment, be seen. I wrote to my mother: "The bitchery which goes on between seven entombed Nazis fighting for the baby spots would put to shame any star actresses of the limelight era."

Outside the theatre, even civilians became a tiny bit war-conscious in their own lives. We had toy blackouts and brownouts in New York. Gas rationing made the Vineyard seem very far away. I had to black out all the windows which could be seen from the sea. Since Gay Head had no electricity till many years later, you simply carried around one oil lamp and a blanket and blacked as you lit, so to speak.

More hoarding of coupons, because for three months I did a radio program every morning at 9:15 from CBS on Madison Avenue while living, most of the time, at Westport. I suppose this was when car pools first began, convening at the Merritt Parkway (there was no Thruway) to get us to the early train. It must have been toward the end of "live" radio—and not very far from the demise of all intelligent radio in the United States. My program was not sponsored, and therefore not interrupted; it was "highbrow," consisting of the reading of thirteen and a half minutes, Monday through Friday, of Charlotte Brontë's *Jane Eyre*. In these days when almost everything is pre-recorded on film or tape it is hard to imagine the grim, ineluctable, predestinate discipline of "doing it live"; no cutting, splicing, going back, retaping; if you made an idiot of yourself you did it instantly, publicly and irretrievably. But I respected the medium, as I do still, for its delicate fidelity; I regret that, in the United States, so little—except for good music—is left of it. I think often of Eva Le Gallienne's lapidary comment, when refusing a shoddy radio series: "I have a foolish distaste for entering other people's homes bearing unworthy gifts."

In an article called "Solitary Child" I tried to describe my experience:

> I think it is the loneliness that gets me: perhaps since I am reading the story of *Jane Eyre,* a forlorn and solitary child, this is a fitting emotion. . . . My previous experience in radio has been concerned with plays, discussions or quiz programs; there have been others besides myself clustering round the mike in a friendly though subdued manner, rather as if we were all congregated at the bedside of a sick friend. Sometimes orchestras have shared our studio, and often a flesh-and-blood audience. By these means the faintly church-like atmosphere has

been ameliorated; I have not consciously missed the carefree racket of theatre dressing-rooms, or the muted bustle in the wings. But Jane Eyre and I are hermits indeed; to an old "legit", the solitude is practically oppressive.

There is no sound but my own voice. Sometimes I wonder if I am not simply talking to myself. Of course I am not. Actually, I am coming closer to you than I have ever done from my accustomed habitat behind the footlights, closer than if you were seated in the studio itself; I am in your very homes. In my remote, sub-aqueous world I am sure of only two things: that you can switch me off if you want to—a sobering possibility on which I prefer not to dwell—and that a large proportion of you are according me only one ear and less than a third of your full attention. . . . I am the more determined to hold it; but I realize that I must be very faithful to her and to you. I cannot trick you; the mike records with the uttermost precision the quality and ring of truth.

And I have none of the actor's physical equipment at my service, none of the resources of the eye; I have only my voice; and so, I realize, I must use it more delicately, husband it and deploy it with the most varied and subtle use of nuance and shading. I learn a great deal about the employment of its resources, more than I have done in other radio experiences, because I am not merely being myself, not even interpreting a single character. I am being six characters at once and a narrator and commentator into the bargain. Often there is no "he said" or "she replied" on the printed page: I have to tell you which is she and he by implication. Sometimes phrases or words which are clearly comprehensible in print fall oddly on the ear. How, for instance, am I to differentiate such a phrase as "Mrs. and the Misses Brocklehurst"? How am I to clarify the description "Guyp-like"? . . . I find the attempted solution of these problems fascinating.

The most touching response I got to this article was signed in rather shaky pencil "Margaret Webster." She said that the article had made her feel she owed me a letter; that for six weeks, "since Jane Eyre was a little girl," she had allowed nothing to come between her and me and Jane, except, once, the piano-tuner. She went on:

Curiously enough, you really do seem like a friend, and I must admit valuing this pseudo-friendship most highly . . . have I not been sitting at your feet day after day, completely absorbed in this exquisitely beautiful story which you are reading so superbly? [She added in a postscript:] I am enclosing a picture of Venus and me. . . . I thought that a celebrity might just possibly be a little curious about another bearing the same name. I remember gazing with considerable interest at a picture of you about three years ago, shortly before I lost my sight.

Venus, of course, was her seeing-eye dog. Not all the marvels of man-on-the-moon television have ever, for me, superseded my gratitude for the little miracle of this.

2

My most affectionate memory of the theatre during these years concerns a production of Chekhov's *The Cherry Orchard* in which I was a little bit of everything. I was part of the management with Carly Wharton, a most harmonious and happy partnership with a shrewd and able lady; part of the direction with Le Gallienne; and briefly, part of the company when I had to play Lyubov Andreyevna while Eva was in hospital. (This, I may say, was one of the most difficult things I have ever had to do. Her performance was subtle, moving, stylish, in the best sense; impossible to imitate, impossible to vary, basically, because the production had been molded to it. To put your personal truth into somebody else's pattern is a testing thing.) Eva herself has given a charming description of *The Cherry Orchard* in her book, *With a Quiet Heart*. It was good, I believe. As a director and as an actor I have found Chekhov the most delightful, touching and, in some respects, satisfying of all the dramatists I have known. Also, to everybody's astonishment, including our own, we made money out of this production—not much, but some. It was hard enough to scrape the capital together in the first place, Lord knows; for despite Carly Wharton's high reputation and all her skill and blandishments, Chekhov on Broadway did not sound like a gold-mine.

Eva could blandish too, when occasion required, though she hated doing it, as I did. While we were still in the planning stage, she was on tour, and during the Pittsburgh week some friends told her of a very wealthy man "greatly interested in the arts" who, they felt sure, would be eager to help us with our highly cultural enterprise. A party was arranged at his house one night after the show, and in a carefully accidental tête-à-tête Eva gave her host a glowing and seductive account of *The Cherry Orchard,* a play he had never heard of before. At the end of her performance he said, "But I'm not interested in fruit." Paling slightly, she answered, "Oh, it's not about fruit. It's about real estate." I hate to record that she didn't get the money.

The process of translation was a new experience for me, and highly instructive. Nowadays everybody and his brother undertake a new translation of Chekhov with only the slimmest qualifications, but in 1944 there were few translations, the best being still the earliest, by Constance Garnett. It remains so, I am told, one of the closest to the true Russian feeling; but it is a bit on the stately side. Eva had taught herself Russian when she was very young, and had used the Garnett translations at the Civic Repertory Theatre, but this time she enlisted the help of Irina Skariatina to make a new one. Irina was a Russian of the old nobility, now married to an officer in the U.S. Navy. She was gentle, fragile and enthralled with the task. She had known the villages of Chekhov's Russia, the peasants, the landowners, the doctors or students with the liberal philosophy, the Old Nurse who had been with the family for years. She would supply the authentic background; we would test the translations from the actor's point of view.

We tried to avoid contemporary slang, since it gets so quickly out of fashion, and yet to find phrases which sounded easy and un-starched. Often a sentence would emerge accurate, literate but not easy to *speak.* So many translations are written to be read, not to be heard. The problems were various and fascinating. "What does it mean," Eva would say, following the Russian literally, " 'Petya's asleep in the bathhouse'? It sounds as if they'd put a mattress in the tub." Irina would laugh. "No, no, no! We all had bathhouses—separate buildings, where there were steam baths and massage rooms and cubicles where you could sleep. Everyone had them." So clear and yet so difficult! It was the same with such a word as old Firs's epithet which, phonetically rendered, sounds something like "needyatyoper"; in spite of our efforts to avoid Elizabethan English, we couldn't do better than "good-for-nothing." Some of the existing renderings made Irina laugh till she cried. There appeared to be an offstage character called "Squint-eyed Petrouchka." "But it's just his *name,*" she would say, "Pyotr Kosloi—like . . . Stephen Armstrong—he doesn't *squint!*" And then we would get lost in a passionate discussion of some adjective—did it carry the Russian meaning, did it convey the same thing in English, was it meant to be funny? *was* it funny?

We cheated a little on the stage directions in preparing the acting script. "Yawns" says Chekhov, meaning a tiny indication of boredom —and the actor will subside into a state of somnolent amnesia. "Through tears" runs the stage direction, indicating a few drops of an April shower, swift, volatile, as much joy as sorrow. But the actor tends to remain sunk in grief for the next ten minutes. We omitted some of these. The tradition that Chekhov is gloomy dies hard, though every good production proves that he is, on the contrary, gay and even farcical, tragic and ridiculous in a breath. In Eva's garden, sunny, blazing with roses and punctuated by her far-from-silent dogs, we tried to recapture the essence of the play; it was a fascinating labor of love.

So, indeed, was the whole production. In my experience, the playing of Chekhov tends to promote happiness. One falls in love with those little, foolish, eccentric, bewildered people whom he drew with such merciful penetration, so pitiful, so unconsciously heroic. The company grew together easily. Joseph Schildkraut was perhaps the best Gaev I have seen. Not trusting himself, however, he insisted that the property master spray his eyes with something to make him cry before his entrance in the third act, and the sight of these enormous tears would reduce Eva to dry-eyed exasperation. We were forced to tell him we thought the stuff would probably damage his eyes for life; whereupon he stopped and Eva could cry once more. A dear actor, "Bogey" Andrews, played Firs. He was eighty-six, having been born two years before Chekhov himself. But at the New Haven dress rehearsal he appeared with his little, withered-apple face covered with heavily applied wrinkles to bring his age up to the stipulated eighty-seven.

The process of double direction worked well. It is one which I mistrust and had never experienced before—nor have I since; and though Eva and I had known each other so long and talked theatre plans so often, we had never actually worked together. But the translation process had brought us a very harmonious understanding of the play. Eva knew it much better than I, having done it at her Civic Theatre, when she played Varya with Nazimova as Mme. Ranevskaya. The basic concepts were hers and the early rehearsal period entirely in her hands. Gradually, as she became more absorbed in her own performance, it slid into mine; I could be eyes for her, a judge of balance and result. To me fell the lighting, and the orchestration of that symphony of offstage sounds with which Chekhov's plays are always filled—the distant music, the dogs that bark, the wheels-on-gravel and those all-important tragic sounds which embody and end the play—the "breaking harp string," the workmen singing and the noise of the axe against the trees of the cherry orchard.

After a tremendous struggle with several unions we managed to get permission for an actor with a musical saw to make the harp-string sound. The rest was union-made, but live. I don't believe, all scientific evidence to the contrary, that sound on prefabricated tape can adjust itself to a live performance and a live audience as can the clumsy but responsive instruments of human eyes and hands. Naturally, we had a big struggle with the Musicians Union over the four pathetic members of Lyubov's "orchestra" at her dance on the day the orchard is sold. We only just escaped being a "musical"—the *Tempest* classification was yet to come. And the chaise-longue in the old "nursery," which had molded itself over so many years to Gaev's recumbent back, the dusty, worn object on which Firs lies down to die—how I raged as I watched Schildkraut practicing being gracefully at ease, and old Bogey Andrews carefully balancing himself with every muscle tense, on the three hard chairs, side by side with gaps between them, which was all we were allowed to use. What Stanislavsky would have thought of our enforced servitude I shudder to imagine.

Once the audience was in the theatre they surrendered to Chekhov as they always have. But by way of preliminary propaganda I tried to reassure them as to the "gloom" and the too-too-Russian atmosphere I knew they feared. I stressed that Chekhov had called his play a "comedy" in the true sense; Dante's *Divine Comedy;* the dictionary definition of comedy as "an amusing and enlightening event having a dramatic turn or suggestion . . . serious works whose purpose is to portray truth or life without leaving a painful or tragic impression"; and that "comedy" could be an accurate definition even of a play which hadn't been written by Noel Coward or produced by George Abbott. I said:

> Time and history have given an added excitement to the truth and life of *The Cherry Orchard*. We too, especially in the South, have known the old families, the Lyubovs and Leonids, who have seen their great estates and cherished, gracious way of living pass before the

inexorable pressure of the Lopakhins. We too have laughed and talked till the hour came; we too have heard the axe against the trees of our orchard. We too have seen history through the perspective of little things, petty annoyances, distractions, triumphs. We too, thank heaven, have not forgotten how to laugh.

Of course I quoted Trofimov, the "eternal student," little knowing that he would speak to—or for—the young people of America even more directly in 1970 than he did in 1944: "In order to live in the present we must first expiate our past, finish with it; and we can expiate it only through suffering, through extraordinary, unceasing labor. . . . All Russia is our orchard. Our land is vast and beautiful." And the glowing prophecy about the advance of humanity, of mankind's future happiness: "If we never see it, if we may never know it, what does it matter? Others will see it after us."

I embodied these things in an "Open Letter to Anton Pavlovitch Chekhov," and a few weeks later the *New York Times* published an unexpected reply:

Moscow

Dear Margaret Webster,

It was with the greatest interest that I read your imaginary letter to Anton Chekhov, and I felt I would like to send you my friendliest greetings. It gave me sincere pleasure to see you address Chekhov as a contemporary, and deepened my conviction that the creative work of the Russian writer of genius is deathless, not only for his fellow-countrymen but also for you who speak and think in another language. Evidently Chekhov's stories and plays can be understood and can move the American reader and theatre-goer. I convinced myself of that when I visited your country twenty years ago with the Moscow Art Theatre. . . .

It was very truly remarked by you that the principal content of the plays is the author's belief in man and in the better future which will dawn for mankind no matter what sufferings and deprivations some generations have to endure on their way to happiness for all.

Now, when our country, the United States, and Great Britain are struggling for this brighter future, for true independence of all freedom-loving nations, Chekhov's profound optimism is more keenly perceived by us all. You say in your letter that his plays are hard to read; that they are written for the stage; of translations this is certainly true, but in Russian they are much easier.

I think that like all really great dramatic works they belong both to the spectator and the reader. . . . But undoubtedly—I agree with you here—Chekhov's art gives actors the opportunity for disclosing in their roles beauty, spiritual experience and feeling. The most convincing proof of this is the Moscow Art Theatre's Chekhov Repertoire, which gave our great teachers of the stage art, Konstantin Stanislavsky and Vladimir Nemirovich-Dantchenko, the opportunity of creating that most delicate instrument of acting—psychological reality.

I am writing these lines a few weeks after a performance of *The Cherry Orchard* which we played at the Moscow Art Theatre on Jan. 13, 1944, to mark the fortieth anniversary of its first performance. For forty years now I have been playing Ranevskaya, and, though forty years is a long period, I find new shades of meaning each time, and I cannot speak those long familiar lines without emotion.

I send my sincere wishes for your success in your production of Anton Chekhov's plays and will be delighted to be present at them when the fighting alliance of [our] great countries is crowned with victory over Hitlerite barbarity and when cooperation and friendly relations between our peoples are still further strengthened and flourish in the soil of culture and creative work. Let us believe, as Chekhov believed, that the brighter day of triumph for democratic mankind is not far off. A hearty hand-shake.

Olga Knipper-Chekhova

How much of this was actually written by Mme. Chekhova and how much was the U.S.S.R. public relations officials I do not, of course, know. The historic ironies are as self-evident as they are depressing. What I could not have expected was that, only a very few years later, it turned out highly dangerous to have sought cultural relations with the U.S.S.R., and a hearty handshake from Chekhov's widow might just as well have been a snake bite. Nevertheless, despite all fears and enmities, the Chekhov plays retain a high place in the American theatre—not, of course, on Broadway, where they could no longer be attempted, but Off-Broadway and in the professional repertory companies outside New York. *The Three Sisters* is among the most frequently revived of all classic plays. Chekhov is timeless and international, perhaps to a greater degree than any other playwright except Shakespeare.

The brief tour with which we followed our New York run proved that his American audience was not confined to Manhattan; it didn't make our fortunes, but it didn't lose them either. The only trouble was that it turned into a dog show. Eva had a cairn and a Manchester terrier; Schildkraut two Chihuahuas; there was the poodle that played in the show and the poodle that understudied her and an indeterminate character belonging to the stage management; when I visited the company, I had a cairn too. It was wartime; the trains were jam-packed; dogs were forbidden except when carried in dog boxes and altogether taboo in Pullman cars, unless you had a private "drawing room," which you couldn't get. My dog became hysterical at the mere sight of a dog box; Pepi Schildkraut equally hysterical when forced to stand, with his, outside the Pullman on a swaying platform. In Chicago there was a rabies scare and none of the good hotels would accept dogs at all. I offered to take Eva's home via a drawing room. She refused, with hauteur. "If the inhabitants of Dover," she said, "can live in caves for three years, I can live in the 'Planters' Pub' for three weeks." Finally, we all got out to Milwaukee. Still refusing to be parted from Chico and Vixen, Eva fought her way into a bonded mail van and traveled as a parcel.

3

The following is a timetable for two weeks of my life in September 1945:

		THERESE	TEMPEST TOUR
Monday	3rd	Day off for Co. Crew in New Haven	Rehearse Co. all day, N.Y.
Tuesday	4th	Co. travel to N. Haven Travel to N. Haven by 2 p.m.	Rehearse 10–12 noon
Wednesday	5th	Reh. and dress reh.	* * *
Thursday	6th	Reh. and open	* * *
Friday	7th	Reh. and see show Return to N.Y. after show—drive if possible	* * *
Saturday	8th	* * *	Reh. day and eve.

		THERESE	TEMPEST TOUR
Sunday	9th	* * *	Reh. day and eve.
Monday	10th		Rehearse a.m.
		Travel to Boston by 7 p.m.	
		See evening show	
		Poss. reh. after show	
Tuesday	11th	Early a.m. train to N. Haven (fly??)	
			Scene and dress reh., N. Haven
Wednesday	12th	* * *	Scene and dress reh.
Thursday	13th	* * *	Reh. and open
Friday	14th		Reh. a.m.
		If *Tempest* show smooth, travel Boston for eve. show *Therese*. If not, see *Tempest* eve., travel Boston night or early a.m.	
Saturday	15th	Poss. reh. a.m.	* * *
		See mat. and eve. shows	
Sunday	16th	Reh. if necessary	* * *
Monday	17th	Reh. whichever needs it most	
			See *Tempest*

I doubt whether the art of being in three places at once has ever been more convincingly demonstrated.

Therese was an adaptation—not a very good one—of Zola's *Thérèse Raquin.* My mother came from Hollywood to play Mme. Raquin—she was then eighty years old. Eva played Therese and Victor Jory Laurent. If my mother sometimes envisaged Eva and me as the two small children who used to play together in a garden at Chiddingfold in Surrey, her theatre manners were too good for her to show it. Nevertheless, she told an interviewer, "The last time I was in Boston I was teaching Peggy to speak. This time she's teaching me to act." The first bit was true, or at least I believe so. I have a hazy recollection of crawling about the floor of what must have been a hotel room proclaiming "Pebby, Pebby, Pebby" with egotistical monotony, and have no reason to doubt my mother's assurance that this was in Boston. The second statement, though a good rhetorical balance, is not strictly a fact. My mother had been on the stage some sixty-four years to my meager twenty-one. I have always thought that when a director receives the gift of a fine actor, let alone one with sixty-four years' experience, all he can do is to make it as easy as possible for the actor to act as well as possible.

We had worked together before, of course, three times in all, including *The Trojan Women;* but oddly enough, this was the first time either of us had been paid for it. We tried not to let it overwhelm us. Our relationship, as ever, was easy and professional. I would suggest that Mme. Raquin should do such and such a thing, and Mme. Raquin would seldom demur. She sometimes got annoyed with me if she thought I was withholding or softpedaling criticism, because it gave her a feeling of insecurity. I suppose I went to the opposite extreme, for I remember that once she wailed, *"Now* you never tell us when we're *good!"* I pondered this and thought there was truth in it. I detected in myself a tendency to let things alone when they were all right and only talk when they weren't. I supposed everybody would know I must be satisfied. But this is not enough. Reassurance is generally in order. I have watched more carefully, since then, for the judicious mixture.

Therese was only a fair success in New York. Mme. Raquin is by far the showiest part in it, including a spectacular last scene played in a wheelchair. Given my mother's old expertise from *Night Must Fall,* she had no difficulty in picking up the play and wheeling it off with her to great acclaim. She wrote my cousin Jean a characteristic letter:

> I am still very fussed over and regarded as the cat's pyjamas—and it's pleasant of course, but [I am] unmoved—it is a bit late, you know. I go out a great deal to lunches and yesterday to a huge cocktail party given in my honour, most exhausting, didn't know a soul, just had to sit and smirk—I tottered back at 7 and from then till 1:30 a.m. wrote letters and sorted correspondence, didn't even stop for a meal or a drink.

She never worked in New York again, though the following year she did a summer-stock tour of *Night Must Fall* and made several pictures. Although the wartime activities had diminished, there were always other committees and other causes. The day of television was just beginning to dawn—she would have plunged into it with enthusiasm. She did a good deal of radio. Lehman Engel, who conducted her recordings of *The Snow Goose,* has described her rehearsal routine: she would sit on one side with a table improvised by the property man and her little blue writing case, busily doing her letters until someone said, "Dame May, please—we're ready for you now"; whereupon she would lay down her pen, pick up her script, walk briskly to the microphone and do the whole ensuing section without ever causing a second take.

John Van Druten wrote of her:

> No one was ever a better guest or hostess than May, because she loved people so. I think it is the thing by which she will be best remembered. That is, of course, why she was loved by them. She loved to have people around her—old people whom she had known all her life; young people whom she had only recently met; and talking to them of other people whom she had known in her long, full life. . . .
>
> I myself was a late-comer in May's life, as the years went. It is my regret that I knew her only twenty of them. But in those years I saw a great deal of her; in work, at parties, and—in later years—very frequently alone. In those hours alone we talked of many things. [He gave her a copy of *Who's Who in the Theatre* inscribed "With love, and to save argument."] I was amazed always at her interest in and knowledge of everything that went on in the world; it was so far, far greater than my own, so many years her junior. She would talk of politics, of religion, of theatre and poetry . . . but always in the end our talk came back to people. . . . Sometimes she told me that I did not love people enough. It was a lesson, I think, we could all learn from her.

But Ben was aging far more rapidly than she; it troubled her deeply. His memory was going; he seemed vague and unhappy; he always felt he ought to be doing something—generally something for her—and couldn't remember what it was. His eyes, May wrote, grew clouded and dim, "those blue eyes which always looked as if there were candles behind them."

In February 1947 May agreed to do a week of *Night Must Fall* in Mexico City. Two young men, friends of hers, were courageously trying to start an English-speaking theatre there, and she was to be the star of their opening production. I was in New York, heavily entangled with the American Repertory Theatre—playing in three of the productions and preparing the lighting for the imminent new one. My father was taken suddenly and acutely ill and rushed to hospital. Mercifully, my cousin Jean was with him. I managed to extricate myself for forty-eight hours and flew to Los Angeles. May, it need hardly be said, was in anguish—redoubled by her Christian Science fear and horror of doctors, hospitals and all "materia medica." We talked to her on the telephone, trying to reassure her that Ben was not in pain, only totally uncomprehending and bewildered—he was eighty-two and had never been in hospital before. May's whole heart and soul yearned to take the next flight back; but "How can I?" she said, "these two poor boys . . . their first show . . . there's no understudy, they'd have to close . . . how could I do this to them?" She finished the last three days of the engagement.

I had to leave the day she arrived. Ben, heavily drugged, still knew her. She wrote to me: ". . . those smiles, his blue eyes lighting up, he gave them to me all the time till he went into that coma—and at the moment of passing they opened and looked straight at me, but blank, he didn't see me or anything. I'm so thankful I was there and alone with him and it was so quick at the end."

The following day, February 27, was the centennial of Ellen Terry's birth (Ellen Terry, who had loved him and called him "beautiful, bountiful Ben"). I had written and arranged a special broadcast in commemoration of it—"live," of course. Stars such as Helen Hayes, Jane Cowl, Ingrid Bergman, Eva Le Gallienne, Cornelia Otis Skinner, were to do excerpts from her famous parts and I was the Narrator. The close was to be by John Gielgud, on tour in Baltimore, through a long-distance hook-up. It was the lament from *Cymbeline,* once spoken by Ben Webster and Gordon Craig, golden young men, for the Imogen of Ellen Terry. I finished the introductory sentences and we all stood, listening. There was a moment's agonizing silence; then, through the distance and darkness, came John's familiar voice:

> *Fear no more the heat o' the sun*
> *Nor the furious winter's rages.*
> *Thou thy worldly task hast done,*
> *Home art gone, and ta'en thy wages.*
> *Golden lads and girls all must*
> *As chimney-sweepers come to dust.*

A few days later May wrote to me: "It seems years since he was here in this place and centuries since we were really together—the time here is as if it had never been." After her own death I found among her papers a little clipping from a newspaper on which she had marked the following memoriam: "I would like to place on record my abiding love and thanks for the wonderful love, devotion and tenderness and courtesy my husband has always shown me during all the perfectly happy years of our married life."

I never thought she would outlive him for long, nor that she would want to. She continued the routine of her life, seeing people, attending meetings; she made three more pictures—*This Time for Keeps, If Winter Comes, The Sign of the Ram*. She played a week of "stock" in La Jolla. By this time she was in considerable pain and because of her Christian Science beliefs it was a long time before I could persuade her to see a doctor and let him, at least, ease it for her. That was the utmost she would allow.

Although she was a devoted Christian Scientist, and had been so for nearly forty years, she was by no means lamb-like in its tenets. (I fear she never ceased to deplore Mrs. Eddy's prose style.) I remember that one night her practitioner came to see her and do some silent "work" with her. I went upstairs, leaving them sitting one on each side of the fire. For a while there was a murmur of voices and then silence—a very long silence. At last, I crept out onto the little balcony overlooking the living room and peeped down. The practitioner was leaning back in his armchair, eyes closed, fingertips joined. May was watching him with something strongly resembling irritation; she shifted a little; she waggled her foot; she tapped the arm of her chair; she coughed; at last she burst out, "Jonathan! Are you working or are you asleep? Because if so, wake up and go home and I can go to bed."

I was able to be with her during the last weeks, and they went softly. She was not bedridden, she arranged her affairs, we did not speak of what we knew. She used to insist that even though she were dozing or asleep, we must wake her up at 2:15 p.m. to listen to *Portia Faces Life*. There were several radio serials to which she was attached, but *Portia* was a must. "It's idiotic," she would say, "it's abominably written and the story is perfectly asinine—I could do better myself—but I can't miss it!" Just as she had begun, a very small child, with the serial installments of Charles Dickens's novels, so she was fascinated, despite her informed and fastidious literary taste, by the soap opera of American radio.

She was always absolute for life. Strangely, Christian Science, which had quite literally saved her life, and brought her such faith and fortitude, had never enabled her to come to terms with death. It always seemed to her—or so I thought—something which oughtn't to happen, a theft, a waste. But for very evident reasons, she was perfectly reconciled to her own. Necessary arrangements had to be made. Otherwise it was unworthy of remark. I sat with her through the last nights; I could give no guess as to her spirit's journey. I would sit looking at the eucalyptus tree, black against the window, a thin, fine tracery laid over it by the mesh of the wire screen. I watched the sky grow paler and the carpet of spangled lights below, the lights that she had loved so much, go out. But what I saw was a steep, bracken-covered hillside in Devonshire, my mother and father climbing up the slope ahead of me and I scrambling after on short, sturdy legs. "Mamie" was wearing a white linen hat, and a long rose-colored knitted coat. I saw her stop for breath; my father put his hand against the small of her back and she leaned against it and said, "Thank you, Bennie darling." He took her weight against his hand and they went on up the hill. . . .

There were hundreds of letters, of course, all the way from "Her Majesty Queen Mary desires me to say . . ." to the little movie fans whom she had always thanked meticulously, in her own hand; Christabel Pankhurst, from the Women's Suffrage days, now, incongruously, also a Dame and also in Hollywood. She wrote: "You and I have been extraordinarily blessed in our parents haven't we?" Gordon Daviot, the playwright, describing a "furious letter" May had written her about the New York production of *The Laughing Woman,* "where the very pen strokes were protest and repudiation so that even if you looked at it upside down you would get the gist of it." So many people, as John Van Druten had said, whom she had known in her long, full life . . .

In London Sybil Thorndike and Lewis Casson arranged the memorial service for her at St. Paul's, Covent Garden, under the windows of the flat in Bedford Street where Ben and May had lived so long. All the Dames, said Sybil, sat together. "A Pride?" she suggested, "or perhaps a Gaggle? finally it was decided we were a Tangle of Dames." Lewis spoke of May's theatre career, but even more of her "selfless labour in every cause that would help her fellows," of the founding of British Equity, of all the things "to which she brought not only her boundless energy and deep sympathy, but her shrewd common-sense and her hatred of any form of humbug. And the driving power behind all this was a spiritual and deeply practical Christianity." Finally he spoke of "that dear flat in Bedford Street.

How many troubles has it seen smoothed out by Dame May's kindliness and understanding. How many wanderers has it welcomed to the hospitality of May and Ben. Within its walls how many plots have been hatched for bringing greater happiness and security to broken lives. The last of them I remember was for rescuing a number of persecuted German actors in the days of Munich. For years we hoped that one day, 'after the war,' we should see Ben and May back there at home. Now we shall not any more. For Ben and May, who were together here for 55 years, are together once again."

There is a memorial plaque for them now in that church where so many actors lie, beside the niche which commemorates Ellen Terry. It is inscribed: "They were lovely and pleasant in their lives, and in their deaths they are not divided."

Chapter Seven

Ardors and Endurances

The American Repertory Theatre opened in Princeton, N.J., on September 19, 1946, and in New York on November 6. The repertory part of it finished the following February. The sequent runs of *Yellow Jack* and *Alice in Wonderland* carried it on till the end of June 1947. It lost all its original capital and a good deal more besides. And that, despite some gallant but foredoomed efforts at resuscitation, was that.

The story is twenty-five years distant from me and I was certain my wounds had long ago disappeared without trace; but I find, to my astonishment, that there are still scars, and even that they begin to bleed a little. Eva Le Gallienne's record in *With a Quiet Heart* is definitive and remarkably dispassionate considering that she was writing only five years later. There are only a few drops of spilled blood, her own or other people's. But her account makes dreadful reading, nonetheless. Already she discerned quite clearly the moral to be drawn:

> There can be no doubt that the failure of the A.R.T. will discourage any other similar effort for a long time to come. Its fate is also conclusive evidence of the impossibility of establishing a permanent repertory theatre in this country without the aid of subsidy. Subsidy is imperative to overcome the initial allergy of press and public, to pre-

vent expenses from sinking such a venture before it can become established, and to enable such a company of actors to mould itself into a perfect ensemble.

Government subsidy is not only remote but probably undesirable. Private subsidy is desirable but in these days . . . probably remote. What then?

Twenty years later a good deal of the "what then" has been revealed. It is possible now to demonstrate from the episode of the A.R.T. what was going to happen to a whole segment of the American theatre—and, indeed, what had already happened, only no one had had the wit to discern it. It has become clear that the A.R.T. was launched at a moment in time that could not conceivably have been less propitious. The war years, boom years for Broadway, were over and the tide was receding. The big money, the comparatively easy money, available for New York shows was not so easy now. Private sources of backing were drying up. There had never—with rare exceptions—been enough of a Broadway audience to turn a "classic" into a money-making hit, but there had been enough to keep it ticking over agreeably. Not any more. The out-of-towners who had so recently become Broadwayites wanted hits, not reps.

Looking at the years which followed that season of 1946–47, one can see that classical revivals and repertory companies on a high level were not doomed—they were, and are, only doomed in New York. One can also see where Miss Le Gallienne's "what then" subsidy was to come from: it was to come from the foundations; much later and to a much smaller degree Federal aid would also be forthcoming. There are a dozen companies in the United States today which expect to get, and do get, annually, far more money than we thought would establish the A.R.T. for keeps. Such sources of supply did not then exist. Twenty years before, Le Gallienne's Civic Repertory Theatre had achieved large-scale private backing. Twenty years later, William Ball's American Conservatory Theatre was to receive far greater public subsidy. The A.R.T. sandwiched itself neatly in a vacuum between two theatre worlds.

I think this was true also of plays and playwriting and scene design and ticket prices and many other matters, even including geography. In 1946 theatres which were not within three or four blocks of Times Square just plainly weren't at all. Nowadays the public beetles off cheerfully to Yorkville or the Bowery to see a successful Off-Broadway show. We were actually and literally on Broadway, but we were on it at Columbus Circle. There were three subway lines at our doors, numerous buses and a parking lot. But we might as well have been in Hoboken.

We had plenty of bad luck, but we also had massive good will behind us. We made plenty of mistakes and had plenty of short-comings. All in all, however, the life of the A.R.T., short as it was, and by no means all gay, was not totally inglorious. From its ashes a surprising number of phoenixes have managed to arise.

Eva Le Gallienne's Civic Repertory Theatre sounds today like a pipe dream—indeed, it sounded like one then. It had had no predecessors in America and has had no successors, on the terms she set down for it. Forty plays in continuous repertory, ranging through the centuries, through the languages, Shakespeare, Molière, Chekhov (the first professional productions in America), Giraudoux (also an American "first"), Ibsen, Susan Glaspell—the Pulitzer prize winner; cheap prices—35¢ to $1.50; a "popular" audience which built up over five or six seasons to finish with over ninety percent of capacity —the whole achievement is part of American theatre history. But ninety percent capacity at $1.50 top may pay the operating costs of a theatre—or did, in the late Twenties; but it did not, even then, pay for new productions. The depression years wiped out the Civic's subsidy from private backers and, in due course, the Civic. Eva salvaged what she could from her company and her repertoire and embarked on several long cross-country tours. Like me, she believed in the necessity for getting the theatre away from the narrow, con-strictive and appallingly expensive confines of Manhattan. We began to pool our ideas.

Between us, we drew up innumerable plans and schedules; de-bated plays and casts—and, of course, costs. The scheme closest to our hearts was to establish a circuit of three (or more) repertory theatres, each having a different home base—say, Washington or Baltimore, St. Louis or Milwaukee, San Francisco or Los Angeles; after a given number of weeks in their home city they would rotate to each other's theatres; thus giving the company year-round em-ployment and the citizens year-round entertainment, with a variation of actors, plays and production styles. It still seems to me desirable and do-able. But I have ceased to believe it will ever get done.

In pursuit of this ideal, we approached numberless well-known actors to head the various teams; the emphasis in those days was still on actors, not directors. They all thought it was a wonderful ideal, though perhaps not quite what *they* would be able to undertake. We also visited several cities to explore the possibilities of civic backing. I remember making one such expedition to Chicago armed with a most impressive set of introductions to everyone from the Mayor down—or up, according to your view of Mayor Kelly. I came out with a promise (one) of $500 and the blessing of Claudia Cassidy, then drama critic for the *Sun*. Five hundred dollars were hardly enough to found a theatre on, and Miss Cassidy moved over to the *Tribune* and damned every show of mine that played in Chicago from that time forth. Perhaps she thought I had betrayed Chicago. I hadn't. It never noticed me.

Some of the smaller cities, such as Cleveland, had repertory companies of their own and were very proud of them. Eva got into extremely hot water for suggesting that the Cleveland Playhouse, though admirable in many ways, was nevertheless partly amateur, and its standards not equal to those of the Comédie Française. In several other towns where "nonprofessional" companies were in residence, the idea of a fully-fledged professional theatre was received with hostility. At all events, our splendid schemes never got further than the paper they were written on.

But during our collaboration with Cheryl Crawford on *The Tempest* we found the business drive we lacked and a harder head with similar ideals inside it. There were more discussions. They changed character, however. Cheryl's experience had been almost entirely in New York and we had elicited no response anywhere else, so that the project which emerged gravitated, inevitably, back toward Manhattan. In September 1945, we announced the formation of the American Repertory Theatre.

It is hard, now, to imagine why we thought we could swing it, but we did. We were immensely encouraged by the rave reviews and the public rapture accorded to the Old Vic Company, headed by Laurence Olivier and Ralph Richardson, when it presented four plays in repertory at the Century Theatre. Everybody started clamoring for an American Old Vic. We would be one. None of us was unaware of the disparities or the different problems—a long and blindingly obvious list, including the small point that there was no American Olivier. We knew that it was his reputation, and that of the Old Vic itself, which had caused their six weeks' season to be sold out before it opened, and before anyone knew how good or bad the shows would be. All the same, the outlook for classical repertory seemed good. It wasn't until later that we found out what had gone on behind the scenes—the appalling expense, the union demands, the other problems which could easily have turned the Old Vic's visit into a disaster and did, in fact, cost their backers a fortune. By this time we were committed and could not have drawn back even if we had wanted to.

We held long conferences with the very best legal advisers, financial wizards, benevolent elder statesmen and others as to the structure and form of the organization. We calculated we would have to raise $300,000. We were assured that it would be easier to do this through the investment process rather than by setting up a non-profit corporation. Not that we ourselves expected to make any profit. Contrariwise. But "charitable," and therefore tax-deductible, donations were as yet almost unknown in the theatre world. A show which was a "charity" came under the head of good works and must therefore, automatically, be bad. There was also a complication about the actors' Social Security payments under such a structure. The consensus of opinion therefore was that we should set up a corporation, capitalized at $300,000, on a share-selling basis. We followed the experts' advice. It was completely wrong, and we were idiots to take it.

A leaflet was carefully drawn up, eloquent as to our aims and plans: an initial New York season of six plays produced successively and done in repertory; the following year, a coast-to-coast tour while we rehearsed and opened new additions to our repertoire; then a return to New York, and so forth; an apprentice group and later a small training school. We would work with local educational authorities, doing special performances and readings for their benefit. There was to be a permanent company, employed on a two-season basis. We gave examples of the kind of repertoire we planned to present, and pointed to the success of the Lunts, Maurice Evans, Katharine Cornell and others (including ourselves) in touring such plays successfully. Then comes an astonishing headline. As I read it now, I can scarcely believe we wrote it; but we did.

8. THE DIRECTORS BELIEVE THIS THEATRE CAN OPERATE SUCCESS-
FULLY AND PROFITABLY.

We continued:

We do not believe that it need be dependent on State or Federal
subsidy. We know that we can attract together some of the best creative
artists in the American theatre, who have been waiting for such an
opportunity as this. We have proved that the public will support at the
Box Office fine plays, if they are finely done. The expenses of launching
the project, of conducting the necessary publicity and advertising
campaigns, and of producing the first cycle of plays, will be very heavy.
And above all, the theatre must be absolutely assured of continuity
over a reasonable length of time, since it is intrinsically and essentially
a long-range multiple enterprise and not a single gamble. We have
hopes, however, that the theatre's weekly operating sheet will, from
the first, show a profit, given the variety and quality of its productions.
Although the original capital may take considerable time to pay off,
the costs of new productions should progressively diminish, both in
size and frequency as the repertoire expands and the enterprise takes
root. . . .

There followed a paragraph about our own contributions in
terms of doing practically-everything for practically-nothing, and
our expectation that "the important actors" would do the same (they
did, bless them). We concluded: "We believe that the theatre can
become a self-supporting, business enterprise." The corporation setup
was then made clear (to others, not to me) and the purchase of
shares invited. The entire leaflet was admirably set out, concise, lucid,
embodying impeccable objectives in impeccable prose. It was also,
to quote *Alice Through the Looking Glass,* "wrong from beginning
to end." To prove, however, that we were not alone in our insanity,
we were able to use quotes from the New York drama reporters.
Not only did they welcome the project with the most wholehearted
enthusiasm, but they described the prospectus and its contents as
"sound and intelligent"; "sane, sensible and workable"; its "feet
firmly planted on the Broadway battle-ground"; "Establishing such a
theatre is fundamentally a matter of financing"; and "If I were a
betting Broadway-ite, I would bet on the American Repertory
Theatre." Unquestionably we had the critics' good will. Even if we
disappointed them, the gap between prognostication and achieve-

ment was due mainly to major errors of judgment all round as to the whole trend and potential of the theatre in New York.

We formed a window-dressing Advisory Board, not called upon to do anything but look impressive on a letterhead, which it did. We started the money-raising campaign. We worked like dogs. We wrote, we talked, we appealed. We got ourselves invitations to speak at distinguished Wall Street luncheons, at Women's Club meetings, to Girl Scouts in Wilton and Kiwanis Clubs in Newark. It was frequently funny, but it was also exhausting, crushing, grotesque, endless. We even tried to collect bad debts and invest the proceeds. Frank Fay, the vaudeville comedian, owed Eva $5,000 in unpaid salary from several years before when she had been the "class act" in his show. As he had now been starring in the endlessly running hit, *Harvey,* for many months, she thought he might like to repay her by becoming a shareholder in the A.R.T. It was a vain effort; which later had an unforeseen sequel. Cheryl wrote to me: "I find I'm tired, not physically, but my spiritual bin is empty from money-raising, money-cutting, glad-handing and the grinding repetition of our aims."

The results came from the oddest quarters, not only from theatre colleagues, but from Iceland, from Zaleski, Ohio, from Kent, England. One of our stockholders was a GI, another a nurse, another a college fraternity. It was touching; but it was also very slow and the amounts were usually very small. We began to despair.

I find in my diary for November 2, 1945 the note: "Voisin. Joe." Over a lunch at Voisin's, Joseph Verner Reed offered me $100,000. We were in business.

Then came the actors; the familiar game. In my file is a list of thirty-seven supposed "stars" whom we invited to join us. All of them wanted to—oh, they wanted to, so much, so very much. But none of them did. There was the usual string of insuperable obstacles and excuses. A good many of my list were not really, and never would be, "stars" in the sense of being brushed with that particular and unique theatre magic; fewer still had the training and skills to play the kind of repertoire we proposed. Some have vanished so completely that I cannot now remember who they were in their twinkling days. But we thought the public—no, let me be truthful, we thought the *critics*—would be favorably impressed by their names and that we could implement their technical shortcomings. But we never got the chance to try.

This, by definition, was to be an *American* company. We didn't want to use English actors, even if Equity would have allowed it. But American actors with the requisite qualifications were rare, even in 1946. Such actors have never grown on bushes nor been hidden under them. Now, twenty-five years later, the traditions, the opportunities of learning either by experience or example, have almost entirely gone; the creation of American actors to match those of the European national theatres has ceased.

The A.R.T. did remarkably well. Walter Hampden was the head of his profession in the classic field and did us great honor by joining us. Ernest Truex was a much-loved star comedian. I know of no actress in America, and only a tiny handful anywhere else, who, like Eva, could have played Katherine of Aragon, Ella Rentheim and a light-comedy character part (with a flawless French accent) within one week. Victor Jory had been with us from the beginning —a tower of loyalty, faith and integrity, who was blamed for not being Laurence Olivier, which he could hardly help. There were able actors such as Richard Waring (who had just been playing *The Corn Is Green* with Ethel Barrymore), Philip Bourneuf and others— Margaret Webster, for instance.

Some of the critics decided that this cast was "unexciting," an accusation impossible to disprove, but I think unjust and certainly not widely shared. I suppose they expected us to reach, immediately, the standard of the Old Vic Company, which had recently been in New York. The Vic had been in existence, training its actors, since 1914 or thereabouts, and that visit coincided with a vintage year. In addition to Richardson, Olivier and some very fine "character" actors, they had been lucky enough to come upon an unknown young woman named Margaret Leighton. But it takes time to make a company "exciting." The present Royal Shakespeare Company and even London's National Theatre began with quite mediocre material. Ten years of working together have turned them into very fine ensembles; moreover they have had access to brilliant visiting talents, such as those of John Gielgud, Peggy Ashcroft, Paul Scofield and Albert Finney. Such good fortune was not vouchsafed to us.

There were hundreds of eager youngsters. We auditioned them for weeks and weeks. On the whole, we didn't choose badly. Auditions are desperately difficult at the best of times. When you are trying to pick a company of thirty or so from hundreds of actors previously unknown to you, for a repertory of plays also partly unknown but of a kind for which they have neither equipment nor experience, you will be lucky if you make three good guesses. We did make at least three incontrovertible ones: Eli Wallach, Anne Jackson and—a later addition—Julie Harris. There were quite a few more, such as Efrem Zimbalist, Jr. and William Windom, on whom television has since bestowed national renown. But we missed our big little fish, a very young man, just beginning to be heard of, named Marlon Brando.

Eva has written of his visit to my apartment on 12th Street, shepherded by Richard Waring, who had been playing with him, and his agent, Edie Van Cleve.

He "greeted us with grunts, and thereafter for two solid hours sat completely speechless, slumped down on a low chair, with his feet, encased in rather dirty socks of a hideous shade of green (one of his first acts on arriving was to kick off his shoes), firmly planted on an adjacent table. Every now and then he took a handful of grapes from a bowl at his elbow and chewed them solemnly and vigorously, punctuating his silence by occasionally spitting out a seed. Yet . . . my heart went out to him."

We all wooed him like mad. We lured him down again to dinner, to which he contributed what he called "a sausage concoction" of his own devising. My French-Canadian cook fell instantly under his spell and wooed him too, in her pint-sized kitchen. "Stick around with us," we said, "play a couple of smallish parts and then Oswald or Treplev; and next season we'll do Hamlet for you." He listened to the sirens and said "Ugh." It emerged that he wanted to go to Provincetown and play drums in a band. He sent me a charming, disarming letter in a round, boyish hand, and a jar of shrimp paste to my cook. "You are all unusual women," he wrote—I think he meant Eva and Cheryl, not the cook—"the likes of which one doesn't get the opportunity to know in a life's span. I wish you God's grace and speed. Marlon. P.S. Especially you." But he wouldn't sit around on the chance of Hamlet.

Since we never got that far, he was, as it turned out, right in the short-term sense. But I don't think he ever played drums in the Provincetown band either. He gave himself time to show, in *A Streetcar Named Desire,* that he could be a great actor, and then went to Hollywood and wasn't. (A sigh and a drop of blood here: still no American Olivier.)

We were in the old quandary; you can't get the actors until you know the repertory; you can't establish the repertory until you know the actors. We would have done the *School for Scandal* for Katharine Hepburn (on a one-shot basis, though we didn't much like that), or *Caesar and Cleopatra* for Mary Martin. They each liked the idea, were eager to do it; we geared our plans toward them; they couldn't, wouldn't, anyway didn't.

So we ended up with a "team" company. I believe that if it had come from somewhere outside the United States, and none of the press had ever heard of any of us, it would have been voted a very fine team. Nevertheless, it dictated a choice of "team" plays, allowing each important actor a worthwhile part, but not offering us the chance to try *Romeo and Juliet,* for instance, because we didn't have either. No two people ever agree on choices of plays, and certainly not on anybody else's choice. *What Every Woman Knows* (curtailed to WEWK in our reference language) was thought an odd selection. Actually it is better than is generally supposed, warm and human with a lot of appeal to poor, faithful middlebrows—at least, to the middlebrows of those years, whom we did not disdain. We were sensible enough to realize that it is, in fact, a team play and not a vehicle for "Maggie Wylie." The critics, however, were less perceptive; and subsequently reviewed it almost wholly in terms of how wonderful Maude Adams (whom few if any had ever seen) and Helen Hayes had supposedly been.

We also had the high-minded but slightly dangerous idea that it was not our business to do the best-known plays, such as *Hamlet* and *Hedda,* which were frequently done on a single-run basis, but lesser-known works like *Henry VIII* and *John Gabriel Borkman. Androcles and the Lion* was a good fourth choice, I think, and was the bait which enabled us to get Ernest Truex. Next we wanted to do a new, or recent, American play, and last *The School for Scandal,* probably with a special star engagement for "Lady Teazle"; we planned a long preparatory course in the arts and graces of the eighteenth century, and Agnes De Mille had agreed to help us with it.

In the matter of the new play, we failed through humility. We had two which we all admired and could have got. One was Brecht's *Mother Courage,* not as yet seen in the United States, and the other a first play called *The Sign of the Archer* by an unknown dramatist. It was subsequently rechristened *All My Sons,* and started Arthur Miller on his great career. We abjured them both because we didn't think we could cast them well enough. In the case of *All My Sons,* we were right. But after I had seen Helene Weigel play Mother Courage, I realized that we had all completely misread the part, and Le Gallienne could have done it magnificently. In the end we settled on a revival of Sydney Howard's *Yellow Jack*, a fine play which the critics had applauded to the echo two years before when it had been put on for some special performances by actor-members of the American Air Force. As with WEWK, we hoped to curry critical favor. We were similarly mistaken.

Equity allowed us five weeks' rehearsal. We completed *Henry VIII*, brought WEWK close to the finishing line and "broke in" the early stages of *Borkman*. We opened in Princeton with *Henry*. I think it was the best job I ever did in terms of what might be called "obvious" direction—the script itself (from my Billy Rose original), the crowd scenes, the music, the flash-bang "show." It looked and sounded splendiferous. David Ffolkes did a magnificent job with the sets and costumes. He had just spent four years in a Japanese prison camp in Malaya; he reveled in the lavish resources of New York—and hadn't a clue as to the labor costs. They were crippling. Cheryl, preoccupied with a million other things, let him get ahead of her and we would find ourselves saddled with a bill of $3,000 for a backdrop. Victor Jory's costumes cost $750 each; and there were small, ridiculous items like the soft black caps for the fifteen or so Bishops in the trial scene, which we could have run up for ourselves at a dollar or two apiece, and which worked out at $25 each. It couldn't be helped. The Bishops had to have caps.

It was not Edith Lutyens's fault. She executed everything as economically as she possibly could. This included using furnishing fabrics, as being cheaper than dress materials. The men's clothes were so heavily padded that, when we opened in Princeton in a September heat wave, they nearly killed off the actors. Queen Katherine's train almost dragged Le Gallienne backward off the steps of the throne. The rest of the women (including myself in the tiny part of the Old Lady) used to step out of our costumes at the side of the stage when we made an exit and leave them standing there by themselves till we stepped in again for the next entrance. The angels of Queen Katherine's vision, by which I had set such store in the days of my Billy Rose script-making, were so heavily weighted down in gold cloth that they couldn't possibly perform the choreography arranged for them and finally had to be cut. Eva succeeded in creating the whole vision more effectively than I have ever seen it done, by the miming of her own response and the clear projection of her own imagination. Still, we had wasted $1,000. The reviews, all through our out-of-town weeks, were as good as we could have wished and the public adored the pageantry and carry-on. But in Cheryl's office, with the cost sheets in front of us, we felt a little chilly.

In Philadelphia we added *What Every Woman Knows* during our second week. It was affectionately received. I do not suppose there has been, or will be, a revival where the two young leads (in our case Richard Waring and June Duprez) are "supported" by top stars of the quality of Le Gallienne, Hampden and Truex. It was a good show. We were rehearsing madly all the time, and in Boston we added *John Gabriel Borkman*. We regarded it as our greatest risk, and technically it was the trickiest of our productions. We played it straight through without curtain or intermission. Using our revolving stage, the four scene changes were done in seconds, behind a blackout drop and in a minimal glim of light, and covered by the "Danse Macabre" music which Ibsen stipulates. It was a precision exercise. The lighting was extremely delicate; speed was all-important. The turntable was manual and had to be stopped at exact marks; onstage lamps had to be disconnected and whipped off.

We had only one dress rehearsal, on a Sunday, costing overtime. It was such a shambles that Eva, as director, asked for a scene-and-lights run-through on the following day, when we were to open. Cheryl turned pale, but agreed. We all knew what it would cost; but also that it was absolutely essential.

I was playing Mrs. Borkman. During one of the scene changes I had to watch from a dark corner while a stage hand snatched the lamp from Borkman's desk and whisked it off. (We had had to en-gage an additional "operator" for this one task.) The lamp was very beautiful, costly, with a tinted pearl-glass shade impossible to replace. With almost pathetic urgency, I said to the stage hand "For God's sake be careful of that lamp—make sure you have a clear exit." He nodded. The blackout came. He rushed onto the stage and rushed off again with the lamp—straight into a ladder where it smashed to atoms. I felt a surge of such murderous rage that I really and truly could have killed him.

That night, the Boston local of the stage hands' union sent us a completely different crew who hadn't worked the dress rehearsal at all. Oh, didn't we know? they said; the "night men" had daytime jobs and the "day men" were not allowed to work the night show. I quote Le Gallienne:

That opening was a nightmare to us all. I felt humiliated and ashamed that the critics and first-nighters should blame the many mishaps of the performance on any lack of care or proper respect for the public on the part of myself and my colleagues. I left the theatre that night without seeing a soul. I didn't dare trust myself to speak to anyone, my heart was so filled with rage and despair. After an hour's walk round the Common, I regained sufficient control of myself to go back to my hotel.

As an actress, I think that Ibsen demands more total concentration of the nerves and spiritual energies than any other dramatist. Perhaps Pinter and, sometimes, Beckett ask similar things of their executants. At all events, I found Mrs. Borkman inordinately difficult. I suppose that no one in the English-speaking theatre knows more about Ibsen than Eva; which is not surprising, since she is herself half-Danish and has spent a lifetime studying, translating, directing and acting his plays. Her direction of this one was vastly revealing; her performance of Ella Rentheim moving, delicate and entirely perceptive. The rest of us felt like oafs. Vic Jory, who played Borkman, confessed to me once: "I stand there in the second act, alone, waiting for her to knock on the door, and sometimes I pray that she won't come in." I knew what he meant. I would sit on my sofa at the beginning of the play, knitting; and as I waited for the curtain to go up my hands would sweat with fright till the wool got completely soaked, like seaweed; and this, not merely on opening nights, but at every performance. Eva could never understand this. On *Henry* nights she said she was scared to death; but Ibsen seemed to her simple.

Simple or not, any actor who has tackled an Ibsen part must have found it a hugely exciting challenge: the characters are meticulous in the detailed veracity of their lives, but they are larger than life-size. "No declamation! No theatricalities! Express every mood in a manner that will seem credible and natural," said the author; and yet you must have a force and breadth of imagination which lifts the play onto a higher level—as if you could cast an enormous shadow onto a screen behind you. Eva's performance caught this; sometimes I felt I had achieved it a little. Ernest Truex, as Foldal, perfectly presented one of those little people who, in so many of

Ibsen's plays, are crushed between the giant forces they do not understand.

So. The reviews for all our shows in Boston and Philadelphia were as good as we could have wished. The box office returns were not. We rationalized this in various ways and took the train for New York. We arrived there on the crest of a wave of enthusiasm. On our opening night a paid "ad" appeared in the *New York Times* signed by Equity and every one of the craft unions, the Dramatists Guild, the Theatre Guild, the Playwrights' Company and the League of New York Theatres. It said: "Good luck, American Repertory Theatre." I suppose this generous demonstration is probably unique. To those on whom the pressure of the opening night lay, it added a tremendous feeling of obligation and responsibility. But everything was fine—a blaze—all the technical stuff worked, the cast played beautifully, the audience cheered, speeches were made; I apparently said (though I have completely forgotten it) that "we had a long way to go and a lot to learn"; but the cast, which adored the show and us and each other, all went home very happy.

It is my recollection that I have never been quite the same since the morning of November 7, 1946. Going over what we read in print that day, I am a little baffled by this burned-in anguish of memory. Of course the critics did not *have* to like *Henry VIII;* to be fair, Joe Reed didn't either. On a casual rereading, the reviews seem quite good; most of the critics wanted to do right by us, though maybe a few thought too much fuss had been made over us and we had better be warned. But a more careful reading tells me that our reaction was neither unreal nor unjustified. There is praise for David, for me, for some of the acting; there is "an auspicious start," "a worthy" (oh, dear) "and hopeful occasion." But the emphasis is on what a poor play *Henry VIII* is; that Shakespeare hadn't written all of it (as if we didn't know); that it could be improved (says one) by putting in "copious quotations from the other plays"; another critic apparently thought Shakespeare had written the Holinshed *Chronicle* bits. Evidently one pundit, during the usual intermission conclave, had mentioned the word "listless" as applied to the script. This must have seemed to several others a vivid and neglected adjective. One of them stuck it onto the performance itself. Good or bad it may have been; but listless it sure-as-hell wasn't. Blood, sweat and tears flooded that stage; hearts and souls were up there naked.

Had we been able to run what is known in the trade as a "quote ad" from the letters we received about *Henry VIII* instead of from the printed reviews, it could have gone something like this:

It's not often a person has the experience of sitting absolutely entranced for two hours not knowing whether she is sitting down, flying, dancing or indeed breathing at all. . . . It's the most exciting play I ever saw. (A distinguished historian and biographer)

I do not remember ever spending such an evening in the theatre! I do not ever remember such a combination of brilliant directing, brilliant acting and brilliant staging . . . there came such applause as I have never heard in a theatre. (From a famous radio writer)

. . . it sent me out as pridefully as if I, personally, had had some part in its achievement. The things that are cheap and sleazy and wrong in the theatre faded into nothing—there just wasn't *anything* wrong with the theatre while I sat there! One gets a renewed feeling of the dignity and glory associated with the art. (From an actor)

But this kind of response is hardly to be expected from men whose job it is to criticize. They contrived to find the play "dull." The company reeled somewhat, having had no doubts at all as to what we had accomplished. Cheryl and Eva and I displayed much gallant "never mind" and "tomorrow's another day" and everybody rallied to WEWK. It got pleasant notices; Dick Waring did well, Maude Adams magnificently; the extraordinarily high quality of the "supporting" players was taken as a matter of course. Again, it would have been nicer to quote a fourteen-year-old high school boy:

I told my father and mother I had finally saved up enough money to see Eva Le Gallienne. I endured the long subway ride, bought my ticket and then had one of the most pleasant two hours I have ever known. *What Every Woman Knows* was so unlike every other play I had ever seen; so delightful and "skimming" and what a chance for boys and girls like me, who love the theatre, to see an all-star cast. The actors and actresses looked so at home and since the theatre was not very large it gave me the intimate feeling I was part of the play and not a bystander.

Still, we pulled out a few small printed plums. WEWK was well liked at the box office, and I think we rated it lower than it deserved.

Borkman turned out to be the surprise. It was our greatest "artistic" success. The lack of intermission precluded consultation among the critics. The "sweet Roman hand" of George Jean Nathan was nowhere apparent except over his own signature in a weekly where it didn't matter. The notices read as if their authors had visited several different productions of quite different plays. Some were terrible, some ecstatic, none lukewarm. One condemned us for doing the play at all, another pronounced it a "rare wisdom." We got back the *Tribune* (very anti-*Henry* and luke-WEWK), and Brooks Atkinson broke out some superlatives like "inspired." Robert Garland said we had "embittered" him, and John Mason Brown decided he hated repertory. Eric Bentley wrote to Eva that he had just seen about twenty New York shows as critic for *Harper's Magazine* and "by far the biggest of the lot was your *John Gabriel Borkman.*" A "man unknown" wrote her: "I have seen this play performed on many stages, including the most famous European ones, but your performance certainly tops them all." Some of the press moaned about the "gloom." A group of students from North Carolina telegraphed us asking us to put in some additional performances during Christmas week. They said: "We would rather see Ibsen than eat."

So there we were, with our first three productions, all new, all opened in New York within a single week. None of the press commented on that. They reviewed each one as if it had been done by quite different actors in quite distinct theatres. In fact, it was a superhuman feat which has, rightly, never been attempted since. Courage, of course, does not necessarily equate accomplishment; but I do believe, looking back, that the sustained level of the work done by the A.R.T., both in these first three productions and the three that followed, was astonishingly high for a company in its first season. I have since seen American repertory companies, in Minneapolis or Washington or at Lincoln Center, Ellis Rabb's APA or William Ball's ACT, which blazed into brilliance with individual productions; but none which maintained a higher level of achievement right from the moment of its birth.

In December we added *Androcles and the Lion,* preceded by Sean O'Casey's *Pound on Demand.* Even the critics liked *Androcles.* (So, too, did a West Point Cadet who had seen it "courtesy of the management" and wrote: "There are times when one feels one's own infinitesimal enthusiasm so inadequate. I only wish I were in a position to do more. . . . We are deeply grateful and will stand solidly behind you.") *Pound on Demand* was a choice which didn't satisfy anybody, including us. It is curious that so many young playwrights today are using the one-act form; one hopes it is not because they cannot last out three. In those days good one-acters were hard to come by.

Nevertheless, Eli Wallach collected what I suppose were his first Broadway notices, Truex was fine, the company played very well, the public liked it, everybody was happy. In devising our schedule for the second month we leaned heavily on *Androcles.* The Christmas weeks looked like offsetting the proverbial Broadway "slump" which had been affecting all New York shows. (There is always a slump, unless you have a hit.)

But by this time we were in deep financial trouble. Our production budget, in spite of *Henry,* had stayed close to Cheryl's figures; but our operating losses had been almost unvarying. She had forecast an operating cost of $16,000 a week. It turned out to be $18,500. This was due to an across-the-board increase of about twenty percent for all unions concerned, except Equity, since she had made her budgets. Because there were no established sets of rules governing the playing of repertory, we had had no means of determining exactly what our liabilities would be, and had constantly sought exact definitions. Early in the planning stage Eva had met with the stage hands' union, Local No. 1 of the IATSE, asking them for the same—very liberal—conditions which had obtained at the Civic. They listened and gave no answer. Three weeks later (in June) she was summoned again; again she explained our problems and proposed methods of operation; again the issue was evaded. She has recorded that "at the end of the conference one of these gentlemen slapped me on the back and jovially exclaimed, 'If we want you to have your little theatre, you'll have it, and if we don't want you to, you won't, see?'" It is hard to figure how this gentleman escaped with his life.

It wasn't until we had actually moved into New York, a matter of days before the opening, that they informed us of their final decisions. The two business agents had done their honest best on our behalf. They secured what they felt to be a great concession in allowing us only a one-hour additional crew call every time we changed the show instead of the three-hour change-over call they had imposed on the Old Vic Company. In fact, our shows had been meticulously designed so that they could be rotated and the scenery stacked aside within the normal limits of stage hands' "show time," which begins half an hour before the curtain. It took no longer to clear the last act of *Henry* to a bare stage after the final curtain and set up the first act of WEWK the following night at half-hour than it would to clear the last act and put up the first of any single-run play using more than one set. One of our most important and basic decisions—the choice of the International Theatre—had been made precisely because there was room on its stage to organize our productions this way. Designers, directors and crew heads had all collaborated in making it possible. But we had to bow our heads and be grateful for small mercies.

Other decisions were less merciful. For instance, it was ruled that we must employ the maximum number of men in each department in every show, whether they were needed or not. It happened that *Henry* needed more "grips" than the other two shows, WEWK more prop men and *Borkman* an additional electrician. So we had to employ the *Henry* grips, WEWK props and *Borkman* electrics for every production. When it came to *Androcles,* we were paying eight unnecessary men at every performance.

The ruling might have been understandable if it had resulted from a union policy of steady employment for every man every night. But such had never been the case. Local No. 1 had always exercised the right to send along different or substitute men on any night it pleased. The variations were frequent and sometimes disastrous. There was always at least one octogenarian among the relief men, and the crew heads had to arrange to tuck him away in a corner and get the work done by some more able body. Other featherbedding rules were imposed on us, trivial in themselves, but they mounted up.

We had a foreseeable hassle with the musicians. *Henry* was a "drama with music." We knew it would be, and it had accordingly been scored for the eight musicians we would have to use, at an increased pay scale of thirty-five percent. Somehow *Androcles* got itself into this category too on the strength of a waltz between the title roles and a few trumpet calls. The fact that Marc Blitzstein had composed them was probably the determining factor. Unneeded men and extra pay scales again. The Musicians Union 802 made a great virtue of not forcing us to pay sixteen men for every show.

When we reached the point where every dime mattered desperately, we made a careful calculation of what we were spending on labor for nonexistent work. It wasn't much—about $1,275 a week, depending on the variation of the repertory; not an astronomical figure, but just about equal to the combined salaries of Crawford, Le Gallienne, Webster and Walter Hampden. As things turned out, to have eliminated it would certainly not have saved our lives. But it is one illustration of why the playing of repertory in New York had already become impossible; and, coincidentally, why there is no longer any music to be heard in a New York theatre which does not house a full-scale musical.

We took all the measures we could think of. We adopted a reduced scale for serial tickets, which we should have done from the start and had been deterred by our experts who said audiences didn't want to make decisions as to dates and plays ahead of time. In fact the price scale had been a matter of contention between Eva and Cheryl from the beginning. Cheryl argued that we needed, and had to have, the same scale as all the other Broadway theatres. Eva replied that our sort of theatre was not for the people who could afford that sort of price. When she heard (while we were in Boston) that Cheryl had announced a $7.20 top for the opening night and a $4.20 week-night top thereafter, she said, "It is the end of the A.R.T." I tried to mediate between them and, as usual, the compromise solutions (to which I am so prone) satisfied nobody and didn't work.

Looking back, I think Cheryl was the righter of the two. Eva's old audience of the Civic Repertory days, which she had served so well and which had responded with such fervor, barely existed in new New York. The European Statue of Liberty population, theatreminded from their childhood, had been assimilated into American non-theatre-mindedness and into an American scale of price-thinking. Anything cheaper than usual was suspect—and there were, of course, alternatives for cheap entertainment which had not existed in the Civic days. We tried to cater to students at the Saturday and Sunday matinee prices and through our schools program. Eva deplored the lack of enough cheap seats. But no evidence emerged to indicate a surplus demand for them.

News of the A.R.T.'s troubles spread fast—and didn't help business. At a meeting of our sponsors in January 1947, we summarized the factors working for and against us. We stressed the audience enthusiasm, the response to our educational program, the invitations from England, France and Holland to send our company to their festivals, the possibilities, which we were pursuing, of radio and television programs. But we did not attempt to minimize the gravity of the situation:

> We have concrete plans for the immediate future. We are giving a reading of Euripides' *Electra* for our patrons on January 31st and we are already in rehearsal with Sydney Howard's *Yellow Jack*.
>
> But this is the immediate issue: *We must have time*—time to arouse a public generally ignorant of the special value of a repertory theatre; repertory play-going has its difficulties; we were always aware that the public must have time to get used to them. We did not know that time would be so costly. We must have time, also, to explore the different possibilities of achieving a really substantial endowment for our work, of a firm and lasting nature.
>
> We have no reserves. If we cannot survive the coming weeks, the vast amount of work and achievement already attained, as well as our plans for the future, will be irretrievably wasted.

Theatrical New York was greatly shocked. We received the most moving and extraordinary offers of help from both individuals and theatre institutions. ANTA, once more led by Robert Breen, offered its facilities as a channel for tax-free donations. The American Theatre Wing and Equity itself (to the fury of some of its members) each contributed $5,000; the Theatre Guild offered to circularize its membership. Volunteers from our own company sat up all night addressing envelopes and sending out leaflets. We received innumerable widows' mites, sent anonymously. We appealed to the foundations—such as then existed; it was before the days of Granma Ford.

Eva approached Mr. John D. Rockefeller, Jr. with an admirable proposal to set up the A.R.T. and its world-wide repertoire of plays as a United Nations Theatre, housed in the complex of buildings for which he had provided the site. He replied very cordially: "There can be no question as to the significance of the matter of which you write. What you have done over a long period of years to carry out your dream and thus to serve mankind in a large way is beyond praise. For these reasons I the more regret that I am unable to help you." He then explained that he had nothing to do with the use to which the United Nations would put the site he had given them and that he could not "enter new fields of activity";

he added his "deep appreciation of what you have done for your fellow-men" . . . and hoped that "the aims and ideals to which you have given yourself so generously may be brought to fruition."

It was a splendid tribute to Eva, like many others she received from lesser men. But it was of no practical help. We ourselves did everything we could think of, composed the most convincing prose in articles, reports and appeals, made the most moving curtain speeches—a perfectly useless and loathsome activity which Eva and I hated but Vic Jory loved and did excellently. But it all added up to a smell of failure and this does not sell tickets.

We were forced to the conclusion that we could not continue to play repertory. We would put on *Yellow Jack* for a solid run and save ourselves the repertory expenses till we could reorganize and consolidate our assets in some sort of new plan. The actors who were not cast in *Yellow Jack,* Hampden, Truex and June Duprez, very gallantly allowed us to terminate their contracts. Not so the stage hands. Local No. 1 contended, first, that we must dismiss two of our three production crew heads who, though members of the IATSE, had not entered it as members of Local 1. They were wonderful men, old buddies of mine since the Maurice Evans days, who had put every ounce of their hearts and energies into our enterprise and whom we dearly loved. Second, we were told that since we would continue to use our permanent stage equipment (black velour surrounds, switchboard, etc.) *Yellow Jack* would continue to be classed as repertory and subject to the same union requirements. Our two boys went to the National Board of the IATSE for a determination and Local 1 was overruled. *Yellow Jack* proceeded as a single show, and they stayed with us.

But we were by no means out of the wood. Remembering the rave notices which had greeted the Air Force production, we imported its much-praised director, Martin Ritt (a change, we thought, from Le Gallienne and Webster) and one of its leading actors, Alfred Ryder. The other, Philip Bourneuf, was already in our company. The rest of the play was very strongly cast. But the press decided that it was only a "reasonably interesting documentary" after all. Mr. Garland, who had been one of its most lyrical advocates, couldn't imagine why we had revived it and criticized violently "whoever the programmed Martin Ritt may or may not be." (His subsequent movie fame has enlightened many people.)

We wiped the sweat from our brows and kept on keeping on.

A flag of rescue had appeared. Miss Rita Hassan had been a devotee of *Alice in Wonderland* from the days of Eva's historic first production at the Civic Repertory. She offered to finance a revival to succeed *Yellow Jack*. It was redesigned and directed by Eva with magnificent results and a fine press, amply deserved. I did the lighting and played the Cheshire Cat and the Red Queen, whose make-up (pre-latex) almost destroyed the skin of my face. It moved to Broadway proper, playing 110 performances before the summer (pre-air-conditioning) closed down on all New York theatres: a respectable run, but not enough for such a high-cost show.

The move to the Majestic Theatre, besides breaking our hearts in the abandonment of repertory, almost cost me my life. While we were lighting—the electrician up on a high A-ladder and me a few feet away on the empty stage, judging the focus—a sandbag broke loose from a rotted rope eighty feet in the air and smashed to pieces an inch from my toes. I can still remember three green-white faces staring at me—the conductor, who happened to be down in the orchestra pit, the electrician up on his ladder and our master carpenter in the wings, who had probably saved my life by not calling out. He had seen the sandbag falling and figured it would just miss me so long as I didn't move. I combed the mess out of my hair and went on cutting the shutters on Leko 67.

In June, Cheryl withdrew from the A.R.T. In a very sensible and entirely friendly letter she said that "the experience and observation of this year has left me no faith that such a theatre can exist under present conditions and I see no way in which these conditions can be substantially changed." She added that she found it difficult to function where she did not have single and complete authority: "Perhaps I can only be decisive and properly executive when I have to make up my mind alone and stand or fall by that decision." I think that Eva, by temperament, felt somewhat the same way. I didn't. I don't want executive decisions to be mine alone—not, that is if I respect my colleagues. It is only within the strict limits of my directorial functions that I cease to be democratic; and even then I can be persuaded—sometimes.

The problems of multiple control affect, unavoidably, almost all publicly subsidized theatres. Boards of directors are a misery to the gifted individual who is running the show—three gifted individuals can also be tough for each other. In the case of the A.R.T. no one had believed that a trio of women could run such an enterprise without arriving rapidly at the point of "pistols for three and coffee for one." In fact, this never happened. We disagreed, but we ended, as we had begun, with mutual respect. Cheryl Crawford has continued to hold a high place in the American theatre: an instigator of the Actors Studio, producer of some of the most literate musicals of our time, doggedly trying to translate her ideals into hits, doing a man's job in a world where even men can't do it, facing every kind of misfortune with indomitable courage. She may well have contributed more by cutting her losses with the A.R.T. than Eva and I did by trying to keep it alive. But we couldn't help it. All that hope and faith, not to mention the "charitable donations" from Equity and the rest, seemed to place us under an inescapable obligation.

Rita Hassan, gloriously undaunted by warnings as to costs and expenses, determined to do a full season's coast-to-coast tour of *Alice*. We had made a set of recordings which we hoped would be released simultaneously and that each would help the other. The recordings, made on the old 75-speed waxes, came an eighth of a jump ahead of the 33-speed LP's, and sank without trace. The play opened in Boston to superb notices and lost $3,500 during the first week. Rita Hassan decided to cancel the tour. We couldn't blame her. But we had all lost a season's livelihood, and all the planning, personal and professional, that went with it. For the second time Eva and I were faced with the dreadful task of telling the company. Most of them were old stalwarts of the A.R.T., loyal and loving to us as they had always been. If anybody ever tells you, "Dear Reader," that actors are invariably self-seeking, vainglorious, disloyal and notoriously ungrateful, deny it, please, in the name of the valiant and devoted members of the American Repertory Company.

We still held on, I feeling desperately responsible; Eva, I think, was just plain determined. We made various fanatic but forlorn attempts to resuscitate the enterprise in some form or other, and, after a series of torturous experiences, gave up. The American Repertory Theatre was officially dissolved in May 1948. Some of its assets, such as the electrical equipment and the mantle of Elijah, descended to me for the formation of the "Marweb Shakespeare Company," its first-born heir.

A failure? From the financial standpoint, yes, total. Judged by the quality of the work done, I think no. A knowledgeable woman of the theatre wrote to me:

Please do not regard it as a failure. When I think of the long succession of beautiful plays which you have brought to us, I feel that the mere fact that the venture failed in its money-making effort has little to do with its real success. I sat in the theatre and watched the audiences. They were spellbound with the beauty and power you gave us. . . . I have been a very small contributor but I certainly do not regret my share in it.

The generous enthusiasm which prompted the crusade for the A.R.T.'s survival would not have been aroused solely on the theoretical value of our work. People had seen us by then. We were being endorsed on the basis of accomplishment. Had we been able to continue, we would have molded our company into something really fine, like England's Royal Shakespeare Company. (In parenthesis, I saw a recent *Henry VIII* of theirs, highly praised by the London critics, which did not seem to me comparably as good as ours. Even Dame Peggy Ashcroft, probably the best English-speaking actress there is, did not bring to Katherine of Aragon Eva's nobility or tragic stature.)

But time was the essential. We could have developed our young company—we had even begun to do this. On Friday nights, after the show, they would do scenes for us of their own devising. In this way we discovered the really remarkable talents of *Alice in Wonderland*'s small White Rabbit, named Julie Harris. We could have improved our methods, adapted our repertoire, attracted other directors, playwrights, actors, explored all the possibilities we had originally described in such glowing terms. What we had, in fact, demonstrated was illuminating, but negative. We had attracted an audience passionate for our kind of theatre, but we had proved that it was a small, minority one, not, as in most European countries, large and general. People of the theatre had shown that they were demonstratively eager for theatres like ours to exist; but that only a tiny proportion of them could be induced to give up the financial returns their talents commanded to help create what they so much desired.

We had made it clearer than ever before that New York was the very worst place to start such a venture; it was, and is, the most expensive base to work from, there is the heaviest competition from massed "commercial" theatres and there is almost no sense of "community" or belonging. Also, the critics feel it their duty to "criticize," not to foster. These lessons were not lost on Tyrone Guthrie, forerunner of the professional repertory companies which have since come into being. He began his campaign in the United States by stating that he would choose any city able and willing to support his theatre, provided it was far enough away from New York. The Vivian Beaumont Theatre at Lincoln Center ignored them, and has since proved the same things. It has been able, with substantial support, to do some fine work, but not repertory.

It adds up to what Eva had said from the beginning, that subsidy was essential; Cheryl believed that we could become self-supporting once we had become established. In proven fact, the subsidy has to be continuous, with no terminal date. Nobody doubts that nowadays, or would dream of starting from any other premise. I wrote at the time of the A.R.T.'s demise: "It is the inability to survive for a minority audience which is the root of the matter. This, basically, is why the A.R.T. is now a dismal past instead of a hopeful future." What is too often ignored is the immense importance of the minority.

In this chronicle of our misfortunes I seem to have laid stress on the critics. It is unavoidable because then, as now, you cannot reach your target, the audience, without them. There have been very few, in my lifetime, whose opinions would have seemed to me illuminating, constructive or in any way noteworthy had they been expressed by a private individual at a cocktail party. I might have thought them witty, amusing, repeatable even; but I would not have reposed trust in their makers' hands, far less power. I do not know whether it is preferable to have the life-or-death verdict pronounced, as it was then, by a jury of nine or ten or, as it is now, by a single Supreme Court Judge, originally appointed ballet critic by the *New York Times.* The whole system has always been absurd, and always apparently inescapable.

The critics did badly by us—meanly, anyway; or let us say simply that we failed to enchant them; as if there could be a more humiliating objective. Eva thinks that they could have given us "a fighting chance" had they reacted differently; but I do not believe we ever really had one. The whole climate of the time was against us; not only did we make inevitable—or in some cases "evitable"—mistakes, but the odds were too heavy. We could have been a lot worse than we were and fared no worse than we did; we could have been a lot better and succeeded no better.

By this I do not mean to denigrate our work. If I had not thought it good, I should not have been so hard hit by its being wiped out; not, of course, that it ever really was, or could be. Catherine Drinker Bowen wrote a reproachful letter to the critic of the *New York Times*. She said:

> This is an age when we don't believe very whole-heartedly in the nobility of man. Why should we, after living through the last ten years? Watching Wolsey, watching Katherine, hearing those trumpets from the orchestra pit—something proclaimed itself. Something I for one had wanted to hear more deeply than I realized. All night it stayed with me, and for many weeks to come. It may sound a trifle fancy, but I kept remembering John Locke, where he remarked a couple of centuries and a half ago that mankind, contemplating itself, might expect from the future only Egyptian darkness, "were not the candle of the Lord set up by himself in men's minds, which it is impossible for the breath or power of men wholly to extinguish."

What more can a play do, anyway?

BY BUS AND TRUCK

I have before me a Chon Day cartoon from Lord-knows-how-many years ago. It depicts two convicts cozily chatting together on a prison bunk. Says one to the other: "The trouble was, I completely lost sight of the non-profit aspect of the enterprise." It still makes me laugh. All the memories of the bus-and-truck period of my life make me laugh—or most of them. It cost me a lot of my own money (the A.R.T. had taken only a modest slice) and about three years of hard labor—I do not mean in the prison sense. Our non-profit-making enterprise ended in bankruptcy but not in jail.

The productions we did with this Marweb Company would not challenge comparison with Europe's national theatres, nor even with my own New York productions. The commercial renown was nil; the other rewards were enormous. I have not the slightest doubt that it was the most valuable contribution I ever made to theatre in America. And looking back, studying all the records of hell and high water, of financial failure and general "hideosity," I still feel exhilarated. To write about the A.R.T. wrenches my heart a little;

to write of "the gymnasium circuit" (as it came to be called) makes me laugh.

Nevertheless, the ultimate addition sum ought to depress me. The enterprise was, again, unfortunate, or vulnerable, in terms of "time when." Like the A.R.T., it bridged a gap and the bridge broke under us. The gap between success and failure was, financially, slender to vanishing point; a matter of less than $1,000 a week, which some ingenious adjustments on all sides (booking office, management, "consumers" and—minimally—unions) could have equated. Dear old Granma Ford, or Title 3, or half a dozen benefactors not then in existence could have tilted the balance from loss to profit (or anyway, survival) without blinking so much as an eyelash. We were not dependent on press notices—generally we were out of town before the Podunk *Courier* came off the stands, and the larger-city critics (San Francisco, Detroit and so forth) wanted theatre to flourish and were not concerned with demonstrating its shortcomings. The union conditions, though often tiresome, sometimes costly and occasionally absurd, were never the crushing load they had been in New York. Part of the source of my laughter is that I know actors relish the sort of ridiculous life we led, the sort of pioneering we did. They enjoy it, as I had twenty years earlier in the days of the Ben Greet Players, and as I did still. The laughter dwindles into silence when I reflect that this is a life they can no longer lead.

During the first decade of my work in the United States, it was plain to see that professional theatre outside of New York was withering on the vine. Excessive costs were killing off the old "road," what the movies had left of it, and the nonprofessional resident companies, though they held the fort gallantly and in some cases well, were not as good as they thought they were. The art of the theatre is not a part-time avocation. The educational and college theatres reinforced them, doing an invaluable job in putting on plays which the professional theatre no longer performed. How well they did them was another matter. In 1942 I made the first of many lecture and recital tours, and became more acutely aware than ever before of the dearth of good theatre outside of Manhattan Island and a few other metropolitan preserves.

When I got back, I had several conversations with Sol Hurok, the great impresario of ballet and concert tours, about the possibility of getting a drama to play similar dates—not the old "Number Ones" or even "Number Twos" which the United Booking Office had handled for road tours, but "concert bookings" of one or two nights, with guaranteed set fees, like those paid to concert artists, instead of a gambling percentage on box office receipts. These dates, however, were exceedingly difficult to reach for a large outfit traveling by railroad, as all theatre companies then did, and prohibitively expensive on that basis. Hurok was interested; but nothing more came of the idea.

It was revived by the A.R.T. During our desperate struggle to continue our work or find avenues for its future we sent out exploratory leaflets and got replies from all the (then) forty-eight states. In preparation for the abortive *Alice* tour we mailed a fresh shoal, which included questions as to what plays communities, schools or colleges would most like to see. We planned, during the tour, to set up advance bases in all the cities we visited. The results of the questionnaire were interesting. Five hundred and fourteen plays were mentioned; *Romeo and Juliet* and *King Lear* headed the list; *Mourning Becomes Electra, Peter Pan, A Doll's House* and *Winterset* were among the top dozen. Thank Heaven we never had to choose from that wild list.

In November 1947, after the collapse of poor *Alice,* I went to see Hurok again. We decided that any projected tour must be primarily for schools and colleges and that Shakespeare was, therefore, our man. Under the guidance of the Hurok "Concert Division" another mailing was sent out to possible sponsors in this field, asking a lot more questions about local facilities and potentialities. The response was wide and enthusiastic. On the subject of plays (confined, this time, to Shakespeare), *Hamlet* and *Macbeth* came out way ahead of all the rest—predictably, since these two are most commonly done in high schools. Too often, they are the only ones which are done at all. We decided to start with them. We also decided that we couldn't possibly travel by rail. This outfit, like Hurok's smaller dance companies, would have to go by road. I felt a stirring of my "rogue-and-vagabond" blood. In May 1948, as the A.R.T. expired, Marweb was born.

Money again: Joe Reed once yet again, with incredible loyalty, making a pretense of hard-headedness by styling his backing a "loan," pending our eventual objective of setting up a non-profit-making corporation. I made my usual speeches and appeals. Once, in an excess of zeal, I announced to an interested assemblage that we should visit the forty-eight states, covering many thousands of miles, and traveling by truss and buck. I joined the AAA (nothing to do with Alcoholics Anonymous) and pored over maps, which are my passion. I began to make elaborate charts—also my passion. The final Hurok contract was set up on a basis of stipulated flat fees from the local organizations, minimum weekly guarantees from Hurok to us, and a sliding scale of commissions from us to him. It also contained supposed safeguards as to maximum travel distances, etc., and an option on his side for a second season. It looked as if we couldn't lose. But we could. What looked foolproof on paper proved impossible in practice. Much of our contract was illusory.

Unions: Equity gave us concessions as to rehearsal time, the playing of two plays, an extension of the contractual Christmas "layoff" days and permission to use actors, at additional salary, to help with the setting up and taking out of the shows. We agreed with the IATSE to take three crew heads and a wardrobe mistress at union scale. We asked that colleges be permitted to provide the "help" in small towns where no stage hands' local existed, but undertook to present a "yellow card" (the union hiring requirement) in cities where there was an established local. This was agreed—or so we thought.

We acquired a company manager at union scale, but we couldn't afford a union advance man. It turned out impossible to do without one and easy to find a dozen of exactly the type we needed—but from outside the ranks of the ATPAM, the managers' union. It was not the sort of job their members cared about, but very much the individual, freewheeling type of thing that lots of young men relished. We had a hard time about this, since the union was not prepared to let such a newcomer in. No touring company of our sort had ever before come within the provisos of the craft unions. There had been college companies, wholly nonunion, and Robert Porterfield's Barter Theatre group, operating from an out-of-New York base and ambling round their Southern territory in an unorthodox, freewheeling kind of way, with which the unions had never interfered, but there were no precedents for us.

At about this time a man of destiny arrived on the scene. It had become very clear that a full-time general manager in charge of all the financial and executive side was going to be essential, as well as the union staff. Joe Reed and I, at a loss to find such a character, decided to ask Edward Choate to take the job, if only "to get us started." He had had vast Broadway experience, but his heart had always been with "classical," and preferably repertory, theatre. He had handled the Old Vic Company's visit and given me many valuable pieces of information for the A.R.T., gleaned from that experience. When he became managing director of Marweb, he contributed his knowledge, his time, his office space and also his heart and soul. In fact, he fell in love with the whole scheme—so deeply in love that his judgment was sometimes overruled by his determination to keep the enterprise in being. His faith never wavered, his optimism was unquenchable. He never believed we could possibly fail until long after we had.

Hamlet and *Macbeth* were designed for the special problems of our bus-and-truck locomotion and one-night stands. The scenery was built in New York at union-labor costs. Wolfgang Roth had devised an ingenious set of small rostrums which could be arranged in different patterns and heights, and a series of heavy metal posts connected by rods. We had two sets of curtains, each double-sided, which could be hung from the rods, closed or left open, providing a wide range of the use of space and color. We had the A.R.T. black "surrounds," but hoped to use the local drapes wherever we could. More often than not they proved to be made of hideous orange velvet or light, tan-colored cotton and hung in all the wrong places.

Roth also planned to use projections; the slides were designed and made, the lamps hired; but we never used them. It proved impossible to hang or set them with the right angle of throw and the necessary protection or precision. I had always feared this would happen, so I smiled through my tears and didn't say "I told you so." Modern lightweight metals and plastics would have solved many of the problems which, very literally, weighed so heavily upon us, saving space, time and labor. The same was true of the electrical equipment. Small, portable, electronic switchboards with "fingertip" dimmers were already beginning to be available; but we were assured (experts again) that we mustn't take them since they wouldn't operate on DC current. It turned out that no one had DC current, except in New York where the old-style contractors come from. We had a small board especially designed and built, with three portable "booms" and the requisite lamps, and I devised a lighting plot of infinite cunning.

We were lucky with the costumes. Maurice Evans had kept the *Macbeth* set and very generously lent them to us. I had decided to do *Hamlet* in a costume of "no period," trying to combine some of the pictorial glamour of a royal court with the stripped lines of modern clothes. Now, in the Seventies, they would look quite ordinary. By some ingenious finagling we managed to get them made by an out-of-town college from whom we then "bought" them, saving thousands of precious dollars.

Lehman Engel arranged the music from material of his own, mostly composed for naval documentaries during the war and never commercially recorded. It had to be done on disks—yet once again we were just ahead of the beginning of a new era in technical resources and tape was not yet available. We trundled around our own clumsy turntable and, once again, hoped to make use of the local resources. They were generally dreadful.

Actors. The old story. Hundreds, literally, of eager youngsters, especially women of whom I needed exactly three; dozens of Guildensterns and First Murderers; never a Hamlet or Macbeth. In Hollywood I went through the whole list of exiled, stage-struck malcontents, who came up with the usual regretful refusals for the usual unsound reasons. In the end, I achieved Alfred Ryder (late of *Yellow Jack*) for Hamlet. I also found a young man, not well known, who I thought would be very fine as Macbeth and Claudius. Later, a couple of weeks before we started rehearsing, he asked me to release him to do a tour with Judith Anderson. She added her pleas to his, and like a fool I yielded. Since it was then too late to be even remotely choosy, I replaced him by an actor who was a darling man, but a disaster; a Donald Wolfit without the wolf. For Gertrude and Lady Macbeth, I got Carol Goodner, a very fine actress, well known in both London and New York, who had never played Shakespeare and wanted to and rather liked the idea of the "vagrant, gypsy life."

Thelma Chandler stayed with me as stage manager (I don't think I would have done the tour without her), and there were half a dozen other stalwarts from the well-trained ranks of the A.R.T. Twenty-two in all; when you added up their (tiny) salaries, it seemed like a lot. But when I sat down to plot *Macbeth* and *Hamlet,* it didn't look like so many. In the *Macbeth* banquet, it was tough to make two servants and eight guests look like a reception at the White House; and when I'd juggled my way through *Hamlet* and come to the final speech "Let four captains bear Hamlet like a soldier to the stage . . ." I almost gave up. *Four* captains, yet! Still, I thought, Shakespeare's men are supposed to have done it with sixteen. (How well, should we now think? I've often wondered.)

In casting I tried to weigh very carefully the personal qualities of those concerned. I knew that being shut up in a bus together for thirty-some weeks was going to put an enormous strain on all of them—"like being married to twenty-nine people," as one of them afterwards said. One bad piece of character miscasting could seriously endanger the stability of the whole. I made one.

More questionnaires to the sponsoring organizations: date, place, fee, sponsor, local "contact," auditorium, stage specifications (six sub-columns), electrical and sound resources, capacity and availability of auditorium and stage, hotels, "Other"—a wide column. My charts overran the sides of the sheets. You'd think we knew everything. It took us a while to discover that most of the answers were meaningless. The answerers wouldn't know what a "pros opening" was, let alone "2 hot lines and 1 neutral"; nobody thought of mentioning that the auditorium was on the second floor with no means of access except a spiral staircase, or that the stage "depth" was cut into by two large buttresses and a clutch of organ pipes.

We budgeted with meticulous care. It seemed as if our weekly guarantees must substantially exceed our operating costs and that we couldn't go wrong. We bought a truck and chartered a bus. The truck cost a lot—$1,875, I had been told. Nobody mentioned to me that this was just for the engine and chassis. The body cost another $1,280. We devised all sorts of ingenious ways of packing the scenery, and it was built and measured so that it would, supposedly, fit in. The costumes were to go on racks at the back of the bus. But it became apparent, even before we started, that the truck was going to be too small; it also became clear to me that a third vehicle was going to be necessary so that the crew and stage management could travel on a different schedule from the actors. A brand-new station wagon was added—another "loan" from Joe Reed.

We rehearsed in New York in expensive rehearsal rooms bracketed by band rehearsals and other noisy troupes. A school in Richmond kindly offered us their auditorium for dress rehearsals. We began to learn the facts of life. The switchboard, small as it was, wouldn't go through the rear entrance to the building and we had to take the door off its hinges. The curtain rods fell off their supporting poles. Eva, a benevolent visitor, invented some hook-attachments which had to be especially forged the next morning. The truck was packed within inches of its life.

At last, one fine Sunday in September, the assemblage came together on West 47th Street, the actors (looking very like actors), crew, management, bus, station wagon and truck, proudly emblazoned "THE MARGARET WEBSTER SHAKESPEARE COMPANY IN HAMLET AND MACBETH." Quite rightly, I thought, a newspaper columnist commented that I had become "Shakespeare's Henry Ford." We got everything and everybody packed in with all their luggage and appurtenances, and were, quite literally, "off to Buffalo." It is a long way, Buffalo.

We opened with *Macbeth* on the stage of the Erlanger Theatre, where I had once pinch-hit for Judith Anderson in the same piece. The show was hardly as good. The stage was too big for our little set, and we had not yet learned how to disguise this handicap. The performances, with a young company, unused to each other, Shakespeare and me, were necessarily more rough than ready. A month is not enough to rehearse two such plays to anything like "concert pitch"; and, alas, in the case of *Macbeth,* I was trying to get a good production with the best actors playing Macduff and Malcolm.

Hamlet was much better. Ryder had gone to Constance Collier for coaching, and she had imparted something of her old-time skills to his febrile, modern youth. The costumes didn't quite succeed because the fabrics were too lightweight and nylonesque; but the idea emerged, and you could see the company's potential. We played eight performances, mostly to prebooked school parties. It was too many. A pattern began to be discernible. "Real" theatres in "real" touring cities were no good to us. Audiences in such towns had grown used to musicals and Broadway hits with names. They had got out of the habit of theatre-going and were not going to buy tickets for anything different—let alone something which sounded like culture.

We moved on. In Toronto we were housed at the hideous Eaton Auditorium, enormous, aseptic, meant for a convention hall, not a theatre, with damnable acoustics. The high school audiences were tough. One contingent sat in the front row wearing huge bow ties which lit up when you pressed an electric button. Another bunch brought a football along. Once Al Ryder lost his temper with them and stopped the show, and there was a great uproar in the press and much public apology, which at least aroused interest. But the poor company were undergoing an ordeal by fire.

Kids, especially in bulk, have always been tricky audiences—as I remembered only too well from my Ben Greet days, when they were more literate, better mannered and authority was less permissive. They are sharp-eyed and extremely alive to anything extravagant or phony; this makes them laugh. Sometimes, too, they will laugh because they are moved, and feel embarrassed accordingly. They are uninhibited and not yet theatre-broken. I tried to teach my company some of the tricks of control—and above all not to be stampeded and not to get into a shouting match. They are lessons which can only be learned by experience, and the cast gradually learned them; all except my dear Macbeth, who was a sincere, honest-to-God shouter and amused the kids tremendously. I tried to tell everybody what a magnificent audience the young *can* be; but in Toronto they found it hard to believe me.

After the Saturday matinee we went on again, a weekend jump to New London, Conn., a tiny matter of six hundred miles. We were to spend the night at a hotel en route. The truck and station wagon set off ahead and the bus followed, with me and the actors. Some fifty miles out of Toronto we came upon the station wagon pulled forlornly off the side of the road like a stranded fish. Apparently major surgery was indicated; late on a Saturday afternoon in the wilds of Ontario. Only two people were expendable, me and the master carpenter, who had already decided that the job was too much for him and was going to be replaced in New London. He and I stayed behind; the bus went on its way, promising to inform the next garage and send a camel or something to tow us out.

It turned out to be a bad case of clutch-collapse, and the problems of getting a new clutch for a new model only just on the market, on a Saturday night, miles from anywhere, were considerable. The garage which sent to pick us up was alone on the prairie—a self-contained unit of house, garage and tiny café. Somehow the owner managed to connect by telephone with the main Ford depot in Toronto and had his son drive in for a new clutch. They offered us hot dogs and various chairs and sofas to sleep on. I beguiled the waiting hours by writing to Eddie Choate:

I have now seen these shows put up and taken down three times and made two (and a bit) bus jumps. . . . And one thing I now know without possibility of doubt or evasion: it is completely impossible for us to exceed the maximum travel limitation in our contract of 250 miles in 24 hours by so much as 100 yards! . . .

As a matter of fact, the clause itself is impossible . . . although I was assured at the time that the 250-mile limit would only be used in cases of extreme necessity and *very* rarely; whereas, as it turns out, it is not only utilised but exceeded six times within the first two months and closely approached on three other occasions. I blame myself for having accepted it and for having done everything to try and play along with the dates as arranged. . . . But some of the proposed jumps are quite simply impossible and we must face that inescapable fact *now*.

Let us consider quite simply the number of hours in the twenty-four. We now *know* from actual experience how long it takes us to do a move, and here it is:

Take down after show, load bus, truck, wagon	2 hrs
Unload and put up show (We have never yet achieved this even with my help but I am assuming we will)	3 hrs
Play show	3 hrs
Make-up etc. before show (actors)	1 hr
Travel 250 miles (based on extensive experience of bus driver)	7 hrs *at least*
	16 hrs minimum

This leaves a total of eight hours for meal stops, breakfast before starting, getting into and out of hotels and sleeping. It doesn't add up. . . .

The bookings are insane. . . . We rush 500 miles North to Buffalo, 600 miles South to New London; three days later 400 miles North to within twenty miles of Buffalo again . . . then 275 East to Saratoga. It is likely to lose us our entire company and crew.

Having got this off my chest, I waited for the new clutch, and on Sunday evening George (the carpenter) and I set off again. He didn't drive, so I did; all night, through the hilly and devious Catskill roads. There was no Mass. Turnpike then, no New York Thruway or Route 95. I dumped George off at the railroad station in Beacon when we crossed the Hudson, and reached New London in time to check the setup. Then I went to sleep.

Of course we shortened those early schedules by a very large slice, once we had mastered the take-in take-out routines. During the second half of the tour we acquired a much larger (and more expensive) truck and evolved far better techniques of packing and loading. Also, the problems of travel mileage, forced on us by the booking office, were greatly eased when we got away from the crowded roads of the Eastern seaboard. On paper it had looked quite possible to fulfill a schedule which, in the Middle West, required us to do seven shows in seven states in seven days; and indeed it, just, was. But the great transcontinental roads where you can bowl along at seventy miles an hour were not yet built; and the AAA schedules had allowed no margin for road repairs, detours or other miscalculations.

We tried all we knew to make things as easy for the company as possible, but sometimes we couldn't do what they wanted, and often they didn't know what they did want. Some preferred to make the short jumps at night after the show so that they didn't have to get up in the morning; others only yearned to get to bed. On weekend trips some wanted to beat it all the way through, others to stop midway for the Sunday night.

Two things were certain: there was never the smallest measure of agreement as to where to stop and eat. ("That looks good. . . ." "Oh, no, it's a dump!" "What about that one on the left?" "Too late— we've passed it. . . ." "Let's go on till we get to Elmira. . . ." "Let's stop now, I'm starving. . . .") We could have prompted the Howard Johnson menu from coast to coast. Well do I remember one miserable café on which the bus, for lack of an alternative, finally disgorged its load. "Oh, my God!" exclaimed the single, pallid waitress, "I just prayed that bus wouldn't stop here!" The second certainty was that no sooner were we well and truly rolling than someone would cry out for a "mercy stop"; and then seventeen men would line up for the one available "facility" and our time-schedule would be disrupted for the day. Whoever invented and installed chemical toilets at the backs of buses can have my vote at the next Presidential election.

The bus soon got a cozy, lived-in look, with thermoses and cameras and books and knitting and crossword puzzles and decks of cards and newspapers and bags of food. People settled themselves in their own seats and only unshipped the barest minimum of their belongings. Don Allen, an A.R.T. veteran, got the Busman of the Season Award.

For thousands of miles he stood in the stair well beside the driver. "I don't like sitting," he said, "it makes me stiff." Laundry was a fearful problem. Ophelia became chief laundress (too much of water, perhaps), and Carol Goodner was voted Best Barber.

Hotels, of course, were among the worst of our troubles. We tried to get all the advance information we could so that the actors could choose between "Croxton House—dump but bearable" and "Susquehanna—expensive but good." Often they hated what they saw when they got there and went off somewhere else without telling us. Don Allen did this once, before a *Macbeth* matinee. He was playing one of the Witches. By ten past two we started phoning the hotel for which he had signed, but he had never checked in. By twenty-five past two I was wrapping the witch's cloak and ragged hood over my street clothes and telling electrics to keep the scene extra-dark. At 2:29½ I was huddled on the stage with my two rather less Weird Sisters and Thelma was about to give the curtain cue. Suddenly a dreadful thought struck me. "Stop!" I hissed, "which witch am I?" It turned out later that Don had found a different and much nicer hotel and gone to sleep.

Very often the auditorium would be miles from the center of town and by the time the bus got its load back to their hotels all the coffee shops would be closed. When, as sometimes happened, the company was asked out to supper, our hosts would stare in astonished disbelief as dishes loaded with food were cleared in moments down to the bare glaze. Tom Barrows, our first company manager, reported that once a university president and his wife invited Hamlet to supper. Fourteen Princes of Denmark turned up.

If food and hotels preoccupied the company, stages and auditoriums preoccupied the technicians, and us. Their infinite variety—and unsuitability—baffled description. In New Paltz, N.Y., the stage was so tiny that the Macbeths' party had to take place in the wings with only one visible guest. At Purdue University the stage was so vast and the prop table so far away that a servant, going off to fetch a second helping of boar's head for the guests, never got back until the scene was over. At a college in Texas it proved impossible to get the switchboard inside the building. It had to be left in the yard and Thelma gave cues by semaphore from a window. Some of the "auditoriums" were huge basketball courts with bleacher seats; others had dirt floors and a tin roof; others parquet-floored stages where you were not allowed to use a stage brace.

The toilet facilities were often half across the campus "in the Music Building," they would tell us reassuringly. Once or twice Hamlet quite literally "whipped out his rapier, cried 'A rat! a rat!'" and put it to use—or tried to. Sometimes the dressing-room lights—exiguous at best—blew out and the actors dressed by feel. Once Thelma, alert as always, spied Donalbain rushing to make an entrance. The play in progress was *Hamlet*. Once again, the brave pioneers were ahead of their times. Colleges, universities and—especially—high schools have now acquired splendid, new auditoriums. Many of them are built to a robot pattern, "faultily faultless, icily regular, splendidly null," but at least sanitary, and comfortable for the audience to go to sleep in.

The company managed to enjoy itself in spite of everything. The work was killing, but it was exciting, and never twice the same. College audiences were the best—more eager and attentive than the usual adult audience. Only about twenty percent of our performances were given for high school audiences alone, and the company gradually learned how to tame these wild but lively beasts. We were greatly disturbed, at first, by the rustle of candy containers, crackle of potato chips and crunching of popcorn. But we found out that the more the audience enjoyed itself, the more it ate. When it had given us a particularly generous ovation at the end of the show, we would find, as it trooped out, mountains of paper wrappers and assorted crumbs. The audible conversations during the play were disconcerting; but sometimes they were due to partisanship and relevant argument. The "good guys" earned, sometimes, unsophisticated applause. Our high school public was, quite simply, not theatre-broken. Being used to movies, its members had no idea that we could hear them as clearly as they could hear us—often more so. I learned to detect what sort of a "house" it was going to be by the quality of the noise it made coming in. Once, fairly early on in the tour, I realized the going would be rough and I decided to make a curtain speech—a practice of which I disapprove strongly, on principle, because it tends to substitute the classroom for the theatre. But I said something like this—spontaneously the first time, but I was to find it useful afterwards ("Never waste a good line," said the "theatre-ape" inside my head) :

"A little while ago the movie of Laurence Olivier's *Hamlet* was shown in this city, more than a year after he had actually finished making the picture. He had worked on it for many months, preparing the script, shooting it, cutting, editing, until at last it was finished. The film was put in a can—many cans—and sent forth on its travels.

Whether it was ever shown in your town; whether you went to see it; whether, if you did go, you liked or disliked it; whether you sat still and listened, or whether you munched peanuts, blew bubble gum, giggled, coughed or talked to your next-door neighbors, is a matter of total ignorance and supreme indifference to Laurence Olivier. It didn't affect the movie in the very smallest degree. *But*. If he were here tonight, actually playing Hamlet on this stage, you would be the only people in the world who mattered to him. He would play for you alone—a performance which had never been identically the same before and never would be again—*your* Hamlet. If you listened quietly, attentively, understood what he was doing and saying, helped him—gave him wings—you might perhaps enable him to play the best of all his Hamlets. But if you did all those things you do at the movies when you are bored and restless, his performance would be ruined. He would act very badly—not *for* you, but in spite of you. 'Your' Hamlet would be a bad one. That's what makes the performance you are going to see something they call 'live.' See how good you can make it."

Sometimes they made it thrilling.

The travel, though grinding, was occasionally glorious. Along the coasts of the Northern Pacific states, Thelma, Johnny-Higgens-Electrics and I seized on the station wagon and managed to make some wonderful scenic detours through country we had never seen before. I do remember that, driving over the mountains from Seattle to Yakima, I got into a skid on the snow-crusted precipitous curves and thought they might both be killed, peacefully asleep behind me, before I ever got out of it. But I also remember that Yakima hadn't seen a professional theatre performance for thirty-five years, and the response was very well worth the roller-coaster journey.

Up to this point I had been with the company for much of the time; but in Walla Walla, Wash. (a rhythm I have always liked), I had to leave them and go to England for the production of a play of mine—an adaptation from a German original—which I had written many years before. In London I got news of snow in Denver, tornadoes in Kansas, floods in Oklahoma and finally, from Chickasha in that state, a telegram which said: "CAROL GOODNER LEFT SHOW WHAT SHALL WE DO?" Carol had scooped up Osric also, having married him during the course of the tour, and removed him along with her. She must have known that had I been on the same continent, I would have been making Lady Macbeth's next entrance before she had made the last exit. From across the ocean it was more difficult. I managed to get an old friend and able actress, Carmen Matthews, to replace her, Mady Christians to help her with the Queen in *Hamlet,* Eva to do the same for Lady Macbeth. My guardian angel must have been hard at work; also the stalwarts of the crew, stage management and company. The vehicles kept rolling (despite a breakdown or two), the shows showing, and a month later we all met again in Poughkeepsie.

The "romantic" side of the tour is summarized in an article I wrote for our Souvenir Book—a synthesis, but truthful, called "Soliloquy in a Station Wagon":

It is nearly five o'clock in the morning, the time when all vitality is at its lowest ebb. I wonder to myself crossly how I have any vitality left to ebb. I glance at the seat of the station-wagon beside me; Pete, our Property Master, is hunched up asleep with his head against the door. In the glim from the instrument panel he looks very weary. It is cold, and sometimes there is a light film of ice on the road. We have a heavy load behind us: coils of cable and iron stands, and some actors' suitcases of the largest size. If I apply the brakes at all suddenly the whole load shifts forward against my seat, which tilts under the pressure and wedges me against the steering wheel. This begins to annoy me.

It has been a bad day. Who could have expected to have to play *Macbeth* in a B-29 hangar without stage, proscenium or dressing-rooms? The platform they had put up wasn't too bad, but the masking between it and the side walls . . . ! every piece of spare black material in the State, I should think, strung and nailed and pinned somehow. And at that, the audience caught generous glimpses, through the gaps, of the Thanes of Scotland in various states of undress, with their costumes lying about on the earthen floor because there was nowhere to hang them. The place was so vast that the actors looked like marionettes and the set had the dimensions of a fireplace.

I find myself trying to think up ways of expanding the show to make it more impressive in a large auditorium; I begin to get ideas. Then I remember that tiny stage last week where we had to leave out half the rostrums and I had to alter all the entrances and exits to avoid a pile-up of actors in the "wings". After that I had spent many hours thinking of ways to make the show smaller. Apparently these are Gulliver's travels. How can we ever give our best under conditions like these? How can we possibly capture the magic and the glory? Why do we try?

I become exceedingly depressed and sorry for myself. I realise that I am outrageously tired. There is a blue-ish tinge in the sky and I begin to distinguish the outlines of low, rounded hills. The trees look intensely, profoundly, black. I catch myself wishing our velour backdrop could ever attain that alive blackness. I see a couple of trucks drawn in to the side of the road and a light beyond them. Coffee. Thank heaven, I pull up behind the trucks. A huge suitcase bumps me gently in the back, without rancour. Pete stirs, snorts, bangs his head against the door-handle and wakes up.

We go in and have coffee. Is it really the best I ever tasted or just the context in time and circumstance that makes it seem so? There is a lighted stove in the corner and the little shack is filled with a kind of steaming glow. A couple of truck drivers sit at the counter and Mac, behind it, is a jovial fellow. We exchange friendly conversation in gruff early-morning monosyllables. They give us advice about the detour up ahead. When we come out, the air is as cold as glass; the sky is lemon yellow at the horizon and a dark slate-blue overhead, without cloud.

Pete says shall he drive for a bit, and does, very fast. I hinge myself into a sort of pen-knife position on the seat and try not to look at the road. I begin to think about the audience last night. There must have been about three thousand people—standees too—and that echoing roar of applause at the end—it seemed thunderous; I remember the little group that came and spoke to me afterwards—they said they lived on farms nearly a hundred miles away and had driven in to see the show. They'd never imagined it could be like this and when would we come back and do another? Come *back?* I shuddered.

Though as a matter of fact, *Macbeth* did have a sort of added excitement in that vast, dim place. And the actors certainly rose to the challenge magnificently.

I shift my left shoulder, which is intolerably cramped, and remind myself sharply of all the effort and discomfort. Certainly out of all proportion. I decide firmly that even that tiny little beast of a place last week was better. And none of those kids had ever seen a Shakespeare play before, they told me: many had never seen a play at all. (They sat through three and a half hours of *Hamlet* without moving.)

What a superb play *Hamlet* is! How lucky I am to have had the chance of living with it. The sun must be coming up. We don't need the headlamps any more. What a wonderful experience, seeing one's first *Hamlet* . . . I wonder what we should do next year? What on earth do I mean, next year? We shall never survive this one. Wish

I'd brought a pillow. . . . *Julius Caesar?* a comedy, perhaps? Lord, I'm tired . . . wonder if we've got enough gas . . . wonder what sort of a place it'll be tomorrow—no, today, not tomorrow . . . wonder . . . what . . .

I become dimly aware of a lack of motion. I grunt, turn, bang my head against the door handle and wake up. We have arrived.

So much for the romantic aspects of our travels. Other aspects of them were more realistic and grimmer. By Christmas we had realized that our anticipated profits were not going to be what the paperwork had said. A lot of small things nibbled away at them. We had had union troubles. One of our crew kept sending the "yellow card" ahead of us even to the small towns where it had been agreed we could use the college or school "help." Somebody would dredge up a set of grandfathers who had once, years ago, worked in the Bioscope booth. The local sponsor would be furious because his auditorium had got involved with union labor costs for the first time and he feared they would be stuck with it for ever after. Our own actor-stage-management crew would be furious because the local senior citizens only wrecked their well-rehearsed routines and the rest of our union crew would be furious for the same reason. Our wardrobe mistress plainly threw her supposed helpers out on their venerable ears.

(It is worthy of note that the finest team we ever had was from the faculty of a small Wisconsin college who formed an assembly line of unprecedented vigor and efficiency, put up the set, ran the cables, unpacked the crates and distributed the costumes, all in record time. They were nuns.)

It was apparently impossible for the Hurok office to book us adequate dates for the weeks before Christmas and during the subsequent vacations; the same was true of the Thanksgiving week and the January examination period, when we were reduced to our barest minimum guarantees. Paying the company during the Christmas layoff almost wiped us out. Eddie wrote to me: "We have received an average operating profit of $72 each week while Hurok averages a commission of $917. We have to pay a balance of $2,000 on the new truck, and actors' salaries of $4,600 during the layoff period. This will reduce our working capital to $425 with which to start the New Year." Easter was later to prove an equally crushing festival for us.

But the travel expenses were still, in every way, our main problem. I decided to seek Equity's help. I asked the Council to set up a Committee to examine the whole set of ambiguous and obsolete "bus rules" and draw up a new bus contract. I added that I was being quite selfish. If Equity said the company was not to travel more than so-and-so many miles (or hours) a day, Hurok could not make us make them.

The Committee took evidence from the actors, crew, company and stage managers, bus driver. Its report was both shrewd and fair. The preamble stated:

> The information we obtained was chiefly biological. In fact the word "bus" was rarely used. We did learn that different towns and areas have different waters and their chemical constituencies affect actors differently and individually and never at the same time. We also learned that actors have to sleep and eat. And further that managements . . . are aware of all this and that they would like a set of rules that would be practical and feasible.

In the end, a set of rules was drawn up which did give some protection to us all, though it bristled with intricacies which were to prove a headache for the company manager and Equity deputy alike. They could not, however, be applied to bookings already in existence. Hurok had begun to arrange a second tour long before the Committee concluded its labors, and we had to rely on threats rather than facts.

Anything, however, we thought would be better than the existing muddle of fringe regulations, subject to continuous argle-bargle and acrimony. When everything was added up and agreed upon at the end of the first tour, we found we owed the company a distribution of some $1,800. Heaven knows, they had earned it; but it was a severe depletion of our resources. In addition, a subcontractor who had taken over the Pacific Coast dates from Hurok defaulted on his contract and turned what should have been our four best weeks into our four worst ones.

Nevertheless, at the end of the first season we did show a profit. But it was far too small to enable us to repay our loans or to finance two wholly new productions. Joe Reed, most understandably, had reached the limit of his generosity; he could only give us his blessing. Eddie Choate and I underwrote fresh loans. I put up the Equity bonds. Eddie devised a complex scheme of amortizing what should have been the production costs (scenery, costumes, printing, insurance, etc.) over the tour as operating expenses. As might have been anticipated, the operating profit was never enough to get them paid off. It nearly was—very nearly; but not quite. We tried to cover the weeks Hurok couldn't book (Christmas, Easter, Thanksgiving) with "commercial" dates in such cities as Princeton, Baltimore, Indianapolis and Detroit. Vividly do I remember joining the company in Indianapolis. We had to play a huge, stadium-like auditorium where we had been preceded by a circus and the elephants had left their signatures. At the end of three performances I had to get us out of town with my personal check for $1,500. To cheer us all up, we had a hideous journey to Detroit, plagued with snow and road repairs; I thought we'd never make it. It would have been better not to. We got an excellent press, as we did in all the big cities we played, but we sustained heavy losses (from $1,000 to $2,000 a week—heavy for us). This could wipe out weeks of small profit.

I was not with the company as often as I had been the first time—it was not necessary. Many of the dates were repeats and much of our route was no longer terra incognita. The questionnaires we sent out to the new customers were more specific; we had found out how to ask for the information we needed. Above all, the shows were infinitely better. The most valuable members of the first company agreed to come back again and were greatly strengthened by the addition of Larry Gates, Louisa Horton and Kendall Clark. This time, also, no one was enamoured of troublemaking. I managed to do *Julius Caesar,* Forum scene and all, with two fewer people than I had needed for *Hamlet.* (In making, recently, a count-up of the personnel from *The Taming of the Shrew* program, I came across the name of Dooley Horton as Troilus. "Who in the world was Dooley Horton?" I thought, "And who's Troilus?" It was, of course, Petruchio's spaniel, played by Louisa's far-from-spaniel dog.) The crew was better too. To my dear friend Johnny-the-Switchboard was added Joe-the-Bus and Lou-the-Props. I loved, love, them all.

I wrote:

We are doing *Julius Caesar* in modern dress. This is not a stunt nor is it our intention to draw an exact parallel with a particular dictatorship either of the recent past or possible future. . . . We shall try honestly to interpret what seems to us Shakespeare's thinking in terms which bring it close to our own minds and our own society. . . . The themes [of *Julius Caesar*] do not belong only to the period of classic Rome nor to that of Elizabethan England. They belong to us too.

I knew I was sacrificing some of the stature of a classic interpretation. But I thought our paramilitary guise—not battle dress, in which the actors can be as indistinguishable as they are in togas—sharpened their individuality and helped to differentiate them in the hierarchy.

The Forum scene was populated by the entire cast, including Portia and Calpurnia—suitably disguised, of course—and I wrote a complete "score" for the crowd, exactly like the chorus of an opera and divided up into "voices" in just the same way. It ensured that there would be, at every given moment, the right kind of noise and of the right length and volume; that the actor (Brutus or Anthony) could be sure of what was going to happen next; and that nobody would be left in an unexpected silence floating out some silliness like "Well, look who's here!" or "Anthony for President!" It is astonishing what effects can be achieved by a few very simple words in counterpoint or in sequence on the "three-blind-mice" principle.

The semi-modern dress justified itself—at that time. It would have to be done differently now. (It could be set in present-day Greece with dreadful ease.) Part of our tour coincided with the President Truman–General MacArthur controversy. High school students immediately seized on the analogies and wrote essays about military heroes versus civilian power, the limitations of democracy and the dangers of dictatorship. Of all Shakespeare's plays, *Julius Caesar* is perhaps the one most startlingly applicable to any period in which it has ever been performed.

The Shrew was fun. We knew all about "Enter Strolling Players with packs," and I did it that way, with a troupe of Victorian "strollers" aided by picaresque bits and pieces of costumes. I used the additional Christopher Sly scenes from Shakespeare's source-play (known as *"A,"* as against *"The," Shrew*), and Larry Gates played the part wonderfully. *The Shrew* doesn't happen to be a play I much care for, but directors are always garnering praise for doing it "brilliantly," and it is, in fact, hard to go wrong and easy to be entertaining.

Ben Edwards did a light, ingenious pair of sets, admirably suited to our needs. The costumes were "evolved" or hired. The hiring bill was a millstone. Mileage, though curbed, remained enormous. During one week the bus speedometer registered 1,291 miles. For part of our California safari we were accompanied by a team of photographers from *Life,* who took some spectacular pictures, which were never published. A hurricane nearly blew us off the Sierra Nevada. It became common to have to send the crew ahead by plane or train—costing money, naturally. There were the usual quota of terrible auditoriums and faulty local arrangements. But we had a better "advance man" now, accepted by the press agents' union, and we knew the ropes. Morale remained high.

Louisa Horton wrote to me:

> I have never been happier. All the Hedgerows, Broadways, Cleveland Playhouses, Hollywoods or self-organized acting groups on or off Broadway can't touch what this company offers. . . . It keeps moving, it pays salaries and the plays give the actors and the audience a chance for more drama than either of them could get from any other company in America.

Larry Gates was the ANTA representative—a job he found singularly unrewarding owing to the vagueness of the parent organization and the apathy of its local branches. In a letter to me, accompanying his mid-tour report, he wrote:

> After the war I had to find for myself more reasons for continuing my work in the theatre. I discovered the challenge of the theatre to my own American civilization. . . . In the United States we need the theatre more than we need engineers, automobiles, home laundering devices, etc.; we need it not only for immediate spiritual happiness and well-being; we need it for our very survival. We live in danger of decadence and death, like many civilizations before us, because of unwise minds and unfeeling hearts.
>
> The theatre, at its best, addresses itself perhaps more directly and more literally to the hearts and minds of men than any other human heart or instrumentality. And, in our troubled world of today, people are looking to their hearts, to their feelings, to their spirits more than ever before. I thought, and now say, why not really enlist the help of the theatre, for it has proved throughout the ages that it can bring to life and comprehension more vividly than any other art the great life-building emotions of courage, compassion, understanding and laughter.
>
> You remember, Peggy, we discussed this in one of our letters during the war. Well, this is one of my biggest reasons for battling as an actor in the American theatre for something which is fine and worthy of the American audiences.

It is over twenty years since Larry wrote this letter. Comment would be superfluous.

In one respect we needed all the loyalty and leadership we could get. I had decided to use two black actors: Edmund Cambridge as Pindarus and the Soothsayer in *Caesar* and smaller parts in the *Shrew;* Austin Briggs Hall as Lucius and Biondello. Nowadays this seems unworthy of remark. But it had never been done. We didn't want to court publicity. We wanted to prove that it was possible to take two ordinary Negro actors—not stars like Robeson and Canada Lee—on a coast-to-coast Shakespeare tour; and to do it without fuss, as a matter of course. The last is the operative sentence.

We knew, and so did the two boys, what we would be up against, especially, but not exclusively, in the Southern states. I doubt whether the rest of the company realized it. They accepted Austin and Eddie into the freemasonry of actors and assessed them as players and as people. Actors, thank Heaven, are very generally color-blind. The two pioneers dealt with their problems with calm and nerve. We enlisted the help of the NAACP in the matter of housing, eating and so forth. Everything went smoothly. It worked. Until we reached Natchitoches, La., home town of the (then) Northwestern State College of Louisiana.

Less than a month before we were booked to appear there, I received a letter from the faculty member in charge of the arrangements:

> It has come to our knowledge by the grapevine that there are two Negro members in your troupe, which will appear here. . . . Accommodations for them have been secured in the home of . . . one of our most prominent colored citizens. [He was, in fact, the local representative of the NAACP and a close friend of the Lieutenant Governor of the state.] We are certain you can understand and appreciate our concern over the particular parts these two people are to play. Unfortunately, we feel that we are entirely too far in the Deep South to have them appear on the stage. While this letter is not the place or occasion to philosophize on the evils of segregation, suffice it to say that to date, Negroes have not appeared in our auditorium (in companies of their own, much less in mixed groups), and we frankly feel that the time to begin the practice in this area has not yet arrived.

I replied, after consultation with Louis Nizer, our attorney, that this was an artistic matter of the casting of two actors, that I had never encountered any objection from anywhere else in the South, and that I couldn't possibly change the cast. The college representative then wrote to the Hurok office, putting the situation up to them:

Our institution is for young ladies and young gentlemen of the white race and without expressing any opinion one way or the other about segregation, we are compelled to consider the ideas and sensibilities of our students, their parents and others in this area. . . .

We have written to Miss Webster without result. . . . If we are to continue our hitherto pleasant relations, we ask that you discuss this matter with Miss Webster and see what can be done before we consider taking steps to cancel the contract.

I refused, of course, to change the cast. There was a certain amount of legal argle-bargle about whether or not the college had the right to cancel the contract; they claimed that a "general statute" on the books of the State of Louisiana enabled them to do so. We were supported by Equity and the NAACP, but we failed to stiffen any particular spines in the Hurok office, and we could hardly play the date by main force. We could, I suppose, have made a big press issue of it and instigated a riot. Today, indeed, we could hardly have held panthers or other wild creatures in leash. But in 1950 the situation was very different. To raise hell was not the object of the exercise. We wanted to prove that what we were doing could be successfully accomplished without any hell at all. We bypassed Natchitoches and proceeded to Texas.

Only then did we release the story. I am reported as having said (though the voice sounds a little Nizerian to me now): "I have the feeling that the authorities have imposed their prejudices on the students. . . . I do not think the citizens of the South will approve the action of this college, for they know that there is only one thing more expensive than education, and that is ignorance." The case got headlines from coast to coast; Louisiana students in Natchitoches and elsewhere held big protest demonstrations; the company in its bus and truck rolled on and we never recovered our fee.

We had, of course, told them the whole story; but I think the reality of what Eddie Cambridge and Austin had gone through only came home to the rest of them weeks later in a Northern city. An Indianapolis hotel refused admission to the two black actors. It was a risk we had taken great care to avoid; and the white actors who saw it happen were taken completely by surprise. Louisa Horton wrote: "The surprise brought varied reactions . . . good intentions were rampant. It was not handled efficiently by any of us, but it was not bungled."

One way and another, a good many people got a little more educated. In our feeble-kneed "liberal" way, and thanks to the courage
and steadfastness of Eddie and Austin, we succeeded in proving our
point. We hoped, in doing so, to open avenues for the more general
employment of black actors; yet we never—and I would stress this—
cast them in parts which they could not legitimately play without
distorting or violating the original intentions of the author.

The tours were unquestionably a public success. We got a good
press even in the big cities which cost us so much money. "Will
Shakespeare rides again," proclaimed a splendid fellow in St. Paul,
Minn., "large as life and twice as funny" (it was *The Shrew,* not
Macbeth) "spear-heading the long awaited revival of the theatrical
road. If lusty, lively, expertly staged and acted productions like these
can tour through the country . . . the living theatre need have no
fear of celluloid and the video screen." Alas, "if" turned out to be the
operative word.

By the end of the second tour we were more deeply in debt than
ever. The weekly profits had not been enough to pay off initial costs
and the tour ended with some miserably booked weeks. Hurok himself lent us $1,500 to tide us over, since there were insistent requests
for our return the following season, as well as offers of new dates;
The Shrew especially was in demand. It seemed to us all that we ought
to be able to play more performances in one place and not have to
move so often. A third play for a third season became our slogan. We
proposed to keep *The Shrew,* add *A Midsummer Night's Dream,* and,
a little later, a non-Shakespearean play, *Saint Joan.*

It is one of the drawbacks of the "gymnasium circuit," as it is of
lecture tours, that you have to book them nearly a year ahead of time.
In December 1949 we were trying to set up the season of 1950–51
without knowing what the second half of our current tour was going
to do to us. We hoped for the best and planned accordingly. I entered
into negotiations with Bernard Shaw—that is to say, we embarked on
the sempiternal arguments about his royalties. I have a postcard from
him dated June 18, 1945:

My dear Peggy,

　　There are repertory theatres all over the place, actually or projected, especially projected. I do nothing to discourage them. If they
get going my shop is open; and they can all buy licenses to perform
whatever plays they want. No repertory gets any exclusive rights;

they can all play any play of mine just as they can play any play of Shakespear (the Stratford Shaw) except that they must pay 5% royalty on the receipts when they do not exceed $250, 7½% when they run up beyond $500 and 15% when they exceed $1500, which they rarely do.

I need not say that if your project comes to anything you will be an especially valued customer.

My kindest regards to your gifted parents. I have not seen them for ever so long. I'm on the verge of my 90th year. Can you believe it? I can't.

G.B.S.

I cannot now even remember which of my many "projects" this was; evidently Shaw was right and that is what it remained. However, he was already a little confused as to the grosses necessary to successful operation in the American theatre. By the time I applied to him for the bus-and-truck *Saint Joan,* there were further complications. Maurice Evans had been writing him about a revival of *The Devil's Disciple* and the Theatre Guild was intervening about some other play. The result was I scooped the pool. He sent me a license to produce any or all of his plays outside of New York for the ensuing year—under certain conditions. "My dear Peggy," he wrote me on December 2, 1949:

> You have given yourself a lot of trouble for nothing. My 15% applies only when the takings exceed $1500, which means playing to capacity on Broadway. For any takings you are likely to get my royalty is 5%, which is the least I can do with, as authors have to live on their work as well as players. If you cannot afford this you must either go out of theatre business and peel potatoes or confine your repertory to the plays of dead playwrights. . . .

His figures were wildly out; $1,500 per performance on Broadway would have spelt bankruptcy inside a week and was pretty nearly "the takings" I needed to get. I bowed to the inevitable and tried to follow his cheerful advice to "go ahead." But it wasn't that easy.

Eddie Choate and I had calculated that if we could get the shows rehearsed and the scenery and costumes made outside of New York we would enormously reduce our production costs. We were offered what appeared to be a solution. There was a charming theatre in the

Catskills, at Woodstock, New York, which we had, in fact, used for dress rehearsals and preview performances on our second tour. The owner was prepared to go into partnership with us, he to underwrite operating losses (or so we thought), we to contribute our productions, and share in the expenses of the other summer productions. Woodstock is an area heavily populated by artists and "intelligentsia" who, it was thought, would eagerly devour the kind of fare we would offer. How we could so have misjudged the artistic appetite I do not know.

We worked out a season of great distinction, mixing a few respectable potboilers with the first American performance of Giraudoux's *The Apollo of Bellac;* Chekhov's *The Three Sisters;* and our pre-tour productions of *The Shrew* and *Saint Joan.* Eva came to us to play *The Corn Is Green* (the best of the several Miss Moffats I have seen) and to direct *The Three Sisters,* in which I played Masha. We kept most of our touring company and added, among others, George Roy Hill. He played Tusenbach most admirably and subsequently married Louisa Horton and attained great fame as a movie director. (The bus-and-truck tours promoted a number of marriages and we never lost a father.)

I look back on the Woodstock shows with considerable pleasure and pride. I'm sure I should enjoy seeing them again. I directed only about half of them, but I also played. Masha in *The Three Sisters* was a lifetime ambition. I found her far more difficult than I had expected, but Eva's direction was illuminating and perceptive—an education for us all. The company was working into a fine, smooth ensemble, filled with talent. *Saint Joan* was, by any standards, a production of the highest class. The *Henry VIII* costumes, rescued from storage in a hen-house on Joe Reed's estate, were miraculously set back a century or so and looked rich and beautiful; so did the tapestries from the same source. The local press was dithyrambic. So were those who came.

Only not enough did come. We didn't (you'd never guess) make money. We lost it. "Ah, well," said the hindsight pundits, "far too highbrow." In fact, *The Three Sisters* and *Saint Joan* were our best box-office shows. The potboilers boiled no pots. It emerged that our theatre-owning partner had never had the least intention of underwriting our losses. He and Eddie had been entirely at cross purposes. So far from financing our third tour, the dazzling Woodstock season wrecked it irretrievably. We tried everything we knew and went through the same routine of desperate appeals that I had grown to know so well. But it was no good. At last even Eddie, the most unquenchable of optimists, was compelled to agree that we should have to cancel the tour. "On to the next fiasco!" said our Woodstock partner gaily, having incomparably less at stake.

Yet once again, the margin between success and failure was very slender. Yet, once again, the work was good. I have kept a letter from Joseph Kesselring, the author of *Arsenic and Old Lace,* which is as heart-warming as any epitaph is capable of being:

It's easy to assure you that what you put into that company is not lost effort, lost beauty, lost love, and it's true. I had two guests Saturday night, young farm people who knew little of the theatre, and you literally cut a hole in them and filled it with something from a better and unsuspected world, and I know that you've played to thousands of "young farm people". But I also know that it is a bitter thing to pour into one's work what you must have poured into that company and be rejected. Of course, for you it's a passing tragedy. You'll go on to bigger and better things . . . but it's still a tragedy and, unreasonably, very depressing to me personally.

It is hard, in the theatre, to present proof. You cannot say "Go and see for yourself—look at the picture—read the book—listen to the recording or the score. . . ." You can only say "It 'cut a hole' in the hearts of some young people . . . it made a dent on the mind of a sophisticated Broadway playwright . . . and I liked it." I'm not sure that I've done "better things."

There was little we could do about poor Marweb. Fortunately our contract with Hurok had been made dependent on our ability to raise the additional capital, which we plainly couldn't do. I yielded up my Equity-bond money; Eddie and I cleared off our debts. Hurok and his colleagues made it as easy for us as they could, and I undertook to give some lectures for them, allocating fifty percent of my fee in repayment of their loan to us. We managed to preserve some of the dwindling A.R.T. assets, including the *Saint Joan* costumes, curtains and scenery. They lived to fight another day in a production we did for the Theatre Guild, and were accidentally burned soon afterwards, in the Guild's storehouse, uninsured.

We circulated sponsors of the tour and the press of cities where we had played, trying to get a crusade going to reactivate the Shakespeare company. We spoke of the "proved value of our work in preserving plays of classic stature on the stage and presenting them to students who might otherwise never have the chance of seeing them professionally performed."

We went on the foundation rounds again, such as there then were, stating that, despite the enthusiasm which had greeted our performances, it had been conclusively proved that "a professional company of our quality and size cannot function in this [the school and college] field without some help." College budgets were limited, and prices for individual student tickets (when they were not part of a series-subscription) had to be kept low. "The additional yearly income which would enable us to turn red figures into black is very small. It could easily be made up by one of the Foundations interested in preserving the humanities."

But it wasn't; and a couple of our melancholy prophecies came true —that in consequence of our failure no enterprise of similar stature would have the courage to try; and that the field would be left to the nonprofessional companies—mainly from universities and colleges— who had previously monopolized it. This happened; nor do I mean to condemn the results. It is part of a great university's business to turn its abler theatre students into a company which will provide theatre entertainment and education for the surrounding area. But it does not provide the men and women for whom acting and theatre is a lifework with a field in which their skills can and should be utilized.

Since our day many public and foundation subsidies have arisen, and many offshoots of professional centers, such as those in Minneapolis, Seattle and Stratford, Connecticut, have begun to cater for schools in many different ways. I doubt that there are a large number who have played Manchester, Indiana, or Moscow, Idaho. But the seed was sown and has sprouted in ways we did not foresee. I am quite often startled, and gratified, to meet a senior member of a college drama faculty who tells me he saw his first Shakespeare play in Yakima, Washington, or Marysville, California, and has never forgotten our bus-and-truck. Neither, I am sure, have we who rode it.

It did not, as I had hoped, pioneer a new touring "road" for other sorts of professional companies. For a while bus-and-truck outfits started off, with stars ensconced in them—and Thelma Chandler almost invariably in the stage manager's seat—to try and travel Broadway hits like *No Time for Sergeants* or *The Dark at the Top of the Stairs*. But they gradually disappeared. Too much hardship? too great expense? The fact that you were out of town before anyone had had a chance to find out how good you were? A larger question remains: What is the future for an American theatre audience? Will there be any?

I do not mean an audience for muscials or the fashionable theatre hits which you have to see and talk about. I mean the audiences we played to on our bus-and-truck tours. The A.R.T. had proved that if you can reach college-age audiences, and if what you give them is good, they devour it—once you can get them inside the doors. At Purdue University, once, we started a performance to a quarter of a house. People kept getting up and going out; grim; but they also kept on coming back again with three friends. After the intermission we were pretty close to capacity.

But theatre isn't good business; it is low, very low, on the lists of "cultural necessities"; lots of other entertainments are supposed to be better and are quite certainly cheaper and more readily available. Theatre-going is a habit. It should be inculcated young, fostered, kept active. None of these things happens. Is it not likely to disappear?

Chapter Eight

"Everyone Suddenly
Burst Out Singing..."

DON CARLO

In February 1950, while my cavalcade was heading West across the Texas plains, I was in New York, doing a production of *The Devil's Disciple* for Maurice Evans. It had originated at the City Center, during one of the seasons to which he had given his services, and had proved so successful that it was transferred to Broadway. Early one morning my telephone rang; Mr. Bing would like to speak to me. (Bing? Bing? surely not the Bing who had just been appointed to succeed Edward Johnson as manager of the Met?) Another voice came on the line, firm, cultivated, delicately accented. This, it said, was Rudolf Bing from the Metropolitan Opera House. He would like to see me; I replied, naturally, that I should be delighted. "This afternoon, then?" said the voice. I gasped slightly. "Well, not *just* this afternoon." *The Devil's Disciple* had opened at the Royale Theatre the night before, Maurice was ill, we had a special holiday matinee, the understudy didn't know the lines, I was going to have to cope. The voice understood. "I suppose," it said, "your matinee will be over by about five o'clock?" Rather faintly, I supposed so. "Very well," the voice replied quietly, "shall we say 5:15?" We said so.

At 5:16 I discovered that the voice belonged to a tall, thin man in a dark blue suit whose general appearance, the New York press had decided, was that of a Bishop, an Ambassador or a wild goose. (In recollection, my eye records the Bishop etc. was indeed tall, and always seemed to be looking at people with his head tilted downward and slightly to one side.) He sat behind a desk in a very small office in a sort of haphazard annex building next door to the Met. He made the setting appear insufficient; as indeed it was. I found myself, without circumlocutory preliminaries, trying to grasp the fantastic idea that Mr. Bing was inviting me to stage an opera for him; and not merely *an* opera, but *the* opening opera of his opening season. I thought he must be mad. I protested total inadequacy. True, I could read a score, I had sung contralto in the school choir and had gone through a period of youthful devotion to *The Ring.* But these did not seem to me sufficient qualification. No, no. I knew nothing about opera. I couldn't possibly. Mr. Bing said would I go and see the performance of *Simon Boccanegra* the following night, and if I really thought I couldn't do better than that, he would take "no" for an answer. I found myself walking down the stairs clutching a libretto of *Don Carlo.* The next night I went to see *Boccanegra.*

Two days later we met at the apartment of Dr. Fritz Stiedry, the conductor. The madman in the blue suit sat sipping cups of tea; they became his trademark with the American press. A pianist played through a sampling of the *Don Carlo* score, with Dr. Stiedry hovering over him, humming, singing, giving the beat, turning pages and sometimes supplying obbligatos on the upper reaches of the keyboard. A young man hurtled through the door; he was handsome, harassed and bursting with a sense of "can't wait." He was introduced as the designer, Rolf Gerard. There was a zigzag of conversation, much of it over my head, ranging from Schiller to how many brasses for the Stage Band. I have an impression of Stiedry never still, Bing never moving, Rolf effervescing and Mrs. Stiedry ministering to us. Finally the voice which so admirably compounded courtesy with iron determination asked me whether I would like a little time, say twenty-four hours, to think it over. I heard myself saying, "That won't be necessary. I'll do it."

Going home in a taxi, I began to recover my senses and was aghast. It began to bear down on me, the enormity—the first production of a new regime, by which it would hoist its first standard; my first opera; and the first time a woman had ever directed at the Met . . . But the humming in my ears drowned out the voice of reason. "Perduto ben . . . " I crooned softly to myself. "Ella giammai m'amo" I growled. Cheerfully and valiantly I whistled the "off to Flanders" duet; a tune much despised by music critics, who begin to talk about organ grinders. I found that I had come away with more hummable nuggets in my head that I had carried off even from *South Pacific.*

I began my schooling. I studied the life of Verdi, King Philip and the history of Spain; I brushed up on the Risorgimento. I asked Stiedry (now becoming known to me as "Amico Fritz") what I must or mustn't do in opera that I would or wouldn't do on the stage. At first he said, "Oh, whatever you want—whatever you would do in a play." Pressed, he would add, "But of course it must *sound.*" This commandment is engraved on my heart. I began to learn the innumerable differences. A "lead" character in a play scene I would maneuver into a position "upstage" of the others; a lead voice in an ensemble must be downstage, closer to the orchestra. Conductors like Stiedry did not trust singers to take their eyes off his baton for a moment. ("You must not think of singers as musicians," he said, "God gives larynxes to stable boys.") In classic opera of the Verdian style, it is a problem to make the singers appear to be addressing each other without losing the conductor's beat. Twenty years ago there was far less freedom in this respect than there is now.

There were no recordings of *Don Carlo,* except for a handful of the famous arias. Stiedry, who was no Horowitz, played a dashing hit-or-miss version on the piano which I took on a wire recorder. I later found that the vocal score and Stiedry's piano version were a somewhat insufficient guide. The first time I ever heard an orchestra rehearsal, and realized what the brasses were up to at the end of Act II, scene 1, I almost fainted. How were those two lonely fellows on the stage, not great think-actors, supposed to live up to all *that?*

Meanwhile, Rolf Gerard's designs were taking shape. We were both trying to interpret the meaning of the opera, not just make a framework for it. I was both reassured by his knowledge and a little envious. He seemed perfectly at ease in this opera world. Great singers and conductors were his childhood friends. He spoke four languages fluently and was full of exciting ideas. He lived in a small studio on 34th Street, crammed from wall to wall with sketches, bits of models, swatches of material, photographs, books, easels, painting gear and a few ragamuffin items of kitchen equipment. How he ever managed to burrow his way into the studio-bed was a mystery.

Pride of place was held by a high stand, with a model of the Met stage. His first objective was to open the proscenium frame vertically, thrusting it upward, contradicting its usual flat picture-postcard look.

I found that he hated frills and trimmings. He saw drama in terms of line, proportion, texture, light. He thought the scenery should say something about the opera. He asked me what I wanted to get said.

The designs, sets and costumes both, had to be finished, approved and sent to the workshops in May, six months before the scheduled opening. We shuttled to and fro between his studio and the offices, conferring with Bing, who took a meticulous interest in our plans, and consulting with the technical staff. I tried to find out a little about past and present stage practices at "the House," and made some startling discoveries. Bing had constantly stressed his desire to "revitalize the staging at the Metropolitan so that it may be brought abreast of the Broadway theatre at its best." He was bringing in stage designers and directors—Garson Kanin for *Fledermaus,* Alfred Lunt for *Così fan Tutte,* Tyrone Guthrie for *Carmen.* A theatre designer, painter and builder, Horace Armistead, was to be head of the technical departments. There can seldom have been five more astonished characters than we were when we first met the Met.

There were no "prompt copies," such as would invariably be kept by any theatre production stage manager—in fact, there was no stage manager; no one was in charge of all stage departments at both rehearsals and performances. There were the music maestros (or -stri) whose duty it was to coach the soloists and who would be distributed around the stage during performances to give them a push when their entrance cues came. I learned, incredulously, that no singer was supposed to be capable of taking his entrance cue for himself. There was a super-maestro, an opera director of the old school, who appeared at performances, majestically attired in evening dress, and gave the curtain cues. He knew all the scores by heart; but he never attended stage rehearsals, other than his own, and it was not considered part of his function to have the least idea of what stage action was supposed to be going on. With the aid of Garson Kanin, next in line for the new-look Met directors, I achieved a genuine stage manager for the first time in its illustrious history.

Don Carlo had not been done at the Met for twenty-seven years, so I hardly expected to find any prompt copies. But I did try to glean something from the records of other operas. It was a vain hope. The markings were entirely musical. If the singers' entrances were marked at all, the entries would read: "Radames from 39th Street"; "Carmen from 40th Street"; "Altos and Basses from 39th; Sops, Tens from 40th." At first I regarded this with some hilarity. Actually, it makes good sense and has strong historical roots. Even in the theatre a lot of confusion is caused—or was, in the days of proscenium stages—by the author's "left" and "right." Stage left and right? or audience left and right? Even I, when I am plotting a scene on a ground-plan, have to turn myself round inside my head. I feel sure it would be much beyond the capacity of the Met's Italian wing. In the French theatre actors still enter and exit "Côté jardin" or "Côté cour" because Molière's first theatre had a garden on one side and a courtyard on the other. In England, scripts are marked "P." or "O.P."; that is, the Prompt-corner, or Opposite Prompt side. This is clear to English actors—though no longer to me; especially as the actual Prompt corner, where the stage manager stands, is frequently on the O.P. side. I often wonder whether, nowadays, the Met casts enter or exit from 65th and 66th streets, or whether their hearts are still downtown.

We newcomers from the Broadway world found the Met staff extremely cooperative, with the notable exception of the chief electrician. He had been at "the House" for God knows how long and had presided over the installation of about the first electronic switchboard ever installed on Broadway. It would now be thought about as prehistoric as the dinosaur. Enormous, sinister banks of machinery slumbered in the depths beneath the stage while the electrician, one of Nature's Niebelungen, stood jealous guard over their mysteries. He dictated the lighting on the most primitive lines. It was terrible. He had had long practice with smoke, explosions and magic fire. But anything subtle or evocative, anything which would pick out the singers without sloshing all over the set, was not within his ken. He'd done it his way for decades and didn't propose to alter it for a lot of Broadwayites with fancy ideas. Also, he couldn't. We found, to our horror, that the Met had no lights whatever in front of the proscenium arch, except for a couple of enormous "bulls" (the name is self-expressive) way up in the roof. Kanin, Gerard and I battled our way to a few timid lamps mounted at almost useless angles outside the proscenium arch so that the "hot spot" was not quite always on top of the singers' wigs.

Bing's executive staff filled me with admiration. They were courteous and efficient in six languages. The House ran on zeal. Even the telephone switchboard on the 39th Street Stage-door side was run with confidence and a charm rare among stage-door guardians. The stage staff were cooperative. However, in the process of changing managements, and in some cases crew, some odd lacunae developed—

for instance, in the prop department. The entire last act of *Don Carlo* hangs on King Philip's discovery of the portrait of Carlo in Elizabeth's jewel-box—presumably, a miniature in a gold or jeweled frame. When, during rehearsals, I asked for the "ritratto di Carlo," it wasn't there. Rolf had done a design, but no more had happened. There was no stage manager to keep an eye on such things. The property master (a newcomer) had nothing among the stock props. I went on and on asking for the ritratto di Carlo. Finally, I cut out a head from a colored postcard of an Elizabethan miniature, found a little frame of my own, bought some ribbon and donated the result to the Met. It lasted through several revivals. But it was hardly what I had expected to be doing at the Great House.

I saw a lot of the General Manager-elect during the planning stages of *Carlo,* and during the next few years, when I worked a good deal at the Met, I got to know him in an affectionate but impersonal kind of way. He always called me "Peggy," as does almost everybody I work with, and I generally reciprocate. But I could never bring myself to call him "Rudi." "*Mi*sterbing," accented on the first syllable, was the nearest I came to informality. Why he should have picked me to direct his first opera I never knew. Neither, when I later asked him, did he; something to do with my British background matching with his in Glyndebourne and Edinburgh, and with my Shakespearean experience in handling crowds.

Crowds! Fresh from stretching Macbeth's eight guests into a royal banquet, I found myself with a Chorus of ninety-eight, plus principals, extras and, in the Auto-da-Fé scene, that miserable "Stage Band" which is visible throughout: some two hundred people to be disposed so that at any given moment they could all see the conductor. I didn't realize that I would get all these characters on the stage together at one and the same time for exactly ten minutes. But I knew that it was going to be rough and that there wouldn't be time to be wrong. Much of the planning had to be done before Rolf could finish his designs or assign how many of which costume design would be what. I got a friend to send me boxes of toy soldiers from Paris and drew up immense ground-plans on which I maneuvered them around.

I was very much foxed about the Chorus. Stiedry told me I mustn't mix them up because sopranos can only sing among sopranos and not when mingled indiscriminately with altos, tenors and basses. Later I learned that this was not altogether true. The Met Chorus is magnificent and each member is capable of hanging onto his or her vocal line in the teeth of three competing Pop groups. There was, further, a hierarchical division dictated by the action of the opera: some were "Dame" and "Grandi" of Spain, others were mere "Popolo"; how many voices of which each? Stiedry and Kurt Adler, the chorus master, had to determine this according to their musical requirements; Rolf had to know exactly who was which in order to clothe them, and I had to juggle with the results, not forgetting his color schemes and the size of the singers.

At which point there was borne in upon me a universal operatic truth: that basses come in very large, long sizes and tenors in very short, wide ones. I made determined efforts to attain natural-looking, mixed-up crowds and not to segregate the sexes more strictly than was absolutely necessary; but the basses always gravitated to the back row and at least three elderly, well-nourished tenors, notably lacking in histrionic talent, were inevitably stuck in the front one.

Rolf and I also made up our minds that we would get something done about the extras. Hitherto, anyone who took a fancy to do so had wandered in through the 40th Street stage entrance; a helmet, much too large, would be plonked on his head, a tunic, much too small, dragged over his shoulders, he would be given a push on a given cue and told to follow the others. Everyone knew the archetypal story of the warrior in knitted-string "chain-mail" who got a loose end of string caught on a nail and unraveled himself to his underpants as he trudged to and fro across the backdrop. We decided to eliminate this mindless mob of misfits, and substitute a register of music students and serious-minded characters who would appear regularly, be cast "to type" and have costumes which actually fitted them. With the cooperation of Mr. Bing, who raised the walk-on fee from $1 to $2 (it is now $5) we eventually succeeded in this.

Working through the score, over and over again, I began to realize that Stiedry's placating advice to "do whatever you usually do" was totally misleading. When an actor says a line, he makes his point and his thought moves on to the next; but a singer has to repeat the same words a dozen times, the emotional shading varying with the music, the thought progressing only in terms of sound. An actor says "Good-bye" and goes; he may even repeat it once; but a tenor stays there singing "Addio" for sixteen bars; the progression is aural; very few singers bother to *think* through sixteen different Addios. The Method is left stranded. How, visually, do you fill these sequences? The answer is generally that it is better to leave them alone, to leave it to "sound" rather than to try and invent something to *do*. To a stage director this lesson comes hard—Heaven knows, it comes hard even in the theatre.

I pondered with concern on the artificial stances adopted by singers for reasons of breath control, and the stately, semaphore-like gestures, which had to do with the raised diaphragm. I schemed to eliminate the worst of these: I planned how to fill the rest bars. (By this I do not mean a union requirement, but a musical measure of silence.) When I got to the big "concertante" set pieces which Verdi loved to write, I knew that I only had to get everyone into the right places before the first downbeat, tell them to face the conductor to their, and his, heart's content and leave them to sing their lungs out. I would then heave a huge sigh of relief, relax and enjoy myself.

The casting, of course, was not my province. I was just "told," and it made pretty glorious telling: Jussi Bjoerling for Carlo, Robert Merrill for Rodrigo, Jerome Hines for the Inquisitor, Fedora Barbieri and Delia Rigal, both new to the Met, for the two women and Boris Christoff, the great Bulgarian bass, for Philip. These were, of course, only the opening-night cast; five or six other singers were lined up to follow each of them. I decided not to think about this. I also pushed aside small tremors about languages.

At last, the technical work was done, the designs approved and turned over to the shops; Bing, Stiedry and Gerard departed for Europe; I would see them again in October. I packed up my score, wire recorder, blueprints and toy soldiers and headed for Woodstock, New York. All through that turbulent summer the ground-plans lay open on my desk with the score beside them. I would return from a stirring session with *Saint Joan* and rearrange the sopranos.

Shortly before *Don Carlo* opened I gave birth to the following plaintive satire, modeled on that stirring piece, Mr. Rudyard Kipling's "If . . .":

If you can stage a scene when all around you	(allegro vivo)
Six Maestros wave and prompt and signal too,	(furioso)
If three-ring circuses do not confound you,	(più agitato)
Nor towers of Babel clutter up your view;	(molto animato)

209

If you can state, three weeks before you do it,   (recitativo)
Which scene you'll run at eight minutes to ten,   (a tempo)
And fill out forms to swear you will be through it   (velocissimo)
At 10:03, since overtime starts then;   (fermata)

If you can dream—and not forget your stopwatch,   (presto)
If you can think of nineteen things at once,   (vivace)
If you can gather singers that are top-notch   (col canto)
And cleared by the McCarrans and the Mundts;   (dim.)

If you can talk with tenors and keep your reason   (sotto voce)
And walk with Bings nor lose the chorus touch;   (maestoso)
If you can learn the schedule for the season,   (accelerando)
And speak three languages, yet none too much;   (con espressione)

If you can fill each costly, priceless minute   (alla marcia)
With a thousand dollars' worth of distance run,   (cresc.)
Yours is the Met and everything that's in it!   (fortissimo)
And, which is more, (pianissimo) *you'll be a*
   lunatic, my son.

(After the opening of *Così fan Tutte,* Alfred Lunt sent me his matching contribution:

> *My blood has gone, but not the tears,*
> *They will remain with me for years.*
>
> *As for the sweat, 'tis flowing yet.*
> *I hope some day 'twill drown the Met.)*

The interviewer to whom I confided my poem followed it with this sentence: "Talking to Miss Webster about this project . . . you notice she repeats over and over again the phrase 'You could do it if only there were time.'"

One of the most frightening moments of my professional life came at the first conference meeting about rehearsal schedules. All unsuspecting, Little Red Ridinghood, I walked into the office of Bing's chief assistant, Max Rudolf, where I found him playing host to Fritz Stiedry and Rolf Gerard, squashed together knee to knee with the three heads of the stage crew, Kurt Adler, and Frank Paola, whose duty it was to make up the rehearsal schedules for the House.

I later discovered that Paola was the greatest genius since Houdini. Everybody screamed at him. Conductors, directors, music coaches all demanded more time, different space; singers flatly refused to do this or that; everyone said everything was "impossible," which it was. Frank Paola always kept his temper and made it possible.

To my astonishment, I learned that the first two days of the first week were to be allotted to putting up and lighting the sets; which, in theatrical practice, is always the last thing you do, not the first. The order of doing this was determined by the master carpenter according to the time he needed to set and strike. The rest of the first week (not on the stage) was placed at Stiedry's disposition for musical rehearsals with the soloists. On the Saturday morning I was to get a crack at the Chorus on the Roof Rehearsal Stage. One week gone out of my precious three. "Now," said Max Rudolf suavely, turning to me, "what do you wish to do on Monday week, the 23rd?" I murmured feebly that perhaps the best way would be (quoting *Alice in Wonderland*) to "begin at the beginning, go on till you get to the end and then stop." This was met with stares of amazement and a few pitying smiles. The facts of life were explained to me.

The sets would have to be on the stage "well marked"—that is, a sufficiency of rostrums, pillars and other objects which had to be stood on or could be fallen over. Crew time was a prime consideration. Since the first and last acts of the opera took place in the same set, these scenes must always be rehearsed together. (This might have made it hard for the tenor to establish a sequence of characterization, but didn't because he never thought of any.)

Then came the matter of Chorus time—the primal, torturing, horrific, ineluctable Deity before which all schedules bowed and broke. The Chorus, poor things, had to learn and rehearse about half a dozen operas at once. Their boss, Kurt Adler, was formidable and extremely able. They also had to dash about the building a good deal and occasionally eat or rest. AGMA, their union, had accordingly, and most justifiably, drawn up a set of rules prescribing regular, and complex, times at which they must be released from their chains, as well as times for transit, etc. Accordingly, all rehearsals came to be geared to "how long can we have the Chorus?" Women only (while the men could be being Smugglers in the Lobby)? Men only, so that the women could go off to the Opera Club and be Valkyrie? Could one make the changing of the set synchronize with the Chorus "rest five"—the mandatory five minutes out of every rehearsal hour? (My memories of all the operas I did are stabbed with vivid pictures of the Chorus deputies looking at their wristwatches as the "rest five" became due.)

It was made gently clear to me that for all these reasons I had to determine just precisely how long each scene would take me to rehearse. All idea of sequence was to be forgotten. There would be little time to repeat, and none to be wrong; and I had never directed an opera in my life and hadn't the slightest idea how it was going to work out. Panic-stricken and praying, I therefore answered Max Rudolf's question as to the schedule for Monday week. I have it still, written in pencil in a shaky hand:

10 a.m.	Sc 11 and 40 [that is, Act I sc I and Act 4] Bjoerling, Merrill.
11:00	Add Rigal, Fil. [King Philip] for 11 and 40
11:30	Add Hines (for 40)
12–12:30	Chorus (men only) 11 and 40.
1:00	Break
1:15	Sc 12 [Act I sc 2] Principals and women chorus
2:00	Add Chorus men, Count, Fil., Rodrigo. (Cut duet if necessary.)
2:45	CHORUS GO.
3:00	Sc 21 Principals.
4:00	FINISH.

"All right," said Max Rudolf, and I looked round fearfully for dissentients; no one uttered. "So. Now. Tuesday?" And on we went, minute by minute, through the entire week ten days before it ever began.

This threw me into a state of shock from which I have never really recovered. Three weeks' rehearsal had sounded quite adequate, even though I knew the stage would have to be shared with other imminent productions. But I had never calculated that I would get just about thirty hours, total, of stage time; nor did I yet know that, out of this, the orchestra and orchestra dress rehearsals onstage are sacred to the conductor alone. All the stage director can do is to dash across a wooden gangplank (laid across the Pit) whenever the conductor pauses to rebuke the cello section about an eighth-note, hiss something into somebody's ear and get out fast, before he notices. This, in fact, reduced "my" stage rehearsal time to some eighteen hours—the equivalent of two and a half days' rehearsal on a stage play.

Even after that dreadful production meeting, I still thought I would have the opportunity of working with the soloists in non-stage time—just talking to them, by themselves—in the evenings, perhaps? This did not, of course, happen. Since the opera was unfamiliar to most of them, they worked hard with the musical coaches. I would often go to these sessions and wait humbly to get a word in edgewise, but I rarely did. It would have been difficult anyway, because the space was often so limited that I had to sit on the floor under the piano. The 39th Street Roof Stage was the only one capable of approximating, even remotely, the stage area, and that was most frequently occupied by orchestra rehearsals. The singers rehearsed in any and every practice room, lobby, foyer, club room, cubbyhole and toilet throughout that warren of a building.

Every day genius-Paola would pin up on the bulletin board the schedule for the next day's calls. I have kept one as a sample. It shows eleven different operas being rehearsed in one form or another in thirteen different locations. I would roam the dim and sheeted vastness of the auditorium and its surrounding areas listening for a bit of "my" opera, like Blondel seeking Richard Coeur de Lion. "Ah," I would think, "*that's* it!" and grope wildly for the nearest staircase which seemed to lead toward the sound. But by the time I got upstairs I would hear nothing but some dismal Dutchman or the Chorus hammering away at "Toreador" in Sherry's Bar, and a soprano valiantly trilling Mozart in the Ladies' Parlor. As for my notion of evenings, nobody had ever heard of them.

In addition, the whole schedule for *Don Carlo* was thrown off just before we began rehearsals because Boris Christoff was refused admission to the United States under the so-called "McCarran Act" governing alien immigration. He was a Bulgarian, and presumably it was feared that he would take time off between King Philip's acts of despotism to try and overthrow the democratic government of the United States. At the very last minute, Bing managed to get an Italian basso who had never sung in the United States before but who was politically blameless. On a happy day for the Met, Cesare Siepi arrived. He posed, however, a couple of minor problems for me. I had had to lay out his scenes before he reached us and he was one of the only two soloists who had previously sung the opera in other houses. He knew what he'd been used to doing and wasn't eager to alter it. Also, he was the only important singer who spoke nothing but Italian.

My Italian is adequate for tourist purposes and had recently been enriched by some antiquated operatic phrases; but it is not fully persuasive. I realized acutely how dependent I had always been on the vocabulary of persuasion. However, we all managed. I talked to Rigal in French, retranslating into English for Bjoerling; with Barbieri, a jolly girl, I spoke French and she answered in Italian and we both gesticulated a good deal and understood each other perfectly. I didn't then realize how lucky I was in having *Carlo* for my first opera. To begin with, the libretto, though much simplified from the original Schiller play, makes recognizable sense and has powerful contemporary themes; and to go on with, the singers had few preconceived notions about what to do and did not disdain help. Within the range of the Met repertoire, this is a rarity beyond price.

In my attempts at communication I achieved one notable victory. I asked Maestro Adler if I might steal ten minutes of his musical rehearsal time to talk to the Chorus. He looked startled and reluctant; but he politely acceded to my request, and on the appointed day I went up to the Chorus stronghold in what the general public used to know as Sherry's Bar. They had just reached the "take five" break in the hour. Someone turned on a portable radio and everybody congealed around it. The World Series was in progress. Joe Di Maggio hit a home run. It was hard to recapture their attention at the end of the "five."

I told them, briefly, what I thought they had to contribute to the opera, whether as Grandi or Popolo, and what they were meant to be thinking about in each scene. I told them what I believed the opera was about—power, to begin with; most obviously, the lives of two lovers smashed between the power of the State and the power of the Church; about the death struggle between these two forces; about the theme of freedom—the freedom of Flanders from Spain, by which, of course, Verdi meant the freedom of Italy from Austria; and, most piercingly, the effect of power on the man who wields it —Philip the destroyer, who is also the slave of power and is himself destroyed. "And," I added, "we are only saved from total disaster because Carlo Quinto hits a home run in the tenth."

From that time on I think the Chorus were mine. No one had ever talked to them like that before; in fact, no one had ever talked to them at all except musically and in the mechanics of enter-exit-raise-your-right-arm-on-the-last-note. They are wonderful people. Their memories are extraordinary. I gave the Court Ladies in the second scene an extremely intricate series of moves and business. Several years later I came back to do a revival when *Carlo* had been out of the repertoire for a long time. I had to split my head open re-teaching myself the moves. But the veterans of the first production remembered every one and told the newcomers what to do. It is true that not all of them are distinguished by histrionic ability; sometimes the tenor section raises one's blood pressure. But they love what they're doing—or they used to in those days—and I do too, so we got on.

At the end of the first week's rehearsal I thought to myself: "I know, now, what is going to happen. I have adapted myself painstakingly to the Met's schedule; in other words, I am thinking in terms of Chorus overtime, crew overtime, orchestra overtime; the availability of space and maestros; the demands of the rest of the repertoire, of the conductors, of the coaches, of everything, in fact, except my own freedom as an allegedly 'creative' artist. I have talked to the Chorus, I have even talked to the walk-ons; I do not seem ever to have had the opportunity of really talking to the soloists. Everyone has been extremely cooperative and kind to me, and hopeful that I might do the very things which I cannot, in the circumstances, attempt. I shall do everything pretty well, except the thing Mr. Bing hired me for—that is, to produce a performance as well acted as it is well sung."

We got to the first "full dress" rehearsal. In the big scene of the Auto-da-Fé I found that I had the whole mob—principals, Chorus, extras and onstage musicians, some two hundred people—all together at one time for precisely ten minutes of rehearsal time. It was spent in getting the trumpeters out of the way of the trombones and persuading the French horns to take their glasses off. At the end, when I went hurtling backstage to give the notes I hadn't been able to stop the rehearsal for, I found that everyone had left the House the moment they left the stage. No one but Carlo Quinto was left. Nor should I get the slightest chance of meeting with them again before they did it wrong the next, which would also be the last, time.

Came the "répétition générale," orchestra seats full, friends, public, all the top press who would then write their reviews; a Saturday afternoon. After that, total shutdown till the opening on Monday night; so much still wrong; I gnawing my nails, helpless. Singers resting. Monday: Dutchmen flying onstage; Chorus pitting themselves against Rigoletto in the Lobby; I lonely, lost, a ghost; only interested characters TV directors and cameramen trying to work out setups for all the evening's shenanigans, on the street, in the Lobbies, Sherry's, the Boxes, the Grand Tier; all the rank and fashion and fuss and furor; I to conduct a succession of interviews onstage during the second intermission, impromptu and in three languages, with the singers, Gerard, Stiedry, Bing, keeping them out of the way of the stage hands and timing it to fill but not overrun the allotted minutes.

I went home and climbed into my new evening dress. I haven't the slightest recollection of what happened after that till I found myself with Bing, Stiedry and the singers in front of that famous gold curtain, gazing out at what must surely have been one of the most thrilling sights in the world—the great, red-and-gold horseshoe of the old Metropolitan Opera House, filled to the aisles, flashing and dazzling, the men in the orchestra pit smiling up, and everyone waving programs, clapping and screaming "Bravo"; Bing very quiet, but unmistakably happy, and all of us bowing out front and then to each other and not knowing who was supposed to get off first and getting entangled clumsily in "no, no, after you," and then the whole thing over again.

The next day, I left for Boston. The Brattle Theatre in Cambridge had invited Eva and me to bring half my Woodstock company and join half the Brattle company in doing our *Three Sisters* production in their theatre (the tiny shack where I had first produced *Othello*). I sat in the train feeling very peculiar. Here I was, after the most glamorous evening in high society, a press furor and several television offers, setting off to play *The Three Sisters* in a little stock-company theatre for next to nothing; and not even to play my love-of-a-lifetime, Masha. Eva and I had had long discussions of a "no, no, after you" nature about which of us should play Masha and which Olga. Masha had been one of her most famous parts at the Civic and it seemed to me absurd for her not to play it again; eventually it was so decided. But I wasn't feeling enthusiastic, that day on the train. As it turned out, I was far better as Olga than I had ever been as Masha and Eva's Masha was far better than mine. I enjoyed the play more than ever and was quite happy to let the Metropolitan tumult die away in the distance.

I made a quick trip back to rehearse the tenor who was to take over Carlo. It was Richard Tucker, a fine singer always, but at that time a less than brilliant actor (who has since transformed himself into a very good one). I still believed that the second, third and fourth casts, who had been supposed to watch rehearsals, had, in fact, done so and would therefore know when they were supposed to do what. Tucker and I and one of the sopranos met on the Roof Stage. I was soon disillusioned. We came to the duet in the second scene. He said, "Where do I take her hand?" I said, "When you say you do." He said, "Where's that?" I said, pointing to the score, " 'Io prendo la tua man.' " He said, "Oh. Is that what that means?" (He will forgive me this story because we became good friends and I admire him, in all ways, very much.) I wished him "In bocca al lupo," which he understood, it being the operatic equivalent of "Good luck" or "Merde mille fois" or "Hals und Beinbruck," and dashed back to Cambridge. After his first performance I telephoned Thelma to ask whether he had remembered the moves. She said, "Well, he may have; but he was much too scared ever to get more than six feet from the prompter's box so you couldn't really tell."

I still, even then, cherished the illusion that the soloists who came into *Don Carlo* after the opening would be properly rehearsed, if not by me, then by one of the assistant maestros. This fantasy was so childish that no one had ever supposed I entertained it. Jerome Hines, who was to sing Philip, and Blanche Thebom, a future Eboli, came to me during the original rehearsals to try and find an opportunity of talking and working on their parts. No one else appeared interested, least of all the Met people. They couldn't be. There was neither time nor space. *Don Carlo* was past; so was *The Flying Dutchman,* which had succeeded it. *Traviata,* not a new production, came two days later; six other revivals opened during the following month and *Fledermice* were very active. Herbert Graf moaned that he was having to restage *Figaro* with four new singers in two rehearsals.

I began to grasp the opera-house routine as practiced at the Met— and certainly by other houses, though few carry so heavy a load or change casts as rapidly. A singer who joined the cast after the original rehearsals got none at all other than an extremely hurried briefing from one of the maestros: "You come on up here, the tenor is down there—you walk over to him at the end of this phrase here—you go off together up center." Compared to this, my own exiguous directions of the original cast seemed like the Method at its most profound. Newcomers never got onto the stage or heard the orchestra or (generally) met their fellow singers. Everyone took this for granted and (miraculously) got away with it. The system is still general at the Met and elsewhere; which accounts for a lot.

But by now I was hooked, and wandered in and out and watched some other rehearsals. What, I wondered, would Tyrone Guthrie do with his tenor during the rest bars? (There are a considerable number after the last-act entrance of Don José.) "Just stand up there, dear boy," said Tony to the tenor, indicating a spot which I knew would be way upstage and almost wholly dark, "and lean against that pillar with your back to us. Don't *do* anything, just suffer. . . . Good—good—*much* better."

The season, as always, was awash with crises. Everyone slaved away calmly. Mr. Bing would solve half a dozen as he strode up the aisle at a rehearsal, followed by his cohorts, between the backstage doorway and Row T. I grew to admire his imperturbable humor. On one occasion I was in his office after a performance, with most of the Met top brass. A New York paper had got hold of an important "top-secret" Met story. An advance copy of the morning edition, headlined, lay on Bing's desk. The rest of the press were clamoring, their deadlines only minutes away, and so were the Met staff. Confirm? Deny? "No comment?" Debate grew hot and tempers thin. Bing remained silent, intently studying the paper—not, however, the headline at the top but a small item at the bottom of the page. For a second the disputants paused for breath and Bing's voice cut quietly into the silence. " 'Baby,' " he read in a fascinated tone. " 'Baby eighteen months old bites snake. Snake dies.' " Everybody laughed, relaxed, reached a solution.

He seemed to work a fifteen-hour day. Often, around six o'clock, when comparative quiet descends on the House, except for a few distant "vocalizzi" from conscientious singers and some muted thumpings from the stage, he would stay alone in his office and have some food sent in on a tray. Almost always he would come through to the auditorium at some time during the evening to listen to a part of the performance, concealed at the back of his box. One night he emerged rather wearily during the first intermission. He encountered a venerable lady, complete in furs and jewels—it was a VIP subscription night. Her eyes swept over his dark blue suit with disfavor. "Are you," she said, "Mr. Bing?" He admitted it. "And why" she asked, "are you not in evening dress?" He thought for a moment. "Madam," he said politely, "if anyone else should ask you that, just tell them you don't know."

The greatest tribute I can pay to the charm of Misterbing is that he asked me to do a new *Aida* to open the following season and I said yes. I was old enough to know better. To accept the challenge of *Don Carlo* had a certain bravado; but to tangle with *Aida* was plain lunacy.

AIDA

All the old problems remained and got worse and one of them reached gigantic proportions. Few of the singers had had preconceived ideas about *Carlo;* but all of them had sung *Aida* literally hundreds of times and neither the tenor nor the soprano nor any of their successors could see the slightest reason for altering anything they were in the habit of doing. This was not true of the Americans, Jerome Hines and George London, nor of Elena Nikolaidi, the Amneris; but Americans were only beginning to invade the Italian "wing" and its original inhabitants were not exactly flexible. The soprano, in this case, was Zinka Milanov, no longer quite at the peak of her powers, but still floating those ineffable pianissimo high C's, and an almost sacred institution at the Met. The tenor was Mario Del Monaco, all flashing teeth and fortissimi, the darling of La Scala making his Met debut and speaking no English at all.

I determined not to be intimidated, as I had been over *Don Carlo.* I would talk to the singers, whether they liked it or not. I would try to get some solid truth out of the acting, which, in a libretto as full of high-flown romantic nonsense as *Aida,* is not easy. I dug for themes —dear old liberty again, the noble savage, the power of the priesthood, character conflicts and, of course, lo-o-ve. I summoned the cast to a reading; a *reading,* I insisted, not a singing. I needed printed copies of the libretto, no score, no piano. The Met, poker-faced, came up with a supply of those dreadful things which used to be sold in the Lobby—ill-printed, ill-translated, with a cover design dating from 1900. They gave us the 39th Street Lobby to rehearse in. The cast (all except London, who had not yet arrived) sat on small gilt chairs, looking puzzled. In the dimly-lit marble vastness the busts of Gatti-Casazza and deceased colleagues frowned down upon us.

I explained the object of the exercise. Jerry Hines seemed pleased, Nikolaidi interested, Milanov sulky but acquiescent. Not trusting my own Italian, I asked the shepherding maestro to translate for Del Monaco. "She says it will do good to read it," he said helpfully in Italian. Del Monaco looked stunned, then rebellious; then he stared at me and shrugged his shoulders. It was the most expressive gesture I ever saw him make. Milanov met his eye. I detected sympathy.

We began. "Si corre voce che l'Etiope ardisca Sfidarci ancora. . . ." said Hines, very sensibly. Del Monaco replied in a flat monotone. On Ramfis's exit, I said a few brief words about the priesthood in Egypt. Del Monaco suffered it. Reaching "Celeste Aida," he indicated the melody, parlando. We proceeded. Pharaoh spoke his piece. The Messenger announced that the sacred soil of Egypt was being invaded by the barbarous Ethiopians. The maestro and I made like the Chorus. "Guerra! Guerra!" I cried, giving it my all. "Everybody goes off except Aida," I said. Milanov peered at the libretto. "Ritor-na . . . vinci-tor . . ." she mumbled, as if she'd never heard the words before. She brought the libretto closer to her eyes. "E dal mio labbro . . ." She stopped. "Excuse me." She picked up a large handbag and fumbled in it. At last she found what she was looking for— her glasses. She put them on and stumbled carefully through the next few lines of the soliloquy—aria, I mean. She lifted her head and frowned up at the dusty chandeliers . . . read another few words . . . looked up again . . . shifted sideways in her chair and held the page at a different angle to the light . . . said a bit more . . . pronounced "Nu-mi, pi-e-tà . . ." as if the phrase were completely incomprehensible to her . . . snatched off her glasses. "Wrong glasses," she announced. I know when I am licked.

The 39th Street Lobby became, for me, the Plains of Waterloo. I met the extras there. I had resolved to eliminate all the muddled milling-around which I had seen when last the Egyptian armies had marched in triumph from 40th Street. I had paced out the width of the Met stage from the wings to where the front of Pharaoh's throne would be. All summer I paced to and fro on my porch, accompanied by the Long Trumpets March on a record player. The army was to be divided into four squads, each with a Captain; each squad was to march to the front of Pharaoh's throne, turn, salute, turn and resume its march to its onstage position as the next squad came into sight.

This simple maneuver had to be precise, yet I couldn't afford to waste one of the thirty stage hours on it. But the extras were working people during the day, and no one at the Met works at night until after the season begins. A Saturday afternoon was decided upon. I arrived to find about a third of the armed forces, the shepherd maestro, no union men in the building and therefore no piano and no permissible rehearsal space except the 39th Street Lobby. The maestro and I became the Band. I explained the drill to the only two Captains present, who looked terrified. "OK," I said, "here we go. 'Da—DAH —da-da-da DUM DUM DUM' (first squad ENTER) 'da-da-da DEE de-dum, diddle dee-de-dum' (STOP—second squad ready) 'dee-DAH, dee-dah, diddle-de-DAH . . .' (GO—SALUTE—no, not you, the first lot) 'diddle-de DEE-de-da,' (first squad TURN, second squad ON) diddle-de-DEE-de-da' (second squad STOP—no, not you) . . ." and so on to exhaustion point. "'Where ignorant armies clash by night,'" I thought bitterly, and gave the bust of Gatti-Casazza a dirty look.

The Chorus, bless them, were as willing as ever. I had got hold of a photograph of the whole lot, lined up in rows, singing Verdi's *Requiem,* with a chart attached giving their names. I tried to learn all ninety-eight of them and probably mastered about fifty. It helped. As usual, there wasn't nearly enough time. Before the first orchestra semi-dress rehearsal I managed to get a few words with the men about the opening scene, where they appeared as Pharaoh's Captains (tenors) and Priests (baritones and basses). I said I knew they had to take Maestro Cleva's downbeat for "Ed osan tanto," but I didn't see why they all had to face him for three pages before it came. During that time, the Messenger was telling Pharaoh that hostile aircraft had been seen approaching Manhattan Island, and didn't they think some degree of agitation would be in order? They agreed.

Neither Milanov nor Del Monaco appeared at this rehearsal— they had, or feared, colds; the tenor and soprano who were next-in-line and were supposed to have attended all the rehearsals had not the smallest notion as to what they were meant to be doing. Accordingly, I stayed on the stage to direct traffic by surreptitious pointing, pushing and hissing in the ear without interrupting the orchestra. I was crouched in a corner when the Priests came on, wearing their white robes and black chin-pieces. The Messenger arrived. They listened dutifully. "Il sacro suola dell'Egitto è invaso dai barbari Etiopi . . ." They turned to each other, looking quite upset and whispered "Jesus!" Afterwards I told them it was a fine effort, but next time couldn't they say "Isis"?

There were scenery problems. Two of the sets were in Rolf's best manner—the soaring white and gold of the Triumph scene, with its clean, unadorned "modern" lines, waiting to receive the riot of color, movement and sound which would fill it; the statue of Ftha in the second scene, huge, in two-dimensional black silhouette, which stood downstage center, back to the audience, so that the Priests could pray to God and the conductor at the same time. Other sets, however, were difficult to work in and I did not solve their problems.

We had costume problems too. Del Monaco had brought his own, as most singers do when playing a variety of different opera houses. They were very bejeweled and picture-book, not at all like Gerard's austere and hieratic Egyptian styles. It took all our combined force, plus that of Mr. Bing in person, to get him out of them, and even then we had to concede a pair of sky-blue earrings. To transform the beautiful but stately Milanov into an African slave girl was quite a project too. Her ideas did not coincide with Rolf's, though he wooed her ardently in German. I would have minded less if she had acted more. One morning, after watching the tremendous third-act scene between Aida, Amonasro and Radames, Bing asked me if I couldn't get her to seem a little more agitated. I answered that I had tried, but it was no good. "La donn' è immobile."

We got through it in the end, naturally. The dress rehearsals involved some derring-do with the Stage Band, who regarded Rolf's fifteen-foot-high towers with plain terror. I went up first and they followed with crampons, ropes, and, of course, their glasses and music. I did the Triumph scene well, the Aida-Amneris scene subtly (by intention, anyway—it is an extremely delicate piece of psychology) and a couple of other things not badly. The ballet was exciting, the singing tremendous; nobody cared what Milanov did or didn't do so long as she "sounded," and everybody thought it was fine—or nearly everybody; I belonged to the minority. After the opening, the trouble really started.

Aida is heavily encrusted with traditional business, international currency throughout the operatic world. Cleva and Bing had advised me to ignore it; and after some investigation I did so in most cases.

But it all began to sneak back. Every boat, train and plane that arrived in New York brought a new soprano, tenor, baritone, bass, who rushed to the Met and sprang onstage in *Aida*. They brought their own old ideas and their own old clothes. Amonasro brought his own chains and refused to go on when they told him, "She says no chains." They tried to make their entrances wherever they had been used to making them and were only stopped by pieces of scenery placed in their path. Amneris couldn't throw pearls to the slaves because there weren't any pearls; Radames couldn't come wobbling on in a horse-drawn chariot because I had forbidden four-footed beasts. But in the big ensembles, they would calmly walk across the stage to their own accustomed positions, mixing up the whole stage movement for the rest of the scene, and a lot of other undesirable bits and pieces began creeping in, dating back to the Nile itself.

I looked in to see the fourth or fifth performance. Afterwards I asked Mr. Bing please to take my name off the program. But it remained there, through the Lord knows what horrible metamorphoses until Nathaniel Merrill's new production in 1963 mercifully superseded mine. Later Bing kept asking me to do things like *Ernani*, which makes the book of *Aida* seem like Shakespeare, and I kept asking to do Mozart or *Louise*, or almost anything less Grand than Verdi, or, if it had to be Verdi, something with a minimal chorus, like *Falstaff* or *Otello*. But it never happened.

He remained devoted to *Don Carlo* and paid me, quite uselessly, to "supervise" two revivals. The first time there was no time to do anything at all except try to retrieve bits of scenery which had unaccountably "vanished" and whose very existence was denied till I produced the original blueprints. Curiously enough, their disappearance always made life easier for the stage crew. I tried to get some better lighting from the head electrician who had succeeded to that post, but he was just as obstinate as his predecessor and a good deal more ill-mannered. The second revival was with George Solti as conductor, and we did have just a little more time. I loved working with him and wished passionately that we could do something together from scratch. He absolutely insisted on the singers acting, or trying to; but one of them, though he sang like an angel, never could manage to remember what he was supposed to be doing, and simply wandered about the stage without coherent thought. I never even saw the Grand Inquisitor who was to sing at the opening performance until he appeared on the stage.

Revivals at the Met are unmitigated torture for the stage director and an almost total waste from his point of view. Much as I loved my first opera brain child, I had to let it go. Misterbing, now Sir Rudolf, chose to revive it for the opening and closing of his final season. I was, of course, gratified by this, as I have been by the laudatory references it has received from the press over the years. But I shudder to think how much, or rather little, of what I put into it in 1950 could still be there in 1972.

This will be nobody's "fault." For Sir Rudolf to preserve what Misterbing wanted to create is impossible. It was, indeed, impossible for him ever to create it in the terms of his original vision, just as it was for me to do the work he had wanted from me. The people who pay the Met's bills get pretty much what they want to buy, however much they may grumble about the merchandise. I once watched a public dress rehearsal of a grandiose new production and wrote: "There's nothing wrong with it that six more dress rehearsals, three weeks on the road and a helluva lot of cutting wouldn't cure." But the press and the Met public thought it magnificent.

A respected English critic, reviewing Benjamin Britten's recent opera written for and on television, remarked that "the visuals bothered him"; and he didn't mean simply the television "visuals." He took care to indicate that when he went to Covent Garden he really preferred to shut his eyes; he implied that this would be true for all real music lovers. The dominant Met subscribers may not go that far, but the principle is not alien to them. As the Bing regime draws to a close, a fair amount of criticism is hurled, inevitably, at the departing General Manager; it is a miracle, to me, that he has contrived to stay alive at all.

SIMON BOCCANEGRA

After all my strictures and grumblings, during *Aida* and the *Carlo* revivals, it surprised me rather that Misterbing asked me to come back during the season of 1959–60; another Verdi, another monster Chorus, a libretto sillier than ever and some more glorious music—

in short, *Simon Boccanegra.* I yielded this time, I suppose, because Dimitri Mitropoulos was to conduct and Leonard Warren to sing. I was told (by the grapevine) that Warren was always having fights with people and was "impossible" to work with. I didn't altogether believe this, and I was right. He was a perfectionist. He cared passionately that everything should be just so. Unfortunately this led him to think that he knew more about everybody else's business than they did and he never hesitated to tell them what they ought to do about it. The fact that he was often justified did not always endear him to them. So far as I was concerned, he bent a beetling brow on me at first, but as soon as he had reached the conclusion that I knew what I was doing, we got on famously—not always without argument, but trusting each other.

Mitropoulos was all that I had heard, but reticent and reluctant to involve himself beyond the strictly musical field of interpretation. I first met him in his 55th Street apartment, the orchestra score of *Boccanegra* spread over a high, steeply tilted desk. He was wearing a kind of monk-like robe, his beautiful ivory head bent over the score in the light of a single lamp. He reminded me of "St. Jerome in His Study." All he needed was a tame lion. Or perhaps Warren, with his barrel-like chest, dark, shabby pullover and old beret pulled down on his head to keep it warm, was the not-so-tame lion.

Since *Boccanegra* was to open in February, and work on it had to be done the preceding June, I met for the first time the complexities of opening a production in the middle of the season rather than before it began. Rehearsals had to be fitted together with the complex jigsaw of performances as well as other rehearsals. The budget, always impossible, had lost any fragment of elasticity it ever possessed and was given to last-minute bursts of unreason. The months-ahead planning was bedeviled by divisive geography and by there being two designers instead of one—Frederick Fox for the sets and Elizabeth Montgomery ("Motley" by trade name) for the costumes. Though she was in New York and he in New Jersey, they couldn't seem to get together, and I, for most of the time, was an ocean away. This caused some confusion. Fox, for instance, designed rostrums for the Council scene which were very small, and Liz robes for the Councilors which were very large. The budget-makers would then decide that only the so-to-speak "Republican" Councilors could afford new robes and the "Democrats" would have to come out of stock. That way, everyone could get on the platforms. Less sensible was a firm refusal of four rosaries for four walk-on Franciscan Friars; I went out and bought some and thought of the "ritratto di Carlo."

Freddy Fox and I had been talking about the opera in terms of the libretto's historical setting—early fourteenth century—and of contemporary Italian art. The more I thought about the highly individual stylization of Giotto and his followers, the more I began—paradoxical as it may appear—to hear Mozart rather than Verdi. I wrote to Freddy:

> Verdi very often seems to me most difficult to translate pictorially for a modern audience in terms which are true to the *nature* of the music plus the supposed period and content of the libretto. The "plots" are often idiotic and the characters highly-coloured cardboard. In *Boccanegra* no-one but Simon himself is more than two inches deep. Add to this the somewhat statuesque, to put it mildly, style of the Met singers—and you must get a certain stylisation, bolder, larger and simpler than life. . . .

> I think you must pass it through your 1959 mind and stylise it for the contemporary spectator in terms which will give the simplified, melodramatic aspect of the story—"love", "honour", "revenge", "power" and the rest of it, terms which are strong enough to carry through, with audacity, all the clap-trap about missing daughters and poisoned goblets and stuff and stuff!

> More than this, there is, of course, the music itself which is sheer nineteenth-century romanticism, having nothing to do with the mid-fourteenth century, except that in pure musical sound it transcends both and reaches basic emotions common to both. The richness of the *sound* means, I think, rich colour and texture—but economically *distributed* if you see what I mean, or we'll all get indigestion. Giotto and kindred stuff . . . seems to me too delicate and austere for this romantic business. Probably . . . the garden scene is an exception. It should be very far from the frenzies and violence of Genoa—all Amelia, and her music which opens the act. I think, too, that Simon should have left the mark of his own austerity and truth of spirit on the "Doge's apartments". The Council scene must, of course, be wealthy and arrogant, magnificent Genoa; the first scene ominous and "charged". By the way, remember we only see it at night . . . always very hard to light dramatically without getting too much bounce from background scenery . . . be careful of light colours. . . .

Another problem arose in the Council scene. The Chorus "Popolo," or mob, had to sing offstage, all together under the conducting eye of Kurt Adler, and then rush onstage, plus a number of Guards and so forth, in exactly four bars of music and start singing again. I kept on stressing this; but Freddy couldn't manage to give me entrances wide and free enough for them all to do it from the same place at once. Heads were shaken. At the new Met, they said, closed-circuit television would be installed so that the mob could be in six places and all see Adler via a monitor. I said we couldn't wait for that and why not reflecting mirrors? This, they said, had never been done, and no one took any notice or did anything else. They came to it in the end. It was perfectly simple and worked like a charm.

There is lots and lots of Chorus in *Boccanegra,* and for much of my planning time I was separated by the Atlantic from my toy soldiers. I took to using different-colored candies and throat pastilles instead. At one point I was puzzled because the grouping on one side seemed so thin. With horror I realized that I had eaten the altos.

When rehearsals at last began, I had the impression that "the House" had greatly changed. The wonderful orchestra manager was gone—though there was a wonderful new stage manager. There was a new character called a "production manager" who seemed to me arrogant and disobliging. Bing seemed tired, harassed and with his old sense of humor worn down (and who shall blame him?). I got a subtle feeling that he was no longer fully in control of his own "House." I was rather shocked to find myself calling him "Rudi." Everyone was distracted by visions of the new Met, already well into the planning stage. Precious rehearsal time was wasted while assembled conductors were called onstage to a measuring out of the new orchestra pit and the seating of the musicians. (No two of them ever agreed.) Time was also wasted while the BBC shot a forty-minute TV documentary on Bing. We had to linger for rehearsal shots— about an hour and a half for what I knew would be two minutes of finished film—while Bing stood in the background looking glum. He said he was expressing enthusiasm. I said, "In that case, show me despair." He was ghostly with fatigue.

I had a love fest with the Chorus again. By now, I had done some work with the New York City Opera Company, and it had dawned on me that in a seldom-sung opera like *Boccanegra* the less experienced Chorus members may learn just as much of the Italian as they have to sing and happily ignore what everyone else is going on about. So I took the Doge's superb aria in the Council scene and carefully retranslated it myself—disregarding the official monstrosity. I read it to them and had copies mimeographed. I said it was vital that everyone on the stage should understand it and listen to it with total concentration. After this, as a bunch of us went down together in the elevator from the Roof Stage, a young man (new to me) said, "I have been telling the world that you should stage all twenty-five of the season's operas because *then* we would know what we were doing." I was deeply touched; but I thought to myself that it would not be an easy death.

Sometimes, though not often, I enjoyed myself. I wrote in a letter to a friend:

> Oh, what a beautiful day! . . . On-stage for the big scene which I had only half-blocked with the Chorus and extras on the Roof Stage and not at all with the principals and I was plenty scared. And at first it looked black . . . the costumes couldn't be got onto the rostrums and Warren arrived . . . soused in gloom and disapproval; and then the Chorus swarmed in and I thought chaos would come again; and I yelled a bit and soothed a bit . . . and mixed high-minded exhortations with jovial jokes and lo and behold! half an hour before the scheduled end I said "Let's run it once straight through and see what we've got"—and we had an entire scene in perfectly good working shape and no chaos and everybody amazed and delighted and not the least me. Department of taking pains; and me so very grateful.

Curiously enough, the fact of opening so late in the season seemed to result in my having more time to work alone with the soloists. Still more curiously, I didn't know what to do with it. This was partly due to the dazzling line-up of singers: Warren himself, "Riccardo" Tucker—singing gloriously, and a very wise and humorous man, good to have around—Giorgio Tozzi, American despite his name, to whom I once said, "There are only two sorts of singers: one, like yourself, to whom it is unnecessary to say anything, and the other to whom it is useless." The soprano was to have been the great Tebaldi; but she had announced that she could not arrive until the second performance, leaving Mary Curtis-Verna to sing the first—a horrible assignment, which she carried through with willingness and gallantry. None of them objected to acting as much as they were able. But I found myself wearying of the stock situations, the stock emotions, the ineffably silly plot, and trying to imitate Stanislavsky—in the Opera Club anteroom. I realized once again that when the music takes hold, the singers think of absolutely nothing but singing their throats out and neither do the audience and the director is swept aside along with everything else; and I supposed that was all right too.

Nevertheless, we all worked harmoniously and Warren was fine. I realized very soon what a fund of knowledge he had. In the last scene, just before Simon's death, I had performed prodigies of skill to maneuver everyone unostentatiously into the right places at the right moment leaving him in what I thought was the "key" spot for his final aria. "There, Leonard," I said, triumphantly, "it's all yours!" He looked at the spot I indicated. "I can't sing it from there," he said. I was terribly abashed. "Why not?" "It's a dead spot on this stage. I can sing it from there." He pointed to a spot not more than a foot away. "There are a dozen dead spots on this stage. I know them all." I didn't question for a moment that he was right.

All the same, I was getting worn down. My letters reveal a startling difference from the starry-eyed novice of eight years before. ("Whither is fled the visionary gleam?") The change may have been largely in the eye of the beholder, but I think not altogether so. The workings of what had always been a tightrope-walking system were much less smooth and far more tiresome.

The designer and the head electrician fought like mad, and Bing clamored constantly for a sky of deep Mediterranean blue, having long ago OK'd (against my advice) a white sky-drop which, of course, couldn't be made deep blue and had to be repainted at the cost of labor, time and general fury. I said I would mediate the lighting and take it over myself if everybody else would "shut up, take notes *quietly,* tell me *afterwards* and not talk to the electrician while he is working a cue." But neither I nor anybody else ever succeeded in persuading Mr. Bing that his master electrician was not the man to lay out or be in charge of the equipment at the new Met, though many people tried. He merely expressed pained incredulity and ended by saying "After all, does it really matter?"

Once I had admired his infinite capacity for making lightning decisions on unrelated matters while diving in and out of rehearsals. Now it drove me to distraction:

We had a fair amount of stürm und drang yesterday, chiefly owing to their absurd way of trying to do everything at once and settle everything by argle-bargle as it goes on and vanishing completely as soon as the rehearsal is over so nothing can be settled by discussion afterwards. The perpetual running to-and-fro of Bing and his minions about *Parsifal* and the orchestra pit in the new House and whether Warren's feet ought to show got on my nerves to such an extent that I wandered off into remote parts of the auditorium where they couldn't find me. . . .

There followed an occasion hideously illustrative of some of the things I had found so disquieting. It is best described by this letter, without any distortion of memory:

Fantastic episode today—wouldn't have believed it without "sensible and true avouch of my own eyes". Mitropoulos tells me he wants to put in all, or as many as possible, of second-cast singers for second half (of orchestra semi-dress rehearsal). I think this pretty silly as few of them have rehearsed at all, but acquiesce. . . . Transpires that Bing and minions think it pretty silly too, and also, for various reasons, unpractical. At conclusion of first half I go up on-stage to give hurried notes to Chorus, while various people (not Bing himself) settle with Maestro as to who shall sing what during rest of rehearsal. Orchestra still in Pit, not yet having been dismissed for break. I turn round to become aware of six-or-seven-way argle-bargle between groups of principals clustered down-stage centre, Maestro in Pit and several executives and staff clustered behind him in auditorium. I return to auditorium and stand by orchestra rail. Warren who wants to sing the rehearsal himself because he feels he needs it—getting very heated and pompous, finally says some silly thing like "Well, after all, Maestro, *we* are the singers and *we* have to give the performance"—a roar of hostile and derisive laughter from the orchestra-pit. Warren swings round on them and says "Well, and *you* didn't play so good *either!*" Uproar!! Since I happened to be the only person present who wasn't talking themselves, I heard an appreciable number of four-letter and combination-four-letter words hurled at Warren from the Pit. Well, various peacemakers intervene confusedly and the "orchestra break" of 20 minutes is called for, during which we agree as to who shall or shall not sing the rest of the rehearsal.

But at the end of the break—there is no orchestra in the Pit. They have sent for their Union delegate and refused to play again until Warren apologises!! Finally, they file grimly into the Pit and a square, belligerent type appears by the orchestra rail. Mitropoulos appears and says that Warren has apologised to him and through him to the orchestra. Bing appears and says that Warren has apologised through *him* to the Maestro and to the orchestra. Silence. One of the

Second Violins then arises and says he thinks they have a right to an apology in person. The square belligerent repeats this. Bing hesitates, says yes, well, and disappears backstage. Loaded seconds tick by. Finally, the gold curtains are parted and Warren appears, bull-like and agonised, steered by Bing, and apologises; but goes into a speech. Michael [the stage manager] and I turn to each other in anguish. "He's going to insult them all over again!" hisses Michael. Bing intervenes smoothly and steers Warren off through the gold curtains. And the orchestra consents to continue.

I am too appalled for speech; subsequently telling Bing that had Warren heard one of the first-desk Violins call him a c--- a---, he could have called the AGMA delegate and required the orchestra to apologise to *him*. But Bing only proposes to demand from the Musicians' Union the 11½ minutes of wasted orchestra time this has cost the Met. Which, of course, he won't get. A humiliating and desperate exhibition if ever I saw one.

The "final dress" came and went—all in order—master electrician and I friends again—singing wonderful—acting passable—Chorus onstage in time—surprise, surprise at the finale, when the next-in-line tenor appeared in a lounge suit without the smallest idea of what he was supposed to be doing. Tucker had taken wing for a concert in San Antonio. Well . . . out of my hands now. "God the source, God the kindling fire, flower of God."

The opening: "The performances," I wrote, "wholly respectable and at no point shaming and it was even quite well lit. I didn't think the audience was especially enthusiastic, though I sensed that it had 'given satisfaction.'" There was the usual applause, the gold curtain, Mitropoulos having to be dislodged from the train of Liz Montgomery's evening dress—a bunch of roses for me from "the supers"—a flood of white ties and mink coats—a splendid party at Leonard Warren's. I grieved that this particular group of singers would never sing the opera together again. The ensemble I had worked on so carefully might be as well sung, or better, but the balance, the detail, the rapport would never come again. Next morning the reviews were well worth gloating over; but the changes were already on their way; greater changes than we could have known.

Tebaldi had arrived, in the utmost secrecy, even before the opening, and we had started the routine of "the Tenor's sitting on that bench and you come on from 40th Street." She occasionally sang a phrase or two in her voice like the wings of a dove and even wrote occasional moves in her score—the only singer I remember who did so. The next performance was to be the following Tuesday, at the Academy of Music in Philadelphia—a special expedition, dreaded by all for its immense complexity, but an ancient Met obligation. Tebaldi was to sing and there was a probability that Tozzi, who was having throat trouble, might have to be replaced. For once the replacement singer had had quite a lot of rehearsal.

Three days later, on March 5, I wrote:

0.45 a.m.

I just got back from a performance of *The Balcony.* There was a message to call Michael Manuel at the Met urgently, which I did; to discover that Leonard Warren died on the stage tonight during a performance of *Forza del Destino.* . . .

I've been fumbling for "Profiscere anima christiana" or whatever it is and praying, in more familiar words that flights of angels (whom he'd surely criticise) would sing him to his rest—on pitch. I try to be glad—am glad—that I was, I think, able to help give him a happy and triumphant last experience and that I did get his wave-length and that I loved him—I really did, the old dinosaur—and he knew it. He called me yesterday, not *wholly* pleased on account the tenor had had such good notices and he thought the proportions were wrong. But I said "We did all right by Verdi, didn't we, and that's the main point isn't it?" and he allowed as how. And I've said to him that what achieved those notices was that he and I cared terribly about this and didn't regard it as just another opera. But it's shattering, shattering and I can't really believe it yet—oh, and his poor, young, very sweet wife—oh, dear God, did you need a baritone that bad?

The following afternoon, I wrote:

Bing seems to have handled the whole thing impeccably, with courage, simplicity and elegance—both with Mrs. Warren, the audience, the press and all the rest of it. Naturally, everyone at "the House" yesterday was in a state of shock . . . they were all hollow-eyed and hollow-cheeked. . . . None of us knew what to say to each other. Most of them I hadn't seen since the opening and we started to congratulate each other in constrained phrases and then just stopped and stared . . . we were making little sense. But, as usual, it was the people who had least to do with it who made the most fuss. Mitropoulos and I rehearsed with Tebaldi and Guarrera, who will have to sing on Tuesday in Phila.

I don't know how the hell they'll sing the end of *Boccanegra,* since it ends with his on-stage death, of which Leonard was inordinately proud and told me numberless child-like stories of how doctors had rushed round to find out if he really *was* dead. . . . oh, it is all *most* macabre and hideous. I shan't go [to Philadelphia] because there's nothing I can usefully do—and also no-one has asked me! If it were a play and a theatre company I would not, of course, leave them for a moment! But it isn't. [Also I developed a bad cold, which settled the matter.]

The depleted company went off, new soprano, new baritone and much doubt as to whether Tozzi or the second-team man would sing the bass. Next morning I called Michael Manuel to find out which of them had. "Neither," said he. "Who, then?" "Jerry Hines." The Met people had decided that they couldn't do without another star singer in the line-up. Jerry had been slated to sing the part at some later time but hadn't, I think, been to any of the rehearsals. He sat up all night studying it and was guided through it somehow. No one had had time to notice what the total performance was really like. I wondered, not for the first time, what the orchestra thought of themselves in relation to the last days of Leonard Warren.

I was filled with admiration for the capacity of the Metropolitan Opera House to weather a Force 8 gale. But I realized more vividly than ever that an opera house run on the lines of the old Met is completely impossible for visiting stage directors with standards and backgrounds like mine. The work can only get done well by a series of lucky accidents, and even then it is destroyed, except for the most primitive elements, as soon as it is accomplished. I never got a chance to see *Boccanegra* again; if I had, I doubt whether I would have taken it. It has been revived, and well received, from time to time. But I do not want to see a clumsy approximation of what was once careful and precise, where the meaning is lost and only a distortion of the mechanics remains. I am, by profession, a maker of delicate instruments, not a traffic cop.

Since I kicked against so many pricks at the old Met, and made no secret of my views, it isn't surprising that I haven't worked at the new one. I have not repined about this. To me opera has always been a huge challenge, involving mountains of preparatory work, always terrifying, with moments of incomparable reward, but perishable, fragile, dust between the fingers. I am told that some of the hazards and horrors I have described are present in almost all opera houses, whether at Glyndebourne, Frankfurt or Santa Fe, but to a very considerably less degree. From all I can gather, the old obstacles are still present at the new Met, plus some fresh ones. The new House is full of architectural amenities and electronic marvels; which I mistrust. I like to know that if the worst comes to the worst, a couple of men hauling on a rope can do something; and the new Met has sometimes been enslaved as well as served by its gadgetry. Nevertheless, it is, of course, much more regulated and convenient and aseptic and spacious and well arranged.

It was quite obvious that the old building had become hopelessly inadequate to the requirements of present-day schedules. No one could ignore the dreadful sight of all that expensive new scenery lying along the pavements of Seventh Avenue being rained on and waiting to be scratched, bashed, torn and battered on its way to the storage warehouse and back again. Then there were the ancient dressing rooms far away up long flights of stairs, the lack of re-hearsal space or office space, the antiquated stage equipment. All the same, there were a dozen ways in which the building could have been used, and used with distinction, by other occupants.

It was a beautiful house, rich (why not?), civilized, lovely, living. I used to think it could perform an opera all by itself if you simply turned the lights on and started to play the overture. It was beauti-ful to be in, to listen, to sing—and also to speak in, if you knew how. Nobody believed that, because it looked so big. But I have seen and worked in modern steel-and-concrete structures, large and small, in the United States, Europe, South Africa, Australia. What-ever acoustical science may say to the contrary, they do not have the responsiveness or the natural resonance of the old wood-and-brick buildings—and of course they do not have the humanity. It is as hard to warm them as it would be to produce a velvet tone from a plastic violin. The destruction of the old Met was a betrayal for which no economics can compensate, a vandalism which nothing can excuse.

Way up under the roof, some sixty feet above the stage, there used to be a railed wooden "catwalk" running along the back wall from the 39th Street Roof Stage to the one on 40th Street. I walked across it alone late one afternoon soon before I left the building for the last time. It was dark; there were just the small, bare lamps over the paint frame and up above the grid, and a lone pilot light far be-low by the orchestra pit. The ropes lay coiled on the fly galleries, running up into blackness. Looking down you could glimpse the

Marweb productions on tour—U.S.A., 1949–50

"The local resources were generally dreadful…"

Hamlet set by David Ffolkes, costumed
"in Shakespeare's own period," 1938

The travelling Hamlet set,
designed by Wolfgang Roth, 1948

Cesare Siepi, Fedora Barbieri, Margaret Webster,
Delia Rigal, on the stage of the Met during the intermission
telecast at the opening of *Don Carlo,* November, 1951

Margaret Webster
coaching singers for
Simon Boccanegra
(1959–60)

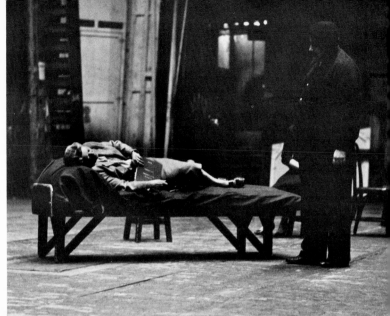

Dying for
Leonard Warren

Being a villain for
Ezio Flagello

Stabbing Warren
for Richard Tucker

Rehearsing the troops

Margaret Webster reading at the Vineyard Haven Tercentennial, 1971

"Dancing" for students in the University
of Wisconsin production of *The Three Sisters,* 1969

"Fighting" for students in the Berkeley
production of *Antony and Cleopatra*, 1964

Margaret Webster contemplating the rain-drenched amphitheatre
at Berkeley just before the performance of *Antony and Cleopatra*

dimness of the empty stage, between the bulk of backdrops and hanging battens. There was the inimitable smell of "theatre." I stood still and listened. The air was vibrant, thronged. The silence beat against your ears, charged with sound—not sound remembered, but alive and present. Brave, I thought, the bulldozer that will dare to smash this living thing. Even the dust will cry aloud as it shatters. There ought to be an earthquake or Wotan's fire.

I said thank you to the crowding presence and walked on and down and away.

THE NEW YORK CITY OPERA

Once upon a time the Met had a poor relation who lived in a hideous old building up on West 55th Street. It was a Masonic Temple which the city had taken over for nonpayment of taxes, and it housed indigent opera, indigent ballet and fragments of penniless drama. Now the New York City Opera Company confronts its rival from an equally stately palace across the Plaza at Lincoln Center. Fountains splash for both alike; distinguished feet cross the patio toward both imposing portals; rival *Traviata*'s resound from west and south; and the New York City Opera very often wins on points. I don't know whether they like each other any better. In my day the Met was lofty and disparaging about the City Opera, and the poor relation was spiteful, envious and resentful about that old rich-bitch downtown. I should be surprised if propinquity has bred affection.

I have said that the old Met ran on zeal. So did the City Center; even more zeal and far, far less money. There were no VIP nights, no white ties and tiaras, but a large "popular-price" audience. Opera was sung almost always in English by mostly American singers. New American operas were produced here often; very rarely at the Met. Of the four I directed, two should certainly have been done by the Met (William Walton's *Troilus and Cressida* and Strauss's *Schweigsame Frau*); one never could have been (Vittorio Giannini's *Taming of the Shrew*); and one *was*—good old Verdi again, with *Macbetto*.

Bing's reason for not doing new operas was that his audience would only support a very limited number of performances, too few to make so much as a dent in the production costs. When he put a tentative toe into the waters of novelty, even so distinguished a novelty as Stravinsky's *The Rake's Progress,* the best he could get from it was seven performances spread over two seasons. The New York City Company gave only five of *Troilus and Cressida,* also spread over two seasons; but they somehow managed to make *Faust* or "Cav and Pag" subsidize a lot more experimental work than the Met ever got out of *Carmen* and *Aida.*

At first the City Opera paid no rent, though it always paid taxes; from 1954 it paid 1½ percent of the gross as rent; but it got no subsidy, ran on a tiny budget, and had to raise funds from opera lovers just like the Met. The President of the City Council, Newbold Morris in my day, was a member of its Board and Morton Baum its ardent moving spirit. The vague aura of public service which clung to it only meant that everyone was desperately underpaid. It was always in a chronic state of deficit—as it is still, on a far grander scale, despite some public subsidy. It played regular seasons at the City Center, sharing the building with George Balanchine's New York City Ballet Company and sporadic infusions of musical comedy or plays. With the aid of short tours it managed to keep together a company which, while not "permanent," was reasonably steady.

I had reason to know "the Mecca Temple," to give it its old name, all too well. I had done battle with its problems twice for Maurice Evans and once (*Richard III*) for José Ferrer during the drama seasons. The auditorium lacked charm to a spectacular degree and was very difficult either to sing or speak in. The stage had reasonable depth but no side space whatever. The electrical equipment had been salvaged from Noah and Sons; but it was less complicated to handle and far more imaginatively used than the Met monsters. The rehearsal space was even more limited, the chorus every bit as hardworked, the pressures were just as lethal—but somehow it was a good deal more fun; perhaps it was because nobody expected so much, and they were always being agreeably surprised.

The first opera I did there, in 1955, was William Walton's *Troilus and Cressida.* The original production had only recently taken place, at Covent Garden. I had not seen it, there were no recordings and no one to play me the score. The libretto was a fine piece of work in its own right. I knew the author, Christopher Hassall, and through him met Walton in London and got permission from the BBC to hear the recording they had taken from a Covent Garden broadcast.

Lots of chorus again, and extras and costumes and complicated scenery, but glorious music and all in English and all new to everybody. The scars of *Aida* were still recent, and this seemed to me enormously refreshing. The singers were all American, the bass a Chinese American, the baritone a Negro. Josef Rosenstock conducted and Phyllis Curtin sang Cressida.

Not least, the composer and author had written the opera with contemporary theatre minds. Hassall was an actor and a playwright as well as a poet; Walton loved words as much as he did notes; and above all, no one had been able to coach the singers in prefabricated, second-hand, "traditional" interpretations. They had learned the score, of course, and were musically prepared, but Dr. Rosenstock and I "got at them," if I may so phrase it, together. I had always thought this was the way things should be. All four of the operas I did at the City Center were entirely new to the singers. At the same time there was a continuity of personnel and musical staff which gave cohesion to the company, and though there were no great singing "names," the cast stayed put. This, however, did involve dangers. When Troilus got a throat infection a few days before we opened, there was nobody else on the American continent who had ever sung the role or even studied it. Mercifully, he recovered in time. The Chorus were as full of effort and good will as they had been at the Met, and there were the usual small, fat tenor and gaunt, elderly bass, always in the wrong places at the wrong time.

There came one really terrible day when I found out that the designer had allocated to the Chorus in the last act a wide assortment of clothing which bore no relation whatever either to who was supposed to be what or to the various vocal divisions. Cooks' sons, Dukes' sons and sons of Earls for whom the City Center couldn't afford belts, jostled each other impartially, mixing first tenors with second basses "irregardless" and hopelessly shattering my careful plans. The only thing I had absolutely counted on was the only thing there wasn't, viz.: an army.

I realized I would have to restage the entire scene overnight, unless Rosenstock would allow me to mix the voices. He was sympathetic, but adamant. The costumes, limited by budget, had been fitted and could not be changed. Working almost all night I managed to get everybody sorted out in time for the day's rehearsal, at the expense of a couple of extra pairs of tights and a slight lack of solidarity among the second tenors. I also discovered that the Chorus had never had a chance to read the libretto and tended to think it was Shakespeare's. They were simultaneously rehearsing *Carmen, Bohème, Golden Slippers* (a new production), *The Merry Wives of Windsor, The Love of Three Oranges* and *Cenerentola.* I marveled. The executive staff worked even harder. They all seemed to have acquired a peculiar yellowish-grey pallor and didn't always have time to get together with a razor.

The opera season opened while *Troilus* was still in rehearsal and every singer was needed to work on some other opera. It was hard to do a sextet with two principals, one understudy and the pianist. Walton arrived, which frightened everybody very much but quite unnecessarily. It was odd to have a real, live composer around; odder still to hear him refer to the tenor's most tenorish aria as "that beastly little tune." He seemed pleased and was helpful except for one rather strange orchestra rehearsal when he himself conducted in the Pit and Rosenstock duplicated from a small podium behind him.

The opening night went well, except for one episode which reminded me of Desdemona's handkerchief. Much of the plot centered around a crimson scarf given by Troilus to Cressida (Act I), by her to Diomed (Act II) and fought over by the two men (Act III). After Troilus's death it was absolutely essential for her to have it in her hands for her final aria, to hide the sword with which she kills herself. Despite Awful Warnings from me to Troilus, Cressida and the two soldiers who had to drag the body of Troilus offstage . . . the scarf got dragged off with him. No end to opera. A swift, silent mass evacuation of the auditorium by me, Julius Rudel and sundry others, a frantic dash backstage; somehow we managed to push it back, under a curtain; somehow Cressida saw it, retrieved it, sang about it, killed herself with élan. I aged several years.

The reviews were fine and the libretto praised as it deserved. But oh, I thought, all this blood, sweat and tears for something which will be seen exactly five times! If it is wearing and dispiriting to direct opera, surely only lunatics with a strong bent toward self-immolation can devote years of their time and talents to writing it.

The next time I came to 55th Street was with dear Verdi's *Macbetto* —text in Italian, Italian conductor (Arturo Basile), Italian tenor (whose only English phrases were "darling" and "no rehearse tomorrow"), charming, gifted young Greek designer, Andreas Nomikos, with whom I had conferred during the summer in Europe. Large chorus, naturally, all quite unused to singing in Italian. At the first rehearsal the harassed, dreadfully overworked chorus master came to me in great distress. "I'm terribly sorry," said he, "I haven't had time to tell them the story."

I borrowed a copy of the Chorus score from one of the baritones. It consisted of a blank stave marked for twenty bars' "rest"; then the notes of "Che parli?"; another fifteen bars' rest; "Orror, orror!"; more rest bars, and so on. One could understand why the chorus seemed so mystified by Macbeth's goings-on at the banquet. I had had my own moments of mystification. The first set of recordings I had been able to get hold of turned out to represent a cut-down rendering of an earlier version of the opera sung by a Viennese company in German. A supposed English translation was attached, but it kept on trying to revert to Shakespeare's lines in places where Piave's libretto made no such attempt. Sometimes it broke down with a bump. "Most sacrilegious murder," proclaimed Banquo, "hath upset the great doom's image." To which the Chorus replied anxiously, "What goes?"

I found that it was better to stop thinking about the play. The opera is swifter, bolder and very much cruder. Melodramatic events fall over each other pell-mell. Psychology is not in evidence, emotion well to the fore. Lady Macbeth is far more dominating, even stealing some of Macbeth's best lines for her own superb aria "La luce langue"; it was fitting, I thought, that her final appearance was heralded as "Gran Scena di Sonnambulismo." I stumbled over minor matters. Duncan is a walk-on. "Macduffo," as a name, conveyed to me more clown than hero. But my chief problem was with what the opera calls "le sorelle vagabonde"—the dear old Witches.

It is bad enough in the play, when there are only three of them; in *Macbetto* they are the entire female chorus, in this case thirty; they still have to "vanish" in half a bar flat. Their music makes no attempt to evoke eleventh-century Scotland; indeed, it always sounded to me more like the fairies in *Iolanthe,* "Tripping hither, tripping thither, nobody knows why or whither." Nobody did, either. I established a Witch-of-the-Month Club award for whoever best mastered the complications of the caldron scene. We became good friends in our mutual efforts, and I was happy to find a number of them at the Met when I went back there for *Boccanegra.*

Basile and I communicated without trouble—my Verdian Italian had improved; nobody could communicate with Macduffo. He sang every rehearsal sotto voce; on the opening night he stepped boldly forward from the huge line-up which ends the first act, and, sing-ing literally "to beat the band," firmly led the whole ensemble a quarter of a tone sharp. My worst obstacle lay in the total inability of the management to make up its mind as to which of two singers was to sing the opening performance as "Lady." This kept us all in agonies of uncertainty, disrupted schedules and destroyed morale. One had the better voice, the other was by far the better actress. And which was chosen? One easy guess.

The production got by, respectably, I don't quite know how. The Macbeth curse wasn't really in evidence, unless you count the fact that I broke my ankle the following morning, just as I was about to leave for London to start rehearsing at the Old Vic. I was not proud of *Macbetto* as an artistic achievement, though I thought it a good acrobatic feat. The City Center budget was stretched dreadfully thin; the Macbeth was by no means the equal of his Metropolitan counterpart, Leonard Warren. And yet . . . and yet . . . When I was beginning to rehearse *Boccanegra* over two years later, *Macbetto* was in the Met repertoire, conducted, designed, directed and sung by their topmost stars, "claqued" to the echo and rapturously received by the audience. I went to see it. To this day I recall my dismay.

> At the end of Act I [I wrote] I went and had an enormous drink and thought, "*Either* I can do absolutely nothing in this house, because its objectives—and not least its audience—are so *totally* alien to every single thing I strive to do, and I had better go jump off Brooklyn Bridge; *or,* however bad I am, or however I get swept aside when the full blast of the music is on, *I cannot possibly be as perfectly terrible as that!*" Matters improved somewhat in the 2nd and 3rd Acts, but I still thought it pretty senseless and incomprehensible and *appallingly* badly lit (this I fear will always be) and generally upsetting. . . . I have, as you know, little conceit of myself as a director of opera and less still for the Threepenny Macbeth we did at the City Center. But oh *dear!* how I longed for Basile and my Witches of the Month and even dear old blundering Macbetto. Altogether I was a most confused character when I faced this morning's rehearsal.

Perhaps it did, in fact, come down to the audience. It was the City Center audience, rather than its galley-slave conditions, which al-ways made me feel more at home there.

Of the two remaining operas I did for them, Giannini's *Taming of the Shrew* was almost a rest cure by comparison—composer alive and well and living in New York, American singers (Phyllis Curtin, happily, again), Julius Rudel conducting, no chorus, Shakespeare recognizable, comedy at last, a pleasant result. The last, Strauss's *Schweigsame Frau,* sung in English, comedy again, a great pleasure. I thought it the nearest I had come to doing what I wanted to do, handled the singers well as actors, and made their rapport with the conductor satisfactory to both him and them. There was only one short Chorus scene which, for once, I snarled up completely at the first rehearsal and felt much ashamed. Neither of the principals (soprano and bass) was really experienced enough for their very difficult assignments; but they tried valiantly and with charm; and the conductor (Peter Herman Adler) and I worked happily together. (I have never quarreled with a conductor. Am I extra cooperative or just a sucker?) We live and learn, I thought, and I learned a lot of pleasant things from this one.

Alas, I never got a chance to put my new skills into practice again; but two things were strongly impressed on me. The first concerned the translation of a libretto into English. I am not a devotee of this. (What I had needed as a director was for *me* to be able to talk to the singers in English, not to have *them* sing to me in it.) I can rarely, as an audience, understand the words, but I understand them better if they fit the notes. I recently heard a *Valkyrie* in which, "owing to unforeseen circumstances," the whole cast sang in English except Wotan, who sang in German. He was the only one I understood. Strauss, I need hardly emphasize, is extremely precise in fitting notes and rhythms to words and stresses. In this opera there occurs perhaps eighty times the phrase "ein-e schweig-sam-e Frau." There is absolutely no way of Anglicizing this except as "a-a si-i-lent wom'n"—in one syllable. The result is horrible.

The second was something I had first to learn and then to teach. It was how a man sits down in an armchair wearing an eighteenth-century skirted coat and dress-sword and carrying a tricorn hat under his arm. Mathematical precision and balletic skill are required, if you are to avoid impaling yourself on the sword, dropping the hat, sitting on a crumpled-up bundle of coat tails and knocking over the chair. Dennis King, an accomplished costume actor, kindly gave me some lessons. It started me on a crusade to get an educational film made on the wearing of costumes and use of "costume props" by the very few remaining actors who know how to wear and use them. The art is vanishing and, in the United States theatre, has all but disappeared. I tried to reach Granma Ford Foundation and other supposedly interested parties. But nothing ever got done. Actors leave off the swords, don't use the hats, rumple up the coat tails and bump into the furniture.

In England the tradition has survived. Dennis had learned it when he was a "call boy" at the Birmingham Theatre from an old actor who had learned it from Samuel Phelps, whose father was of a generation which did all these things as a part of daily living. Once Dennis taught me the routines of snuff-taking, which are of mathematical precision and delicacy. At London's National Theatre they still do this sort of thing beautifully, as they do in France and Germany. The skills survive sometimes in opera, handed down from such great exemplars as Ezio Pinza or Lotte Lehmann, because so many singers are trained in Europe. Some ballet companies safeguard them; which was why the American Repertory Theatre had sought out a choreographer to coach *The School for Scandal*. But they can only be handed on visually; and in the American theatre today practically nobody knows anything about them.

"Visual education" is widely thought to be the most powerful teaching medium for the next generation. You would think that some foundation money, or funds dispensed by educational authorities, would apply their resources to rescue this art from extinction. You would be wrong.

All of which is largely irrelevant to opera. But so is the rest of this book.

Chapter Nine

Of Witch-Hunting

It is therefore our business carefully to cultivate in our minds, to rear to the most perfect vigour and maturity every sort of generous and honest feeling that belongs to our nature. To bring the dispositions that are lovely in private life into the service and conduct of the Commonwealth; and rather to run the risk of falling into faults in a course which leads us to act with energy and effect, than to loiter out our days without blame and without use. Public life is a situation of power and energy; he trespasses against his duty who sleeps upon his watch, as well as he that goes over to the enemy.

Such, in 1770, were the thoughts of Edmund Burke on the "Cause of the Present Discontents." And if you extend "public life" to those whose work is largely in the public eye, it applies to the people of the theatre and its allied industries; and so, in my view, it did and does. But for those who held any principles similar to those of Mr. Burke—however small the scale of their application—the late Forties and much of the Fifties were very rough going indeed. The story that I shall try to tell in this chapter is personal and small; it took place only on the periphery of the main events; it is not a story of which I am proud. But I think it needs to be told, partly because it now seems so utterly incredible, but even more because we need to be reminded that, incredible or no, it could happen again; not in the same framework or with the same weapons, but under the same pressures of insecurity, ambition, hatred, and above all—fear; always, and on both sides, fear.

One of the things I learned from those years was to go through for the first and I think the last time the humiliating experience of fear. But since everything is grist to an actor's mill, I also found myself annotating the physical effects, which, as is usually the case, included the validation of all sorts of cliché phrases, such as the one about the marrow of your bones.

It all began with Equity. I had been one of the early fighters for British Equity in England—on its first Council, and its first Executive Committee—one of those who had had to establish, by their own individual actions, the solidarity of the profession and the principle of the closed shop. When I came to the United States, I acted as a kind of liaison officer between the two Associations; but the outbreak of war in 1939 severed any further active connection with British Equity. In 1941, the Nominating Committee of the Council of American Equity asked me to be one of the regular ticket for new Council members. I was honored and accepted. Then the fun began. It transpired that the Committee had refused two names placed before it—Mady Christians "because she was foreign-born" and Alan Hewitt "because he had been accused of Communism." There was an almighty row and an independent ticket was formed consisting of these two and one other name. The independents also endorsed the candidature of three "regulars," E. John Kennedy, Ethel Waters and me. We, in turn, endorsed their candidates.

Plenty of fur flew, plenty of mud was thrown and there was a "stormy" annual meeting at which I appealed for unity and wrung the reluctant hand of Florence Reed, our chief opponent, and was cheered to the echo by all but Winifred Lenihan, who glared at me with the blazing eyes which had won her fame as Saint Joan, and said it was a "dirty, ham-actor's trick." It wasn't so intended, but I could see her point. Anyway, we all got elected, and the above two ladies, plus Peggy Wood, a vice president, and seven other most distinguished and valued Council members resigned in a frenzy of apprehension. Equity was doomed. Our election "plus the professional bleeding hearts on Council now gives the Communists seventeen votes," declared Miss Lenihan to the press, a little wildly. We all begged them to return and help to counter the dreadful danger; but they wouldn't. Other councilors were appointed and Equity continued on its charted course, sensible, reasonable, a bit stodgy, rather to the right of the middle of the road, argumentative but seldom actively belligerent. I remained on its Council for ten years; and if any of my fellow members were, in fact, Communists, I can only say that as actors they were brilliant, and as minions of the U.S.S.R. totally and utterly useless.

During those ten years I worked for many causes. One was the extension of the professional theatre outside of New York. I wanted Equity to cooperate with the semi-professional "Community Theatre" groups, to increase their quota of professional actors, to improve their quality and standards. I wanted professional Artists in Residence at the university theatres. I strove for the evolution of new contracts to meet their special needs. I was active in devising new rulings for the groups which were forming in New York beyond Broadway, for the Experimental Theatre, for the Equity Library Theatre. I was for anything which would revitalize the shrinking theatre-conscious audiences throughout the United States: "the creation of theatrical companies of the first rank to feed and serve this audience, and the expansion of the profession of theatre to the point where it can provide an outlet and a livelihood for the wealth of talent which is at present blocked out or starved out" (so ran one of my memoranda to Council). "In this task there is no room for petty rivalries, jealousy and false pride." There was, of course; plenty of room. But despite the pitfalls it encountered, the resentments it engendered and even the casualties which sometimes resulted from the advance of a trade union into a new and disorganized field, the policy was good. What it began has born fruit Off-Broadway and in the professional repertory companies which are now established all over the United States.

In what way these convictions could have been construed as following the Party Line it is hard to discern. Nevertheless, the issues of Communism were growing, even during the years when the U.S.A. and the U.S.S.R. were fighting a war together against Nazi Germany. But the energies and preoccupations of Equity and all other members of the entertainment industries who were not already in the armed forces were directed elsewhere—to the USO, the Stage Door Canteen, Treasury Bond Drives, Red Cross Drives, British War Relief, Russian War Relief and a multitude of war-engendered charities and "causes." Among these were two in which a number of theatre people participated, and which were destined to cause as much grief to their supporters as aid to those they supported.

I was never on the boards or committees of either, but I was a "sponsor," attended their public functions from time to time, and made appeals for their funds. One was the National Society for Soviet-American Friendship—or at least, the section of it which was concerned with the arts. During the war years we tried to establish contacts in the fields of theatre, music, etc., looking toward the hoped-for cultural exchanges in the postwar era. The other was the Joint Anti-Fascist Refugee Committee. It had originally been formed to help the anti-Franco Spanish refugees who had been interned, under the most miserable conditions, in French refugee camps and had been largely forgotten among the more urgent demands of warfare. Picasso was its international president, and its cause had attracted much sympathy in America. It happened that this organization unwittingly ignited an explosion which rocked Equity and started a series of chain reactions which damaged untold people and lasted for years.

The man who set fire to the fuse was Frank Fay, who had by now been chasing his *Harvey* rabbit for almost a year; a highly volatile Irish-Catholic, not very strong on logic. His partner was no rabbit but a tiger, Howard Rushmore of the New York *Journal-American.* The story, as you reread it, is so ludicrous that its impact and consequences seem incredible; but they happened.

On September 24, 1945, the Joint Anti-Fascist Refugee Committee held a big meeting at Madison Square Garden to raise funds. Five actors, four of them women and all nonplanetary stars, appeared during the early part of the meeting, after which they went off to their respective theatres to play their shows. Later in the meeting a radio speech was transmitted from London by Harold Laski, the British Labour Party economist. In it he referred critically to the politics of the Roman Catholic Church in Spain.

Powered by Rushmore, Fay rocketed into space. The *Journal-American* proclaimed that "the appearance of actors at a Red meeting which condemned religion is a far cry from the tradition and tolerance of the theatre. . . . The participation of stars in a front meeting such as this deserves a full investigation," declared Fay. "Inexcusable conduct," he fulminated; and at an Equity quarterly meeting which happened to fall on the day following the *Journal-American* article, he declared the five actors to have been "a party to defamation of the Church, the Pope and the Vatican in the greatest insult to religion [he] had ever heard." This patent idiocy was not hilarious. The five members had already filed charges against Fay with Equity under the Association's by-laws which covered "conduct prejudicial to the Welfare of the Association or its members." They claimed that he had "clearly damaged and injured them in their profession."

These charges, of course, had to be heard. There was a good deal of preliminary skirmishing, during which Fay refused to proffer his allegations in writing, challenged the Council's jurisdiction, and simultaneously announced that he had been denied his rights. There were meetings, recessed meetings, evidence given by the five members, much obfuscation and evasion by Fay, vain appeals to him for peace and sweet reason. The five members testified that they had been "physically assaulted, insulted, threatened with violence to themselves and their families, picketed and informed that not only their present plays but any plays, motion pictures or radio broadcasts in which they might appear from now on would be boycotted." The Council and its officers "received more than 1,600 letters and telegrams from individuals and organizations blaming Equity for accepting charges against Mr. Fay and accusing it of attacks on religion."

In the end, the Council ("composed," as we stated, "of men and women of the Protestant, Catholic and Jewish faiths") passed unanimously a resolution sustaining the charges brought by the five members. It ordered that "Frank Fay be reprimanded and censured"; but he was in no way penalized. He took the case to a membership meeting, which resoundingly backed the Council. The Council did its utmost to vindicate "five innocent members who in no way participated in any attack on anyone's faith or religion." But it failed to save them and only involved itself. Henceforth, Equity was a "Red" organization and the councilors who had censured Fay were pinpointed. Among them were some of the most rock-ribbed conservatives in the Association; but also some suspect characters of known "liberal" views, such as Mady Christians, Philip Loeb and myself—"pinkos" was the fashionable derogation—who were more vulnerable. Frank Fay and the Hearst press did not forget us.

Now as then, people believe quite guilelessly what they read in the papers or hear over the air. A lot of interested parties were beginning to get publicity mileage out of this new and patriotic cause, pressmen and Congressmen alike, and millions were sincerely alarmed. The years of disgrace were upon us, of reckless accusations, of endless "smear campaigns," or innuendoes, of that most insidious of weapons, guilt by association. The big guns were trained first on Hollywood. Accusers such as Congressmen Martin Dies and Parnell Thomas confronted celebrated accused—even citizens of such outstanding probity as Frederic and Florence March—with the crime of having belonged to an organization called the Anti-Nazi League, and raised a tremendous amount of blindingly spotlit dust. Investigations and "trials" were the order of the day. In April 1948, ten well-known Hollywood writers refused to answer questions put to them by the Congressional Committee on Un-American Activities in California. They were tried for contempt of Congress and sentenced to jail. Two years later, after a succession of fruitless appeals, they went there.

For the ordinary humdrum citizen, called upon to combat a danger to his country, there was a small weapon called the boycott.

Broadway, being less in the national eye than Hollywood, received less attention at first. I got a whiff or two of grapeshot, but was not much disturbed. Soon after the Fay episode I got a more-in-sorrow-than-in-anger little missive addressed to my "attention" in care of Equity, and beginning:

Gentlemen:

It is with regret that I have read recently in the press that you are "affiliated with 19 communist front organisations."

Your play *Therese* I have seen and I have enjoyed the good acting therein by Dame Mae (*sic*) Whitty, Eva Le Gallienne . . . but in view of the press statements I am inclined to boycott any other play in which your name appears or in which you are connected. . . .

It continued with a vigorous denunciation of the Spanish Loyalists and concluded, oddly, "Might I enquire whether you are a member of the Equity Actors Association?"

I am sure that the writer of this mild and meaningless muddle had no understanding that his letter carried with it the implied threat that because of some unverified press statements, all right-thinking people should prevent me from earning my living and seriously damage those associated with me.

Another such piece of endearing intimidation reached me a little while later, which began by conveying the writer's "best and warmest wishes" for the coming year and continued:

I would like to mention that I am really perturbed and amazed to note that you are "very sympathetic to the cause of the left wing" meaning the Communists, it is the more unbelievable since you are the daughter of such a dignified old Lady Dame Whitty. . . .

The dignified old Lady Dame, a rebellious radical from way back, was outraged. I laughed; but it wasn't at all a laughing matter. The investigators of all those press statements, investigations, boycotts and so on were very far from funny. Perhaps it was the mantle of the old Lady Dame that protected me from them, for a while anyway.

Early in 1947 Frank Fay popped up again. Equity, as I have described, made a very generous donation of $5,000 to try and save the American Repertory Theatre. The donation was channeled through ANTA, of whose Board I was a member. Fay thought this clear evidence that I was "throwing a curve." In fact, neither Eva nor I had felt happy about accepting the Equity contribution, but we could hardly refuse it. I had written to the Council that we "have felt deeply obligated by the faith in our work which was demonstrated by the fund-raising campaign. We have interpreted the donations, especially that of Equity, as an instruction to continue our battle." But Fay continued his accusations, backed by all the extremist and "lunatic-fringe" people who believed as he did. He reiterated his attacks at an Equity membership meeting.

Eva and I began to receive abusive postcards, the penciled original message inked over in various crazy-looking capitals. I have kept one, addressed to Eva:

Protest meeting being arranged by *EQUITY MEMBERSHIP*. You better *RETURN* that $5,000 or want to be investigated by F.B.I.? All-American Comm. See newspapers.

I thought the FBI would be wasting its time, since Eva is just about the most nonpolitical creature I have ever known. I used to tell her that she had never wanted to vote for anyone but Napoleon. But she wrote to Fay, very politely protesting his statements about Equity and the A.R.T. She continued:

But you, dear Frank, who have been chasing imaginary rabbits (both on and off the stage) for a considerable length of time, must surely be in a position to put this whole matter right in a moment—since it seems to cause you so much concern. You have only to write a check for the amount you, as manager of the Frank Fay Vaudeville Show, owe me for my services as an actress, and I will instantly make it over to Equity. Don't you think that would be an excellent way to settle the whole matter? . . . I look forward to hearing from you very soon. . . .

I need hardly add that she didn't.

The climax to this sort of furious folly came a little while later when the Experimental Theatre was in danger of extinction. It was being carried on by ANTA's efforts, but had been Equity's child in the beginning. Also, the Council had recently discovered, to its surprise, the handsome sum of half a million dollars, cautiously kept in a current bank account, as safe and useless as if it had been hidden in a sock under the floorboards. I felt compelled to ask for a little of it on behalf of the ET. To disarm suspicion of some hidden personal gain, I proffered simultaneous resignations to Equity, ANTA and the ET Board. None of them was accepted, the Experimental Theatre was not saved, and by some mysterious Fay-alchemy I came to be regarded as not only a Communist but a crook.

During these years it happened that my two chief guilt-by-association ties were dissolved. The National Society for Soviet-American Friendship perished, predictably, in the cold winds of the cold war that followed the shooting one. The fellowship of artists in the pursuit of a common ideal still seems to me as valid as the fellowship of astronauts, which is becoming increasingly recognized. And it has yet to be proved that the world can, in fact, survive without some form of Soviet-American friendship. My only regret in this connection is that we have never yet produced, or at least been able to exhibit to other countries, theatre companies fine enough to stand comparison with their own national theatres.

The Joint Anti-Fascist Committee continued to make its Refugee appeals; but it seemed to me that the emphasis was subtly shifting from the humanitarian to the political and I ceased to have any connection with it. In 1951, when I saw my name still lying around its letter-head, I wrote stating very explicitly the reasons for my withdrawal. Ironically enough, at exactly this time the Supreme Court ordered that its name should be stricken from the Attorney General's list of supposedly "subversive" organizations, for lack of evidence entitling him to put it there. This was also the case with the Soviet-American Friendship society.

But by this time such fine distinctions had become completely unimportant. Suspicions and accusations began to fill the air like smog. The years of loyalty oaths were upon us. I think the entertainment industry unions adopted them reluctantly and defensively, but they did adopt them. I had a certain admiration for those who refused to sign them, since I did not and do not believe that anyone's freedom of political action should be dictated, or his freedom of conscience delimited, either by his labor union or his employer, but only on the highest level, by law. If Communism was illegal, Communists became punishable under due process of law; and this seemed to me to be the only valid method of judgment or punishment. Sir Thomas More, as I remember, stated much the same case rather memorably.

For myself, I signed them, because I am by nature a truth-teller. But I believe now that more of us should have refused to play with these pusillanimous and meaningless "oaths." If I had really been a Communist, I should, naturally, have signed without the slightest hesitation. To do otherwise would simply have drawn attention to something which I needed absolutely to conceal. I think only non-Communists had the courage not to sign.

Equity at first tried to save a little face by asking its councilors simply to declare that they were "not members of the Communist or Fascist parties." (But by this time nobody gave a damn about the Fascists.) As I remember, all of us signed. Later we had to declare that we were not members "of any parties, organizations or groups which have adopted resolutions or platforms presently in force declared by the Council of this Association to be inimical to and conflicting with the best interests of this Association and its legitimate purposes . . ." and more "to the same defect." Verbose, confused, ignominious and capable of being used to the most dangerous and repressive purposes. The other unions went through much the same degrading processes. Quite possibly the newly-formed radio-and-TV union, AFTRA, hit the all-time low, as late as 1955, with the following resolution, passed unanimously by the National Board and submitted to a referendum of the membership:

NOW THEREFORE BE IT RESOLVED, that the following rule is hereby adopted. . . .

If any member of AFTRA is asked by a duly constituted Committee of the Senate or House of Representatives of the United States, whether or not he is or ever has been a member of the Communist Party, and said member fails or refuses to answer that question, said member shall be subject to the charge that he is guilty of conduct prejudicial to the welfare of AFTRA. The accused may be investigated and the charges may be heard by the Board of the Local of which he is a member. The Local Board may, in its discretion, fine, censure, suspend or expel the accused from membership, in accordance with the constitution of the Local, subject to such appeals as are provided in the Local and National Constitution.

Had we known, in September 1947, what lay ahead of us, we might have had the sense to throw out that cozy little question as to whether or not we had been Fascists. For the logical AFTRA consequence consigns to the winds the Fifth Amendment, the Constitution of the United States and all due processes of law.

(In 1971, while I was writing this book, I checked into the history of this resolution. The AFTRA voting membership is estimated to have been at about 15,000 in the spring of 1955. Of these, just under 4,000 voted for the resolution; just under 1,000 voted against it. The rest were that famous "silent majority" whose apathy, ignorance or timidity cause most of the tragedies of the human race. I feel sure that of the thousands of new members who have joined AFTRA since that date, few are aware that the resolution in question is still a part of the by-laws of their Association. It has never been repealed.)

In 1949 there was some talk of nominating me for the presidency of Equity; but I withdrew my candidature, not because I was too modest to accept the office, but because I knew my candidature would be divisive by reason of the Red fog in the air. By 1950 the heat was well and truly on, though most of it was still turned toward Hollywood, where the Un-American Activities Committee had been busily at work for some three years, branding as "subversive" or "Communist Front" such innocent-sounding groups as the League of Women Shoppers. The big Hollywood producers formed their own organizations dedicated to the patriotic purpose of rooting out Communists. Writers and directors were the first to bear the brunt of the attack. People were peremptorily told to clear themselves of accusations never formally made; contracts were dropped; names disappeared from credit lists; doors were shut in many well-known faces.

In the summer of 1950 a group of former FBI agents published a booklet called *Red Channels,* which was publicly and widely sold. Its target was Broadway and, even more, the radio industry (though the Milk Consumers' Protective Committee got into the act too). There were some fifty pages of "listed" organizations and about a hundred and fifty pages of the names of people who had been associated with them. "Much of the data," said the *Times,* "consisted of press clippings or excerpts from the House Committee reports . . . the publishers of *Red Channels* subsequently acknowledged that they had made no effort to check the accuracy of the data or to give the accused persons a chance to offer their version of events." The results were devastating. Jack Gould, in the *Times* of April 22, 1951, courageously exposed them:

> In radio and television there is a new type of displaced person— artists, writers, announcers and directors who, without hearing, without publicity and without much public interest, effectively are being deprived of their opportunity to make a living. They are living in the never-never-land of today's hysteria, damned if they do anything, damned if they don't. . . .

> Essentially, the story is the unpublicized sequel to the now-celebrated case of Jean Muir, the actress, who was peremptorily dismissed from the cast of "The Aldrich Family". . . . More distressingly, it is the saga of how commercial expediency . . . has played directly into the hands of the foes of democracy, Communist and Fascist alike. . . .

> *Red Channels* in effect became the Bible of assorted groups opposed to Communism. As a star listed in the book was announced for a forthcoming program, the sponsor and the network were promptly deluged with protests. The first victim of any prominence was Miss Muir, who flatly denied any pro-Red affiliations but was removed by her sponsor, the General Foods Corporation, on the grounds that she had become a "controversial personality" who might adversely affect the sale of the concern's products. Ultimately, General Foods decided not to apply its policy of "controversiality" to other persons listed in *Red Channels.* The controversy dropped from public attention.

> But what actually happened is that the blacklist merely has gone underground and . . . it is just much harder to do anything about. . . .

> The way the policy operates now is this: the sponsor or advertising agency simply does not hire a person listed in *Red Channels* or does not renew a contract upon its expiration. Any number of perfectly

normal excuses—a change of cast, etc.—suffice. The individual is just out of a job. . . .

The vicious "controversiality" policy in effect has circumvented all the traditional safeguards of due process and fair hearing. The person named in *Red Channels* is "controversial" per se; his innocence or guilt is now beside the point so far as many, if not most, prospective employers are concerned. . . . His basic and fundamental rights have disappeared into thin air.

Mr. Gould went on to describe a proposal whereby the radio artists' Federation might hope to defend its members. How far that eventually got is illustrated by the AFTRA resolution quoted above.

My lawyer, Louis Nizer, he who had guided my bus and truck safely through the jungle at Natchitoches, had already agreed with me that there was no point in making a fuss about *Red Channels,* for the reasons stated. Even if I could disprove all the affiliations ascribed to me, or prove the innocence of my intentions, or even that I had been legally "damaged" by demonstrable loss of employment, which I thought I could have done, it still wouldn't have got me anywhere. On the day following the Gould article, I was writing to Louis:

> Is there any means of getting well and truly "investigated" and clearing the air once and for all? . . . [This turned out to be an incredibly babyish notion.] How do we disenfranchised citizens ever get out of this net? or are we driven into an ivory tower whether we like it or not? I am not speaking of "gainful employment", though our situation there is, God knows, precarious enough. If the Un-American Committee gets to thinking the "theatre", apart from Radio and Hollywood, important enough to investigate, I shall surely be on their list. But are all of us to be left in a kind of suspicious limbo for the rest of our active lives? My guess [it was correct] is that things will get worse, not better during the coming years. What, Citizen Nizer, are we to do?

The theatre was still comparatively free, and I personally was not deeply concerned in the radio field. I was disturbed and distressed by a quite different occurrence. There was to be a UNESCO conference in Paris at which the American contingent was to include one delegate representing all the theatre unions. I was unanimously chosen and my name forwarded to the State Department by William Green of the AF of L. There came a guarded reply that the Passport Division might not clear my passport. I was not able to make contact with the source of the information. I dug out my extinct British passport and looked at it thoughtfully. I asked the British authorities whether, by virtue of my dual nationality, I could, at a pinch, get another one and was told I could. During the ensuing years, when all sorts of unaccused persons had their passports removed from them, this became a comfort.

Despite the apparent immunity of the theatre, it was later than I thought. On the day of my letter to Nizer, the *New York Times* carried an article about Larry Adler and Paul Draper. Back in 1948 they had brought a libel suit against a Greenwich woman who had accused them of being Communists. The ensuing trial cost them $75,000 and ended in a hung jury. But the result was not important; the publicity was everything. They had instantly lost all possibility of getting work in America. They went to Britain, Europe and Israel. Mr. Adler was quoted as saying, "There is one good thing. I have been able to keep playing." These two were early theatre examples of the great brain drain which had already started in Hollywood. Brilliant men like Carl Foreman and Joseph Losey went into exile, never accused specifically, far less heard. They did not return until years later, after they had made triumphant movies in Europe that should have been made in the United States. Sometimes they did not return at all.

During the merry month of May 1951, *Variety* announced that the Un-American Activities Committee was "getting ready to switch its emphasis from Hollywood to Broadway" and "investigators were already working the Big Town for information." They were accustomed to getting it. The territory was not so heavily spotlighted as the West Coast, but it was fruitful; especially from the years of the early Thirties. These became the happy hunting ground of the Committee.

Then, as now, "the young" had hated, despised and been appalled by the "system" which had so blatantly plunged them into chaos. They were "for" the workers and "against" the capitalist bosses. Theatre was one of their weapons. Among the Workers' Theatre groups were some undoubted Communists; but the true Marxist believers were maddened by the individualism, romanticism and lack of discipline of the rest; also they were often extremely amateur in their professional jobs. Talent attracts talent, and the Group which emerged from the ruck found a playwright with a clarion call in

Clifford Odets, actors and directors like Elia Kazan and Harold Clurman, and a Messiah, not in Karl Marx but in Konstantin Stanislavsky. Nevertheless, they were patently pro-Russian, lively with social conscience, and the years of their glory had acquired very sinister overtones by 1951. Many of them had probably attended a Party meeting or two, some had even, briefly, "carried a card"; it was extremely hard for any of them to prove they had never had coffee with a Communist twenty years before the investigation.

Some, like John Garfield, had begun to attract the Committee's attention in Hollywood. Others were "named" by their "cooperative" former colleagues, like Elia Kazan. Had I been in New York in the Thirties, I should undoubtedly have been mixed up in all this; but by the time I got there the Group had been fractured by prosperity, individual success and political common-sense. Issues had been resolved or burned out; the Party cards, such as there were, had long been thrown away. But this ancient history served as a springboard; the *Red Channels* material was something else again.

In mid-May the Committee summoned three witnesses, Budd Schulberg and Frank Tuttle from Hollywood, and also José Ferrer. "Tuttle and Schulberg," ran the *Variety* report, "admitted being ex-Reds and came through with lists of those whom they had known in the party. Tuttle's list was the longest yet given to the Committee by any witness." They were patted on the back and sent home to Hollywood, where, presumably, they lived happy ever after. "Representative Francis Walter (D.Pa.) said he hoped the studios would not bar from employment those who cooperated with the probe, such as done by Tuttle." (O morality! O grammar!)

Joe Ferrer would not admit to being what he hadn't been and received in consequence "a stiff going-over." "Members told him they could not believe he knew as little of the subject as he claimed he did. Ferrer fought back constantly. They sent him away and told him to think some more, and especially about the names of those through whom "his assistance had been secured." Recalled, and under pressure, he dredged up four: the two secretaries of the Joint Anti-Fascist Refugee Committee (whose names were emblazoned on its every letter-head), Eddie Choate and me.

Why he picked on us I have no idea. Perhaps because the smear on Eddie was patently ridiculous—all he had done was to sign a letter protesting against literary censorship. Perhaps there had to be someone a little more plausible; and Joe was quite correct; I had in fact asked him to speak at a Refugee Committee luncheon—he and my mother; they both did. Later, when I studied the transcript of his questioning, I began to understand a little better. We were in almost identically the same leaky old boat. The things of which he was supposedly "guilty" almost all applied to me too. They read like a black comedy.

He had had good notices in the *Daily Worker* (he hastened to vindicate himself by producing some bad ones). He had voted for Benjamin Davis as candidate for the New York City Council (Davis was black, had advocated a scheme for new types of theatre in New York and ran on no party ticket; Joe claimed not to have known he was a Communist). He had in some vague way endorsed or cheered on a May Day celebration—probably having, like me, old European notions about May Day, of Arthurian antiquity. He had contributed to or supported such suspect bodies as the Veterans Against Discrimination, the Civil Rights Congress, the Committee of the Arts, Sciences and Professions, the Anticensorship Committee, the Artists' Front to Win the War (a meeting at Carnegie Hall urging the opening of a Second Front during the siege of Stalingrad). He had signed protests against the Wood-Rankin Committee and the Mundt-Nixon Bill; and, though not a member of the Equity Council, he had vocally condemned Frank Fay. There was a lot about Fay and the "Kangaroo Court" which had censured him. There was also a good deal about Paul Robeson.

Most of this I did not know until later. But the papers carried the names he had used, and I knew it wouldn't be long now. Surprisingly, nothing happened—to me, I mean. Plenty happened to plenty of other people, sometimes with a big splash, sometimes with a soundless slithering away into the dark, oily waters. Joe Ferrer had been dismissed with a severe caution and had done a little public self-castigation. His studio then bravely carried on with the movie starring his name in which they had already made a considerable investment. Meanwhile, on the political scene, a star was waiting in the wings who was to press a button and hit, perhaps quite unexpectedly, a jackpot. His name was Joseph R. McCarthy, from Wisconsin.

In the spring of 1951 I was planning a production of *Saint Joan* with Eddie Choate and the Theatre Guild. We were to use the costumes and some of the scenery from my Woodstock production and several of its actors. Uta Hagen had agreed to play Joan. She was, of course, a *Red Channels* graduate. The production was to be a part of the Guild subscription series, and they were to provide the backing. Evidently the subscribers became alarmed. I find this letter among my papers, addressed to Lawrence Langner:

Look, Lawrence dear,

On the subject of the letters you are receiving about Uta and me and *St. Joan.* I cannot answer for Uta but only for myself. . . . You are not buying from me my race (which happens to be Irish, Jewish and Anglo-Saxon), my religion (which happens to be a daily and active faith in God not attached to any organised Church), my voting affiliations (which have crossed the Republican and Democratic party lines in what used to be a system of "secret" ballot), my opinions of Hindemith, Saroyan or Picasso, nor my predilections as between the Giants and the Dodgers. You, and your subscribers, are buying my ability to direct *St. Joan.* They have no right whatever to make any further enquiry and you have no right to require any further answer of me.

If you depart from this position, in regard to either Uta or myself, you are, in my opinion, taking the first step on the slippery downward slope which will eventually lead you to the worst follies, the scared ineffectualities, of Hollywood and radio. I will stand on the record— on the Bible saying of "By their fruits ye shall know them." The fruits of my fifteen years of work in the American theatre . . . are perfectly well known to you. It has been, consciously, a question on my part of "service". You know this, and you can say it if you want to. I won't.

Nor will I go into some ridiculous deal about how many speeches I made for the Red Cross or for Treasury Bonds, or how many times I tendered my services to the U.S.O. and so forth. I could do all these things and still be a Communist. I have had occasions in various official capacities to take the non-Communist oath. . . . I have done so, and have not perjured myself. If any of your correspondents care to accuse me publicly of being a Communist I will, of course, sue them under the laws of the State of New York. That is no business of yours. You have hired me to direct *St. Joan.* This happens to be a play about God. I happen to believe in God. If I didn't I couldn't direct the play. I further believe in what Shaw states as the theme of the play: "the protest of the individual soul against the interference of anyone . . . between the private man and his God". If you don't believe in

258

this, don't do the play. If you do, don't ask me to excuse myself to half a dozen Theatre Guild subscribers. You can't have it both ways.

Love . . .

Brave words, if a little on the pompous side. We did the play. There was no trouble—at least, not on the political front (we had others by the bushel and the production fell short of my hopes). I am inclined to think that its mediocre success was due to its own short-comings rather than to any undercover boycott of Uta and me. This was the kind of thing you couldn't ever tell, the unresolved shadow-boxing.

In October, Mady Christians died. She was fifty-one. I wrote the following letter to the *New York Times:*

> Mady Christians was always in her life a preventer of strife, never the cause of it. I do not think she would have wanted the position to be reversed now.
>
> Her death was unquestionably precipitated by the horrible fear of being denied the means of earning her living and by the shock of the recent and brutal evidence of this which she had suffered. She was never accused of anything. Those responsible never, I am sure, thought about her as a person. She was "on a list" and that was enough; she was accordingly refused employment. Whether or not this is a defensible procedure is a question which every man must settle with his own conscience and his own sense of God. Upon each answer the pattern of our society depends.
>
> For Mady Christians herself a last reiteration is important: no one who knew her either personally or professionally, no one who had taken the smallest trouble to examine her background, history, public and private record, could even for one moment have supposed her to be "subversive", "dangerous" or "undesirable" in any way whatever. She was deeply in love with her country, conscious of her responsibilities towards it and concerned for its welfare. She was a fine actress of great gifts which she devoted to the service of her profession and its members. She was a warm-hearted human being who always held out a helping hand to anyone who needed it. It is thus that she would want to be, should be and will be remembered.

In May 1952 John Garfield died, at the age of thirty-nine. He had had a bitter time at the hands of Senator McCarthy's Committee and emerged to find himself without a job, subject to all sorts of subtle, or not so subtle, forms of suspicion, his telephone tapped, "blind" items in the press insinuating that he was to be indicted for perjury. He was a fine young actor, and a loss to the theatre.

Not everybody caught the black death. Suspicion was countered by personal loyalties, good faith and healthy skepticism. I received some questioning letters from people who were trying to make a fair survey of the effect *Red Channels* had had on the entertainment industries. I wrote to one of them:

Your questions are not altogether easy to answer. . . .

1) *Red Channels* has certainly affected my professional life, but not, so far as I can judge, my personal one—except for the general atmosphere of caution which surrounds almost all free discussion of public problems these days. I have quite definitely been debarred from two important radio and television long-term jobs. . . . However, my employment has never been in the radio, television or screen field to any great extent, and in the theatre I have no direct evidence that I have been excluded from jobs. . . .

2) It is my impression that there is a growing tendency to revolt against the whole of the *Red Channels* set of taboos and that the fear and consequent repressive action is centered at the top financial level— sponsors, big agencies, backers, etc. This has not yet lessened, I think. But there are many indications that everyone else would be glad to be rid of the whole mess and that only a small—but very vocal—section of the public cares.

3) No, I have found no way at all of combating these allegations nor do I see any in the present climate of thinking . . . no amount of explanation, however valid and convincing . . . appears sufficient to have any practical effect. The people concerned may believe completely that there is nothing blameworthy in your record, but they do not dare to act on that belief. It is my feeling that time, patience and the ultimate re-assertion of the basic good sense of the American people will finally cause the furore to subside for lack of fuel. . . .

5) It is my personal view that . . . the dangers of having public opinion act in the place of law to circumscribe a man's life and deprive him of his livelihood are only too apparent and have historically been proved, over and over again, perverted, disastrous and usually foolish in the long perspective.

It is an illumination of the times and (a poor one) of myself that I gave my correspondent permission to quote these opinions but preferred that he did not name their source.

If it was true then that my personal life was unaffected, it did not remain so. Your friends began to divide into two groups—those who grasped your hand warmly and seemed a little over solicitous, and those who were polite but a trifle evasive and had that "no-smoke-without-fire" look in their eyes. Once, when I talked of renting my apartment while I was away in Europe, I was seriously advised to go over my books and lock up or get rid of things like John Reed's *Ten Days That Shook the World*. My letters to my mother from Russia in 1935 had best, my friends told me, be burned. Yes, really.

The optimistic views expressed in the letter quoted above were, of course, eventually vindicated; but the interim was longer and darker than I had thought. Times were getting worse, not better. It was certainly not coincidental that during 1952 I had no theatre work. I did some lecturing, and for several months I was in Europe in a tiny cottage I had acquired in the South of France. I didn't bother very much. I had bought a play in Paris, called *Sur la Terre comme au Ciel*. Eva Le Gallienne agreed to do a translation of it, and when I came home I set up plans for its production under the, presumably, nonsuspect auspices of Walter P. Chrysler, Jr. I continued to be surprised that none of the "investigators" had yet got at me. I never supposed I would be immune forever. I wasn't.

In the spring of 1953 I was asked by Lawrence Langner to devise a program of scenes from Shakespeare. Half a dozen stars were to play in it, for nominal salaries, to help raise money for the projected Shakespeare Theatre at Stratford, Conn. I put the script together, directed it and served as Narrator and general mortar between the bricks. We went on a short tour which was to finish in May, with two weeks in Washington. I was then going back to my little cottage at La Colle-sur-Loup. By this time my passport had expired. I had applied for a new one. It didn't come. I wrote and asked why. The day before we got to Washington I was notified that the application had been refused.

This shocked me profoundly. It shouldn't have, because it was so easily foreseeable, but it did. I found it very peculiar to come onto the stage of the National Theatre in Washington, exuding confidence and charm, godmothering a distinguished show and appealing to a distinguished audience for funds to aid a national "cultural" project, while something was ticking away at the back of my skull saying: "Don't listen to me, ladies and gentlemen. I'm a dangerous character. I'm not allowed out. I'm un-American."

Faye Emerson was in the cast. She helped my morale enormously. She told me that while she was married to Elliott Roosevelt they had been "investigated" six or seven times during a couple of years. She cheered me up with all the stories current among her friends on the Washington press in mockery or defiance of the investigating committees. She said to me, "Ring up the Passport Office. Ask to see Ruth Shipley. Now. Yourself. While you are here." Mrs. Shipley was the head of the Passport Division. The climate of the times had made this a position of tremendous power which she wielded, said Faye, with remarkable understanding. I got an appointment to see her.

Of course I was in communication with Louis Nizer. But without an accusation he could not prepare a defense. He told me simply to answer any questions they put to me and hope for the best. Mrs. Shipley saw me in the presence of a senior member of the Passport Office legal staff. He carried a fat folder of documents. They asked me pretty much what I had expected, the *Red Channels* stuff, as well as questioning me on a number of minor matters dating from as long as ten years back, of which I had little or no recollection. I had to answer everything from memory. It was exhaustive and exhausting. Finally, they asked me to write out a statement, then and there, summarizing my life story as I had given it to them. I prayed that I wouldn't "misremember anything" as the children say, or put in anything which Louis would tell me had been "ill-advised." Mrs. Shipley read it. "Oh, yes," she said, wearily but not sternly, "I know. You're a joiner." I admitted rather sheepishly that I supposed I was. They gave me one of the usual "oaths" to sign.

Two or three days later I left Washington. I had a new passport. I went back to New York with a tremendous load off my heart. I walked into my apartment, where some mail awaited me. A telegram was lying on a little table by itself. I opened it. It directed me to be in the Senate Office Building on Monday, May 25, at 2:30 p.m. to appear at a private hearing of the Senate Subcommittee on Investigations. It was signed "Joseph R. McCarthy."

The following morning I was knocking on Louis Nizer's door before the office was open. He assigned to me an extremely able member of his staff, Sidney Davis. We went round the whole mulberry bush. The passport examination had, in fact, been a valuable dress rehearsal for what I could expect. I was shown the testimony of several other witnesses, people whom I knew, including Ferrer.

Some were abject, some defiant, some canny; but they didn't solve my problem. For me, as for them, it was insoluble. The alternatives were limited and all of them undesirable.

You could plainly refuse to answer questions, and become liable to imprisonment for "contempt of court." You could tell all, beat your breast, give as many other names as you could think of, be patted on the back as a cooperative witness and sent home, presumably re-employable. Neither of these alternatives was open to me, since I had nothing to tell or refuse to tell. There was the Fifth Amendment, which enabled a witness to refuse to answer questions when the replies might prove self-incriminating. Many witnesses had used it, not always to protect themselves but to protect the other people whose names would inevitably be dragged into the answers, however innocently. To "plead the Fifth Amendment" was widely held to be an admission of guilt. It might get you off the legal hook, but in every other way you were effectually self-condemned. There was also something which came to be known as "the diminished Fifth," when you agreed to answer all questions concerning yourself but not when they involved other people. This was morally OK but legally dubious. It was no real protection; for names were the crux of the matter.

We all agreed that I couldn't and wouldn't plead the Fifth Amendment. Apart from everything else, I had the obstinate feeling that if the law empowered Congressional Committees to ask you these questions, it also told you to answer them. I thought it dubious law and evilly abused. But it stood, until we managed to change it. There remained the names. Who was present? Who asked you to join? Who was on the platform? Who? Who? Who? Some had divulged, others evaded. I knew very well that Paul Robeson's name, for instance, would crop up. There was nothing I could tell them about Paul which he himself had not widely publicized long before. But there were others as "innocent" as I, but also as vulnerable. If I mentioned their names, they would certainly be subpoenaed, and probably suffer serious damage. Nothing I could read or discover got me off the horns of this dilemma. I decided I would try for the "diminished Fifth" and pray for the best.

The warning which was repeatedly impressed on me was never to say "No." "Did you attend such-and-such a meeting?" "I cannot remember doing so." "Did you give an interview to this or that paper?" "Not so far as I can recall." "Did you subscribe to Cause A or Fund B?" "To the best of my recollection, no." But never "No." Two witnesses could easily be produced to say yes, you did or yes, you had and a suit for perjury was in order. Under the reign of Roy Cohn as counsel for the McCarthy Committee it was well known that "vulnerable" people, especially government employees, were intimidated into accepting the role of informer, supplying fabricated information in return for immunity.

At Nizer's suggestion I drew up a statement to deposit with the Committee, having had an opportunity to verify the information I had already given to the Passport Office. Rereading it, I find it a little self-righteous and rather too explanatory. I had dredged up a list of thirty-one absolutely blameless charities to which I was a more or less regular subscriber and fifteen pure-as-snow organizations for which I had worked. All of these statements were perfectly true, but I felt degraded by having been reduced to making them.

It was agreed that Sid Davis would go with me to the hearing. The witness's lawyer was not allowed to interfere or raise objections or tangles with Roy Cohn, but he could kick his client under the table as a warning gesture. We congratulated each other that this was to be a private hearing, at the Senate Office Building, which was not much frequented by the press. The Committee members were McCarthy, Karl Mundt of North Dakota and Everett Dirksen of Illinois (the Republican majority); Stuart Symington (Missouri) and Henry Jackson (Washington) for the Democrats. It was supposed to be a closed session with no press release. None of us put much faith in that. We were right. The day before I went to Washington, Walter Winchell, that champion of liberty, released the news that Aaron Copland and I had been called before the Committee. It had been carefully "leaked" to him.

That same night Sid Davis called me, sounding a little worried. He said he was going to Washington early "to prepare things." He asked was I all right, and I said yes. And so I was, up to a point. It was all extremely unpleasant and would certainly have damaging results; but I went with a clear conscience and the child-like conviction that "the truth would set me free." I put in my wallet a little piece of paper on which was written: "Surely my labour is with the Lord and my work with my God. Isaiah."

I flew to Washington alone and met Sid Davis at the Statler Hotel. He told me that he had got in touch with the two Democrat Senators. They had never been called to the hearing and had not known there was to be one. I should have been left to McCarthy and his colleagues—not to mention Roy Cohn—without any dissentient voice. I was shaken, but not dismayed, since the danger had been averted. Sid impressed on me his last instructions: say as little as you can, never elaborate, never, *never* say "No."

We went to the Senate Office Building. There we were told that the meeting had been transferred to the Senate Building itself, so that the Senators would be available to vote on a bill which was at that moment being debated. They had been given the use of the Secretary of the Senate's office. This proved to be at the end of the long corridor which runs behind the Senate Chamber and has long windows along its outer side. My memory is that they were recessed; but this may be just because I was trying to retreat into them.

The corridor was lively with people, including many press correspondents and reporters. I had been playing in Washington only days before and was therefore recognizable. It was a kind of publicity I did not, frankly, care for. I pulled my hat (we still wore them) well down over the "audience" side of my face and glared intently out at the view. I have no idea what it was—vaguely green, I think. Sid Davis gallantly stood between me and the passers-by and parried passing questions from people who knew him. We waited for an hour and a half.

It seemed that the Committee was occupied with some subversive persons who were accused of trading in painted feathers and bird's-nest soup with Communist China. (I am not inventing this.) My nerves became stretched very tightly indeed. At last, a small, rather shabby and very battered-looking couple emerged from the "office" and we were ushered in. My impression is of rather grandiose wood paneling and gilt (not guilt) ornamentation; a long, heavy table; Senator McCarthy facing me, with Roy Cohn on his left, both looking very type-cast; on his right, Senator Karl Mundt, toad-like, whose horribly repressive Bill (co-sponsored by Nixon) I had opposed and knew he must know I had; me at the near end of the table, with Symington on my left and Sid Davis on my right. Henry Jackson next to Cohn; the remaining Republican Senator next to him. I must have raised my right hand and sworn something. We sat down.

The questions, from Roy Cohn, Passport Office type, began. Pretty soon he said, "Is it not a fact that you have been refused a passport?" I kicked Sid Davis and said "No" loud and clear. "You mean you have one?" "Yes. Would you like to see it?" (Mentally, I asked God to bless Ruth Shipley in all her works and ways, here and hereafter.) We proceeded; or went round. One question, I remember, was, had I given an interview to the *Daily Worker* in 1939 outside the St. James Theatre, New York? (Fourteen years ago—*Hamlet*—publicity for the show? Probably. Why not?) I said I didn't remember. "You did not give such an interview?" "I have no recollection of doing so." "You deny it, then?" (Oh, no . . . too easy . . . a couple of little clerks at the Department of Agriculture, teen-agers at the time, were waiting at the stage door to see Maurice Evans, and heard me. . . .) "I'm afraid I cannot recall it."

We got to the names. Had I been present at a luncheon organized by the Spanish Refugee Appeal on some date in 1945? Yes. Who else was there? About three hundred people. Who were the speakers? The chairman of the committee, José Ferrer (who'd already said so), my mother, Dame May Whitty. . . . I had been present, had I not, at a so-called cultural conference held by the Soviet-American Friendship Society? In 1944? Yes. "You were chairman of the Theatre Section?" "Yes." "Who else was there?" "Many people from all the arts fields." "What were the alleged objectives of this meeting?" I outlined them, managing to get in the fact that there was a similar society in London whose theatre chairman was Dame Edith Evans. "Please tell us about the others present in New York?" "We-ell . . . the chairman of the Music Section was Serge Koussevitsky." Nobody commented on my curious ability to remember only the names of those who had recently died, because at that moment bells rang and the Senators scurried off to vote. The stenographer came up and asked me how to spell the name of the man who had been one of the most famous symphonic conductors in the United States.

They came back. It went on. Had I been present at a dinner held by the National Soviet-American Friendship outfit—I think it was a victory celebration of some kind. Yes, I had. Who was there? We-ell . . . I sat between the Soviet Ambassador, Mr. Gromyko, and Mr. Thomas J. Watson, President of IBM. Even Senator McCarthy blinked. What had been said? I had said that I hoped we could send an American theatre company to play in Moscow after the war situations had settled; Mr. Gromyko had replied that he hoped so too. On again. The Joe Ferrer stuff. That Greek outfit. I truly didn't remember a thing about it. Very tough about May Day. Always Roy

Cohn cutting in on the answers: "Did you endorse that appeal?" "I'm inclined to think I did, but . . ." "Did you vote for Benjamin Davis?" "I supported his theatre plan but . . ." In spite of the helpful intervention, from time to time, of Symington and Jackson, Cohn was determined never to let me get past the "but." Mundt grunted in a sour way (a Mundt-grundt, I couldn't help a small grin to myself). McCarthy shot a question or two.

At last it came, the no-evasion name. "I believe you were the director of a production of *Othello* in 1944 with Paul Robeson." "Yes." (Now what do we do?) At this point Symington yawned. He addressed the chairman. He said that he saw no point at all in Mr. Cohn's questioning; he thought a great deal of everybody's time was being wasted; and that there seemed no reason whatever for further investigation of Miss Webster, whom he then exculpated in words which I cannot remember because of the relief thundering in my ears. Senator Jackson vigorously concurred. Mundt grundted. McCarthy gave a bark or two and took a vote to dismiss the witness. No one dissented. It was perhaps an hour and a half since we had come in.

Senator McCarthy told me they had decided I was an OK American after all and thank you very much. Everyone stood up and dispersed in various directions. Left alone, Senator McCarthy said I understood, did I not, that no blame attached to me on account of the investigation and that they were grateful for my testimony. I said I hoped Walter Winchell would get to hear this good news. McCarthy held out his hand. To my eternal regret, I took it.

As Sid Davis and I left the building, he seemed to me almost unduly elated. God knows, I was thankful to be out of the place, but, I reminded myself as my knees gradually stopped shaking, I had always known the truth would prevail. Sid said, "I think you're really off the hook now. I don't see how they *can* get after you again." I asked what he meant. He said, "I didn't tell you before because I thought it would upset you. But I happened to run into Roy Cohn at a cocktail party on Saturday. I spoke of you. He said, 'Oh, yes. Of course she'll plead the Fifth Amendment.' I said of course you wouldn't. He said, 'Well, in that case I'll produce two witnesses and we'll indict her for perjury.'" At this point a taxi passed, he flagged it down, gave me his blessing and sent me off to the airport. I went back to New York alone and arrived alone at my apartment. And *then,* then I got frightened.

I kept wondering whether I had slipped in a "no" somewhere in-advertently, whether I *had* given that interview to the *Daily Worker,* whether I *had* voted for Ben Davis etc etc. I convinced myself that it would be only too easy to put together a perjury accusation if any-one wanted to take the trouble, that it had been done dozens of times. I told myself not to be silly. They had bigger fish to fry, or burn. That it didn't matter anyway. "It's OK," I said, "go to jail like your betters. The hell with it." Bravado. I didn't want to go to jail. I conjured up images. Very vivid. My inescapable actor's mecha-nism began to function. I noted that one was cold, and one's nostrils stiffened, that the marrow of one's bones really did feel curiously soft.

I made two telephone calls. Each time I kept hearing subdued clicks and peculiar noises on the line. One of the people I talked to said several times, "I couldn't hear you. There seems to be something the matter with this line." I remembered that a night or two before there had been footsteps and noises on the flat roof of my top-floor apartment. Next day I called Louis Nizer. "Is it possible," I said, "that my telephone is tapped?" "Why not?" he answered cheerfully. "We know there are about 56,000 telephones unofficially tapped in New York City alone."

The following week I left for the South of France by a charming American boat called the *Constitution.* I hoped this was a good omen. But I felt sure that at the bottom, or top, of the gangplank I should see that heavily disguised, instantly recognizable figure in the unob-trusive suit and the felt hat. He would step forward and say "Pardon me" as he produced a card from his wallet or a badge from his lapel; and all that would be left would be to get my luggage back off the boat.

It didn't happen. Lehman Engel was the only person by the gang-plank. Flowers were in my cabin. Whistles blew. We moved out into the river. I have never, ever, been so relieved as I was to see the last of the Statue of Liberty.

To be afraid is a very humiliating experience. I do not mean the lightning second before the car crashes—I'd known that one—or the night before the operation. One copes with that. But to be afraid in spite of your mind, your reason, your convictions, despising what you fear, despising yourself for fearing it . . . that is a very evil thing. It takes a long time to forgive that—not to forgive the people who caused it, which isn't very difficult, but yourself for having yielded to it.

In my little stone cottage looking across the valley to the picture-postcard view of St. Paul-de-Vence I relaxed, wrote an article about Rudolf Bing, worked on the script of *Sur la Terre comme au Ciel,* now entitled *The Strong Are Lonely,* because nobody could think of a better way to avoid the Biblical quotation, and the Bible, as every-one knows, is "box office death." My cousin Jean came to stay with me and I drove her back through France, including Brittany which I had not known before. A different world. Back to New York.

The Strong Are Lonely was a beautiful play, wonderfully played by Victor Francen and Dennis King, designed by Rolf Gerard in what may have been the simplest and finest set he ever did, and quite well directed by me. We played two weeks in Philadelphia and came back to open in New York. On the day of the dress rehearsal Lehman Engel was taking an orchestra rehearsal in the basement while the crew went out to eat. The pit might not be occupied during the mandatory everybody-stop-and-eat hour. I sent for a cup of coffee and stayed to listen. Down the stairs came two of those heavily disguised, instantly recognizable types. They stood silently. I went over and asked what they wanted. The badge-showing took place. They had to talk to me. Now just now, I said; after the opening night. Obligingly, they said I might come to their office on Broadway. We made a date.

And there, "blow-me-down" as the English say, if we didn't start the whole routine over again. By this time, having nothing more to lose and having regained some perspective, I was both gay and sardonic. I said, "But we've had all this. My statement is on file at the Passport Office, didn't you know?" They alleged that they didn't. "Well, the whole investigation is on record in the files of Senator McCarthy's Committee. Have you looked?" They alleged that they hadn't. I said, well, you're supposed to know everything and be the guardians of our liberties. Go take a look and I'll be happy to fill in any missing bits; but don't let's play the same script over again. Oh, and don't forget to make a note of the bit where Senator Mc-Carthy said I was an OK American. I offered them a copy of the statement I had made to the Committee.

We fiddled around with it a bit. We arrived—you'd never guess —at names. One about which they asked me was that of the highly distinguished writer, artist and stage designer, Aline Bernstein. (They called her Alice Berkstine.) I asked them whether they knew that she was partially paralyzed, confined to a wheelchair and, it seemed, inevitably close to death. No, they didn't, but accepted that she was probably not very dangerous. There were others which seemed to me equally foolish. Obviously, by this time almost everybody in New York had been investigated except the statue of Father Duffy in Times Square.

At last they said they were satisfied; I was an OK American. The file was closed. I asked if the FBI would confirm this verdict to any potential employer or other interested party. They said no, they couldn't do that; it was classified information. But, they said, if you have any other friends who are in trouble, just tell them to come to us and tell us all about it. I asked what good that was supposed to do, and walked out. I went home and patted my passport.

The Strong Are Lonely flopped completely in New York, since the press, even beloved Brooks Atkinson, hadn't a notion as to what it was about. Another bit broke off my heart. Victor Francen, who had played it in Paris for a two-year run, went home a sadder and much bewildered man. Silence from the witch-hunters, vis-à-vis me. Also silence from all employers. I did some odds and ends, including, for next to nothing, a very good production of *Richard III* for and with José Ferrer. Some Hollywood columnists rumbled a little, but perhaps we were let off on the score of good works. The City Center of Music and Drama was a worthy cause, blessed by the City Fathers, though scantily supported. No "gainful employment" appeared.

My cousin Jean fell ill. I went to England only just in time to see her before she died; the last of my known Webster relatives, and the last of her father's famous theatre clan of the Broughs. I went to France again, to my little cottage. There I had a letter from a New York agent; it was an offer to direct the Shakespeare scenes in a movie about Edwin Booth, starring Richard Burton. I cabled back that everyone had better check on my blacklist status. They did. My agent wrote that her contact at Twentieth Century Fox felt "since he had the fullest admiration for you, that you should know that they did check on your clearance and were informed that you are 'still active in associations that are on the Attorney General's subversive list'. . . he felt you should know that this is evidently your status in Hollywood, so that if it is not correct you can clear it up on your return."

Oh, yes, well, couldn't I do that simple thing? In fact, I no longer belonged to anything except Equity, the Blue Cross and the Martha's Vineyard Community Services. I told them I thought they better offer the job to Eva Le Gallienne. Which they did. I wrote to poor Louis Nizer again, in some fury, and one of his colleagues replied as follows.

Sidney confirms the fact that the investigation of you by the FBI, as well as by the Senatorial committee is closed. He says, however, that the FBI does not issue letters of "clearance" particularly since its sole purpose is investigatory, and it must refrain from appraising, evaluating or basing conclusions upon the evidence obtained by it. He suggests that in view of the actual completion of the proceeding, it would be preferable not to write to the FBI (which has your file in its N.Y. office).

We do sympathize with your resentment against the continued, and totally unfounded, inferences which some individuals are drawing against you. X's statement is so incredible as to appear to be based upon a complete misunderstanding. If you have gotten any further information as to the source of the misunderstanding, and it appears to be official, please let us know. Otherwise a general inquiry would produce no results and be of no help.

It turned out to be the American Legion which had supplied Twentieth-Century Fox with its completely inaccurate information. But the source didn't matter, neither did the accuracy. Once on the blacklist, you stayed there. I was no longer frightened, but I was sick and tired of the whole business and strongly tempted not to come back. But my life, my work, my friends, my Martha's Vineyard roots were in America. I had a long lecture and recital tour booked for the fall, and the colleges, universities, women's clubs etc., for whom I was to play didn't seem to have consulted the American Legion about my appearances for them.

But there was still fear in the air—or on the air, as, in the spring of 1955, AFTRA so ringingly demonstrated. In September, Philip Loeb died. He had personal burdens which must have weighed heavily on him, but he was neither ill nor old. The root cause was the same malady from which he had suffered more severely than most. I did not know him personally very well, but we had been on the Equity Council together for ten years, Often laughing, sometimes disagreeing—even violently—but never with ill-will. I admired him as an actor, liked and respected him very highly as a man. The *New York Times,* bless it, again afforded me space. I wrote that the tributes paid to him by the Equity Council and others made "slightly bitter reading." The blacklist sickness, which had poisoned him as it had so many others was not, in his case,

> the whole of it, or even the worst of it. He was submerged by the wave of fear and mistrust which swept almost all of us. His motives and public actions were rendered suspect. Even in Equity which he had so belligerently and passionately served, he was besmirched and maligned. He was a man of courage, humour and outspoken integrity; all these things were sapped by the poisons of doubt and suspicion. His zest for service, his purpose in life, were destroyed, and so was he. We must all share in the responsibility of acquiescence.
>
> It is not enough to render him the posthumous tribute of words. We must resolve that never, so help us God, shall such things happen again. This is the only adequate memorial we can offer to the real Philip Loeb, who was unafraid, who laughed at threats and pretences and who fought for his fellow-men.

McCarthy himself had ceased to be a power after the army confrontations and the Senate's censure in 1954; but there were other vigilantes to take up the running. In radio and TV the persecution intensified to an unbelievable extent. One of the compilers of *Red Channels,* Vincent Hartnett, formed an organization called AWARE to "combat the communist conspiracy in entertainment communications." It issued a periodical bulletin in which suspect individuals were attacked and listed as "subversive."

The power behind it was a Syracuse supermarket proprietor named Laurence Johnson. He managed to intimidate program sponsors by threatening to exclude their products from his supermarket chains if the actors named by AWARE appeared on their programs. The sponsors intimidated the big agencies and between them they intimidated the networks. Not a single person, however unimportant, could appear on the air without clearance, and the clearance had to be paid for. At last, one of the sufferers, John Henry Faulk, had the courage to bring suit for libel and conspiracy against the vigilantes team. He also had the good fortune to get Louis Nizer to represent him.

It took six years to get the suit into court. The revelations of the power and pervasiveness of blacklisting were appalling to press and public alike; the jury awarded Faulk the unprecedented sum of $3½ million in compensatory and punitive damages. The amount was reduced on appeal; Johnson himself died just before the verdict. But the power of the blacklist was destroyed. Everyone thought the lesson had been learned. I sometimes wonder.

When light began to filter back into the entertainment world quite a few names were missing from the membership of the writer and performer unions. Some of the Hollywood people blasted their way back from exile or enforced anonymity; some actors struggled back onto the casting lists after longer or shorter periods of time; some stayed away, or went into other kinds of work; some sank without trace; some probably found that they were not "listed" by St. Peter.

To arrive at a fair verdict, or even a summary, of the era through which we had passed is beyond my scope and far beyond the retrospective allocation of praise or blame. Among the "accused" many were gullible or insufficiently watchful; and, undoubtedly, there was a hard core of political "activists." Among those who were frightened into postures of oppression were many just as gullible and probably a larger hard core who sought personal gain or political power behind the banners of a crusade. I believe that no one touched the blacklist, witch-hunt pitch, without being lessened and to some degree defiled; neither those who were injured by the lists, nor those who compiled them, nor those who used them nor those who went along with them. It was a miserable business from first to last; it did lasting damage to the United States and very few people emerged from it with any credit whatever; certainly I was not one of them —I mean, of course, in my own eyes.

Publicly, I seem to have remained respectable and even, as I "age," respected. In 1960 I was invited to do a job for the State Department, and apparently did it with credit and have done a couple since. I have done far less public work since that time; like many others, I am sure, I got cautious—probably too cautious and certainly too late. Professionally, I have no doubt that my so-called "career" was undermined, if it was not ostensibly broken. Personally, it had subtle side-effects, loosening some bonds and strengthening others. I got to know whom I'd like to be in a trench with and whom I'd just as soon not have on my side. All in all, my life did, very profoundly, change after those years, and in part as a result of them. There were other factors.

The American theatre was changing too, very rapidly, as I had always predicted it would. Broadway became almost uninhabitable for citizens of my sort of theatre, and the new professional companies away from New York were only just beginning. For many years it had been impossible to count on making a living in the "legitimate" theatre; probably the last to do so were such legendary figures as the Lunts and Katharine Cornell, lucky inhabitants of a doomed Valhalla. I had long said that none of the next generation would be able to do it; none have. Most of the stars transferred allegiance to the movies or the new young giant, television. The blacklist stopped that for me. It might not have, probably would not, if I had fought back into those fields; but I didn't really want to. They weren't "my thing." Many actors, especially the young ones, post blacklist, found a solace in Off-Broadway and a living in TV. I shifted my ground to other fields—the ones outside New York, whose worth I had so long and persistently advocated, and even across some oceans. I gave up the apartment on 12th Street where I had spent so many happy and fruitful years, though never my tiny fortress on Martha's Vineyard.

Broadway could no longer mean much to me (though I have done some shows there since, both plays and opera), not because I am growing old but because it has grown crustacean. I realized that there really is, in hard fact, a "world elsewhere," to which I still had a contribution to make. I was unimaginably lucky in that the current of my personal life, through this loosening of those professional bonds, brought me fourteen years of total happiness. But for the blacklist I might not have had the courage to accept my enfranchisement. I think it has also enabled me to see, and follow, different paths of service to what I still think of as "theatre."

It is the fashion in the early Seventies to despise "liberals" and liberalism, whether you are a Black Panther or Vice President of the United States. Liberals have always been mown down by extremists from either side in any and every revolution; but they have somehow managed to get up again. There is plenty of justification for despising the "liberals" of twenty years ago. But we are tougher than we look. We shall still be around when a lot of the shouting and the shooting and the burning to the right and left of us has gone with the wind.

Chapter Ten

About and Roundabout

The life of an itinerant lecturer is not a happy one. Retrospectively, with the tongue, or pen, of Emily Kimbrough it can be made to seem funny; there also clings to it, in my case, a slightly Pauline whiff of missionary zeal. In any case it is arduous. I made my first lecture tour in 1940 and have undergone these things periodically ever since. Through the later Fifties and Sixties I endured ten or twelve weeks almost every year; by this time I was giving recital-performances rather than lectures, which is even more exhausting. But throughout this whole period I find that the same themes recur, the same photographs of memory crop up again and again.

To look on the black side, here is a typical sentence in one of my letters: "I am sick of being tired, bored and frightened to death, in sequence and often simultaneously." On the other hand, there are the compensating flashes: a very small town in California—a performance of *The Brontës* to a scanty audience and under disagreeable circumstances—a young boy (ten or twelve) asked to see me; he just stood and looked; then he said in a hushed voice, "I never thought there could *be* anything like that. I could see a lot of people. And it was just you."

Or another instance where I was sharply reminded of a perspective which minor irritations tend to obscure. It was a Chicago Women's Club—a midday "short-order" version of my Shaw program to follow a Luncheon, which, of course, I had refused to attend—a mandatory act of self-preservation. These are conditions I detest, and my irritation was not lessened when I arrived—not a soul in sight to greet or guide me and a cataract of yackety-yak streaming down from somewhere upstairs. I wandered into what seemed a library, full of impressive, little-used books. I almost wrote "Miss Webster was here" and went away again. My eye fell on the contents of the glass case on which the Visitors' Book rested. It was a copy of the Kelmscott Chaucer, open at the sentence "The life so short, the craft so long to learn, the assay so sharp, so hard the conquering." Priorities and proportion returned. I gave a good performance.

Although the essence of this business has not changed, a lot of things have. I myself have completely changed what I do, but the audience, in its various and different categories, has not altered much; the same may be said of auditoriums. Accommodations, since the blessed arrival of the motel, are quite different. So is travel, since planes superseded trains, and this is a major fact or, almost a determining one.

During my first tour, at the behest of Mr. Colston Leigh, I worked out five different "talks"—on Shakespeare, on Acting, on Directing, on Women in the Theatre and a full-fledged history of the American stage called "The Theatre Comes to Main Street" (I might have subtitled it "And Goes Away Again"). This was a load of unnecessary labor. In transit through less demanding agencies I reduced the lectures to three; then I began to turn the Shakespeare lecture into a recital; I felt increasingly that I accomplished more by illustration than by precept. Also, I enjoyed it more. I gradually evolved a coherent shape with a line of development and called it "His Infinite Variety." A cockeyed college printer once set up the programs as "GUS UBFUBUTE VARUETY." Thereafter I noted it in my diary as "GUS."

The lectures on the theatre began to get more difficult in that I never could find a "third-act curtain." The majority of towns in which I spoke hadn't had a live professional show for years; and when I had finished "selling" the glories of theatre art, I could only finish, lamely, by saying it was too bad we didn't seem to have any, right now. I evolved two more recitals, one a set of excerpts from the plays (as well as odd bits from the letters and Prefaces) of George Bernard Shaw. The third and most recent was a kind of story-scrap-book about the Brontë sisters. I played it in London and New York as well as on television.

I find Shaw more tiring than Shakespeare, partly because of the sheer stretch of memory involved and the necessary speed. His torrents of adjectives must be vividly imagined and precisely delivered. They are so exactly placed that if you paraphrase or even transpose one of them you are instantly aware that something is wrong. His acrobatic debater's antics must be lucid and charged with force. Shakespeare will lend you wings. Shaw offers you a powerful machine, not easy to handle. As I trimmed and tailored these two recitals, I discovered that the scenes I picked must be for one main character, the others—one or more—being subordinated to "feeding" the protagonist. You cannot act and react at one and the same moment and the focus must be on and from one person. For this reason I threw out Rosalind-Orlando and the scene in the first act of *Arms and the Man* between Raina and Bluntschli. In this case, also, I found my young audiences completely bewildered; it was entirely beyond their ken that anyone could ever have found soldiers glamorous or war heroic. There was nothing for Shaw to satirize. On the other hand I found that the scene from *Mrs. Warren's Profession* between mother and daughter packed as much of a punch as if it had been written yesterday.

The Shaw and Shakespeare affairs are elastic-sided and can be stretched to two hours or compressed to forty minutes, though they do not make much sense that way. The Brontë anthology is an organic whole, carefully woven together. I find it the most delicate and therefore the most difficult, especially in large auditoriums. It is in some ways the most rewarding, but emotionally the most draining. It is also difficult to "sell." Outside Tulane University I once heard a young man read the poster title aloud to his companion. He added, "What are brontës?"

It is a very special business, this of one-man or -woman shows. It is not quite like acting—more like demonstrating. I feel some kinship with the old-time magic-lantern lecturers. "Here . . ." (click-click—the slide shifts) "is Katherine of Aragon," explain briefly and then go into the speech. The first bit is objective, the second as subjective as you can make it; but you have to interrupt yourself for a short "feed" speech from Wolsey, and then get back inside Katherine's head. The temptation is not *really* to go back—simply to show and not be. The transitions are subtle and they have to be instantaneous. It demands a technique peculiar to itself. You don't have to pretend to look the part. I don't, I hope, look very much like Falstaff; but I can make a picture of him for the audience. I wouldn't dare try it with Juliet; I have the curious and perhaps quite personal feeling that there would be more to contradict.

I do not use "costume," except for a scarf which almost drapes itself by now, to alter the picture a little. Once a student said to me, "I was just waiting for you to thread it through your ears." I wear what used to be known as a "picture dress." Nowadays all clothes are so picturesque that you can almost buy one in the ten-cent store. But I have an idea that if the audience is going to have to look at one person for a whole evening, the picture at least shouldn't be dull. Whatever image you select creates packing problems; and I have developed, over the years, what amounts to a trauma about packing; I should by now have reduced it to a fine art. Instead, it reduces me to a nervous wreck.

Once I am on the stage it becomes, for me, peopled. I know exactly where everybody else is and what they look like. As Charlotte Brontë, I am always aware of Emily, sitting in that chair on the other side of the table. I think I can "conjure" her for the audience too— I hope so. One of the hardest things I ever had to do was a television version of my Shaw program. A set had been devised which necessitated my putting all the other characters in unaccustomed places. I would turn, automatically, to look at Marchbanks, and find I was looking at Morell. It was unbelievably disconcerting.

Too much of this one-man-show business is not, I think, very good for an actor. He tends to become a puppeteer. Micheál Mac-Liammoir says he finds it easier to be on his own and do all the bad acting himself. Not me; I like company. Besides, the nervous concentration of this lonely performing is enormously tiring. Nevertheless, I prefer it to "lecturing." Theatre is something to *do,* not to pontificate about. The change in the type of material I use has also meant a change in the type of audiences I play to: more campuses, fewer luncheon clubs. With apologies to the hundreds of kindly Madam-Presidents, Program Chairwomen and gracious be-hatted ladies, only too anxious to feed me shrimp cocktails and chicken à la king, I do prefer the kids.

The greatest revolution which has taken place during my thirty years of "lecturing" activity has been in methods of travel. I am not a relaxed traveler. I do not turn up at the airport, station or bus stop a casual five minutes before "it" leaves, but about forty-five minutes too early. I am a worrier. I worry about getting the taxi or limousine to "it"; I worry about missing "it"; I worry about whether "it" will arrive on time at the place it's supposed to get me to; the plane frequently doesn't. If I'm driving a "hurt-yourself" car, I worry about having a blowout or losing my way or not finding the auditorium. All this adds up to four or five worry-days a week on the travel basis alone.

In the early days trains were, of course, the principal means of locomotion. I miss them, dear, noisy, reliable old things, interludes of peace where no one could get at you. I liked inserting myself at night into a roomette so small that you needed a can opener to get in or out of bed. I enjoyed the restaurant cars and the whistle-stops and the landscape proceeding past the window at a pace which made it visible and beautiful.

Of course trains seem more romantic in retrospect than they were at the time. Often I have had to leave from some tiny station, remote from any town, in the vastness of the Midwestern plains at three o'clock in the morning. I would huddle over a pot-bellied stove in the waiting room, generally the only passenger, thinking it impossible that a huge train should stop there just for me. At last, I would hear a far-off, repeated hooting, the most melancholy and the most reassuring sound in the world. I would stagger onto the platform loaded with luggage; the thunder and flame drew nearer, the juggernaut bore down upon me, slowed, stopped, huffing impatiently. At the extreme far end of the platform a pair of steps would be pushed out and a white-coated figure descend. Rescue.

Trains in the Middle West were usually splendid things. Not so the Eastern seaboard. Sometimes I would have to scramble onto some dismal milk train, still in evening dress, having been driven from a distant suburb of, say, Baltimore, to arrive in New York at 2:30 a.m., hungry, thirsty, deathly tired and looking indescribably sordid in full, begrimed make-up. As the war years deepened, it became impossible to travel through the bottlenecks of Boston, New York, Philadelphia, Washington. Wartime conditions jammed the trains with soldiers and the hotels with civilians, stripped the stations of porters and denuded the streets of taxis. The armed forces were hungry and you couldn't get into a diner; they were tired and slept crosswise on the seats with duffel bags under their heads. Schedules were chaotic. I would end up standing in a crowded coach on a train I had only achieved by taking the ferry to Hoboken. I gave it up.

In the Fifties train travel was very different, air travel having superseded it. I used it seldom. Surely American railroad depots are either the grandest or the most dismal places in the land. There is nothing to touch the dreary marble vastness of Philadelphia's 30th Street at 11:30 p.m., when the night train is an hour late and the last employee has gone home; except the dingy coziness of Stroudsburg, where you can wait undisturbed for a year or two, while occasional townsfolk drop by to use the facilities or pass the time of day. I was once forced, by adverse circumstance, to use the Lackawanna Railroad from Newark to this city, at night. I wrote:

The station was a desert. Ticket man aiming to be a "character"—large, sticking-plaster patch over one eye, shirt-sleeves, pants slipping down to his navel, laconic and incomprehensible; taxi-driver had to help me up long flight of stairs with bags. But when the train finally penetrated the dark desolation with mournful hoots, it turned out to be most comfortable, full of chrome and cushions. Had long conversation with sweet old conductor about the passing of the Railroads. He lives in Binghamton, has eleven children and was never able to eat Christmas dinner with his family till the youngest was two years old. . . .

Hotel room *minute,* with heat that wouldn't turn off, storm windows that wouldn't open, bathroom so small that you had to sit sideways, and all night long huge trucks roared past, stopped at the light intersection right outside, revved up their engines and started off again. A hellhole. . . . Performance continued in the same vein, with no-one to guide, meet or tell me anything. Beastly auditorium, beastly overhead lights, "assembly" period program, audience of muffin-faced morons as stony as mud. Tried to skip, to be gay, not too sophisticated and yet not talk down, and they *wouldn't* laugh and I loathed them and yelled at them at high speed for the required number of minutes and made them at least sit still and listen, but we parted with, I'm sure, mutual relief. And these are to be *teachers.* I should have thought total loss all round; but nice lady who volunteered to drive me to depot angrier with them than I, but said she thought "perhaps fifty" had taken something in.

If so, it was worth it. But I ended up in Hoboken very sour indeed. It was curious how often an entire segment—journey, hotel, show—turned out to be of a piece in either pleasure or horror. There was one from San Francisco via Kansas City to a small town in Mississippi: the train rocked itself almost off the tracks, flights got canceled and I found myself fifty-second on a waiting list; the hotel was next to the bus station and all buses started from under my window at 6 a.m.; the audience was all dressed up and wore white gloves (which for some reason I find off-putting); the president first sat on the stage with me—very disconcerting—and then walked off in the middle—more so—(it turned out he'd gone to chase away a stray dog)—and when I asked how I was to make my escape in the morning, the hotel manager obligingly called the railway depot and said, "Say, can you find out whether that little ol' train still operatin' jes' about same time she used to?"

Sometimes I drove, most often I flew. I must have missed more connections in Atlanta and covered more foot-miles in Chicago's O'Hare between Gate C4 and Gate G8 than any other "performer" I know. The smaller airlines are still subject to a high degree of personal eccentricity and my agent has a happy knack of getting me on a lunch-hour flight which doesn't serve lunch. I arrive too late to eat until after the show and then I'm too tired. The most exciting flight-catching occurs during October between the Eastern and Middle Western states. You never have the least idea whether you are on Eastern Standard Time, Central Standard Time, Central Daylight Time or Eastern Daylight Time; and often the airport operates on one kind of time and the town on another. But air travel has enabled everybody's agent to send them up and down and back and forth for hundreds of miles in every direction and there is no nonsense about booking dates in the same area in any logical sequence. I offered a prize once to anyone who could locate, without looking it up, the following three cities which I had to visit within a week: Alamosa, Chickasha and Milledgeville. The second is in Oklahoma and the third in Georgia; they were both old haunts of mine. The first is said to be in Colorado; but though I have been there, I still don't believe it exists. Nobody won my prize.

Sometimes, of course, it is better to travel hopelessly than to arrive. Having a good deal of experience from my bus and truck days, I am no longer—or rarely—surprised; but sometimes even I am a little daunted. For instance, I have a memory of a State College in upstate Pennsylvania. I was to "perform" in a gymnasium of vast size; the whole center area of polished boards was empty, as for the basketball games it was intended to house. The audience sat on bleacher seats along each side and a few, a block or so away, in front of me. There was no "lighting," nothing but bars of brilliant fluorescent light which illuminated me and the audience with equal, flattening brilliance. A couple of young men walked out and crouched in the middle of the empty space in front of me, taking photographs.

This dreadful practice is bad enough, even when you are just lecturing; you find yourself waiting for that "click" and wondering whether to turn your head at that moment, or not till it's over. When you are trying to evoke Lady Macbeth's spirits of evil—especially under gymnasium conditions—it is unbearably distracting. I find myself going from coast to coast banishing microphones and fighting photographers. The sponsor thinks he has done his duty if he forbids flashlamps. But the soft, insistent clicking is just as bad—like somebody whispering when you're ill or trying to fold a newspaper quietly when they think you're asleep. The degree of concentration required to sustain a one-man show is total; break it, and you are lost.

The gymnasium-auditorium is also used for "Assembly programs." This means that on the stroke of the fiftieth minute a bell shrills screamingly through the building to dictate that everyone should get up and go somewhere else. I have known it to happen as I drew Cleopatra's dying breath and almost died myself, of fury.

Then there is the chapel-auditorium. I like this better, even though there is no room for Mr. Shaw's desk or Miss Brontë's table as you dodge between the pulpit and the lectern, and there is frequently no place to hang lights which will penetrate the chancel. "Lead, kindly light," I have murmured to myself, "amid the encircling gloom." But the chapel-auditorium has an "atmosphere" which is not gloomy; it is focused. Many of the best audiences I have played to have been in Catholic, or sometimes Lutheran, colleges. I am sure this is not coincidental. It is because there is an initial consensus of thought and feeling; not a unity, exactly, but a perceptible identity. You are dealing, immediately, with wholeness of response, not with a lot of scattered and disparate elements.

In parenthesis I should add that, in my experience, priests are the best hosts and nuns the fastest drivers you are likely to meet. I was driven into Pittsburgh once by my hostesses of the night before and have seldom been more frightened. The chauffeuse was a Benedictine. My nuns regretted very much that "the Mercies" and "the Felicians" from neighboring colleges couldn't come, but "the Charities" were there in force. We overtook a carload of "Mercies" driven by a proper, peak-capped chauffeur, and shot past them as if they were standing still. We ignored red lights—cops waved us on cheerily. I have wondered whether the de-uniformed Sisters of today are not missing some of their former privileges.

Then there is the Women's Club auditorium, a quite different species. Sometimes it has a stage, more often a small rostrum with a tottery little reading desk and a mike for Madam President which has to be got rid of for me. It is usually broad daylight and the ladies are happy and replete. But I remember one occasion when I was dreadfully disconcerted to see that, very soon after I had begun, members of the audience began to get up and creep out—even from the middle of a row—practically on all fours. I thought, "I can't be as dull as *that*—not as *soon* as that. . . ." Presently I was almost equally disconcerted to perceive considerable numbers of them creeping back again. It transpired that it was all a question of parking meters. After the eating and the preliminary club speeches, the two hours were up. Everybody had to go and put in another dime.

Once, at UCLA, the students asked me to do my performance (Shakespeare) in two forty-minute halves for two different audiences. The locale was an enormous ballroom in the Student Union with floor-length windows all along one side (it was a morning show) and an electric drill very busy in the street outside, as well as constant activity from people coming and going at the back of the hall. There was no real stage, just a platform, and when I turned to greet Macbeth, I ran straight into the Stars and Stripes proudly ensocketed in the corner. Fortunately everybody was glued to their TV sets for the sixth game of the World Series, so nobody came anyway.

Staying on campus, as in this case I did, is a mixed blessing. Since, in my view, the object of this whole exercise is to "open doors" for people, it seems churlish to grumble that you cannot lock your own. Nevertheless, one is extremely vulnerable to any and all enquiring minds—as well as to small-hours gatherings with Pop music accompaniment, in the adjoining room. To get breakfast means rising before dawn; and 5:30 p.m. is not, for me, a civilized time for the evening meal. I am speaking, of course, of a several-day campus sojourn, not of the single-recital affair. But the whole food routine often raises problems of insuperable magnitude and had better be abandoned on days of rapid transit. The timetable, on such a day, can well run something like this:

6 a.m.   Woken by alarm clock and hotel operator, seldom simultaneously. Coffee shop not yet open. Finish packing. If in an optimistic mood, reflect that although a woman has to drag around a lot more different clothes and make-up, etc., than a man, at least she doesn't have to shave. Get taxi or limousine to airport.

                Ensuing travel troubles, various, as above described. Lunch on the run while changing planes, or airline-provided plastic meat, apricots born in a can, coffee so weak that at least it doesn't stain your clothes if you spill it. Sometimes it's all you can get.

2:30 p.m.   (say) Arrive. Met, usually, by several meet-ers, including local press. Sometimes by a lone meet-er. You recognize each other by anxious, peering expressions and uncertain smiles. Occasional false starts and apologies.

                You are asked what you'd like to do first. You say maybe see auditorium, arrange furniture and lights (plot sent ahead for simple minimal requirements) so then you could go back to hotel and rest. Problems arise. The hall won't be free till 5:30; the janitor can't be found; the plot you sent ahead has got lost somewhere in the office of the Physics Professor, who happens to be program chairman for that year; there is no furniture in town remotely suitable for the parlor at Haworth parsonage; the student newspaper would like to interview you. When (if) you finally get together with whoever is setting and running the lights, a music student has arrived and is busily practising on the organ. Finally, back to the hotel. Unpack. Pray evening dress uncrumpled.

5–5:30   "A little light food" (not more and not later on account of show—very hard to achieve). Rest??

6:30   Dress and make up—usually only bright light in bathroom. Perch make-up on small glass shelf and stand up in order to see in mirror.

7:15–7:30 Fetched by sponsor, who is late, causing heart failure.

8:00   Show. Good, bad, indifferent. Tiring. Sometimes exhilarating.

10:30   Coffee-clutch—sometimes weak and sticky "punch." Cookies?? a sandwich? mebbe. Much handshaking and thanking and frequently you don't get to sit down while this

284

goes on—which, counting the bathroom make-up, means you have been on your feet for some five hours.

Back at the hotel, you have ordered a cold chicken sandwich to be left in your room. You look at it, buried under several napkins, crowded between flabby lettuce-leaves and glasses of once-iced water. It looks rather like you feel. You decide you're too tired, both of you. You climb out of your regalia, pack it, un-make-up, crawl into bed. A red neon-sign outside your window flashes on and off all night and the trucks roar past merrily. You wonder why you do it?

Well, it's a good question. I answered it, in part, for myself, once, in the following letter:

The performance was rewarding tonight. I returned filled with gratitude to God and Mr. S. I blame myself for dwelling on the miseries. It's a wrong emphasis. One can do much better by creating with happiness. . . . It is better, oh, *much* better, by and large, to enjoy oneself than not—richer all round. You have to give and ex-pect, not get dreary. It's difficult—the conditions are frequently awful, the audiences ignorant and non-civilized, the loneliness tough for an actor who's used to reciprocity. None of this must be allowed to mat-ter, any more than bad notices, a bad house, a bad speech. It has just damn well got to be enjoyed, even if you have to work at it. When you lose this, you lose the lot. . . . That's why I hate it so in New York now—the load of responsibility, costs, fear—there's no fun left.

And then, of course, there is the matter of "opening doors," en-larging dimensions of human understanding, enlivening imagina-tions, a certain evocation of magic. I remember, long ago, being shocked at a small teachers' college in Ohio because the faculty said they thought I should explain more fully about Falstaff and Othello. None of their students had ever heard of these characters. Why did I think they should have? They knew far more than I did about all sorts of things from physics to Pop music. Why should I deplore this particular ignorance? I suppose because to know Falstaff is to participate in a large and healthy climate of laughter; to suffer with Othello is to suffer with mankind, whose blood is the same color under any skin.

The opening of doors is sometimes unexpected and always won-derful. I described one:

. . . a strange little meeting followed by a strange little show to a very undemonstrative Scandinavian-Lutheran college in South Dakota. I think they were quite fascinated by the peculiar, articulate, dressed-up creature who had appeared in their midst. At the coffee-clutch afterwards (revolting, very pale, Scandinavian mixture with egg mixed in) plied me with endless questions and were large-eyed and sat at my feet in all senses. But they gave me no applause at all *during* the show, which makes it a breathlessly long haul. (I don't suppose they knew they were meant to.) A strange, very large young man in a football helmet turned up during the first half and sat in the prompt corner where I couldn't un-see him, as for bird and snake. Asked me in intermission whether Shaw believed in God, and I said Mr. Shaw would talk about that in the second half, and at the end he was speechless with deep thought and pleasure.

(The result, I should say, of a selected bombardment from *Major Barbara, Androcles and the Lion,* the *Man and Superman* preface, *Saint Joan* and one of Shaw's letters to Dame Laurentia of Stanbrook Abbey.)

Naturally, I learned a lot too. I still didn't collect the two states (Hawaii and Alaska) which my bus and truck had missed, but I enlarged my knowledge of the rest and was enthralled all over again by the immensity, diversity and wealth (I don't mean riches) of the United States. ". . . small plane up the Wisconsin lake-shore line —so beautiful—the Iron Mountain 'airport' a tiny shack among the pinewoods, and the Western sky rose-orange and the stars a pale silver and when the plane switched off its engine, the silence fairly roared at you." A morning show—I "fairly good—the audience grave but very attentive." I had time to wander around and mooch about the General Store and learn something about how people got to be here and where they came from—Finnish, until recently, then many French-Canadians; more surprisingly, Italians. Grass roots, when they have no political connotation, are of absorbing interest.

There were surprises. At the height of the New Orleans school-segregation storm, I had an engagement at a state-supported university in southern Louisiana. The first thing I saw was black students strolling around the campus with white ones. "Are you integrated?" I asked the president. "Oh, yes," he replied cheerfully, "but don't tell the press." "How many black students?" He said, "I've no idea. We never ask. We just keep quiet." The same thing, I found, was happening at a state-supported university in Alabama in 1966 under the Wallace regime. The head of the drama department had just returned from an assignment in Addis Ababa; the president was new, and young. Their chief supporters were the medical men of the town, who were mostly Jewish. We all got together over Othello and Falstaff, and I thought cheerfully that there is more than one way to one world. My path is small; but I plod along it.

The most macabre happening I remember was one which befell me on a Friday afternoon in November 1963 at the De Lys Theatre in New York. Its owner, Lucille Lortel, gives, every year, a series of special matinees for the benefit of ANTA. Most people do them partly from good will to either Lucille or ANTA and partly as a showcase. There is always a regular production playing at the theatre. In this case it was one which required a bare stage, open to the back wall behind a kind of wire-mesh screen, flanked by black velour "wings." Not only was it difficult to recreate the Brontës' home within these grim surroundings, but there could be no glim of light at the back or sides of the stage.

The De Lys [I wrote] has developed a peculiar habit . . . of having nobody back-stage—but I mean *nobody*—just me and a couple of dead mice. There's a bearded fellow who does the lights from a booth at the back of the balcony and he came and synchronised watches with me at a quarter to two, and we agreed that at 2:35 he would take the house lights down and bring the stage lights up and I would walk on. There is, however, another fellow-of-all-work, very amiable, who was to "check" with me about fifteen minutes before this. He did so; simply asked if I needed anything and I said no, and he said should he check again, and I said yes, about five minutes before zero hour and he went away, leaving me alone—and the backstage area (except for my dressing-room, up a flight of stairs) black as pitch. A few minutes later I felt my way downstairs and stood about. My fellow materialised through an alley-way side door. He said "You must brace yourself for a bit of bad news." I thought "The electrician's dropped dead!" "The President of the United States has been shot." I said "Is he dead?" He said "We don't know yet," and mumbled something about "extreme unction." I said "Then you'll have to cancel the performance." He said "We've known for half an hour but we didn't like to tell you. The audience know—they all heard before they came in." Completely shocked and baffled, I said "Then you or Lucille must go onto the stage and ask them do they want me to give the show or not." At this he waffled a little and disappeared again. I waited, listening to the quite substantial noise from out front—I figured that of course the show must *not* go on—and at this moment the house lights went out and the stage lights came up and there was a ripple of applause and I realised that I'd put my script down *somewhere* in the blackness and hadn't a clue where—nonsensically I thought I *must* find it in case I *had* to do the show! Every second I expected Lucille or my fellow to come up from the front (it's a stage with steps from the auditorium and no curtain) and make the announcement, but nothing happened. I slapped around in the dark, finally found the script, figured out that if nobody else was going to go on I must, and did. Applause, and I held up my hand to stop it and said *something* about "the appalling news" we had all just heard—and voices called "Is he dead? is he dead?" and I said I didn't know and someone came down the aisle saying that he was believed to be dead, and I said some more, God knows what, and sent them home. It was all quite unreal and absurd, like a nightmare.

Then lots of people I knew came onto the stage and an important-seeming lady, unknown to me, kept saying "You did right, you did right!" and a man who'd flown from Dayton, Ohio, to see the performance and obviously thought it should have been given, and the President of the Brontë Society from Boston, something of the same mind, and many sympathetic friends . . . and finally the smoke of battle cleared as people drifted off in bewilderment.

I added in a postscript: "Did I or did I not write to you from Dallas a month ago saying that it seemed to me a Doom City and gave me the most appalled feeling of horror?" which indeed, for no accountable reason, it had done.

It is not an affectation to say that these recitals make me appallingly nervous. Even if it is a little junior college in Indiana, it feels like a Broadway opening. I am not one of those who think there is anything meritorious in being nervous; and I don't know why it should get worse, not better. I suppose that if I did only one program, and did it consistently, I should get more used to it and mind less. The alternation of three prevents one from settling down. Strangely, the most familiar material is the most nerve-racking. For instance, I had devised the *Tempest* speech "Our revels now are ended" as an epilogue to the Shakespeare performance. I know it so well that if someone were to shake me by the shoulder while I was fast asleep and murmur the first words in my ear, I should mumble through to the end without ever waking up. But the thought of speaking it fills me with such fright that I hardly ever do. I suppose there must be some dark, psychological reason behind this. It's probably better I should never know.

Certainly it isn't the audience, per se, that causes "nerves." They haven't changed much; they are challenging, sometimes (as I once wrote) "tough and cough-y," but generally warm, responsive—and surprised. They laugh, perhaps, less easily than they used to, at verbal wit like Shaw's. Satire is a weapon which rusts in a modern armory, and vocabulary shrinks—regrettably. To keep language a live and beautiful thing is one of my missions, an important one, I believe. We waste so much of this, our tax-free inheritance. People are still moved and astonished by the power and music of fine words set in order.

So that I do have a sense of purpose—which is as well, since my labors in this field must add up to several woman-years. The rewards can be very great—the hush, the silence, the laughter, the response expressed not only in applause, but afterwards in questions and comments, the awareness of the opened door. Sometimes, at the end of a grueling tour, I have taken off my full-dress uniform with infinite relief, but also with a feeling of gratitude that we have been able to do good service together.

Chapter Eleven

Which Side of the Ocean?

1

For some thirty-five years I have been troubled with a malady for which there appears to be no cure. Pamela Frankau, who also suffered from it, used to call it Transatlantic Schizophrenia. For some twelve years, important years of my working life spent wholly in the United States, it slumbered in my blood. In 1952, when I began to revisit England via my little cottage in France, I could feel it stirring again. Two or three years later it became rampant. For a considerable time neither I nor anyone else knew which side of the ocean I was on. "You'll get no promotion This side of the ocean," runs the old RAF song which I had learned to know in *Flare Path*. It is for certain that you will get none on both sides at once.

Even though the ocean may be crossed in a matter of a few hours, people, understandably, prefer to deal with someone on the spot who can be chatted with informally, without prior notice, and who, in New York, can be caused to dicker around with tentative fantasy-projects which involve no obligation. The payment of a transatlantic fare implies a certain solidity. Moreover, the English, on their side, are not very hospitable to their returning sons, let alone their daughters, as many well-known expatriates have discovered. They have, after all, got on very well without you. "Why, *helloh!* How nice to see you—where have you been all this time? oh, yes, of course, America . . . Well, we must make a lunch-date one of these days." Period.

At the end of March 1949, I left my bus and truck in Walla Walla, Wash., and flew to London via New York. It was my first transatlantic flight. The plane—it was a DC-3—seemed to me beautiful and enormous. You could put about twenty of them inside one of today's Jumbo Jets. I had beginner's luck. The flight did what it said it would when it said it was going to. I thought this was usual. During the ensuing years I learned better. Heathrow Airport was a collection of small army huts—it had not existed at all when last I had been in England, eleven years before. The nostalgia of memory had deceived me. I had just come from the agreeable climate of Seattle and the Oregon coast, and I had thought about "daffodils that come before the swallow dares, and take the winds of March with beauty." I brought lightweight spring clothes. Folly. The winds of March were whistling around all right, but not so much as a snowdrop had ventured above ground. Rationing was still in force and I had, of course, no clothing coupons. I shivered continuously for three weeks until, a few days before I left, I managed to buy a Jaeger coat.

I had dreaded seeing London; but never has it seemed more charming to me. Shabby and battered, pock-marked with bomb fragments and blast damage, not yet repainted though a good deal tidied up, it filled me with profound humility and respect. Sometimes, of course, it took me by the throat. I remember walking down Bond Street from Oxford Street and thinking "But it's still here—it's exactly the same . . ." and then I reached the crossroads of Conduit Street and Bruton Street, which weren't there at all.

I walked about feeling transparent. I thought, "Perhaps it will be like this after one dies, walking the familiar ways, invisible." My old home in Bedford Street was still pretty much intact, though with bits of brickwork chipped and pecked away, showing orange-colored cavities; my mother's name still on a brown-green brass plate below the bell of the top flat, offices now. The theatres were recovering much of their old look. Edith Evans was giving a luminous performance of *Daphne Laureola* at Wyndham's; across the alleyway Laurence Olivier and Vivien Leigh were playing *Richard III* and *The School for Scandal.* Ralph Richardson and Peggy Ashcroft were at the Haymarket (home of my illustrious ancestor, Old Ben Webster) in *The Heiress.* (I tried in vain to convince Ralph Richardson that the ancestral home of the character he was portraying was pronounced "P'kips-y" and not "Powkeepsie"; he preferred his own version.)

Terence Rattigan had written a play about Alexander the Great; Gwen Ffrangcon Davies was in it with a young star, new since my day, named Paul Scofield, whom I thought likely to become the finest actor of his generation, as indeed he did. An American play called *Dark of the Moon,* which I had seen in New York, was being directed about nineteen times better by the young Peter Brook, recently down from Oxford.

I visited the Old Vic. It had suffered severe bomb damage in the first blitz and was still not usable as a theatre; but the Old Vic School was established there, conducted by an illustrious trio, Michel St. Denis, George Devine and Glen Byam Shaw. The whole floor of the auditorium and the stage area were bare. Dance and mime exercises went on in some corners. Scene plans were spread out on the floor while students crouched over them. Sounds of music came from distant parts of the building. I found myself glancing automatically in the direction of Lilian Baylis's box and wondering if her busy ghost was bustling around somewhere muttering encouragement or, more probably, blunt but trenchant critical comment, badgering God to get the school some more funds.

Lacking her prodding, God didn't—or not for long enough. The master plan of a school, Young Vic and Old Vic, in escalated order, had been evolved by Tyrone Guthrie. I used to audition American students for the school—and found, among other talents, the Canadian Leo Ciceri, who became an actor of true stature. But the school part of the scheme was dropped while everybody concentrated on getting enough money to rebuild the theatre and rehouse the main company. Now it is in working order once more; so is the school and the Young Vic. When the National Theatre moves to its grand new home a few blocks away on the South Bank, London will not be so stupid as to lose the old building, as New York did the old Met.

The whole strength of the British stage had been scattered during the war and post-war years over the entire area where English-speaking troops were stationed—India and the Far East, the Mediterranean (later, France and Germany), the mining villages of Wales, remote naval bases in the islands north of Scotland. Probably more people saw more fine actors during that time than ever had before or will again. Now the theatre was reassembling itself very much in the old, familiar patterns. I realized afresh the tenacity and flexibility of the English stage traditions. It is said that in Germany theatres sprang up in cellars or dugouts among heaps of rubble almost before the bombs stopped falling. There had never, in Britain, been evidence of that kind of fanatical enthusiasm, and the theatre had never been supported from public funds. But now this was beginning to happen.

Wartime entertainment organizations had proved themselves essential—not only the paramilitary ENSA, English counterpart of the American USO, but the Council for the Encouragement of Music and the Arts. This organization had been initiated by American funds, provided by the Harkness Foundation and the Pilgrim Trust. (The Harkness had never donated so much as a dime to any form of theatre in America; but it gave $200,000 for this purpose, via the Pilgrim Trust.) Under the leadership of Lewis Casson, CEMA had done such magnificent work that it had been awarded matching funds by the British government and these were gradually superseded by entirely government funding. It became the Arts Council, of which the drama section was a part. It was, and remains, unhampered by political influences or bureaucratic interference and was already beginning to prove itself the most vital, life-giving force in the British theatre.

I did not have time to take in all this immediately. My own play had already opened its try-out weeks. It was an adaptation from a German original, called *Royal Highness,* which I had made several years before and which had been blocked by the censor on the grounds that it dealt with some distant—and deceased—relatives of the Royal Family. Either society had since got less Royal or the protagonists were more deceased; anyway, the censor had relented and it was playing in Cardiff. Thither I went, wrapping myself round myself to keep warm in the train. Few of the cast were known to me; I privately thought it very badly acted, except for two or three of the smaller parts, and abominably directed. But I took infinite pains not to be a back-seat driver. I did a few minor rewrites as requested and tried to behave like a pleased first-play author.

At the hotel, I practically went to bed in my clothes to defy the cold. On the breakfast menu I saw good old English "sausages and bacon" and ordered them with nostalgic enthusiasm. Alas, the sausages consisted of bread and sawdust encased in lightly browned plastic. I felt deeply ashamed of my disappointment.

The production was in the hands of the powerful organization known as "H. M. Tennant Ltd.," which mainly consisted of Hugh ("Binkie") Beaumont. His record over forty years of management is staggeringly impressive, probably unique both in quantity and qual-

293

ity—even though he held a monopolistic power which was the despair of those who did not come within his orbit. He had acquired the Lyric Theatre, Hammersmith, for the production of "experimental" plays, or those of dubious commercial value, by a non-profit subsidiary called The Company of Four. His enemies called it a way of getting cheap try-outs by paying the actors small "try-out" salaries. It was a gamble and a showcase for the actor and I wished we had some in New York. The theatre itself was old, beautiful in a florid, red-plush and dusty-gilt way and had a lustrous history. It had been un-damaged by German bombs but has since been demolished by de-velopers with the blessing of the London County Council.

My play added little to its illustrious record. Being only the author, I felt under no obligation to endure the torture of an opening night, so I made my way to the farthest suburb of Outer London and did a television interview from the Alexandra Palace. Meanwhile, my bus and truck were bleating wistfully for my return; so I set out for Heathrow once more, just as the incomparable young green of the English spring was sweeping across the London parks, and the gardens were edged with a froth of pink and white blossom. The daffodils had come and gone, the lilac was beginning. I longed to stay and smell it. But I had a tryst with my truck in Powkeepsie.

2

It was three years before I came back, this time via France and by boat. Among other things, I drove to Devonshire to see Sean O'Casey about a projected production of *Cock-a-Doodle Dandy* in New York. He was most amiable and wholly uninterested. I seized the chance of visiting some of the magic places of my childhood, such as Woola-combe, marvelously unchanged. Rationing had gone, everything looked tidier and more prosperous, the people seemed a little less polite. I went to Stratford, and saw Gielgud's magic *Much Ado* in London; the Old Vic was home again. The Dames (Thorndike and Evans) were playing together in *Waters of the Moon,* a play to which London audiences flocked for two years and wouldn't have run in any other capital city for two weeks. It was only a brief visit. I made another the following year because of the death of my cousin Jean, my only near relative. Nothing much happened except that I almost got killed in a car crash and I saw *The Mousetrap,* then a tot, barely six months old. In November 1972 it will be twenty.

Meanwhile, the Met had uplifted me, my truck demolished me; I had done several Broadway productions, including *Saint Joan—* disappointing work—and *The Strong Are Lonely*—disappointing and saddening result. The blacklist was still black. I was sure, anyway, that Broadway was never again going to be a place where I could earn a living doing the kind of thing I wanted to do. I rented my apartment and brought the script of *The Strong Are Lonely* to England and showed it to Binkie Beaumont, who liked it, but only if we could get a certain star. We couldn't. I also showed it to Donald Wolfit, who liked it, cast himself in it and said he would present it under his own management. It would have to wait a few months because of his film commitments. I rented a flat in London with Pamela Frankau and prepared to re-Anglicize myself.

I had known Donald for many years. We had been at the Old Vic together; I had played with him in his first tentative managerial venture—some special performances in his home town of Newark of *The Master Builder* and *Arms and the Man.* (The then totally unknown cast included John Clements and Margaret Rutherford.) I was godmother to his younger daughter. I respected his splurging power as an actor and admired unreservedly his total dedication to the theatre. But Donald was born just a little out of period. Had he been one generation earlier, he would have flourished as an actor-manager such as Fred Terry, Matheson Lang or Martin Harvey—he had been trained under the first two of them. He would have played Shakespeare, a lot of costume melodramas, an Ibsen or two, a "powerful" new play now and then. In fact, he did all of these things and became the last of the actor-managers. But the glory had a little bit departed. The style of the theatre had changed.

Like his predecessors, he reveled in being king of his own castle. His staff and cast were servitors rather than colleagues. He threw himself heart and soul into everything he did—and his work in the provinces was of great value, as was his "Lunch-time Shakespeare," which he maintained throughout the London bombings, much as Dame Myra Hess maintained her lunchtime concerts at the National Gallery. His knighthood was a deserved outcome; and none, I am sure, has ever been more richly enjoyed.

There should be a dictionary of theatre metaphors. Why should "to lay an egg" mean the same thing as "to be a turkey"? Is it sinister that nowadays "we bombed in New Haven" means what we used to do when we simply laid an egg in that city? Why is "a smash" antithetical to "a bomb" and "a blockbuster" more like the first than the second? *Variety* terminology has always been both antic and arcane. At any rate, to be "a ham" means—though it is less often used nowadays—to be an overactor and, by overtone, a bad one. Donald Wolfit was, could be, an extremely fine one; his detractors called him a ham; but at least he was not pallid. His King Lear was, I thought, quite magnificent. His company was simply dreadful—and that was the trouble. While John Gielgud invariably surrounded himself with actors of the highest possible quality, Donald did not. It is perfectly true that managers such as Bronson Albery and Binkie Beaumont placed resources at Gielgud's disposal that Donald never had.

Donald paid his companies very badly indeed, and his physical productions cost as little as he could possibly manage. He never understood that it can be rewarding, even essential, to spend money. He was as parsimonious to himself as to his company and staff. I should be surprised if he took a taxi more than a dozen times in his life. He employed a company manager mainly for the reason that this character managed to commute between Donald's cottage-office in off-Hampstead and his multiple assignments in the West End without ever taking one. He was also supposed to double as an actor, which he wasn't.

Some aspects of this mentality are, obviously, admirable, but it was not "West End." His resentment against what he considered the "West End clique" went very deep. He had a profound conviction that Binkie Beaumont, John Gielgud *et al.* conspired to keep him out of London. You could not have convinced him that Gielgud, that gentle and generous man, had no reason to be afraid. But there was an element of truth in his beliefs. The kind of work he wanted to do and the production standards he was willing to accept did not suit them; nor would he have been willing to accept any degree of subordination, nor to play for them the kind of parts which he later played with such outstanding brilliance in movies and television. Also it would be hard to deny that he heartily enjoyed being persecuted.

Though I had known Donald well in the old days, I had lost sight of him for many years; and when I began to talk to the important actors we needed for the other leading parts in *The Strong Are Lonely*, I was disagreeably surprised. I invariably got the same answer: "Yes, it's an extremely interesting play and a fine part; but who can play with Donald? All he wants you to do is to stand downstage and throw him cues." At last, I took my courage in both hands, gave him a plain account of these reactions and asked, "Is it true?" He made me a very convincing answer; that he wanted good actors, needed them, was prepared to pay both for their abilities and the box-office value of their names. He asked whether the people to whom I had been talking had ever, in fact, been in his companies? No, I thought not. Then it was all hearsay; a slander deliberately put about by Binkie Beaumont and John Gielgud to keep him out of the West End. Naturally, I discounted the last bit, but I was nevertheless impressed.

The next day I had asked Ernest Milton to lunch—surely the most mannered actor since Irving, and capable of great brilliance; a Shakespearean star of one-time magnitude. He said the usual things. I made Donald's speech back at him and ended "In fact, Ernest, *have* you ever played with Donald?" A pause. "Nu-uh-uh," said Ernest, lingering out the monosyllable through four different cadences, "nu-uh-uh." "Well, then?" Another pause. *"Huh's* played with *muh."* Milton did accept the part and gave one of his most glittering performances in it. The character was the Father General of the Jesuit Order, who visits the Jesuit settlements in Paraguay, disguised as a Spanish nobleman, and ends by ordering the Father Provincial (Donald) to destroy the work to which he has given his life. (The analogy with the hierarchy versus the Catholic Radical Left would give the play a sharper impact today than it had then.)

A duologue between the two men in the second act is the core of the play. For much of it Ernest had to sit in the Father Provincial's chair of office behind his desk. It was mandatory; he plainly had to. Ernest would sit writhing, twisting his neck into impossible coils (and complaining of fibrositis) so as not to turn his face away from the audience, while Donald, footloose and actor-free, would gravitate steadily toward the rear wall. Ernest, when released, would spring, panther-like, to the very backdrop. In vain I would beg Donald to let us please take a look at his expressive back; in vain assure Ernest that there would be no light that far upstage. Kenneth Tynan is a critic whom I do not at all admire; but he absolved himself, in my eyes, for many sins by his comment: "I shall long recall these two expert players stealthily upstaging each other 'to the greater glory of God'!"

Donald asked me—quite rightly—to put the last two scenes into one. It held the tension better; but it also involved some problems in doing onstage what had been covered by the scene break. For instance, what kind of wound, eventually mortal, could cause the Father Provincial to become unconscious (for eleven minutes and fifteen seconds—Donald clocked it) and eventually to die without a lot of fussy bleeding and bandaging? also permitting extreme unction and a death speech?

After expert consultation I found out—the Father must be shot in the right side of the abdomen, resulting in internal bleeding but not instant death. Unfortunately, Donald's re-entrance "shot" had to be with his left side to the audience. To my horror, he came staggering on at the dress rehearsal with his cassock torn open to the navel, revealing a white ballet shirt plentifully daubed with red paint right over the heart. I told him that if he insisted on being shot through the heart he'd have to die right away and we'd have to end the play without him. Very reluctantly, he yielded the point. But when I revisited the play, unbeknown to anyone, after an absence, and snuck in at the end of a matinee, there was Donald shot through the heart again. He just couldn't bring himself to forgo that bloody ballet shirt. (I cannot believe that the deep springs of Wolfit-Milton behavior have been expunged from the mechanism of star actors. They certainly function "on camera." But I wonder how they handle this particular problem on thrust stages or "in-the-round"? I had a Brandeis "summa-cum-laude" graduate with me in a recent production. She didn't know what "upstage" meant. I should add that she didn't know very much else either.)

We used Rolf Gerard's designs from the New York set. He gave me all his blueprints and other specifications, but he couldn't come himself. A "technical assistant" was outside the Wolfit philosophy, so I inherited the designer problems. When Rolf and I had first talked about the play, he did his usual careful research into the architecture of the place and period; he then told me that the set would be simple, massive, extremely austere: black-brown wood for the door and window frames, floor-cloth painted in terra-cotta tiling, everything else completely white. I was horrified. Light thrown onto a white, or even "off-white," painted surface throws back a "bounce" which makes the faces of those who move in front of it almost invisible. Rolf let me in to a trade secret which he had learned from the great French designer, Christian Bérard. The set would be faced with bleached burlap (or "Hessian"), a coarse, open-weave fabric, not a true white but nearly so, and backed with black duck cloth. This gave it the texture of a sponge. It mopped up light. You could "paint" it with light—blues, warm pinks, cold daylight colors—and there was no bounce at all. It was the most glorious set to light that I have ever known. My New York electrician taught me a couple of invaluable tricks too, and the result was beautiful.

In the Wolfit context, however, two drawbacks were involved. One was that I had to fight a bruising battle to the very last ditch to get an electrician for the preliminary touring weeks; the second was that, after six weeks or so of traipsing around the provinces, how was the set to be cleaned for the West End opening? Normally you get a "touch-up man" from the scene-painting studio for a swift and simple operation. It wouldn't work in this case, because there was no paint. Someone suggested employing a firm of cleaners. Donald almost had a fit. Other procedures were rejected for similar reasons. It ended with me and the stage management climbing up ladders and scrubbing away at the canvas "walls" with Somebody-or-Other's Stomach Powder. As I rubbed away, on my precarious perch, at two o'clock in the morning, I wondered what would have happened if we had tried to do the same thing on 45th Street: an explosion of the stage hands' union of a size to decimate Times Square.

The play wasn't a "success," but it wasn't a failure. Our tenure of the Piccadilly Theatre was limited by the onset of Christmas pantomimes, which cause most serious theatre in London to go into retirement. After "the holidays," we were able to reopen at the Haymarket, an unusual tribute. A respected critic of a London paper remarked, rather bemusedly, "This strange play seems determined to get itself liked." Our tenure was only for a few weeks, pending the arrival of Binkie Beaumont's newest production. But Donald was as delighted as a child to be occupying the star dressing room in the great, historied Haymarket Theatre. I gave him a playbill of Macready's Farewell Performance from more than a hundred years earlier when my great-grandfather was the actor-manager there. Donald was as awed by his predecessors as he was belligerent about his contemporaries. He was a theatre romantic, touchingly vulnerable.

At the Haymarket he contrived to believe in all sorts of abstruse persecutions; the BBC, he firmly said, would broadcast pessimistic and unfounded weather forecasts about rain, snow and fog just to keep people at home watching television instead of going to the theatre. Our having to leave the Haymarket (though he had known all along that his tenure was limited) was, of course, a conspiracy and a cabal. The play had, indeed, won a deserved audience; but even Donald's courage and tenacity could not achieve a third home for it. He revived it later for some "fringe" performances at the Edinburgh Festival, with a lesser cast and no director.

I saw him only a few times after that. He lived much at his charming little cottage near Andover. He made many excellent movie and television appearances and played a really wonderful Pastor Manders in Ibsen's *Ghosts*—by far the best I have ever seen. It was not his own management. Shorn of the blood-stained ballet shirt he could be a superb actor, and had he been able to edit his own performances, or allowed someone else to edit them for him, he would have ranked very high in the British theatre. His death was sudden and deeply to be regretted; there was much for him still to do. As it was, he fought a dramatic rear-guard action for a kind of theatre which, whether for good or bad, had ceased to exist. He was the last of his line.

3

My next two engagements were of a very different nature—with the Old Vic and the Shakespeare Theatre at Stratford-on-Avon. The former had not yet been absorbed by the National Theatre, nor had the latter acquired its London home and greatly expanded non-Shakespearean program. They were embryos of their present selves; but each with a long and rooted history without which their present development would not have been possible. The transformation which has taken place in both cases is the clearest possible evidence that ongoing, onward-looking theatre comes from a growth, a flowering, not from deracination.

Glen Byam Shaw was at that time in charge of Stratford, and doing an exceedingly fine job. The theatre was still a "seasonal" affair, beginning in early April and running through the autumn. Like all such theatres, the cast and repertory had to be set up months ahead of time. Toward the end of 1955 he asked me to do one of his two opening productions for the following spring—it was to be *The Merchant of Venice,* and the stars were Emlyn Williams and Margaret Johnson. I brooded a little. The British do not like women directors and they do not like people who have made reputations in America, and *The Merchant of Venice* has been done so frequently and invites so many comparisons that I thought I was probably buying trouble if I accepted the challenge. But I couldn't run away from it.

A very potent reason for my acceptance was that I wanted to do the Trial scene in a way I had never seen or had a chance to try, though I had written about it at length in my book, *Shakespeare Without Tears.* Briefly, I thought (think) that the scene has lost much of the impact it had when it was first written because we all know the plot; we all wait for Portia's "this bond doth give thee here no drop of blood" and it seems extremely sadistic of her not to have mentioned it earlier and saved Antonio and Bassanio a lot of needless agony.

But since neither she nor her mentor, Bellario, had ever seen the actual contract, it is legitimate to suppose that, although forearmed with the legalities of punishment, she had to find the flaw in the bond for herself. Shylock blocks off all the avenues of escape or evasion on which she had counted; she herself grows increasingly desperate as it dawns on her that she may not be able to save Antonio at all; only at the very last moment does the solution leap out at her—"Tarry a little! There is something else. . . ." The focus, for the audience, is shifted from the known answer to the excitement of watching her find it.

I asked Glen Byam Shaw if he had any objection to my staging the scene this way; he had none. I asked Emlyn Williams, who looked vague and agreeable. I asked Margaret Johnson, the Portia, and she was enthusiastic. I signed the contract. The sets were designed, I did my homework, all was in order. In February, a week before we were to begin rehearsals, Glen telephoned me. "Maggie," he said, "has decided she can't play the Trial scene the way you want. I've argued with her. But she won't do it. She's offered to give up the part." This, of course, was nonsense as she was under contract to play the leading women's parts throughout the season. I didn't take it very seriously. I said I would persuade her. But I couldn't. I thought her arguments were very silly and mine grew in cogency as I enlarged on them, but she still refused. I suggested that she should let me lay out the scene in rehearsal, with all the subtle shifts of emphasis involved for the other actors, and see if I couldn't make it work for her. Would she wait and see? No, she wouldn't.

Probably if I had been a few years younger, vainer and a fraction more dictatorial, I would have refused to go on with the job. It would have caused the maximum of inconvenience to everybody, and after the first burst of self-righteous indignation I should have regretted it. If I couldn't have convinced Maggie that the scene should be played "my way," she certainly wouldn't have convinced the audience. Comes the opening night, the actors have to do it. The director can't. I gave in. But I felt exceedingly despondent.

We started rehearsing, Maggie very nervous. ("Expects me to raise hell," I thought.) After a few days I asked her if she would like to work with me on the Trial scene in the evening, alone, not even with the stage management. She looked panic-stricken, but agreed. I made no attempt to depart from the orthodox handling of the scene. Sometimes when you are working with an actor, you make no headway at all, you elicit no response whatever; but sometimes you choose the right words, find the right images, touch the right nerve. Magic happens. It did that night. After that, I think she would have played the casket scene standing on her head, if I had asked her to. She was an excellent Portia and got excellent notices; so did I. But I still haven't seen the Trial done "my way."

Nevertheless, I enjoyed Stratford. Because *Hamlet* was being re-hearsed at the same time, I had a certain amount of leisure and Pamela and I would drive round the beautiful Cotswold country which we both knew and loved. She was working on a book, and at intervals we returned to London and house-hunted—with eventual success. Meanwhile *The Merchant of Venice* began to unfold.

It is not always easy for a visiting director to work in an existing repertory company. You have to accept prearranged casting and pre-established methods, and sometimes the company are a little "set in their ways." But in this case they were most of them young and talented and new to Stratford. Several have since attained stardom— one as a Labour M.P., with, reputedly, the loudest voice in the House of Commons. Anthony Nichols was a strong and authoritative An-tonio. This was important to me. One should not ignore the title of *The Merchant of Venice*. I began the play with the lonely figure of

Antonio watching, apart, the chatter and bustle of the Venetian scene, and ended it with him, still alone, as the happy lovers dance away in the early dawn at Belmont.

The theatre was beautifully run and everything went smoothly—or nearly so. The set for the Trial scene (Alan Tagg had designed the play with decorative invention) was quite different from any of the other stage pictures. It consisted only of a translucent, painted "ceiling" with hanging ribbons, making a light suggestion of a colonnaded background, attached to the same iron pipe. There was nothing else but a black velour masking backdrop. On the opening night when the lights cue arrived, nothing happened. I went rigid. After a few seconds they came on—revealing nothing but the actors and the black velour backdrop. I catapulted out of my seat and tore backstage. There was nothing to be done. The ceiling ribbons had got entangled with some other hanging stuff and the stage manager had decided (rightly) simply to go ahead without it. Afterwards I apologized to Emlyn Williams. "What for?" he said. "The Trial scene set." "What about it?" "It wasn't there." He answered, "Oh, wasn't it? I never notice the scenery unless it actually hits me."

Before I crossed the Atlantic again the Old Vic approached me to do a production of *Measure for Measure* the following season. I had seen the play several times but never acted in it or directed it. I wasn't sure I knew what it was about, or what I would try to do with it. I delayed my answer until I thought I had found out. I studied all the critics and commentators. They were exasperatingly unhelpful. All they did was to pick the play to pieces without indicating how it was to be put together again. I went back to the text, as one should, and just soaked in it, mindlessly. It began to take shape. There emerged, I thought, a Heaven-Earth-Hell pattern, probably derived from the medieval mystery and morality plays which must have been so familiar to Shakespeare, not used specifically, but as a sort of cosmic frame. I thought, too, that the play was concerned with triple identity: every man is three people—the man he would like to appear, his public image; the man he himself likes to think he is; and the man he *really* is, the basic stripped essence. And further, that there is a theme about the use and abuse of power, running all the way through from the Duke to little Elbow, the constable. Lastly, fortified by all the commentators' assurances that the author had written the play piecemeal, at different times, and put it together rather like a jigsaw, I ventured on some textual transposition to bring the second Isabella-Angelo scene a little later and not lose sight of him for so long in the second half of the play.

The designer (Barry Kay) and I tried to work out these various notions. We evolved a built-up unit set, the Duke, at the opening, entering on the highest level, and "Hell" being the dungeons. The theatre at that time utilized a flight of steps leading down into the orchestra pit, very handy for this purpose. We tried to follow out my triple-identity theory visually. Angelo, for instance, first appeared dressed soberly in a scholar's black gown; was invested with the robes of office; and, in the last scene, stripped of them, leaving the unadorned "man." (I have since thought that today's permissive nudity could have made a valuable statement here; except that for an actor to wriggle out of a pair of tights onstage in view of the audience would not have been either dramatic or impressive.) Similarly, in the scuffle attendant on the arrest of Lucentio, his elegant, golden hair proved to be a wig which came off, revealing a bald and scabrous skull.

Having set in motion wheels such as these, I left for various American assignments, leaving myself exactly two days between the opening of *Macbetto* at the New York City Center and the start of rehearsals at the Old Vic. On the first of these days, I broke my ankle. Fortunately, Pamela Frankau was with me and got me home by plane and wheelchair. There was no margin of time to have a plaster cast made and left to set, so for the first week I was on crutches. This was not helpful. Nor were the actors. They were a fine company, whom I greatly admired, but from my point of view two of the most important parts were not cast as I should ideally have liked, due to the unavoidable exigencies of repertory. Also, they were all strangers to me, except Tony Nichols, the Duke. They had all the virtues which ensemble playing engenders; but there was also a very perceptible feeling of a club, closed to non-members, to which I had been graciously accorded a temporary visitor's card.

Because of my crutches, I could not dash around with my usual agility, demonstrating what went on where, nor, more importantly, was I able to trot across the road with them during the lunch break and fraternize at the local pub over a glass of beer. I never really got on terms with them until one day when, in a clumsy effort to do everything at once, I knocked one of my crutches overboard into the orchestra pit and let fly a fully-charged four-letter word. The PA communications system happened to be on, and it was broadcast all over the theatre, including the dressing rooms and the offices. Everyone was much nicer to me after that.

I have been impressed—an old but reinforced impression—by seeing how many of that company have since grown into extremely fine actors—Judi Dench, for example, and Barry Ingham. There is raw material in the United States with an equal potential, but neither equal opportunity nor, I think, equal dedication. However, the lesson I learned from this Old Vic experience—again not new but reinforced—was how much a fine play (Shakespeare, Sophocles, Sheridan) reveals itself when, and *only* when, the actors bring it alive. Then, for the first time, the text yields up secrets which you have never uncovered before; layers of obscurity peel away, revealing something quite blindingly simple. I had spared no effort over *Measure for Measure,* and it was an effort to *understand,* not to superimpose fancy theories needing a program note or a lot of gimmickry. But I found out a lot of things too late to put them into effect. Later, there was to be a corollary to this. I did a production of the same play for an American university, thinking that *now* I could demonstrate my discoveries. But I couldn't. I didn't have the actors.

In 1969 I saw a brilliant production of *Measure for Measure* by David Giles at Stratford, Ontario, with a vivid, startling Angelo by Leo Ciceri—all quite different from mine and all splendid. I marveled once again at the infinite adaptability of Shakespeare; and the primary importance of actors.

4

The day after *Measure for Measure* opened I shed the plaster cast I had by this time acquired and crossed that ocean again, feeling as vulnerable as a soft-shelled crab and making much of my supporting stick. I was to direct a version of Shaw's *Back to Methuselah.* Arnold Moss (my Prospero of *The Tempest* days) had very skillfully condensed the five plays into one evening; he had used a great deal of Part One (Adam and Eve), virtually nothing of Part Two, some of *The Thing Happens* and the *Elderly Gentleman,* and, alas, a fragment only of *As Far As Thought Can Reach.* The connecting Narrator was made up—you'd never guess—as G.B.S., and played—surprise, surprise—by Arnold Moss.

The parts were distributed among five other actors: Tyrone Power as Adam, and sequent characters; Faye Emerson as Eve etc.; Arthur Treacher—no, not as the Serpent, but importantly as the Elderly Gentleman and other things; Valerie Bettis as that Serpent *et seq.;* and a young man in the Cain "line." The producing management was the Theatre Guild, in collaboration with . . . Arnold Moss. Triple crowns have never been easy for their wearers to support in any form. Arnold's was no exception. The production was designed for a three months' bus-and-truck tour of one- or two-night stands before coming into New York. Thus, supposedly, it would pay off its production costs on the strength, mainly, of Tyrone Power's name, and have nothing to lose on Broadway.

Tyrone had been on a semi-bus tour of *John Brown's Body,* a rather grandiflora affair, though sufficiently tough to give him the general idea. Nobody except me had ever done battle with the real thing. The booking management, of course, understood only too well what they were after, which was money. They trusted to the capacity of actors to suffer the insufferable and accomplish the impossible. Only, as has been observed before, the impossible takes longer; and on a bus-and-truck tour you don't have longer. Everything was therefore laid on for trouble.

There were some unforeseeable additions. We opened during the first week of January in Orlando, Florida, and it snowed. The auditorium was gymnasium-type Grade A horrible, and we had to turn out of it between the dress rehearsal and the opening night for some intervening community activity. Our first jump was to Sarasota, some 120 miles, to play a matinee. The rain fell from the sky in cataracts. There was only enough "juice" for one of our two switchboards, and it had to be placed behind screens on the auditorium floor. I sat with the electrician, a heroic type who had driven the truck all night, and we made up the lighting as we went along. The head carpenter got drunk. The next day we did a little two hundred-and-some miles to the opposite coast, where the local union wouldn't let the trucks be unloaded unless we called more men. Much similar bus-and-truckery ensued.

The bus was often quite denuded. Arthur Treacher's wife was with him (darling people, both) and they drove in their own car—a loss of ballast on the bus, for they were a center of imperturbability.

The stage management and/or crew sometimes had to travel ahead, much as mine had done. A car donated for the use of Ty Power (and resultant publicity) was diverted to them and Ty got another. The stress and fatigue of travel, on whichever kind of wheels, the vast auditoriums, the long and difficult show, bore down on everybody.

Arnold Moss's triple-threat position was a source of constant friction and I almost exhausted my supply of oil for pouring on troubled waters. Faye Emerson was under considerable strain and, though normally a gay and gallant lady, developed a tendency to fly into rages and throw things at people—quite without malice. The boy who played Cain had to be replaced, and the assistant stage manager said he couldn't stand another minute of it and must give in his notice. I said he must stick around and gain inestimably valuable experience in what not to do and how not to do it. He would be a producer himself one day and it would come in handy. He was William Ball, who has had his own companies for years now, and I hope he has used what he so painfully learned.

The saving grace was Ty Power himself. Gentle, considerate, shrewd, humorous, humble about his work, firm when he needed to be, he was one of the best people I have ever known. I had never before worked with a real movie star who was, literally, mobbed whenever he appeared in public. Complex arrangements had to be made to get him into and out of hotels or restaurants; I had to get a police pass before I could penetrate the stage door. The Beatles had yet to show us what mobs of hysterical teen-agers could really accomplish; but Ty's fans were quite bad enough. He handled himself and them admirably, with good temper and good sense. He had great strength under the courtesy and kindness, as well as charm, talent and good looks; not bad equipment. He was very proud of his theatre ancestry. His great-grandfather, Tyrone Power the First, had acted under the management of my great-grandfather, Ben Webster the First; probably a unique repetition of a pattern. We worked well together.

The show finally staggered into New York; it was moderately good, got moderate notices and had a moderate run. A year later, suddenly, shockingly, wastefully, Ty was dead.

5

There seemed to be an odd pattern about my eastward journeys across the Atlantic: I was always doing an opera and being ill. In 1960, while I was working on *Simon Boccanegra,* I received an offer to do *The School for Scandal* for the Birmingham Repertory Theatre, which I accepted. The cold which had afflicted my last days at the Met turned into flu; and I had letters from Pamela Frankau telling me that our London home had got dry rot. ("Our bathroom floor is being burned in the garden. 'Have any of your readers had a similar experience?'") During my few days at a London hotel, when I was too ill to smoke, I decided (for the fourth time) to stop, and did; this time for good. But I arrived in Birmingham in no very sturdy frame of mind. Smoking, for me, had always been a rehearsal accompaniment of (I thought) absolute necessity; the deprivation was plainly hellish. But for the first time I really wanted to stop more than I wanted to go on. Until you reach this point, all "cures" are a waste of time. In fairness I should add that six months *later,* for the first time in my life, I got bronchial asthma. I also put on twelve pounds in weight. Nevertheless, Dear Smokers, stop it. You will have won a great freedom.

Pamela and I installed ourselves in huge, old-fashioned rooms at the Queen's Hotel, right above the railway tracks of Birmingham's main station. The loudspeaker was forever announcing the departure of trains for Kidderminster, which must be the most sought-after town in Britain. She wrote all day on a book called *Pen to Paper,* one of the most stimulating books on the writer's craft that exists, instructive and witty. She would read bits aloud to me when I came back from rehearsal, using me as a sounding board; I would spill out my rehearsal problems and watch them rebound, much diminished, from her good sense. We found, as we had at Stratford while she was writing *Ask Me No More,* that the craft of the novelist and of the theatre director are astonishingly close. The writer must interpret the men and women of his own imagining on paper; the director has to translate the creations of other writers in terms of flesh and blood. But the process is more alike than is generally supposed. We were very good for each other. And, as was invariably the case, we laughed a lot. It was not just frivolous laughter; it involved perception, self-criticism, irony, a sense of proportion—and, on occasion, guts. I think it may well be the most precious thing that two people can share with each other. I cannot possibly, ever, be thankful enough for this rich gift Pamela brought me; there will always be a halo in my memory around the echoing name of Kidderminster.

Crossing a bridge over the railway lines, I was within two minutes' walk of the theatre. The Birmingham Repertory Company was one of the earliest repertory theatres in England; it was founded by Sir Barry Jackson just before the First World War, in the wake of Miss Horniman's two pioneering theatres in Manchester and Liverpool. In the Twenties it had enjoyed a period of great fame; it was the nursery of many of England's most famous actors, such as Cedric Hardwicke, Ralph Richardson, Gwen Ffrangcon Davies and Laurence Olivier. It had sent to London many long-running successes, such as John Drinkwater's *Abraham Lincoln, The Immortal Hour, The Barretts of Wimpole Street* and *The Farmer's Wife* (1,324 performances); it had done the original productions of several Shaw plays and was the springboard for the Malvern Festival, which revived many more. In my youth it had been one of my greatest ambitions to get into one of its companies; but I never did. Now, at last, I passed through the stage door.

The building was the same, an oblong-shaped auditorium, very steeply raked, with no balcony, seating less than five hundred people. Sir Barry Jackson had retired from active management and had donated it to the city. It was supported partly by his endowment, partly by Arts Council grants and partly by the city itself. Each tax payer was therefore paying something like one farthing (a quarter of a U.S. cent) per year. The great majority of them never came (it was then a city of something like 1¼ million), but everyone had the right to grumble on account of that farthing. The upsurge of new repertory theatres in England since the war had left it simply one of a dozen or so of similar quality; there were startling newcomers, like the Belgrade in Coventry, only a few miles away; but it was still among the best. Its series of plays were, by that time, usually played in succession for three weeks each rather than in repertory, but it cast a wide net (classics, recent successes, a few new plays) and had a solid permanent company and director, with occasional visitors like me.

It was excellently and smoothly run. The designer was a famous little elf of a man called Paul Shelving, who had designed many of Barry Jackson's most famous productions, and he did me a series of light, charming, elegant sets. Some of the actors were excellent. The Lady Sneerwell is now one of the leading ladies at Stratford. (It has taken her eight patient years to reach that eminence, which is a long servitude for an actor, and she had far too much talent and skill to make it necessary.) There were some admirable character actors, as, for instance, those who played Sir Oliver and Crabtree. I was impressed by the fact that some of the best of them were happily settled down in Birmingham and weren't at all anxious to fight their way into London's West End. They had continuous employment, good parts in good plays—why should they? But, of course, this is a static situation which cannot last. New acting blood has to be brought in; audiences want new faces as well as old favorites. When British television established out-of-London bases, it drew heavily on the pool of trained repertory-theatre actors. New types of play have come into fashion, new kinds of theatre buildings arisen; there is a variety of activity and great vitality in such diverse cities as Oxford, Glasgow or Stoke-on-Trent; Birmingham itself has a new building, though not as yet its old glory. But the debt owed by the British theatre to Barry Jackson can never be repaid.

A couple of years later I worked for a quite different type of British "rep," the Theatre Royal, Windsor. This is a darling little building of antiquity and elegance, nestling under the Castle walls. It usually does plays which would be guaranteed not to shock "the Royals" if, as is quite frequent, they care to drop in, and which would always entertain the merry burghers of Windsor. Like most other English provincial theatres, it is "rep" only in name, but what the Americans call "stock" in fact. Like American summer-theatre companies, it does fashionable successes with casts specially engaged for them, each play running for two weeks. Four or five times a year a new play will be done, and my production was one of them—a dramatization of Pamela's book, *Ask Me No More.* The play had flaws, so had the acting, and the star hated the young man we had chosen (now very well known) and adopted a "he-isn't-going-to-do-it-like-that-is-he?" attitude which stultified both him and me. But the standard of the performance was high, and the theatre, once more, beautifully managed—and solvent. I found this very remarkable.

There is much health in the British repertory theatres. During the past decade they have gone from strength to strength. They come in all kinds and sizes. The elegant "stockbroker" variety often act as try-outs for London's West End. They have no permanent companies, but they are a valuable outlet for new plays or neglected classics. I later directed *Mrs. Warren's Profession* for the Yvonne Arnaud Theatre at Guildford with two star actors—a better performance, I thought, than the one at the National Theatre which shortly afterwards followed suit. They are the kind of theatre American Equity has always been so afraid of—"undercutting salaries" and all the rest of it. So far as I can see, they have done nothing but good.

Others, more experimental, have started up in industrial towns like Stoke-on-Trent or Sheffield, with a working people's audience. The companies in Nottingham and Oxford have won national fame doing a wide variety of work. In Greenwich, a suburb of London, the theatre is supported to some extent by the local Borough Councils, and largely by a membership recruited through door-to-door canvassing. Within a year of its opening it had sent two extremely interesting new plays to the West End.

But before American readers get too envious, they should remind themselves that not one of these theatres could or can exist without the very substantial support of the government-funded but wholly nonpolitical Arts Council of Great Britain; and that its Board of Directors consists of men and women at the head of the arts professions, without a single political appointee.

6

Interlaced with all the assorted frenzies of the Met, flu, dry rot and getting off to Birmingham was the beginning of another activity, one which I enjoyed more than any job I had had in England since my return there. It also completed an interesting small-scale spectrum: I had worked for the last of the old-style actor-managers, for both the national repertory theatres, for a provincial "rep"; now I was to come back to the West End, directing a play by the Westest Endest living author, Noel Coward. It was called *Waiting in the*

Wings. The management, Michael Redgrave and Fred Sadoff, had sent it to me in New York. It is a play not at all in the usual Coward vein, about a home for retired, aging actresses. I thought it compassionate and touching—with a quota of "pastiche" Coward songs thrown in for good measure at a Christmas party scene.

When I first got back from New York, and was able to climb out of bed, I went to see Noel; I was weak, cigaretteless and distinctly nervous. I had "known" him since forever in that casual semi-social way theatre people have; you never know anyone "just" socially, because you also know the plays they have written, the parts they have played, their public sayings and bits of their private lives; there is always a professional overtone. However, I had never worked with him. A hundred years before, I had auditioned for a part in *Cavalcade:* I had never been so courteously treated; I left the theatre feeling taller, even though I was certain I wouldn't get the job.

Noel was relaxed, friendly, funny of course (it is the speed of the comment that dazzles you—it is always instantaneous as well as right in the middle of the target), and he seemed to like the idea of my doing his play, which pleasurably astonished me. I knew that Binkie Beaumont had read the script and was reported to have displeased Noel by asking for some extensive rewriting. I therefore tiptoed on eggshells toward this subject. Little as I liked it, I felt I had to. I said would he please explain something that had been puzzling me. He had set up a whole chain of circumstances leading up to the outbreak of a fire in the "Home"—quite a small, manageable one, not a conflagration; then there was a scene break, and a whole other chain of circumstances leading away from it again. I said I knew that he must have had some very strong and valid reasons for not carrying straight through the scene itself, which obviously he must have considered, but, please, I should love to know what they were? His eyebrows rose very high, his eyes opened very wide; I trembled. He said, "Darling, I never thought of it." That night, he rewrote the scene.

The duration of Noel's visits to England is (or was then) determined by the Inland Revenue Department. He is a nonresident of the most heavily tax-burdened country in the world. ("Unpatriotic" some people have called it. Speaking as one who has experienced the double-taxation machinery in a modest way, I would suggest that the patriots try it for themselves.) His stay in London was to be very brief; he would return for final approval of the casting and go away again; return for the last three days of rehearsal and the opening two weeks—in Dublin. The one thing which had to be settled this time was the identity of the stars. Marie Löhr was to be one—I had first seen her playing at His Majesty's Theatre in *Pinkie and the Fairies* when I was three years old.

For the other starring part we all wanted Sybil Thorndike; she and Lewis Casson never played without each other—and since she was then seventy-eight and he eighty-five, it was unlikely they would break the pattern. Fortunately, there was a part for Lewis too; but (we were only too aware) it was a small one. Some competition was in the offing from a play about St. Teresa of Avila, with a much better part for Lewis. He came to my hotel to pick up the script while I was still flu-bound; he stood beside my bed in his old blue beret and was gruff and affectionate and I couldn't at all get used to the idea that I, who had started my professional life in the Chorus of *The Trojan Women* under Lewis's direction, and had understudied Sybil in *Saint Joan,* could possibly become their director. I prayed to St. Teresa of Avila to wait a little. While she and the Cassons were still considering, Noel left for Switzerland and I, less glamorously, for Birmingham. A few days later came a telephone call from Fred Sadoff—the Cassons would do the play. Next morning there was a note from Sybil: "Darling, it will be so wonderful to be working with you again." I couldn't find the right words for a reply.

After my return to London, and a certain amount of deck-clearing by Fred Sadoff and me, Noel came back for the final discussions about casting, design and the rest of it. I can only begin by saying that he has the most impeccable professional theatre manners I have ever encountered. I think I can hear cries of dissent. I have been told of occasions when "the Master" flew into rages of dreadful dimensions—indeed, I witnessed a couple of them. Once we raged together, shoulder to shoulder, and once he and Lewis raged at each other in strangulated politeness. Noel turned purple and Lewis turned bright crimson and they both swelled up till I thought they would burst; but that night Sybil and I defused the two bombs and they returned to their normal shape and color. These two incidents apart, I found Noel's courtesy, professionalism and saving-grace humor a matter for profound admiration and gratitude. He could so easily have been a dictator; but he never forgot the dignity of the other human being.

To me he behaved beautifully. He was never a back-seat driver.

He never gave the actors directions or criticisms over my head or without my knowledge. "Would you mind, darling, if I talked to So-and-so about that speech?" or "Don't you think we might tighten up that bit?" He was always amenable to cuts—or additions—and we nearly always thought alike—which of course does make for harmony. I don't know that I would much like to have Noel "agin'" me; but I'd have the uneasy feeling that there must be a good reason.

Some of the casting had been decided before I reached England—Norah Blaney, for instance, as a character who had to play the piano in the show, and who was in fact a pianist of concert quality, as well as being a "top-liner" in the old music hall days. She and Sybil, if allowed to reach the piano together, would settle down to a four-handed Bach jam session which took a lot of stopping. There was also a Canadian actor, William Hutt, whom I didn't then know, but everybody else seemed to, who was to play Sybil's son. For the rest, we settled down to long discussions about distinguished ladies, long retired, who had been stars when I was at school. Often a question would arise as to whether they were still "available." I would eagerly suggest a name. Noel would shake a mournful head and point upward. "Really?" I would say, shocked. "Are you sure? It seems to me she was around last year." "All the same, darling, no good now. Feathered choir." Less grimly, arose the question: can she learn the lines?

We would invite the "possibilities" to the amicable surroundings of Michael Redgrave's flat. Some were Coward stalwarts from previous productions whom he knew he wanted and I knew he wouldn't have wanted them if they hadn't been fine. There were gales of laughter over "Do you remember when . . ." with Fred and me smiling and looking at our watches. Others, like Edith Day or Ada Reeve, had been stars of past musical comedies. Noel would launch into the lyrics of their hit songs, remembering every word and note of them, and they would tinkle happily along with him. They would all go out smiling; but often I knew that Fred or I was going to have to write a horrid, misery-bringing little letter the following day. Naturally, there had to be some stage readings, hellish as always. Often, to make it easier, I would read with them myself, trying to kind of nudge them into the right mood or tempo and "feed" them as nourishingly as I could. Noel sat out front and was polite and charming. We seldom disagreed as to the verdict; except about one young woman, a newspaper reporter in the play, and Noel turned down my candidate. She was a young Australian, newly brought to England by Tyrone Guthrie, named Zoe Caldwell.

Finally, we were all set but for the smallest part, the least important of the "retired ladies," carrying an incredibly meager salary—I think £12 a week. Someone suggested Mary Clare; we stared incredulously, thinking of her many years of top stardom in London productions—including Noel's *Cavalcade*. All of us knew that she had the reputation of being "a perfect bitch" in the theatre; but I reflected that my cousin Jean had talked of Mary's great kindness to her; and one should never take these "bitch" and "bastard" reputations on hearsay. They often involve all sorts of extenuating circumstances and whole coveys of other bitches and bastards. We were told that she needed the money. We got in touch with her.

She arrived, looking vague and gracious and beautiful, with snow-white hair, and said that of course she would love to do the play; but I thought she had better read it first and not be left to discover, too late, that everyone else had a better part. I gave her the script and said I would telephone her in the morning as Noel was taking wing for Switzerland. I had some trouble reaching her, and when I eventually did so she apologized. "You see," she said, "I had to go out to try and hire a tape recorder for my little dog, which talks." I said well, yes, of course, why wouldn't it, and she explained that the dog—a Pekingese—was psychic, would go into a trance while on her bed at night and, after a little snoring, deliver messages from people in the other world. Mary's late husband, Lionel, had been the first to get in touch. "You wouldn't think, would you," said she, "that a Pekingese's larynx would be able to say 'Lionel'? Now Ivor is much easier. He often brings messages from Ivor." I resisted the temptation to ask whether Ivor (Novello) had written any new songs for the Peke-medium; I asked would she play the part. "Oh, yes, of course," she said cheerfully. I cabled Noel: "MARY CLARE WILL PLAY HAS LITTLE DOG WILL UNDERSTUDY."

As it turned out, she always appeared looking benevolent and benign, left the clair-audient dog at home, and couldn't learn a single word. She would sit, smiling, in a large armchair downstage left, utterly oblivious of her cues; except when, occasionally, a flash of mischief would light up her face and she would chirp in with somebody else's line—always a good one. As rehearsals progressed and her lines didn't, the others became understandably frantic and I came under considerable pressure to "let her go." But I simply couldn't face it. I tried everything, including prayer; the Catholic church next door to the theatre was where my Jean used to attend Mass and it seemed a propitious locality. Eventually God sent an ecumenical answer in the shape of a Quaker, Mary's understudy, who had been a schoolfellow of mine once upon a time. She took Mary in hand, coached her, cosseted her, steered her to her entrances, whispered the next lines, crouched behind the armchair in the prompt corner, nursed her through. I wish I could say that Mary's benevolence lasted all through the run, but her colleagues, I fear, would not agree. Anyway she stayed in that armchair.

A single set and a smallish cast; it sounded like a breeze. It wasn't. The whole action took place in one room, where, obviously, the inhabitants would tend to gravitate toward their accustomed chair or sofa; yet I had to avoid a monotony of pattern. Several activities had to go on at once—a game of bridge, someone playing the piano, two or three people having a discussion or quarrel. It was the kind of play for which a small theatre was essential (there aren't any in New York any more—or very few); and yet the room necessitated a good deal of furniture, including a grand piano; a staircase to the upper floor; an entrance hallway; two other doors; a fireplace; and a bay window which, in the last act, sprouted a visible solarium outside it. If anyone thinks this is an easy jigsaw, let them try.

With the very skilful aid of Margaret Harris (Motley in English), this got done, and I worked out everything very carefully not only because English actors tend to want to know where they're going before they can really figure what they're thinking about, but because in this particular case I didn't want to muddle anybody. Noel likes his actors to know every line by heart at the first rehearsal. I hate it. As an actress, I like to let the lines grow inside me; and as a director, I find that nobody is listening to the play, each other or me; they are not relaxed or receptive, but only tense with the effort to remember what the next cue is and what they are to say then. But in this case I realized that the learning of lines becomes much more difficult as one grows older (I know it now from personal experience) and that one needs the assurance of knowing them. Marie Löhr and Sybil had both devoted weeks to learning; I didn't want to complicate anything. I got it all set as smoothly as oil.

The scenery was already more than half built when the management announced that in London we were going to have to come to the Duke of York's Theatre—a darling little house for the audience (except for a small outcrop of pillars) but an extremely teasing stage. It is not only small, but alive with sticking-out bits, crooked walls and sloping ceilings. How Granville Barker ever managed to house his famous repertory company in it is an abiding mystery to me. At all events, our set had to be entirely rearranged. I canceled a weekend's rehearsal, and shut myself up with Margaret Harris and a streaming head cold. We managed to salvage almost all of the pieces of the set, rearranged in different positions, and I altered every essential departure point of movement while contriving to leave the actors' moves as undisturbed as possible. We proceeded.

Most theatre generalizations are fallible and misleading; I will venture on one which seems to me less fallible than usual: it is that American actors like to sit and sit and read and read and talk and talk before they start what is called in America "blocking"; English actors prefer, as I have said, to go into rehearsal feet first. This, obviously, is not true of the long-range companies like the RSC and the National, nor of the way-out gymnasts, nor of productions directed by Peter Brook; but I think it is very generally the case in "ordinary" plays. There was an interesting example of it in *Waiting in the Wings.*

William Hutt (now a leading actor and director at Stratford, Ontario) arrived for rehearsals a week late. It didn't matter, since he had only one scene, a duologue with Sybil in the last act. He was supposed to be her son, who had been taken to Canada by his father when a child and had never seen his mother since. His scene did not affect the other actors. Nevertheless, he had missed, such as it was, the "talking" stage of rehearsals and he wanted to talk—about the character's childhood, his father, his present occupation, status, income, way of life and—obviously—attitude toward his mother, who had been a famous actress and was now reduced to living "on charity." All this was perfectly in order, and I sat down with him and Sybil to do it.

But I found that he and I were doing all the talking and she just sat. She looked peaceable but far away. Bill would make quite a long speech and turn to her eagerly—"Don't you agree, Dame Sybil?" She would start slightly and say, "Oh, yes, dear, yes, I do." Sometimes I would try to ensnare her with a question: "Do you suppose that when he was a child you used to drag him around on tour with you?" "What? oh, yes, darling, yes, I should think very likely." Occasionally she would flash disagreement with a quite definite "No,

I should hate that" (meaning the character, not herself). After a while I would detect a faint "I-wonder-what-time-it-is" expression on her face, and presently she would jump to her feet and say briskly, "Yes, well, shall we rehearse now?" She was deeply sympathetic toward Bill's problems, but she wasn't really interested in all that introspective bit. She knew by instinct, deeply and wholly, who she (the character) was and what she was thinking and feeling; all she needed was the mechanics of doing it.

And she didn't want to discuss it; she was afraid—subconsciously perhaps—of talking it into the ground—of analyzing, reasoning, blueprinting, methodizing—killing it. (Pamela used to say the same thing about her books while she was in the early stages of creating them.) I believe this is a quality common to many of the best actors and too little cherished by directors. A good actor is equipped with very delicate antennae; he has fleeting, sensitive, half-realized instincts and promptings of emotion, intuitive responses that he is shy of displaying or explaining. A director must perceive the "visionary gleam," make space for it, nourish it—but frequently not talk about it. Even praise must be edited. "It's beautiful, the way you turn your head and look at him—perfect"—the actor becomes self-conscious and may quite possibly never do it quite like that again.

Sybil Thorndike, as all theatre-lovers know, has been capable of tearing into a part with such furious energy and verve that the whole play trembles. But in *Waiting in the Wings* she was very quiet, very simple. At the first walking rehearsal she came into the "room" and paused for a second, looking round. The expression on her face was so totally revealing that pages of dialogue could have said no more. "Oh," I prayed inside myself, "If only she can keep it . . ." She did. I was careful never to mention it until the run was over. I found that in this whole play all I had to do was to place things (furniture or people) where they wouldn't get in her way and (mixing the metaphor) keep the orchestra together. It was a wonderful "orchestra"—merry and willing and sweet to me, who had been only "May and Ben's little girl" when many of them had their names in lights. Nor were they—as might have been expected—in the least "bitchy" to each other, either off the stage or on it. No stealthy upstaging (or downgrading) here. (Indeed, the only thoroughly bitchy cast I have ever directed was composed, all but one, of men.)

We began by rehearsing in various halls at various clubs to which the stage management brought hamperloads of "props." I was divided between grateful admiration, combined with wonderment at their being allowed to do so by the stage hands' union, and a guilty feeling that Equity oughtn't to let them be so overworked. For the last week the management did something rare even in London, unthinkable in New York. They hired a "dark" theatre and put the set up in it. I do not know whether this was due to the eminence (and nonresidence) of the author or to a realization that a cast also eminent and mostly aging would find it difficult to adjust to staircases, complex entrances and fire-scene hazards at the usual inadequate dress rehearsals. The result of their generosity was that by the time we got to the opening night, the actors were completely used to their surroundings and had started to live in them instead of glaring at them in horrified astonishment. It was a beneficent miracle and I wish it could be copied.

Noel came back a few days before we left for Dublin. I don't know how frightened the actors were, but they can't have been half as scared as I was. I should have known better. He was pleased without being effusive, critical without destroying confidence, stimulating and constructive; oh, and it *is* of inestimable value to have someone around the place who, in moments of dynamite tension, explodes laughter. I wished he could give lessons to all managers, producers, authors, directors, backers and other interested, loud-mouthed parties who charge into productions late in the proceedings and recklessly destroy what is not yet made. But then they would have to have Noel's skills and qualities, which limits the field.

We had the usual dreadful dress rehearsals in Dublin, technically made more than usually difficult for me for two perfectly silly reasons. One was this British "Prompt-O.P." terminology. The Prompt corner was on the O.P. side. All right. But the lighting instruments (British and even Irish theatres have their own permanent installations) opposite the Prompt corner were also called "the Prompt Perches"—or whatever other lamp it happened to be. The O.P. Perch, operated by an idiosyncratic Dubliner whom—despite my Irish ancestry—I could scarcely understand, drove me to distraction. The stage manager and our own electrician got into the act on technical as well as national lines of division. At last a weary voice from the front proposed a solution. "Look, darlings," said the voice, "why not just call it Muriel?"

The second plague was the impossibility of getting from backstage to the auditorium during a performance without wasting about two minutes going upstairs, downstairs, along passages and through concealed doors. "Never mind," said Noel, soothingly, "change at Limerick and take a box lunch." Such trivia are not as frivolous as they may appear. The safety valve they provide should be a priority item in every theatrical enterprise—indeed, I believe, in every enterprise which marks the progress of mankind from barbarism to the civilized conduct of its affairs. Has anyone written a book called *I Heard David Merrick Laugh?*

We had an uproarious time in Dublin (who doesn't?), sobered up in Liverpool and Manchester (a very sobering city), and finally got the set onto the stage of the Duke of York's Theatre with the aid of a lot of ingenious shaving and squeezing. The cast all, but all, had to share dressing rooms and these were up several flights of stairs. They did their quick changes, of which there were a great many, in the boiler room or under the prop table. Nobody grumbled, once they realized that we weren't being mean to them—there were just plainly no alternatives. On the morning of the opening, Marie Löhr went into the church of St. Martin-in-the-Fields for a little dedicatory prayer. Coming down the steps, she slipped, fell and broke her arm. (There is a saying which Pamela used to quote: "No good deed goes unpunished.") She played that night. She also played for many weeks thereafter with her arm in a sling. Throughout almost all her scenes she was supposed to sit doing petit point. She did it. She had quick changes. She made them. Her, and our, enabling genius was once more my Quaker schoolfriend, whose name will never appear on the top of a playbill, except perhaps St. Peter's. For the record, and in gratitude, it is Molly Francis; not that I suppose St. Peter will need reminding.

The play was received with what might be called modified rapture and had a modified run. I'm afraid I think it was damaged—though not as seriously as it would have been in New York—by an anti-Coward press, which seems now to have yielded to his years and his knighthood, even though he has done, in my view, no better work since. Fairly soon after it opened I had to cross that ocean again for two or three weeks and Noel of course, was once more carefully non-resident. By chance, we returned on the same day and saw the same performance. The next morning I telephoned him. "Don't you think," I said, "that we better have a little practice?" "Yes, darling, I most certainly do." I called a rehearsal and asked him to speak to the company first.

What he said was not at all what they, or even I, expected. He emphasized truth of feeling, simplicity, reality; not the tricks of the trade. He begged them not to press for the laughs. ("Don't try to squeeze the orange in the first act; there are two more to come.") His sharpest criticisms were for the most apparently popular effects. Anything phony he was onto like a knife. I thought, for the thousandth time, that fashions in acting change; techniques are lauded in one cycle and covered with ridicule in the next. They are all different means to the same end, whether the exemplars are Stanislavsky, Grotowski or Noel Coward. Provided you are indeed aiming at the highest attainable goal, "the way to heaven out of all places is of like length and distance."

Chapter Twelve

Interlude in South Africa

1

The decade of the Sixties involved me in a good deal of locomotion. Apart from what I came to regard as our local ocean, the Atlantic, the major journeys started in 1961, to South Africa, and ended in 1969, to Australia. Both had the blessing of the State Department, by whom I had apparently been cleansed with hyssop or some other detergent. The first was directly sponsored by their "American Specialists" program—an activity of the highest value about which far too little was known and which was always the first to get axed when Administrations started cutting budgets. My fellow "specialists" visiting South Africa at about this time were an athletic coach and a track runner. The sponsorship on the South African side was also on a governmental level, since I was to work for the "National Theatre"—a euphemistic terminology which meant that the South African government did make an allocation of money to a loosely organized theatrical set of enterprises, zealously served, as always, by the actors and executive staff concerned, without, as yet, much political connotation.

I was supposed to direct an "American classic" play with a locally recruited cast; obviously all white. The choice of play was more difficult than might be supposed. I canvassed opinion far and wide (being on a recital tour at the time). Many recent successful plays of what might be called "classic" stature, by optimists, had already been done by local theatres in South Africa—the best work of Tennessee Williams and Arthur Miller, for instance. Others, such as *Our Town,* were a bit too "regional" for non-Americans to tackle successfully, or so we thought. There were other special difficulties; I did not contemplate asking Lillian Hellman if we could do *The Little Foxes* with the two Negro parts played by white actors in black-face. MacLeish's *JB,* a recent Broadway "artistic success," aroused singularly little enthusiasm. Eventually O'Neill's *A Touch of the Poet* was decided on. I was assured that there was an extremely fine Afrikaner actor who would play the leading part splendidly.

I knew a certain amount about South Africa through English friends who had toured there, visited or even settled there, or who, in England, were of South African origin. In the United States nobody seemed to have heard of the country. It had only recently seceded from the British Commonwealth (which, naturally, was no crime in American eyes), and the National Government's policies of apartheid were only beginning to be recognized as one of the infamies of the world; nor had the inevitable corollary yet been revealed: that a police state was going to have to implement them. All the same, I was staggered by the totality of American ignorance: that a high proportion of the white population spoke Afrikaans as a first language; that the "colored" people of the Cape were not black, but descendants of white settlers who had intermarried with black, or Asian, blood; that when "Africans" were spoken of, Bantus or other blacks were meant, and that "South Africans" were, by definition, white—these things alone created instant bewilderment in most American minds.

When I tried to buy some winter clothes in June to wear in Johannesburg, everybody thought I was mad. I tried to explain about the seasons—about Johannesburg being high and the sun due north at midday. People stared. The South African Consulate was not much help. I thought it would be polite, though of course unnecessary, to learn a few phrases of Afrikaans. They were stunned. No such thing as an Afrikaans phrasebook had ever been heard of. In 1961 many Americans were still only dimly aware that we ourselves had a racial problem in our midst and took little interest in anybody else's. We are hideously wiser now. This did not, of course, apply to the State Department, and I was carefully briefed on questions of procedure and the already strained relations between the United States and Dr. Verwoerd's government. I did a lot of homework, consulted a lot of people, thought myself reasonably well prepared. I wasn't;

least of all so far as the theatre situation was concerned. The following article, written shortly after my return, epitomizes some of the
surprises that were in store for me:

It is my first public appearance in South Africa, a Sunday night,
forty-eight hours after my arrival. Scene, the Brian Brooke Theatre
in Johannesburg; present, a considerable proportion of all the actors
and theatre people in the city, assembled by invitation to hear M.W.
talk about "The Theatre in the United States"; and here I am—scared
to death. I have been briefed by the Embassy people to be cordial but
careful—especially on racial topics; I have been briefed by the head of
the National Theatre Organisation (over six cups of tea of ferocious
strength) to "say whatever comes into your head." Nothing much has.

It is a small theatre: on-stage, a tiny, pie-shaped piece of *The World
of Suzie Wong,* much encumbered with a raised "revolve" and exotic-
looking fixtures; the lights tend towards dark-strawberry, amber and
blue. A distinguished member of the Embassy staff introduces me, with
many flattering references to how much he admired me long ago when
he was in High School. I feel exactly like Mother Goddam.

Thank Heaven for the free-masonry of theatre people all over the
world. This is an audience of friends, not strangers. I begin by telling
them a little of the romantic frontier-story of the American theatre,
and they are evidently surprised and moved. There is a kinship between our forefathers, blazing a trail across the plains of the West,
and the Boer farmers who trekked North into empty and unknown
lands. Only with us, the actors came too, or soon after. Not with them.
The Bible forbid.

When I come to the Broadway of today, I sense that translation is
needed; Unions, economics, Equity salaries, stop-clauses, production
budgets, the shrinkage of the professional theatre and the rise of Off-
Broadway . . . I begin to realise that I am assuming a shared experience which does not exist. Television, for instance; I talk of its octopus
universality, of the inroads it has made on the other entertainment
media. I find out later that there is no TV in South Africa. There is
radio in English and Afrikaans, a government-controlled network and
a commercial one; some Bantu programs too; but no TV. The accepted explanation is that so many programs would have to be supplied
ready-made from England or America that they would swamp the
home-made, and, above all, the Afrikaans product.

The question period provides enlightenment for me as well as for
my questioners. It is funny, friendly and en rapport. The patches of

thin ice are rare; but the disparity of experience recurs from time to time. For example, I am asked about touring; isn't it bad for the actor? I reply sturdily, referring proudly to my bus and truck. A couple of weeks later, I am doomed to ride in N.T.O.'s touring bus, a Volkswagen known as a "Combie". It is only thirty miles from Johannesburg to Pretoria, but I arrive voiceless from the effort of talking over the noise of the engine plus the actors, and without one single vertebra in alignment with its neighbour. An American actor would take one look and go home. Only then do I realise that the actor who had asked me that question about touring was probably a cripple from Combie-travel. I realise that my own company is supposed to do its first jump by Combie—1,000 miles. I avert this.

These developments are still, of course, hidden in the mists of time. I am aware, however, that the ice is successfully broken; that my audience is friendly, if slightly bemused. I have a feeling it has reached the conclusion that all American theatre people, from David Merrick to the relief flyman, are (a) crazy and (b) millionaires.

The next two weeks: shuttling between Pretoria and Johannesburg, giving lectures, recitals, talks, interviews, as well as casting and setting up the play . . . I give auditions. I have been told that "everyone" in the South African theatre wants to be in this production, and I assume that "everyone" means a lot. Blithely, though I hope with courtesy, I reject the first three applicants for any given part, none of whom seem to me a bit like it, only to find "that's all there is; there isn't any more". In the case of the leading part, "Con Melody", the actor on whom we had counted has died of a sudden illness. I am told not to worry; Mr. So-and-so will be ideal. Alas, this is not the case. He is too young, too stiff, too lacking in temperament. Who else is there, I ask. Nobody. Not anybody at all. Desperate, I enquire into the possibilities of getting someone over from the U.S. What salary, I ask, would the part carry? Answer, the highest star salary paid by N.T.O.; this proves to be the equivalent of Equity's touring minimum.

In the end, I emerge fortunately. Marda Vanne, a South African actress and a friend of mine, well known for many years in London and New York, has recently returned to her home country and is available for the part played by Helen Hayes in New York. An extremely talented young woman who could have been an actress of note in any theatre, Fiona Fraser, is the daughter. A "Con Melody" turns up, of Afrikaner derivation but with experience in the English classics. I have just as much trouble—more—in rounding up a couple of American-seeming toughs in the small parts. I am no longer choosey—just prayerful.

Rehearsals . . . oh! the world-wide similarity of rehearsals! The theatre we are using is "dark"; walking into it from the pale, bright sunshine is like walking into an ice box. Johannesburg is six thousand feet up and bitterly cold at night; the theatre conserves permanently this night-time témperature. Its owners evidently share the general South African conviction that because the climate is hot in summer, no central heating is necessary at any time of year. [It is a Southern Hemisphere delusion. Melburnians endorse it.] The usual bare stage, but reasonable lights; as in England, part of the theatre's permanent equipment (not that dreadful New York 2000 watt work-light which blinds everybody and lights nobody). It is further equipped with a family of mice in the O.P. (shades of the British Raj) corner. I try not to tread on them as I climb from the auditorium to the stage. Tea or coffee breaks are frequent and mandatory. Supplied with these stimulants, the actors are prepared to work their heads off. They prefer to rehearse in the mornings and evenings, with the afternoons off; so do I; and there are no Union regulations to deny us this arrangement. Much good work is consequently achieved.

A great gap is revealed—no stage manager. Nobody appears to have any clear idea as to what I mean by a stage manager. Can't the actors do it between them? with an assist from the amateur carpenter who's helping to build the set, or the boy who's going to drive the truck, or a stage-struck youth from the University who'll come to rehearsals when he isn't engaged in the inter-Varsity fencing championships? Two weeks of nagging and no-saying net me an extremely charming fellow of many talents, stage managing being not, as yet, among them; but a couple of weeks of good will on his part and hard work on mine, and we are in business. Understudies? Honestly? Unheard-of! The notion ranks as news in the Rand *Daily Mail*. But I press on. . . . A week after the play has opened, the leading man is ill and three actors have to be moved up into the parts they understudy. I am regarded as a prophet.

Dress rehearsals at a town called Springs have a certain sporting element as the company commutes from Johannesburg and the crew and technical staff from Pretoria, an equivalent distance of some forty miles. . . . I stay at "The Lion" and spend anxious hours scanning the horizons for my colleagues. Otherwise, the hideous try-out passes much as it always does. . . . The opening night in Johannesburg— audience acclaim—supper-party—morning papers (only a few drops of cold water) . . . all familiar ordeals—the performance, I think, is pretty good. A few days for the play to settle down, and I am off on my own tour.

It is grinding work . . . one week I do seven "shows" (recitals or lectures) in four days; but it is passionately interesting; kaleidoscopic at the time, but gaining, in retrospect, some sort of perspective. There are certain constants; for instance, the perpetual whistling draft, straight from the plateaus of Antarctica, which is mercilessly directed at my shoulder-blades whenever I get into evening dress; no matter what the auditorium, the draft never fails me. As universal are the flowers, the gifts, the books, the souvenirs, the beautiful courtesy, dignity and charming manners of my South African hosts . . . their reactions of enthusiasm and gratitude out of all proportion, it seems to me, to what I have been able to bring them.

But if there are constants, there are also, naturally, violent contrasts; some occasions stand out vividly in my mind. The Great Hall at "Wits", for instance—the University of the Witwatersrand in Johannesburg—because it is very big and this is my first Shakespearean recital. Also because it is one of the few, the very few, auditoriums in the country to which a nonsegregated audience is admitted. Also because a party is given afterwards at a private home, attended by Americans, English, white and black South Africans; my companion from the Embassy gleefully warns me that there could be a police raid and we would all be liable to arrest because liquor is being served to African guests. Alas, this does not occur. [This regulation, like many others, has been altered since the time at which I wrote.]

Not many memories of mixed audiences, but a few. In Pietermaritzburg I give a Shakespeare recital at a hall in the Indian township. Here are Indians, Bantu, Coloureds and a good sprinkling of students from the (white) University. . . . I am welcomed by the Indian pastor, who was trained for the Ministry in Edinburgh and at St. Augustine's College, Canterbury. While the audience is coming in, a beautiful girl in a white and gold sari operates a small record-player in the Prompt corner; from it issues, scratchily, a medley of songs by Noel Coward.

Sometimes I appear before wholly Bantu or Indian audiences, and am disconcerted at first by the impression of total blackness where the pale smudge of faces should be . . . a wonderful response, though; Falstaff is perfectly at home. There are Coloured audiences too. Since apartheid, they must live in restricted areas, attend separate schools and colleges and be subject to all the bitter deprivations of racial segregation—worse, probably, because, hitherto they have always been accepted as European. There is a teachers' Training College outside Cape Town, and here I am booked to do a Shaw recital—a morning program, never my finest hour. To my horror, I find that contingents from the adjacent High Schools have also been invited—twelve and thirteen-year-olds, an age group for which my Shaw program was not really devised, even in more sophisticated surroundings. I ask the Principal does he *really* want Shaw? wouldn't Shakespeare be more appropriate? no, he wants Shaw. He had heard that it went very well at Cape Town University and his people would like it too. Well, but . . . unexpurgated? *Mrs. Warren's Profession,* for instance? Yes; let them know the facts of life.

I cast a nervous eye at the tots of twelve squirming slightly in the front row and take a deeper-than-usual breath. The hall is full of bright daylight; the suburban railroad fulfills a relentless schedule a few yards from the open windows and I am unglamorous in ordinary day clothes. But I start the "Ra" prologue to *Caesar and Cleopatra,* and the laughs come, just where they always do. For an hour and a half G.B.S. commands a perceptive and intelligent response, though a slight sense of strain becomes manifest in the front rows towards the end. I find myself questioning whether a similar age-group in England or America would be as good.

Afterwards, I talk with the Principal and some of his staff. *A Touch of the Poet* is about to open in Cape Town in the tiny Hofmeyr Theatre—the only playhouse in this great and beautiful city which is still devoted to drama alone. It is owned by the Dutch Reformed Church and the lease stipulates that only white audiences shall be admitted; but I am told that performances have sometimes been permitted for non-Europeans only, without whites. I ask my hosts whether they would attend such a performance if I could arrange one. No; they would boycott it. What, I ask, is the alternative? To come to *them.* "But you have no stage." "Then give integrated performances in Cape Town." This is impossible, as they know; it is not allowed. "Very well, then. All white audiences must join with us and boycott all theatres which do not permit integration." "And you think this could happen?" "We think so."

I wonder; I wonder, too, about the extremely precarious state of the theatre in South Africa—its tenuous footholds, so hardly won; it wouldn't take much to dislodge them altogether. Closing the present theatres would probably do the job. I wonder how many people would care. There are many other pictures, a wide cross-section of Universities, Women's Clubs, Rotaries, the High Command Staff College in Pretoria—an Embassy request. Then, there is a school-full of eleven hundred Afrikaner children listening to an author they had studied but never before heard; and the comment of one, going out, "but it sounds wonderful—not a bit like Shakespeare!" There are remarks like "we need not only books or even records, but the living voice".

The most vivid memory of all is of something which came about, unplanned, a performance squeezed in between journeys because I met the local Education Officer at Port Elizabeth and he begged me to do something for "my children". . . .

I am in a little church in the Bantu township; it is filled with black children, aged about thirteen to fifteen; morning again, very bright, no evasion of the wide, watching eyes, nowhere to put my script, an embarrassingly fulsome introduction; and I can't imagine which bits of my full program to select for this shorter one; and I am as scared as I was the first time, in the Great Hall at "Wits". . . . I pray to do it right.

Anyway, I begin. The black faces stare at me, intent, unwinking, no-body moves, nobody breathes; I try to make it real, I try to make it funny, I try to make it sing and be a music to remember; and there is never the smallest smile or stir, and I go on, feeling like a blind man. . . . Finally, it is at an end, and I am too much thanked and have to leave in a frenzy to catch my plane; and I still don't know, and people say to me indulgently, "oh, I don't suppose they took any-thing in", and I wonder . . . and then my friend the Education Officer writes to me: "I employ one of the High School boys in my garden each week-end. When he came on Saturday he said: 'Sir, that lady from America was too wonderful.' " The Education Officer adds "Tell your Ambassador we value this more than dollars in African educa-tion."

Once again I render thanks for Mr. Shakespeare.

2

I spent the winter of 1962 in New York, vainly trying to get Wendy Hiller and Maurice Evans to believe they were playing in the same play. It had the same title, *The Aspern Papers,* but they did not seem to agree that it was the same one. Françoise Rosay, as Miss Bordereau, sat in her wheelchair between them, casting a beady eye on each. I attempted miracles of diplomacy, spending one whole evening in my very best French, papering over the cracks—as I hoped, successfully. As we parted, she smiled, thanked me for the visit, and said "Bon soir, Madame Talleyrand."

The adaptor, Michael Redgrave, was in New York, playing in another play, and behaved with extraordinary gentleness to all those (not including me) who thought they could do a better job than he had. A leading performer quit, two weeks before we opened in New York, for the very simple reason that she had been offered a more lucrative job in Hollywood. She offered neither apology nor excuse. "Where your treasure is, there will your heart be also," said I to her. I hope she hurried back to her hotel to consult the Gideon Bible, but I doubt she recognized the quote. The experience was not, all in all, a happy one. It was the first venture onto Broadway of David Black, and it is to his honor that it did not permanently deter him. It did not make me feel a passionate longing to return to this overrated area.

So, weighing drawbacks against accomplishment, I agreed to return to South Africa to do *A Man for All Seasons* for one of the few remaining private theatre managements there. The play is one which I admire deeply, and I thought its message urgently needed a hearing in South Africa. It was to be the first dramatic production in the new Civic Theatre in Johannesburg, a tremendously impressive building with a restaurant and lobby rivaling the marble halls of Lincoln Center. It was to open with a month of opera; I went to the first night. The auditorium looked beautiful, paneled with glowing wood from the native South African trees, steeply raked floor, not too big. I was suspicious of the acoustics, but couldn't really judge because, of course, the orchestra pit was open and in use; for plays it would be covered over. The stage was enormous—it had been thought desirable to leave sufficient width at the sides and back to move in whole stage-size sets on sliding trucks. There was a new electronic switchboard installed by the London firm of Strand Electric.

The casting problem was no longer a surprise to me, but it was just as acute. William Roderick had come from London to play More; he had understudied Scofield, and afterwards played the part on the American national tour. The rest was the mixture as before —four or five admirable actors, all but one of English extraction, and then—an abyss. We were ten days into rehearsal before we could find anyone, but anyone at all, to play Henry VIII, or even to put on the costume and walk onto the stage looking like him.

A second problem, not immediately recognizable, grew to such dimensions that ever since, in cases of panic, I think to myself, "Well, it's not as bad as Johannesburg." The technicians of Strand Electric had departed, having set the operas going, and presumably instructed the local man (there was only one). I knew nothing about the working of electronic boards; as it turned out, neither did the theatre electrician. *A Man for All Seasons* depends on swift and frequent changes of lighting to indicate total changes of mood and locale within a unit set. They never happened. We went over and over it; the margin of time grew shorter and shorter; "electrics" and I worked longer and longer. I developed an ulcer (who shall blame me?), and Taubie Kushlick, the management, brought me gelatinous substances and thermoses of chicken soup, and I kept cutting the actors' rehearsal time (which was desperately needed) to get the lights right. The time margin diminished, narrowed, was gone. On the opening night "electrics" said, "Will you sit in the booth and help me?" I agreed.

But I knew that, beyond a certain point, I couldn't. Whole sets of lights had to be preset together on master dimmers; one cue missed and the whole thing would be out of sequence—the "river" would blaze with light, More's garden be in blackness, the dungeons effulgent, the Trial invisible. (It happened once, in London, in the early days of electronic boards, on the first night of a famous actor's Hamlet, and irretrievably wrecked it.) It almost happened that night. Halfway through the first act "electrics" turned to me. "I'm lost," he said. "What shall I do?" At this moment an angel appeared. He looked like Michael Grobelaar, who had been my stage manager in *A Touch of the Poet,* and was house manager of the new theatre; but I knew him for an angel. He picked up the cue sheet instantly and began dictating from it. "Set the White Master with this—this—this . . . . dim out the Red Master—" (to me) "when?" *"Now!"* "Now. Dim up the White. Reset on the Red. . . ." We were in business again. I sweat still in recollection.

The irony was that, being in the light booth, I couldn't judge the acoustics. It was the first time we had ever had the auditorium filled with people, so nobody could have known; but it turned out that they were totally, unbelievably impossible. I had realized they were going to be bad, and already started a lot of "come downstage and face front," which I detest. I had tried everything I could think of to block off the wide-open spaces at the sides and back of the stage. But this was plain murder. You could sit in Row E 4 and hear nothing whatever; in M 26 you could hear perfectly; in T 19 intermittently; in J 23 not at all. There was no rhyme or reason to it. It was a "rogue" auditorium. There ensued, of course, a good deal of furor and recrimination and hasty palliatives and the addition of panels and louvers and the rest of it; but nothing could be done quickly enough to save our production. Moreover, I had always thought that if the Afrikaner press "got the message" of the play, they would hate it; and they did and they did. The English papers did their best for us (the Rand *Daily Mail,* like its counterpart, the Cape *Times,* must be one of the most courageous newspapers in the world). But you cannot fight ideologies with one ear and acoustics with the other, and between them they were too much for us.

3

The National Government of South Africa, like most authoritarian governments, is not partial to criticism. My feelings about its treatment of the theatre will probably render my future presence within its territory unacceptable. I would be sad not to see South Africa again; such an unimaginably beautiful country—such warm, hospitable, charming people; audiences brimful of enthusiasm; dazzling scenery; unshakable sources of wealth buried deep, miles deep, under the earth's surface; the sand-silver, flat-topped mountains, man-created, which are the first things you see as the plane circles in over Johannesburg, and the last glimpse you get of the city as you peer over the top of the exotic farewell bouquets with which your hosts have loaded you on your departure. If you like adjectives, you cannot fail to enjoy South Africa. Let me proffer a last one. Vivid; this applies to all sorts of jumbling memories.

A luncheon was given for me in Pretoria during my first visit at which were present a small group of women who were the wives of Cabinet Ministers, or themselves holders of positions of power and authority. By far the least impressive persons at the table were the American Ambassadress and myself. We were the best-dressed (or she was—I have never been sartorially distinguished), the most urbane and amusing. But we both seemed diminished. The talk ran much on a series of wall tapestries being woven by these ladies for the new Government Hall at Pretoria. There was an air of certainty that competition from the Gobelin factories need no longer be feared. There was an equal certainty that whatever these formidable ladies in hats wished to get done would get done.

Only democratic governments have ever neglected the theatre, or left it to go bumbling inefficiently along in a circus-and-commerce manner by guess and (with luck) by God. The National Government of South Africa has known what to do with the theatre, in line with what it wanted to do on the national scene. It has wanted a bilingual country, and it has therefore fostered Afrikaans theatre, especially schools programs. There is only a meager amount of Afrikaans dramatic literature, but the supply of Afrikaans-speaking actors has increased both in quality and quantity. Acting pay scales have been greatly improved as the structure of government-supported theatres grew. Independent managements still struggle with the old problems —few actors, fewer directors, high costs, geographical distances. Ironically, they are forced to rely largely on "light entertainment," since the subsidized theatres can offer longer runs and better terms to the fine plays; for the government has known that it is good to have theatre on your side.

Money has been allocated to four different areas, self-governing and geographically divided. Theatres have been built—not only the acoustical disaster at Johannesburg. The latest (to date) is the Nico Malan in Cape Town, which proclaims itself in an impressive document. "You are seated," it tells the audience member, "at the moment in the finest theatre in the Southern Hemisphere." (Until the Sydney Opera House gets to seating anybody, this may well be true. Mind you, the scale is small—an "average attendance of 244" is a prideful accomplishment.) "With the evolution of four full-scale performing arts boards in South Africa, the acting profession has gone 'respectable.'" (Gracious, how nice! and how's the acting?) "The actor or actress can now plan a full year according to the parts offered, and then happily 'commute' from province to province." Should this forecast prove accurate, it will break the historical precedents of several millennia.

There are warning notes—or rather lacunae and deceptive adjectives. A few samples: "CAPAB Drama, in common with the remaining regional boards, has to exercise keen discernment in the choice

333

of material it presents to the public." Quite right. Whose keen discernment? Not, of course, censorship. An interesting case has been
that of Athol Fugard, the author of *The Blood Knot* and of *Boesman
and Lena.* This author, so the Nico Malan leaflet informs us, has now
been "entrusted" (I like this word) with a version of *Oedipus* for the
Malan Theatre. Mr. Fugard's status has been extensively juggled
with. He was "in," he was "out." His plays were produced successfully in London and New York, but he was not allowed a passport
to go and see them. However, the South African government discovered, somewhere along the line, that Mr. Fugard's plays were
not overtly anti-apartheid, but simply anti-poverty and could have
been written, *have* been written, in most of the other countries of
the Western world. Mr. Fugard was "in" again and was "entrusted"
with a passport; also with the task of working for the Malan Theatre
by dramatizing the story of Oedipus, who put his own eyes out three
thousand years ago. The government acquired a liberal image.

There is another slightly ironic comment in the brochure of the
Malan Theatre in Cape Town. "As you settle back," it says, "in the
luxurious seating . . . for this performance, ponder the fact that
your seat represents a cultural investment of R 1.65 [about $2] by
CAPAB Drama over and above the price of your ticket," you lucky,
pampered, white, repeat white, theatre-goer. Ponder perhaps also, the
reported information that, in 1969–70, PACT (which is the Johan-
nesburg-Pretoria theatre province of government-subsidized theatre)
received a subsidy of R 142,000 (about $170,000) for drama, in
addition to huge subsidies for opera, ballet and orchestra. Nine hundred and one performances were given, of which thirty were for Indian, Colored or African audiences. A highly distinguished visiting
English star told me, however, that in Cape Town a special preview
performance is given for a nonwhite audience; which, she thought,
answered my question "Is there any opportunity for [British] Equity
members to play for nonwhites?"

There is a slightly less publicized activity—almost certainly not
so good, in terms of theatre art, as Sophocles or Anouilh in Cape
Town. A duo of actors—one of them an actress of first class talent
—have put together a program of Shakespearean scenes, so jazzed
up and made comprehensible that Joe Papp himself might well have
presented it proudly in Central Park; but with a difference: in Central
Park everybody could have come in for free and nobody's skin pig-
mentation would have been examined. The actress writes to me:

Within a month we hope to play to about 18,000 African and non-white students. Were a set, or even drapes, essential to the performance, we wouldn't have been able to stage it under the primitive conditions that exist in the township halls. . . .

Of the pitifully few legal avenues that still exist for communication between races in this country, the theatre must be one of the most direct . . . and the Africans want us desperately. Initially we offered to give two free performances of our Shakespeare programme in the townships, but many more were requested for which the Africans offered to pay ten cents a head. We agreed to this but said that after covering expenses we would like to donate the profits back to a fund for African education. We were thanked, but told that such a gesture was unnecessary. It was more important that we come to act for their people. If we made a profit they felt we would be encouraged to return and other white artists might follow us to the townships.

Playing to African students is not easy. . . . Our theatre is very foreign to them. Trying to reach their hearts and heads with the words of Shakespeare is very hard, but it can be done. The desire to reach each other is very strong. . . .

It should perhaps be added that it has also been hard for white groups to get passes to enter the townships at all; and that any breath of political propagandizing, by anybody, is apt to imperil all permissions granted to everybody else. A further ironic footnote is that the boycott exercised by many authors against the performance of their plays in South Africa because of audience segregation is felt by the Africans themselves to bear most hardly against them since they, too, are cut off from contemporary dramatic literature. Some independent managers try to give performances for nonwhite audiences; but the costs are so great, the facilities so totally lacking and the return so minimal that it is next to impossible.

In contrast to the government's theatre policy, concerted and implemented, actors and actors' organizations have made all the wrong guesses and done, in effect, nothing. I am speaking, of course, of visiting actors. Those who were born in South Africa, or have settled there, must either approve the conditions imposed by government policy, acquiesce in them, doing the best they can, or leave. Visiting Americans just plainly do not visit. This is largely a question of economics; the same situation obtains in Australia. "The Southern Hemisphere" (to borrow the Cape Town phrase) has never seen American companies. They cost too much. But it is also true that a member of American Equity can hardly make it his proud boast that no member of his Association will play to a segregated audience in the United States and then go off and do it in South Africa. Pop singers and groups have done it for all-black (or nonwhite) audiences. Indeed, it was a bitter joke in Cape Town that a lot of whites "blacked up" to get into the blacks' theatre to hear a black American.

British Equity has been in a more difficult position. In the old days many British companies visited South Africa. Indeed, there was little home-grown theatre. Since the government's apartheid policies came into force there has been much debate and several changes of policy. "No one in any country should be excluded from any theatrical entertainment whether as spectator or performer by reason of race, color or creed," declared the Association boldly. A boycott was instituted with the object of increasing the very small number of desegregated theatres which—in the late Fifties—still existed. Predictably, the government then closed them. The boycott was abandoned.

It was widely felt that a labor union should not try and dictate to its members on what was fundamentally a matter of individual conscience. Was it better to go to South Africa and try to keep the lines of communication open, or stay away and shut them? Equity decided to ask its members voluntarily to sign a statement which declared: "I will not perform in South Africa if I am forbidden to play before multiracial audiences." Most of them did so.

Over the years, however, it has become abundantly clear that there is no way of playing to a desegregated audience and very little chance of reaching a nonwhite one. Nevertheless, Equity's pious resolution seems to be widely disregarded by individual actors, even those who signed it. Many others either do not know of its existence or regard it as a meaningless platitude. Like the boycott, it has failed to achieve its aim even though, in my view, the principle remains entirely valid.

The theatre has never taken kindly to regimentation; but it takes very kindly indeed to audiences of whatever color. Inside South Africa, cracks begin to appear in the barriers of prohibitions. Organized efforts begin to be made to improve facilities in the townships and, as one group puts it, "to co-ordinate and assist in the interchange of performances between white and township areas." The indomitable Professor Elizabeth Sneddon, backed by her University of Natal, raised sufficient private funds to train and equip a troupe of fifty-five Zulu actors and send them to the 1972 World Theatre Festival in London.

The government allowed them out—under bond to come back again.

But in the same week the "Coloreds" in Cape Town organised a boycott against Margot Fonteyn and her ballet. A single performance had been offered for nonwhites only, at a different theatre. They declared they would rather not see her than accept this act of "charity" with the endorsement of segregation it implies.

The pressures for freedom grow. Conditions change. But the basic dilemmas remain as sharp as ever. They must, of course, so long as apartheid is accepted as a principle of government.

Next year, so the government says, television will be allowed for the first time in South Africa. Nobody knows where this will lead. Television, like radio, will do as it is told. There will be much more employment for actors and they will have to accept whatever form of censorship is imposed on the medium. The powers that be will no doubt use it "with keen discernment." Actors may well find themselves dubbing *The Forsyte Saga* in Afrikaans. At least, let us hope, they will not have to earn their living by enacting fatuous "commercials" of which they do not believe a word.

Visual education is the medium of the future. Its power and importance are limitless, especially in South Africa and Australia, so sparsely populated, so meagerly supplied. Let us pray that wisdom will go with power. I cannot seem to feel very hopeful.

Chapter Thirteen

The Groves of Academe

BERKELEY

What with lectures and bus tours, I have probably visited more campuses than anyone in the American professional theatre. Most of the time this has meant only a recital or a talk and generally an informal meeting with the students over some convivial coffee. Sometimes I have stayed for several days, given a couple of public shows, talked to or with or at members of the departments of theatre, speech, English or other interested segments. Three times I have done full stage productions within a university context, once with a professional company linked to university sponsorship, and once after having been thrown bodily into the university dishwasher for a whole semester. (I begin to sound like St. Paul again ". . . once was I stoned, thrice I suffered shipwreck . . . in journeyings often, in perils of waters; in perils of robbers; in perils by mine own country-men . . . in perils in the city; in perils in the wilderness . . ." Sometimes it felt a little like that.)

In 1964 the whole United States became involved in a fever of celebration because, four hundred years earlier, the wife of a small-town tradesman living in Stratford-on-Avon had given birth to a son, christened William. In fact, the activities of the great Quadricen-tennial year had got under way many months previously. In this, as in other matters, the University of California at Berkeley was ahead of the game. It was Travis Bogard, chairman of the Department of Drama, with a Quadricentennial look in his eye, who first introduced

338

me to Berkeley's Greek theatre, while I was on tour in the Bay area in 1962.

I had heard of it, of course; and it proved to be a very formidable monument. I gazed at it; it gazed back impassively; the rising tiers of stone seats; the lawns and trees beyond, climbing up into the sky; the enormous, flat, pillared stage, about three times as wide as the Metropolitan Opera House. I saw a name graven large on the stone wall. Sophocles? Aeschylus? No. William Randolph Hearst. "Shakespeare!" murmured Professor Bogard, persuasively. "One of the Roman plays; the Quadri—" I said I knew.

I looked doubtfully at the entrances, a brisk five minutes' walk away from stage center; the level, circular "orchestra," some fifty feet in diameter; the "front row," only just within hailing distance. I pondered. "How are you fixed for *Antony and Cleopatra?*" I demanded of Mr. William Randolph Hearst. He met my eye, stony but baleful. "Well, *I* think it would be very exciting," I stated belligerently. Battle had been joined.

In the fullness of time I was appointed a "Regents' Professor" at the university and prepared for the fray. It was not to be, strictly speaking, a campus production. The casting was done from the whole San Francisco area and rehearsals took place during July and August 1963, while the university was not in full session. There were some undergraduates and graduate students, some faculty, some nonprofessionals from the many theatre groups around the Bay, one or two ex-professionals, including Cleopatra, a faculty wife who had been the golden girl of her year at Carnegie Tech and later joined William Ball's ACT company. Many of those involved had daytime jobs or summer classes, so that rehearsals were restricted to evenings and weekends—except for special sessions when I would grab anyone I could get and rehearse anywhere I could find. The sets were by a professional designer, the costumes by the university costume department—both excellent.

The problems presented by the stage were enormously interesting to me and the fluidity of the semi-thrust, semi-Greek arena offered as many opportunities as it did problems. We interrupted the wide, flat stretch of stage platform with a group of tall pillars on either side, some of them broken, suggesting that they had preceded the protagonists of this play and would outlast them. We concentrated the lights within the area thus defined. I was therefore enabled to meet the play's demand that Rome and Egypt should advance, recede, hurl

339

themselves against each other like breakers of the sea. The entrances, though fantastically difficult to time accurately, could be made from "outer darkness," and the protagonists of one scene overlap the disappearance of the actors in the preceding one. The forward thrust of the platforms gave me an area on which to play the intimate scenes. It is not realized, as a rule, that the earlier exchanges between Antony and Cleopatra belong to the genre of *Private Lives* rather than of antique tragedy; comedy, irony, satire, deadly political cut-and-thrust dominate most of the play. It soars into tragedy only at the end—and, of course, because, as in *Oedipus,* we know that the "hero and heroine" are doomed from the beginning.

Berkeley does not have the marvelous acoustical properties of the true Greek theatres; the architect allowed them to slip away sideways in a great gap below the stage platform and on each side of it. Subtlety, therefore, slips away too. But the stone steps plunging down into the arena are wonderful for pageantry and on-rushing battles; and it is greatly to the credit of the Berkeley Theatre Department that its actors are made to play without mikes, and do so remarkably well. The department is thereby involved in minor wars with "Grounds and Buildings"—to divert the traffic, stop the bells from the Carillon Tower, and turn off the rushing mechanism of air-conditioning in the neighboring Science Building. It even tangles with local airport authorities in an effort to rearrange plane routings. But, all in all, the production area endowed the play with a dramatic, even an epic, quality which made it vital and exciting.

My first instinct, that it would be a battle, was proven entirely correct, and there were many times when I felt certain it would be lost; but for my fellow fighters, it certainly would have been. Even the elements joined to oppose us. Sunday was the only time when the entire cast could rehearse by day as well as by night. From noon until 5:30 we would sweat under a blazing sun without a scrap of shade. Then we would go home, to give the temperature a chance to drop thirty degrees, and change into heavy slacks, topcoats, mufflers and gloves. We would return to toil through the evening hours, while the mists hovered round us and a mean, sneaky little wind blew crosswise through the amphitheatre and whipped over the pages of our scripts whenever we stopped clutching them.

"Toil" is the operative word. We had decided to build a series of platforms in descending levels, thrusting boldly out from the stage over the circular arena space. I "sat," in theory, at the inner rim of the stone benches, facing the center of the stage. I began to "block" the play for its eighty or ninety actors. Before every entrance I walked some one to two hundred feet, up the ascending platforms, to organize and demonstrate its mechanics to the actors concerned; then we all covered another quarter of a mile or so while I showed them just where to go; then I completed the round trip back to home base. At the next rehearsal most of the actors had forgotten where they were to go or how they were to get there, so I did this all over again. "Enter Caesar's army" might involve only one main-line trip, but about sixteen whistle-stops.

In the later stages of rehearsal I would check for visibility and audibility from farther away and higher up. Like true Greeks, we disdained microphones. The audibility problem was therefore considerable, and I ran round and round the amphitheatre in ascending circles like an agitated ant. If I had to give a stage direction that involved "showing" and not just telling, I had to walk down from the third floor, so to speak, to the cellar and up again. I began to echo Cleopatra's cry "Let me sit down! O Juno!"

Rehearsals drew on; locomotion grew less. The weather was extremely "unusual"—it never prevented us from working. The sun baked the amphitheatre till it retained its warmth even at night, and we gleefully cast aside our topcoats and began to think perpetual sunshine was quite normal.

Miraculously, costumes appeared—something like a hundred and fifty of them. They necessitated a renewed bout of climbing up and down in order to demonstrate how to walk up steps wearing a long robe and carrying something, or how not to get the sword between the legs when sitting down. Props occurred: splendiferous standards, spears, canopies and huge poles sixteen feet high; they duly refused to go through doorways or to be held aloft throughout a whole scene without wobbling. A pole-bearer fainted in the middle of the dress rehearsal and would have brained his neighbors if the pole hadn't been made of cardboard.

Light towers grew tall a mile or two away on the heights that ring the amphitheatre, and bravely threw their beams, like Portia's little candle, at the distant stage. An orchestra cropped up, and so far as I could see, would have to be accommodated somewhere in downtown Oakland, there being no nearer place for it. Last of all, and only just before the final dress rehearsal, the steps and rostrums got painted, very effectively, in black, flicked and veined with varying reds. They weren't completely dry when we began the first "full dress," so we flung down tarpaulins and pieces of canvas where people had to sit, fall or die, having in mind Iras's gauzy garments and Antony's snow-white tunic.

Came the day: grey, lowering, full-bellied clouds; whitecaps on the waters of the Bay. It began to rain, softly at first, then steadily, torrentially, with satisfaction. Around four o'clock it stopped, grudgingly. The clouds still hung, watchful, a few feet above us. Armies were conscripted and swept the platforms clear of the deepest lakes. A good deal of the red and black came off on our mops, brooms, feet and hands. It was clear that Antony would meet his death wearing a red and black checkerboard, and that Iras would probably catch pneumonia. "Don't worry," said Professor Bogard, "the risk is only hypothetical. Just look at those clouds over the Bay." "You mean we won't be able to give a show?" "I shall decide at seven o'clock," he replied, sounding remarkably like General Eisenhower. The clouds lifted just enough to clear the light towers, and in the west the sky was bright—or at least palely silver. At seven o'clock he signaled the great armada. It made ready to sail.

I hadn't the smallest hope that an audience would appear, but it did; equipped with rug, thermos flask and stadium boots just as if it had been a Big Game. Play—I mean *the* play—did finally begin. All went well, if damply. And then came the fog. Down the hills it swept, and up from the Bay; the colored beams of light caught and held and were defined by it. Out of its mystery, armies came into view, unheralded, seeming immense, took the stage and vanished. Magically, Cleopatra appeared, bringing Egypt with her, as Rome was swallowed up in darkness. The cardboard poles, painted a gleaming black, grew from the floor of the stage to create a gigantic prison for the dying Queen. And from the upper levels of the theatre you looked down upon a swirling caldron of mist and small, gallant figures, caught like moths in the brightness, and the great lines came singing upward like arrows. . . . Had the play been *Macbeth* instead of *Antony and Cleopatra*, the effect would have been stupendous.

"C'est magnifique, mais ce n'est pas la guerre," the author might fairly have commented. But I doubt whether he would have been surprised, except by the chance magnificence. The vagaries of the weather must have been a commonplace to the Lord Chamberlain's Men; he must have groaned many times over such mishaps as these. And he must be subjected to them all over again. They are a part of the four hundred years of life, the price of escape from being petrified as the Immortal Subject for Examination. The actors—eager, generous of themselves, dauntless under fire; the stage managers and electricians and costumers and carpenters, slaves of the lamp without whom its flame would die; the audience, who are also the creators and "onlie begetters"—all are touched with the recklessness of an adventure. It may not always be gloriously successful, but it is very seldom dull and never twice the same.

There were negative aspects of this experience. For instance, the matinee performance was overloaded with schoolchildren whose "attention span" was definitely overstretched. They found the death of Eros pretty funny and the botched suicide of Antony uproarious. It wasn't the actors' fault; and to some extent it is a normal, though primitive, reaction. In South Africa I had been warned, when I was about to play to a Bantu audience, that if they were impelled toward tears they would probably giggle; and they did. The American young can be somewhat the same. Nevertheless, I do not think it is a good idea to push them in bulk into a large theatre and compel them to listen to high tragedy without giving them some indication of what they may expect and what is expected of them. The long weeks of school performances which the actors at Stratford, Connecticut, have to undergo before they reach their adult audiences can be very damaging. There is no possibility of delicacy or finesse; and there are so many pitfalls to be avoided that it becomes impossible to play a love scene—or sometimes a death scene—as you would really want to play it; you are too busy avoiding the laughs. On the other hand, broad comedy will score more than it is worth and the actors will be severely disillusioned later on. It is a pity that school audiences cannot be mixed in with adults, so that each could pick up the reactions of the other—the kids becoming better-mannered and the adults more impressionable. Within a university context, it should not be impossible to achieve a degree of this sort of "integration."

The Berkeley assignment also included a seminar for a small group of school and community theatre directors from the Bay area and even from Sacramento, where the Eaglet Theatre is a model of its kind. I did vast amounts of preliminary reading and probably learned more than I taught. But it was rewarding—and misleading. I was to learn later that one seldom has the chance of teaching under such specialized conditions. The Theatre Department itself was very ably staffed and, at that time, abominably housed. It has acquired its own buildings since. Some of its graduates had managed to acquire a good deal more experience than many Equity members, in that they had played a lot of important parts in good plays, not only at the university but in the many nonprofessional groups of the San Francisco area. The standard of these groups was, to say the least, variable and, no doubt, occasionally lamentable. There are the inevitable questions as to the advantages of high endeavor and therapeutic value as against displays of vanity and low standards of accomplishment. They cannot be answered by generalizations. But the chairman of the Berkeley department was perfectly clear and specific in his aims. He was not trying to train people for the professional entertainment industries. His interest lay in educational theatre. He thought that more interesting plays were done, more experiments made and more appreciation of dramatic literature gained in a university context than in the professional fields. I thought it a deplorable viewpoint, but there was too much truth in it to be disregarded.

BOSTON

In Berkeley I had not been working within the normal university structure. The first time I undertook a production cast solely from students of the Theatre Department was the following year at Boston University. The department had only very recently been taken over by Mouzon Law. Since we were now truly in the Quadricentennial zone, the play had to be by Shakespeare. I chose *Measure for Measure,* partly because I wanted to do it again myself, putting to use what I had learned, and partly for the good reason that the play has a number of equally important parts and does not depend on a tremendous Macbeth or a scintillating Rosalind.

What followed is not what would happen today. Mouzon Law had already started to transform the shape and purpose of the department's program; he has since made it into one of the finest in the country. He holds a philosophy quite different from that of my Berkeley friend. He has never ceased to make experiments and explore possibilities for liaison between the drama student and professional actors, playwrights, directors, designers, to forge links and establish

344

bridgeheads between schooling and professional practice. The introduction of visiting directors like myself was an early step. I think both he and I learned from it.

To begin with, the audition process was nonsensical. Dozens and dozens of students were hurled onto the stage during the course of one afternoon and evening. They "did" a few lines, of their own choosing, and were carried off on a conveyor belt. They ranged from sophomores to graduates, anyone who wanted, come one, come all. From among them I was supposed instantaneously to short-list the "possibles," and to set them speeches from the parts for which they might be suitable, to be read on the following day. Since I had never set eyes on any of them before, it was impossible to fulfill this very important task satisfactorily. The help and advice of the other faculty members was most kindly proffered me, but I had no time to seek it.

In Berkeley they had made a short list of "possibles" for me before I arrived. Perhaps this may have eliminated a few individuals in whom I might have thought I detected talent, but the job had been carefully done and I should think the errors were rare. Heaven knows, a very long "short list" was left. At least it safeguarded me; I do not mean my time or labor, but my capacity for judgment. Some directors, producers and other "choosers" allege that they can make instant choices without undue effort. Not me. I try dreadfully hard to concentrate on everybody. My eyes, ears, sensibilities become so blunted, my memory so stretched beyond reason, that I end by praying for the next comer to be terrible so that I needn't try to remember him. I scribble feverish word-sketches: "Blonde, blue sweater—long straggly hair—good voice—poss.—not for this part." I ask her to come tomorrow and read another part. A girl appears in a red dress and head scarf hiding her hair and I have no recollection of her whatever. I am infinitely relieved when I can write my code for oblivion: "N D T." It means "no discernible talent." (Subconsciously I have, even then, hedged the bet.)

I have attended singing auditions, where, of course, there are certain ineluctable standards of technical skill; the same is true of dancers. But acting is an accomplishment nearly impossible to categorize except within wide and elastic margins. Since auditions are almost the only gateway to a vastly overcrowded profession, they should be treated with far greater care by those who arrange them, judge them or even participate in them. The Theatre Communications Group has made a valuable contribution to this end in arranging regional and group auditions; but the method remains, I suppose inevitably, fallible in the extreme. Perhaps a newcomer to the theatre had better be trained from the beginning to accept injustices, bad judgment and bad luck as a part of his chosen profession.

In Boston, to return there, the standard seemed to me shockingly low; but in the outcome my cast delivered a remarkably good performance. Their zeal and capacity for hard work were unbounded. In Boston I met for the first time a condition which I am sure is general in most large universities. The students chosen for the "big productions," such as mine, get no additional time to devote to it. They have to fulfill their entire quota of classes, lectures, theses and other assignments—and get the rehearsals in as well. My children (I soon grew to love them with possessive affection) would have worked from 8 a.m. to 3 p.m. before they ever got to me. They had to come from another part of the campus, a subway ride and a longish walk from the theatre we were using. They were already tired out. After I let them go, never later than 10 p.m., they had to write their theses or do their other preparatory work. Naturally, I did everything I could not to call anyone I didn't need and not to keep them hanging around unnecessarily; but this is a tricky business and not every director will be bothered with it. Also, they should have been able to learn by watching; but they hadn't time. They got no official credits for their work with me. What should have been the high point of their training became an extracurricular activity. This is widely true and patently absurd.

Naturally, the students were a little wary at first of an outside director; but we soon got on terms of easy communication. I found that they were terribly aware of criticism by and from each other, since mutual criticism was (and I'm sure is) much used in classes. I am inclined to think this is a dangerous method. To criticize from knowledge, constructively, is never easy; to criticize from ignorance, destructively, is much too simple; and since an actor's instrument is not a slide rule, but himself, it may result—as it had in some of these students—in an inhibiting self-consciousness. Their chief problems, though they themselves did not know it, were plainly in the perception of images and the lucid speaking of words with fluidity and understanding.

The technical departments were headed by two men of renown in the professional theatre, both of whom I had known. Horace Armistead did the sets; he had run his own scenic studios, designed many productions and been technical director at the Met when I first went there; a Yorkshireman with an ingrown accent, humorous and purposeful. The costume department was in the hands of Raymond Sovey, once Gilbert Miller's head designer, an aging man now, full of theatre lore and theatre love. The technical and design students were admirably trained. I have found this to be true in many colleges and universities, though they are rarely fortunate enough to get two men such as these. But the requirements are concrete: a faultily built set will fall down and a badly cut costume fall off, so teaching is kept to hard, disciplined standards. There is no room for muddled "improvisation" and self-indulgence.

In spite of having clarified and extended my ideas about *Measure for Measure,* I was only able to make them partially effective, and that through the design departments. But I did have an Isabella who was, as I am convinced she must be, truly young, innocent, passionately dedicated to becoming "the bride of Christ"; unless this quality can be made real the character is meaningless. I also had an Angelo who showed considerable potential ability in this exceedingly difficult part. He afterwards got as far as an apprenticeship at Stratford, Conn., and then got lost in the vast, sprawling shuffle of the entertainment industries; a waste of talent, all too common.

THE NATIONAL REPERTORY THEATRE

My next experience in the university field touched it only tangentially through a professional assignment. Nevertheless, it contributed to questions which have grown increasingly important in my thinking, namely: Is a college training essential, or even especially valuable, to anyone who plans to work in the professional theatre and its related arts? If so, are current academic programs providing the training they should? To what extent should they, can they, do they fill the void left in the cultural life of the United States by the diminution of professional theatre?

The National Repertory Theatre had been founded by Michael Duell and Frances M. Dougherty in 1959, with Eva Le Gallienne as its main star. Its objective was to bring back fine plays, other than

current Broadway successes, to the old touring routes; and, by extension, to send out companies playing more than one play in repertory.
The first tour was a single play, Schiller's *Mary Stuart,* with Eva as
Queen Elizabeth, in a production originally created by Tyrone
Guthrie at the Phoenix Theatre in New York. It included a great
deal of bus-and-truck life, and the usual adventures, such as getting
snowbound in the middle of South Dakota; it was particularly tiring
for Eva, whose make-up as Elizabeth took over two hours to put on.

The following tour, building on the enthusiastic reception of this
one, comprised two "Elizabeth" plays, the Schiller, and Maxwell
Anderson's *Elizabeth the Queen.* To this rather hollow piece Le
Gallienne's performance lent extraordinary magnificence. There were
still some long jumps and short half-week dates, but the tours were
settling down into a longer-playing routine. After a year for re-
organizing and taking breath, the NRT launched into "real repertory,"
with three plays, *The Seagull, The Crucible* and *Ring Around the
Moon;* Eva played in two and directed one—*The Seagull,* which she
also translated; the following year, again three plays, of which Eva
directed two but did not play herself. Then came the season in which
I joined them. The program was to be *The Madwoman of Chaillot*
and *The Trojan Women,* both of which I was to direct, with Eva
playing the Countess and Hecuba, and *The Rivals,* under the direction of Jack Sydow, with Sylvia Sidney as Mrs. Malaprop.

The idea of taking plays like this across the country was beyond
praise. It had not been done since the days of the old actor-managers.
It was just what we had wanted to do with the A.R.T., but of course
it was hopelessly uneconomic and needed an amount of subsidy which
its founders had great difficulty in raising. Having no home base, the
National Repertory was nobody's child. It had to face, as we had
done, the crushing burden of rehearsing, building sets and making
costumes in New York at the highest possible cost. Michael Duell
accordingly formed a liaison with the University of North Carolina
at Greensboro, and subsequently with Ohio State at Columbus.

The arrangements varied slightly, but the broad principle was that
the university paid the National Repertory Theatre a fee plus rehearsal and performance space for the final week or so of preparation
and the previews and opening performances of the repertoire. In
return for this, the actors were made available for class discussions
and seminars, some rehearsals were open to students and some performances given free for them, as well as some for the local patrons

and public. In Greensboro they also helped with the putting-on of the shows. It did not lift a great deal of the financial load off NRT's back, but it did help. It also meant that the final stage of work took place in a setting outside of New York, where the actors could concentrate on their work without other distractions; or that was the hypothesis.

For myself, I found that "the Greensboro connection," if I may so phrase it, was a mixed blessing. The fact that actors were always having to go off and address classes of students was disrupting to the rehearsal schedule; Eva plainly said she could not do it; that the creation of two parts like Hecuba and the Comtesse Aurélie was a more than full-time job, even though the rehearsals of the third play afforded her a certain amount of technically "free" time. She was, in this sense, perfectly right. She also opposed the admission of a floating student audience to any but the final dress rehearsals; and, again, there is much to be said on both sides of this question.

George Bernard Shaw, who was hardly an introvert and was not averse to public appearances, pronounced firmly, "Remember, no strangers must ever be admitted to rehearsals"; the secrecy surrounding them should be absolute. He spoke as a director and as an author but also on behalf of actors. It may be, no doubt is, of interest to students to watch a director and actors in the throes of creation; but actors are self-conscious and easily thrown off by premature observation. They are reluctant to try things out for fear of making fools of themselves in public. The director is generally less subjective and sometimes is not averse to showing off to the only audience he will ever get. But for myself, if I have anything delicate or probing to say to an actor, I will not call it out for all listeners to hear. Even talking to the company as a whole is generally better done quietly, sitting together on the stage. What you shout aloud from the auditorium is the least important part of what you do. Learning from rehearsals is a difficult art, even for the initiated. Conducting them publicly can be done, and valuably done, as a deliberate class exercise or demonstration; but not when, as with the NRT in Greensboro, you are trying to prepare a show for public performance in a minimal length of time.

Nevertheless, I think the Greensboro students gained by association with the NRT. Many of the company talked or worked with groups and classes; some of them did it well and some badly. But enough of the genuine theatre "feel" got around to be instructive and useful. Far too many students emerge into the professional field without the foggiest idea of the concentrated labor which will be required of them, of theatre discipline, custom, even terminology. Not that I think the NRT company were an object lesson in theatre discipline. We all lived in rooms or cottages belonging to the same motel; and it seemed impossible to persuade the actors that they could not learn lines, give talks, dress-rehearse, perform *and* sit up being convivial till three o'clock in the morning.

The Greensboro experiment was only one of many efforts to evolve cooperative effort between a university and a theatre company; it was only on a small scale; but perhaps for that very reason it was, I think, worthwhile for both sides. I found it a fruitful experiment. We opened *The Madwoman of Chaillot* first, immediately followed by *The Rivals,* which rested Le Gallienne and me and enabled us to do a considerable amount of work on the third play, *The Trojan Women.* We then moved on to Columbus, where the NRT was under the aegis of Ohio State University. We did not play on campus, but in the delightful old Hartman Theatre, which had once been a regular "Number One date" for touring companies. Now it was "dark" for most of the year, shabby and faded; but it retained an indefinable "inhabited" quality from its days of glory.

We opened with the shows we had already done in Greensboro and completed rehearsals of *The Trojan Women.* The university's demands were easier to meet because only a few of the men were needed for the new production and the rest of them were therefore free. I got a little burdened at times, but mostly because the play was so close to my heart and spirit and drew so much from me.

This was the third time I had tangled with *The Trojan Women.* The first time, my first professional appearance, was in Sybil Thorndike's company. I was highly romantic and emotional, overwhelmed by the greatness of Sybil's playing, by the sweep of pity and terror and tragedy, and by my own first immersion in professional theatre. The second time, which I have described, was during the Second World War. The impact of the play was more immediate, contemporary, sharper, but also, in a sense, narrower. This time I found myself aware of a slight shift of emphases; all the rest was there as before, but as if set against an overwhelming irony—the waste, the unalloyed wickedness of war, the totality of loss, for the "victor" as well as for the vanquished. Dean Fuller, who composed the music, evolved a theme, light, percussive, sinister, which we called "the Greeks will not make it" motif. At the end of the play, as Hecuba and the women go off to exile and slavery, the Greek soldiers stood with lowered spears in the thickening smoke and darkness; in the gateway of the burning city the shadow of Poseidon stood once more, as when he had prophesied "How are ye blind, ye treaders down of cities . . . yourselves so soon to die . . ." and there came the soft, dreadful tapping of "the Greeks will not make it" drum. I had never before been so aware of what the play's author must have felt—that the Trojan War was not only the tragedy of Troy, but an even greater one for Greece.

Eva's Hecuba was perhaps the finest performance I have ever seen her give—quite different from Sybil Thorndike's, smaller in scale but finer in grain, very austere, very piercing. When Talthybius came on bearing the body of the dead child, she looked at him, perfectly still. I used to wonder how he could endure to stand there, confronting those terrible, annihilating eyes. The Chorus (nine people, all fine actresses) I handled as simply as I could, with a good many lines spoken by a single voice or a group of two or three, only rarely chanted in unison. I was proud of the production, as I think was everybody in it. The climax was a very peculiar rock-and-roll experience, heightened, of course, because we were all deathly tired; I had a kind of flu bug which had been decimating the company for a couple of weeks, and our hotel was infested by a convention of juvenile maniacs who yelled and shrieked in and all round it through the hours of supposed sleep.

On the night of our first technical run-through everything was ragged, but I knew "it" was there, hiding away and darting out every now and then. "The management," present for the first time, said not a word. The following night magic occurred. It reminded me of the final run-through of *Hamlet* on the Munich weekend, or the opening of *Othello,* except that there was no audience. I cried like a fool. The management *still* said nothing. Eva and I were infinitely depressed and furious. The next day it transpired that they had said nothing because they were incapable of speech, having wept themselves silly. I warned the company that the same sort of exaltation wouldn't happen again, or only occasionally, and that they were likely to have a letdown.

What we did have was a free student performance, a requirement for those taking certain courses; twelve hundred denizens of Ohio State filled the theatre, coughing and whispering and seemingly as bored as they could be. Le Gallienne withdrew into her tent and became inaudible from sheer rage; whereupon, of course, they coughed and shuffled more than ever, until she emerged and blazed at Helen and mowed down several rows of the orchestra. To help us all, Cassandra's torch, filled too full of Sterno by a zealous prop man, scattered burning bits all over the stage which were mostly put out by the "dames of Troy" with little or no assistance from the Greek army, and all of this amused "the young" of Ohio State hugely. It was a memorable evening.

Afterwards I met some of the faculty of the university, all full of shame and apology for the behavior of the audience. Their analysis of the reason astonished me; it was that their students had absolutely no conception of the horror of war or of suffering other than on the narrowest personal level. This, in retrospect, seems incredible, since the catalytic effect of the Vietnam war must have been within inches of explosion. Such, however was their reading of the situation, and the behavior of the audience confirmed it. The students who attended the other performances we gave in Columbus were mixed in with the outside public; and during the rest of the tour there was never a repetition of that second evening. Neither, I think, was there ever a duplication of the first. You cannot violently assault a newly-created, still tender living thing without leaving at least a faint scar.

The National Repertory Theatre did one further tour, which ended, as had been the case once before, with a brief engagement in New York. Each time they were respectfully received and lost a good deal of money. They had decided to try and do without star names, partly because (the old story) there were so few stars who would commit themselves to a long tour, and partly because they were trying to keep together a semi-permanent company; indeed, they already had some very valuable actors who deserved promotion. The repertoire they chose was not entirely successful, and they were then lured into becoming the first company to try and operate the newly reconstructed Ford's Theatre in Washington. This experiment did not work at all. The reconstruction of the famous site of Lincoln's assassination had been planned more as a museum than as a working theatre; it was hedged with restrictions, including the installation of equipment faithful to the Lincoln era but fatal to this one. Complex problems converged on the same result—the end of the National Repertory. It was a loss; for it should have filled a genuine, and serious, gap in the reach and scope of theatre in the United States.

The end of the university experiment was a loss too. Partnership, or mutual understanding and help, between educational and professional theatre still seemed to elude all attempts to make it work.

MADISON, WISCONSIN

It was not until the fall of 1969 that I really met a great university head on. If I seem to be ungracious to my hosts in my account of this collision, I hope they will forgive me, especially since the theatre section of the Speech Department has changed its ways a bit since I was there. But I learned a lot which enlightened me as to the profound, possibly unbridgeable, abyss between the academic and the professional attitude of mind. This has nothing to do with the personal kindness and magnanimity with which I was treated. The chairman of the department for that year, a research professor on whom the domestic chores for the year had been off-loaded, subsequently asked a former colleague of mine from another university, "Is she always as difficult as that?"

He got a negative reply. Nevertheless, in his experience I *was* difficult; this was largely out of ignorance. I had had, for instance, no idea that the chairman of a department does not necessarily know anything about its component parts other than those within his own sphere. Since I had gone to great trouble to define and summarize what I was going to try to do, for the benefit of those students who wanted to join my classes, I was knocked completely off balance when this same chairman, greeting me at my apartment on the day I arrived, sunnily inquired, "Well, now, Miss Webster, and what are your classes going to be about?"

The wires had got crossed from the beginning. Despite a valued fistful of honorary doctorates, and, as I have said, more campus-visiting than any other "pro" I know, I have never been through the exceeding-small-grinding mills of American college educational processes. Nobody at Madison could have guessed that I was so profoundly ignorant, and nobody seemed to be as anxious as I was to establish preliminary conversation. Geography and disrupted airline

schedules, summer vacations and the lying-around of important communications on the wrong people's desks contributed to the general
misunderstanding.

Two basic and major foundation-stones were out of alignment. I
was supposed, had agreed, to conduct two seminars of not more than
fifteen people each: one composed of senior undergraduates or graduate students, about "Styles of Production"; the other, of a similar or
smaller number, was to be confined to graduate students and/or
faculty members and was to be about Shakespeare. I took pains to
define, within a paragraph, my objectives, and I was assured that the
enrollment could and would be controlled in certain ways so that—
especially in the case of the first seminar—I could get a cross-section
of aspiring directors, authors, actors, designers who would participate
in work and not just be talked at.

To secure this, I took the very excellent advice of Lillian Hellman,
who had had experience in the field, and did two things; one was to
define my objectives, and the other was to issue a questionnaire to
the proposed enrolling student so that the seminars could be, as I had
been assured, hand-picked. More by good luck than good management, my questionnaires turned out to be extraordinarily well devised
to expedite the selective process and give me the information I needed
about the interests, previous knowledge and ultimate objectives of my
"audience." But alas, nobody ever saw my definitions, only the sketchi-
est attempts at enrollment control were ever made, the questionnaires were neither seen nor filled in by the class until its first session
was actually in progress and my two high-level seminars had turned
into "Dramatic Interp. IV" and "Shakespeare V" (or something like
that) and consisted of thirty-four and twenty-six members respec-
tively. These were drawn from every college level, between junior-
year students who really were beginning at the very beginning and
Ph.D. candidates in their late thirties who had already taught in other
colleges and had considerable experience in other American or
European universities or even in professional companies.

This meant that I had to throw away my whole planned framework
and start over again. I was determined that, despite their size, the
classes should be kept on a level of participation and not just be
talked at by me—even had I been able to talk as long and as often
as would have been necessary. I was also determined to break through
the academic "grading" procedure; paperwork exams and grades
dependent on paperwork were almost entirely irrelevant to what I

was trying to do or get the students to do. The department was very cooperative in allowing me leeway to evolve my own eclectic standards of judgment. But so long as grades and paperwork are the pillars of the academic system, it is very hard to teach "theatre" within it.

I found I had to check all my assumptions. I had thought that I might be made very much aware of the much-vaunted "generation gap," but I never was—possibly because I was of the grandmother generation, which "the young" seem to find more generally acceptable, or forgivable. I thought I should appear irretrievably "square," and/or that I should not understand what they were trying to do when it lay in directions strange to me. None of this happened. One of my firmest fellow workers was a wild young man with all the visual appurtenances of rebellion who came to me after my first talk (which was on the importance of language) and said he hadn't agreed with a single word of it. I said that was fine with me and would be stimulating for everybody else, which I think it was.

I had assumed, also, that there might be complicated disruptions, since the University of Wisconsin at Madison was a notoriously militant campus. There were, indeed, quite a few "incidents" while I was there. They varied. Some I found solemnly impressive; others pointlessly arrogant. One such demonstration, in the English Department, involved the disruption of classes, invasions of private files, "sit-ins" in professorial offices. It was designed to secure tenure for a certain member of the faculty, popular with some of the students, partly on account of the "pot and pop" parties he gave for them.

I wondered if the students concerned understood the weird rules of "tenure" as laid down by the American Association of University Professors. They would do well to take a short refresher course. Twenty-five years hence, oh, file-destroying, sit-in students, your children may come to this university. They may be compelled to sit at the feet of an aging mossback, irremovable, unless they remove him with dynamite. Who endowed him with sacrosanct "tenure"? You did.

I thought the university authorities handled these demonstrations very well, on the whole. The state legislature was in session in Madison; it was the focus of much student antipathy, and the university was shot at from both sides. So far as I was concerned, I went on teaching, which was what I was there for, and the great majority of my students went on studying, which was what they were there for. This point of view appears to be gaining ground.

I had been warned about the dope problems—had been sternly advised that today's kids were "very bright—much brighter than we were." I did not find them all that doped or all that bright—minorities of each; no gaps that could not be bridged with a modicum of effort and, above all, trust. By the end of the semester I had got to know some eighty kids—remember their names and something about them outside the classroom. The over-all impression with which I am left is that they were alive, questing, eager to gobble up all you had to offer them, indescribably hard-working. They were also stuffed by "the system" with huge hunks of useless academic knowledge and amazingly naïve, touchingly ignorant—in areas where you least expected it.

Every nonacademic going to work in a college field should start by checking his assumptions; or not making any. So should the college.

Once I had evolved a way of dealing with my unwieldy groups we did fine. I read a lot more and they wrote a lot less than either they or I had expected. Those whose interests lay in writing, all graduates and mostly Ph.D. candidates, did some admirable work—of the sort that could be put on paper. The design students, only a handful, showed a high degree of imagination and technical awareness—they, too, could demonstrate it in concrete terms. The would-be directors were more elusive. They were hamstrung for the same reason that I was—there may have been acting talent, but, at least on the undergraduate level, there had been absolutely no acting training or genuine instruction in the use of an actor's tools. In the department of theatre there was virtually nothing to contribute to the making of an actor. So there were no tools for a director.

My questionnaires had revealed some interesting things. For instance, I had asked in what field the student wanted ultimately to work—professional, educational, community, children's theatre, or "other"? and in what primary capacity—writer, designer, director, actor, executive or technical, teacher? It turned out that of the undergraduate students (a proportion of about five girls to one boy) almost all wanted to be professional actors; on the graduate level, among the M.A. and Ph.D. candidates, almost none. The great majority wanted to work as teachers in the educational field, some as directors of community theatres, with, of course, a certain amount of crisscrossing. Wisdom, I thought, had been rapidly acquired.

The undergraduates were able to take a large number of elective courses and had neither asked for nor received much in the way of guidance as to what they might sensibly "elect." Many subjects which would have been useful, even essential, to them were outside the department, such as dancing or fencing (Phys. Ed.). Singing, naturally, was the prerogative of the Music Department. It hadn't occurred to anybody that an actor benefits from the study of costume, as revealed through art appreciation, or language, as revealed through foreign ones. Since the students were not allowed to take more than a given number of credits within their own department, these outside credits would have been useful; but few took advantage of them for any coherent purpose. On the other hand, all sorts of students who had no serious interest in theatre whatever meandered through theatre courses in order to pick up a few easy credits to supplement their own majors. There was plenty of the study of dramatic literature as literature, but not of how to get it on a stage. There was plenty of "Improv." and "Interp." "Improv." descends (quite a long way) from "the Method" and involves very useful exercises in self-expression and group therapy; it is an invaluable part of training. Repeat, part. A younger member of an acting faculty has written to me:

> I have thought a great deal about the value of all this improvisation and have come to the conclusion that it is more suited to a movement class, and must, in any case, only be indulged in by the actor after he has learnt the disciplines of technique. I am constantly suspicious that it is really an escape from the drudgery of basic training, especially vocal and physical. I begin to plan my courses at the beginning, with the script . . . knowing that that work is being backed with vocal training and body movement.

This makes, I think, excellent sense. "Interp.," which might be defined as interpretative reading, or theoretical interpretation, is also valuable; but it does not constitute the whole equipment of an actor or a director. Voice training you plainly cannot do without; and at Wisconsin there was none at all.

After a couple of introductory talks to my Shakespeare lot, who were all graduate students, I asked each one to pick a speech of his own choosing, not necessarily one that he or she considered would be a suitable part for them to "play" themselves, prepare it and read it aloud. Out of twenty-six about half a dozen read reasonably well; it later transpired that three of them had had training outside the

357

United States and the rest in community or even professional companies. A few others read—what shall I say?—acceptably? It depends on what you accept.

The rest were a total loss, even from the limited standard of translating Shakespeare into intelligible language and leaving out of account entirely the music-psychic-sound values on which the author relied. They might have been reading Beginners' Japanese. Yet, as I later discovered, most of them were highly intelligent, aware, susceptible, eager to be dedicated. The majority planned to be teachers; and Heaven knows that requires dedication. But of this particular means of communication they knew almost nothing; yet it has been tremendous, ever since the first cave man said "Ugh" and his female said "Gook." Speech remains primary. I have read that, even in this present day, more than two-thirds of the world's population can neither read nor write, though human beings have been possessed of language since time immemorial.

In Madison, as on many other campuses I have visited, the Theatre Department is only a subservient section of the overall Department of Speech. "Rhetoric," or learning to make a good speech, does not necessarily involve speaking lines seductively. Poets often read their own poems very badly. Courses in "rhetoric" do not train an actor to do well by Aeschylus, Congreve, Tennessee Williams or Harold Pinter—not as an interpreter, that is; the acting courses, on the other hand, might help speech-making politicians to get elected; a dangerous potential. I saw no signs of its being used.

In my "Styles of Production" class, about halfway through the semester, I tackled the subject of stage movement. Good actors ought to be good athletes; the acrobatics employed by the most avant of the avant-garde are valuable. Greek actors walked up and down steps practically on stilts; Elizabethans were expert swordsmen; clowns and all the circus-ancestors of today's players were practiced gymnasts. Even my mother, in her youth, was automatically expected to do a back-fall off a table or down a flight of stairs without damaging herself; you couldn't be a heroine of melodrama without getting knocked about a bit. Today both chorus and principals in musicals are required to have learned a high standard of singing and dancing skills—far higher than ever before. If they were able to come by these things on the Madison campus, it was more by good luck and their own determination than by any curricular activity. There were a couple of way-out groups organized by the students themselves, who

leaped and pranced and fell about like mad, to the glory of the theatre gods. But they did it for themselves and the results were unpredictable.

There was a brilliant and devoted professor who taught, with
fanatic, obstinate expertise, the arts of the Japanese and Chinese
theatre. He imported teachers from the East. His teaching (since, of
course, it also involved the most abstruse and quintessential art of
standing still) extended to such contemporary playwrights as Mar-
guerite Duras. The university funded his program; but not under the
Theatre Department, with which he was perennially at odds; it was
shifted to the Department of Asian Studies. He preferred that his
students not mix at all with the contaminating mishmash of campus
"theatre." He would not have risen high in the diplomatic service.
But he was a unique asset.

This matter of stage movement affected me in that everyone who
mixes with theatre—teaching, community, educational, whatever—
will certainly, sooner or later, be required to wear costume. Nothing
even remotely connected with this was either taught or contemplated.
I have referred before to the quite primary physical problems involved. Walk upstairs tomorrow morning in a floor-length bathrobe
and carrying the breakfast tray and see. On the other hand, try
sweeping around in a long cloak, or flipping off a wide-brimmed hat
in a flourish of salutation, and see how gratifying it can be. In my
"Styles of Production" course I had chosen *The School for Scandal*
as one of my cross-section of plays, largely because I wanted to talk
about, and demonstrate, the use of eighteenth-century costume, probably the most difficult of all.

I began with the snuff-box routine, as taught to me by Dennis
King, and had brought with me a gold snuff-box which had belonged
to my great-grandfather. I went on to the use of a fan; I had brought
two, my mother's from the period of the Eighteen-Nineties—a
little large for my purposes, but they had texture and balance. (One
member of the class had been taught how to use a Japanese fan
under the "Asian Studies" bit.) Then came, as I have previously
described, the matter of a sword. I asked the costume department if
they would please get me an eighteenth-century dress-sword (or replica thereof) with belt and hanger. The head of the department was
a young woman of wide, accurate and cherished knowledge; her
chief assistant, experienced and skilled; they knew exactly what I
wanted. After prolonged effort the best they could come up with was

a Sam Brown belt and a Civil War saber. I borrowed a fencing foil from an enterprising student who had strayed over into Phys. Ed. for a fencing course, stripped the belt of its accoutrements and put together a hanger with some string and ingenious gadgets from the ten-cent store.

By this time I had almost abandoned the notion of doing very much in the way of rehearsing scenes for this class; most of them had not reached a standard where I could have achieved anything without taking almost the whole semester to do it and wasting the time of the nonparticipants. I did odd bits and speeches, however, and in the Shakespeare class considerably more than that; but it was still a skittery, surface-of-the-ice affair. However, to make my point about *The School for Scandal,* I thought I must at least put Act I, scene 1 (a short scene) "on its feet." I cast as Joseph a lazy but talented young man in his senior year whom I had just seen play Higgins in the all-campus production of *My Fair Lady;* he had been very "acceptably" good. When it came to his entrance, I told him to come on and bow to Lady Sneerwell—not a full court bow with all the trimmings, but an ordinary "afternoon" sort of bow. He said, "I'm very sorry, no one has ever told me how to bow." Four years in the Department of Theatre and as yet no bow. I never came across a mime class, though there may have been one; if so it was not reflected in any fluency with gesture.

Of course a lot of this was my fault; I had laid on a program which, even in its revised version, was far too ambitious and assumed a concentration of theatre studies for theatre students which didn't exist and wasn't supposed to. Having shifted the emphasis, unavoidably, from the rehearsal toward the teaching method, I found there were extremely few textbooks. I was trying to present the whole stage background of my selected plays—what sort of society the author lived in, what sort of theatres he worked in, what the acting of the period was like, who the audience were. When I analyzed the plays, I did so from the point of view of how they should be transferred from the printed page to the stage. It was an unorthodox sort of approach. But unorthodox books do not get into paperback and are not therefore available to students.

I drew on my own book (*The Same Only Different*) for some invaluable information about the nineteenth-century theatre. But this is not a book which has been acceptable to paperback publishers. It is not, they say, "course-oriented." A book was recently projected which was to contain half a dozen full-length prefaces to famous plays—not just the usual thimbleful of introductory notes, but considered analyses from a stage point of view. The first three contributors were to be Tyrone Guthrie on *Oedipus,* Eva Le Gallienne on *Hedda Gabler* and myself on a Shakespeare play; three other well-known theatre people were to write on Sheridan, Molière, Chekhov. The proposal was widely rejected. One publisher said the authors would be too dissimilar in their views; another that it sounded as if it were too much about the actor and would not "be learned enough for the English and Humanities students who are our market." This came as a slight surprise to Doctors Guthrie, Webster and Le Gallienne. But there it is: no courses, no texts; no texts, no courses.

Halfway through the semester I embarked on what turned out to be by far the most successful project of my Wisconsin sojourn, a production of Chekhov's *The Three Sisters* on the Main Stage. Even this began with some disenchantment. I remembered the theatre well; it had been designed and built by Lee Simonson, the Theatre Guild's chief scene designer, and opened in 1935 by the Lunts in *The Taming of the Shrew.* It had one of the first electronic switchboards in America, with the operators sitting in a "goldfish bowl" at the back of the auditorium. It had a capacious stage and an orchestra pit on a lift, which could serve as a forestage. For many years it had housed the best professional touring companies, including mine.

I discovered that it was now greatly despised. Thrust stages are the fashion. They are not, in fact, easy to speak from, but they look easier than Lee Simonson's very deep auditorium with its high, steeply raked balcony. He had assumed that actors would know how to project. Since theatre-in-the-round came into general use, this is no longer felt to be essential. At some point the original switchboard had been moved backstage to a position where its operators had no room and the stage manager was unable to see either them or the stage. Most disconcertingly of all, the Theatre Department had no privileges with regard to the theatre; we had to rehearse in what had been designed as a concert hall, on a stage which resembled the "Main Stage" in no way whatever, and rent had to be paid for all occupancy of the real building. Perhaps the only thing which *The Three Sisters* rehearsals had in common with a professional production was this miserable handicap.

But the contrasts between the professional and the university approach were plentiful. One of them concerned auditions. It was an extension, in the worst possible direction, of what had happened in Boston. This time I was supposed to audition the entire campus. The Main Stage productions were open to everybody. During the course of two afternoons and evenings I was to hear anybody and everybody who thought it would be fun to be in a play, pick a cast, and go into rehearsal with it two days later. I got difficult again.

I could not, of course, negate the basic practice, sanctified by time, but I argued it. A great big free-for-all is perfectly in order; and no doubt there were—are—dozens of people on the Madison campus with histrionic talent which they would like to unleash when they can spare the time from their engineering studies. But when you have only five or six full-scale theatre presentations a year they should, I think, be reserved for highly selected members of those who are studying, teaching or intending to practice theatre—the culmination of their training, the showcase for their attainments. Moreover, the public should not be asked to pay good money to watch other people's fun-and-games. You would not expect to sell tickets for a performance of Beethoven's Ninth executed by enthusiasts who had once played the fiddle in school or sung in a home-town glee club. Nor was I, a quite expensive luxury for the university, imported to teach beginners' acting at Chekhov's expense to those who never intended to be actors.

Other members of the faculty generously agreed to take two preliminary auditions and to guide my choices from their own previous experience. I was forced to cast Vershinin and Anfisa outside the department, because I could not find within it actors who would be as good. I laid myself open to the accusations that I had overburdened the rest of the faculty; that I had favored graduate (i.e., experienced) students over undergraduates; that I had dislocated the usual rehearsal schedule because I had insisted on a gap of a few days between final casting and first rehearsal so that the chosen candidates could have a chance to read and study. It was all true. I did all these things. My single and sole objective was to do Chekhov's play, *The Three Sisters,* as well as it could possibly get done. I am a pro.

None of this surprised me very much. But a further disillusionment was in store. The technical departments were fine, taught by young men and women of great talent to students, more than one of whom seemed to me to have considerable potential, and who also seemed willing to work a twenty-hour day. They were supplemented by volunteers from the department who did manage to "fulfill a requirement" or get a credit of sorts by reupholstering a chair, whereas they would have got none by playing Masha. The technical director, in charge of all the mechanical labors of execution and the final physical production, was terrifyingly efficient. The day after my arrival in Madison he asked me if I had a prop list, though we were not going to begin rehearsing for the next six weeks. Awe-stricken, I made one.

At the dress rehearsal a considerable proportion of the most indispensable props still were not there. To fulfill teaching requirements and what is so nauseatingly known as a "class situation," the rehearsal-prop people had been replaced by another team to whom I had never had the chance to explain what I meant or wanted. The same thing happened about the sound tapes, delicate and immensely complex. The lighting of *The Three Sisters* must be one of the most intricate and subtle ever demanded by a dramatist. A student was assigned to work the switchboard who had never in her life seen a switchboard before. She was limitless in good will; the learning experience, I have no doubt, was invaluable. I went nearly out of my mind. The dress rehearsal was thought splendid; I barely survived it. I was rescued by three or four dedicated stalwarts doing what they weren't supposed to. An ardent young heroine worked the antiquated tape machine; she was ensconced in a broom closet where she could neither see nor hear anything. Liaison with the Music Department was loving, voluntary and extremely intermittent.

One final case of frustration and wasted effort: I had hoped to set up an understudy cast, even a second cast in some instances. Since I was perfectly aware that I was in Wisconsin to teach and not just "be a pro," I thought it would be good to try and teach as many people as possible. I accordingly picked a "second cast," including two or three of the actors playing a maid, an orderly or an "itinerant musician," and prepared to take the necessary trouble to make the rehearsals fruitful for them. It came to absolutely nothing. No one who wasn't playing a good-sized part could afford the time from credit-making courses to come and try to learn from what, rightly or wrongly, was supposed to be a rare opportunity. The near-walk-on people were never there unless they absolutely had to be, and quite often not then. In this case they had other extra-curricular fish to fry; shows directed by each other in which crude but stimulating directorial ideas were being poured away onto the sand because nobody knew how to execute them; the blind were leading the blind with great excitement into a variety of ditches.

But with all that said, and all that undone, *The Three Sisters* was a beautiful show; I would back it to challenge comparison with other productions I have seen done by well-known companies. We had a wonderful time; Chekhov, again, having much to do with it. We enjoyed ourselves, we opened doors to each other and to the audience, most of whom had never seen Chekhov before; we did not, of this I am quite sure, do any dishonor to Anton Pavlovich. I felt very amply rewarded, and so did the other people concerned in the production. We all felt deprived when it was over.

I am not sure that the faculty can have enjoyed my presence so much. They were unfailingly courteous and helpful; they even invited me to an hour's radio discussion with the chairman, the head of the department and the dean, who was entirely charming, and, as chairman of the Athletic Board, far more interested in Saturday's Big Game than in anything the Drama Section might be up to—as is only right. I warned them that I should raise a lot of awkward questions, and I did. These were picked up by many of the students, who asked me to address a meeting about it, and I did. In fact I was generally subversive. I should add that this did perhaps help to "start something." The Theatre Department has undergone changes and is, I believe, undergoing more. I have sounded, unavoidably, very critical of what I found; I should probably never be as critical again because I should never be as surprised. I know, of course, that there is a very great difference between a huge state university like the Madison campus and a small college with comparatively high fees, a small enrollment and a more sharply directed focus. There is one such, Beloit, only a few miles south of Madison where "theatre" is taught—and practiced—astonishingly well. Madison, being the capital of an agricultural state, would not be likely to lean heavily toward the performing arts. In fact, its university has no liaison at all with the Milwaukee Repertory Theatre only a few miles away; and I found that very few of my students had taken the trouble to visit either the Guthrie Theatre, not so far off in Minneapolis, nor the available theatres in Chicago. In those respects the university is more fortunate than many of its counterparts across the country. In many other ways it is typical of them. One of the questions I asked of my colleagues was this: "The professional theatre today offers very limited opportunities to young people. Community theatres, too, are relatively thin on the ground. What are you, in the educational theatre, trying to do either to train actors or to introduce theatre to rural communities? or aren't you trying to do these things at all?" The future of the American theatre must largely depend on the answer.

I left Madison better educated than I was when I arrived. For instance, in my efforts to bring my sights into alignment with those of the degree-seekers, I "read round" *The Three Sisters* far more thoroughly than I would have dreamed of doing for a professional company; and though I am not sure that I really directed it any better, I gained in the process. My classes caused me many intensive hours of library study by which I benefited, without doubt. Nevertheless, I was confused among the twisting groves of Academe. Fears and scruples which I had long harbored were sharpened into hostility. In the end (after I had left the Madison campus), they hardened into something like fury.

The cast of *The Three Sisters,* as I have said, were almost all graduate students, many of them in pursuit of that Ph.D which is the academic union card and which dictates years of grinding and largely useless labors. Several were young men and women in their thirties, who had been teachers, and I'm sure extremely good ones. Three or four were of experienced and proved ability as actors; I would have welcomed them in any repertory company of which I was in charge. There was a young man of great sensibility who, I thought, would not ever be an actor to set the Hudson on fire, but who was already amply well equipped to teach or to direct. This he had already done in several community theatres; but the head of the directing section of the department had refused him admission to the directing classes and set him to studying something quite irrelevant to his purpose. All of them were forced to rush away and write theses in corners whenever they were not engaged in the scene we were rehearsing. They didn't want to; they had to.

Shortly before I left the campus a leaflet was circulated concerning the funding of Ph.D. programs. I learned to my horror that in the Liberal Arts fields an average of ten years elapses between graduation and the acquisition of a Ph.D. Yet nobody—well, *almost* nobody!— really wanted it; they couldn't get the top academic assignments without it. They had to leave their jobs and come back to school to acquire these magic, Open Sesame letters. Often their wives had to take domestic or clerking jobs to help pay the bills.

Before they even got to the thesis-writing bit, they spent a couple of years imbibing terrifying amounts of knowledge. Some of my able and talented cast of *The Three Sisters* attended a drama seminar from whose sessions they would return pale and shaken. One week they had received an assignment to be completed in fourteen days: they were to read Bergson on Laughter, Aristotle on Comedy, fifteen plays very rarely performed on any stage, and write a thesis of not less than ten pages. (There is a dreadful emphasis on prolixity in academic circles.) This, of course, would not bring them one milli- meter closer to becoming Edith Evans or Lynn Fontanne or Mike Nichols or Danny Kaye. It was not meant to.

For the crowning glory of this Ph.D. business is the thesis and the essence of the thesis is its much-ado-about-nothing-ness. The essential determining quality is that your theme should never have been writ- ten about before. This means that your subject must be of an almost unimaginable triviality. Incredible as it may seem, this has even led people to write their final dissertations on such a subject as "Margaret Webster: Her Theories of Directing as Reflected in Her Productions." In three cases, for reasons I now find it hard to imagine, I have been trapped into concurrence—generally because of the writer's heart- rending pleas about the time he had already spent on this foolish labor, and of the dire results which would ensue if I refused to co- operate. The truth began to dawn on me in Madison; only later was it fully revealed.

I had been too innocent to realize three things: First, that the resultant minutiae would be deposited in university libraries where they would be available to anybody who cared to pay $11 for a microfilm copy. Second, that although I always stipulated that the thesis should be shown to me before being submitted, it never was. Third, that because the subject chosen was so recondite and of such minimal interest that the examiners hadn't the least idea what the examinee was talking about; they therefore let by, and by implication endorsed, a number of unimportant but egregious errors of fact which have now become part of the record. At Wisconsin, I offered to supply the library theatre collection with a list of errata to be attached to a thesis by myself, its subject. The librarian recoiled.

"Well," he finally and reluctantly allowed, "if you *really* want to . . ."

The committee of examiners will require of the candidate that he should write to my friends and former colleagues, such as Maurice Evans, Uta Hagen, Helen Hayes, Paul Robeson and so on and so on, requesting their answers to a long and involved questionnaire which would embroil them in hours of time, thought, labor and often research if it were to be answered adequately. Most of them are sensible enough to refuse categorically and on principle; many will simply pitch the request into the wastepaper basket, which is already filled with half a dozen others of the same nature. A few fools like me will occasionally fudge up some hurried, inadequate and often inaccurate replies. The eager examinee will feel astonished, annoyed, "chagrined" (it is a quote) by the lack of response. I wish that examining committees could be persuaded that we have other things to do with our lives than to write several dozen theses a year for any and every doctorate-seeker.

Foiled, however, in his private life research, the candidate will, of necessity, plump up his thesis with extensive quotations from my books (which can be read by anybody who is interested). He will then pronounce on how my productions reflect my theories. He never saw my productions. He has not the slightest idea of how plays get put on the stage under professional theatre conditions or who is responsible for what or how the praise or blame should be allocated. He will plow (God help him!) through endless files of the *New York Times, Tribune, Post, News, Telegram, Journal,* the fringe dailies and the more important weeklies, perpetuating views which were generally valueless to begin with. (It is a dreadful thought that this will involve endless repetitions of the platitudes and prejudices of Clive Barnes, echoing ever more hollowly, throughout the book stacks of eternity.)

It probably will not occur to this potential Ph.D. that there is a richer and untapped field among the critics outside New York, and fine men among them: "H.T.P." of Boston, who was before my time; William McDermott of the Cleveland *Plain Dealer;* Richard Coe of the Washington *Post;* Elliot Norton, also of Boston; and many others. Their opinions may even be of greater worth because they started—as a rule—from the premise that it would be nice if the show were good and that people would enjoy it and that an audience would come to keep alive the fragile theatre life of their cities. They were not trying to exercise destructive power, though they did not forgo judgment. In any case, the Ph.D. candidate cannot assess my productions by reference to any critics unless he can also assess the critics. But he can probably satisfy his examiners by filling half the page with *"Ibid., Ibid., Ibid., Op. cit., Op cit."* By this means any industrious mole can become a Doctor of Philosophy. There was a time when the degree stood for genuine, valuable and original research. In the field of science perhaps it still does. More often, I think, it entraps the unwary into an arid medieval scholasticism which will bury their best years in library dust. It shouldn't have to. There was a very gifted young writer in my Wisconsin classes, the holder of a Shubert Fellowship in playwrighting. You'd think he might be empowered to write a play for his Ph.D. But he wasn't. He had to dissertate.

It is nice to believe—and I do believe—that the worst aspects of the Ph.D. fetish are in decline. I was interested to read very recently that the United States Commissioner of Education was urging more vocational training, more broadly placed and accorded higher status and respect. "We have hypnotized ourselves," he is quoted as saying. "We are so preoccupied with higher education that it has become a national fetish . . . the notion that someone who goes to college is better than someone who doesn't go must be changed . . ." I applaud this with all my heart; adding that everything, but everything, can be focused on the training of an actor—music, history, art, languages, sociology, physical training and enough mathematics to calculate deficits. Ph.D. programs are coming under very severe scrutiny and have even been refused further funding in New York State.

However, I am easily intimidated; and for three months in Madison I had been struggling hard to adapt myself to academic standards, viewpoints, methods of approach and assessment. I had begun to feel defensive. However, a few days before I left Madison something happened which threw my whole laborious academic effort entirely into the discard and rendered all doctorates irrelevant, leaving me an old pro, just where I started. I went to see the Lunts.

They lived an hour's drive away, in Genesee. It was December, deep snow. I drove wearily, tired after the Herculean efforts of *The Three Sisters* and the usual post-production letdown. Also I felt as if I had been running for thirteen weeks, striving to understand difficulties, to perceive virtues—whether in an academic older faculty, a Methodized younger one or Grotowski-inclined students; trying to adjust, to compensate. Genesee is so small that I was past it before I realized it was there. Finally I located the reticent white house, back from the road, a Victorian jewel casket inside, elegant, idiosyncratic, unique.

The "help," for some reason, was away; Alfred, a Cordon Bleu cook, insisted on concocting a most elegant lunch, although he had to wear a pirate patch over one irretrievably damaged eye, and was limping from an injured foot. Lynn firmly declined all offers of assistance. We settled down to talk. They knew far more about the theatre than I did, having just returned from visits to London, Paris and New York. Their accounts of what they had seen were illuminating and astringent. I tried to describe my university life. They swept aside my uncertainties and scruples. I am sure neither of them had ever done a single one of the "Improv." and "Interp." exercises now thought so essential. Bergson on Laughter and Aristotle on Comedy were not their bedside reading.

We discussed the problems of *The Three Sisters*. I had failed, I thought, to help the young actress who was playing Masha with that hideously difficult entrance in the last act—perhaps, I said, through being insufficiently "Method." But I had played the part myself and should have known. "Remind me of it," said Lynn. Well, even Chekhov fails totally to help the actor. "Enter Masha" is all he says; meaning a running, flying entrance, at the highest pitch of agony, straight into her lover's arms. She has exactly one line, "looking into his face": "Good-bye"; one stage direction: "a prolonged kiss"; he has two stumbling sentences and goes, taking her whole life with him. The author gives her no words—just one more stage direction: "crying bitterly." That's all. Lynn thought about it for a moment; then she said decisively, "I don't think I should find that difficult." And, God bless her. I am sure she wouldn't.

They were glorious and trenchant and right, the Lunts. Their absolute professionalism was like rain in a desert to my parched and drooping spirits. I said good-bye gratefully—grateful for the day and for many remembered days. I drove back to Madison, where the *Three Sisters* cast were giving a party for me. I found myself cheerfully exceeding the speed limit by very wide margins and scattering shards of academic endeavor all over the road. Moreover, I was singing; at the top of my voice . . . an old hymn from the school choir:

369

All things bright and beautiful,
All creatures great and small,
All things wise and wonderful,
The Lord God made them all. . . .

And so He did too, I thought, to the rhythm of this jolly tune; and all of them are in the world of the theatre . . . my world. . . .

Epilogue

Letter to a Young Actress (concluded)

Well, dear Miss Worthington,

There it is—as much of the story as I yet know. For what is to come—to see, learn, experience—I subscribe to the credo of Bernard Shaw, though, Heaven knows, I don't always live up to it:

> This is the only true joy in life: the being used for a purpose recognised by yourself as a mighty one; the being thoroughly worn out before you are thrown on the scrap-heap; the being a force of nature, instead of a selfish little clod of ailments and grievances, complaining that the world will not devote itself to making you happy.
>
> And also the only real tragedy in life is the being used by personally minded men for purposes which you recognise to be base. All the rest is mere misfortune or mortality. This alone is misery, slavery, hell on earth.

Since this book has been a story and not a treatise or an academic pronouncement or a Sunday-pundit prophecy in a magazine supplement, I must hand over to you now. I don't know what the future of the theatre—in the United States anyway—is going to be. Any guesses I might make would be outdated within six months. You, if you decide to defy your Coward-minded mother, will have to determine it for yourself.

You know the facts as well as I do—probably better: the decline of Broadway, the struggles, compromises and divagations of Off-Broadway, the thinning-out of public subsidy on all levels, its misapplied effects as well as its high aspirations; you see the "gorgeous palaces" built at such cost and opened with such fanfare; and "these our actors . . . melted into air, into thin air." You even witness the current grim little footnote about the reluctance of audiences to go to shows in New York (once the most flourishing theatre city on earth) because they're afraid to go out at night.

Maybe you think the grass is much greener on the other side of the ocean. Well, in some ways, so it is: the theatre is more tenacious, rooted, yes—"established," in every sense; but it is ready to change, develop, it is not unreceptive to new ideas. And yet . . . and yet . . . British Equity has been so alarmed at the number of Miss Worthingtons who *are* "determined to act" in a field where, as Noel Coward said, "the profession is overcrowded, the struggle is pretty tough," that they have discussed or tried to put into effect all sorts of preventive measures known as "regulated entry." "Rep" companies are to be allowed only a minimal number of young, not-yet-Equity members; there are proposals to limit the number of students graduated from "approved" drama schools; university theatre departments are to be warned that they are not regarded as "approved" vocational training and that between a degree in drama and an Equity card is a great gulf fixed.

These efforts to limit supply to the dimensions of a shrinking demand may well prove impracticable—even illegal. Mathematically, I should suppose that, if they were carried out, the British theatre would rapidly become geriatric. But theatre has a way of breaking out from bonds artificially imposed on it, and genius escapes elimination. Gielguds and Ashcrofts might fail the first audition round, but they would get through somehow. Talent, however, could easily be lost; talent is elusive, hard to detect and often vulnerable when asked to display itself; the personal qualities of judges and judged at an audition may simply not match each other.

(Be careful of auditions, Miss Worthington; not that there is very much you can do; luck, or fate, are factors of dominant importance and there is nothing you can do about them; so keep calm and—if you are given your own choice—do something *you* like and believe in rather than what you guess might please "them." If you are asked to come back a second time, wear the same clothes; unless of course, you discover that the part is that of a pampered Boston

Brahmin, rather than the hippie in blue jeans whom you had originally impersonated.

If you do decide to go ahead, to go "on the stage" regardless of
the risks and obstacles, there will be plenty of things going with you,
or for you, and a lot of heartening optimists who manage to persist in
spite of everything. I had a letter the other day from one of my
"Trojan Women" of the National Repertory Theatre days, one who
has had a very tough time since then; but "here I am again," she
says, "still tilting at windmills." I asked Larry Gates how he felt
now about his gallant sentiments of the bus-and-truck years, which I
was proposing to quote. He replied that they sounded a bit "turgid"
to him now, but that yes, he still felt the same way, and yes, he would
make the same decision in 1971 as he had in 1940 when he hiked
from Minneapolis to New York in order to get into the theatre. I
have a friend who works for the New York State Arts Council; she
writes: "I'm having a wonderful opportunity to learn through seeing
and talking with the experimental crowd some of the things I never
had time to investigate before. It isn't always my bag—much is
simplistic beyond belief . . . but some of it is very exciting and
most importantly, I believe, will in perhaps unforeseeable ways be
incorporated into the work to come." (This I, too, most powerfully
believe.)

So there's life in the old theatre yet, plenty of life teeming with
good will and desire not only for self-expression but for social
service, bursting with commitment. It leaps through devoted gyra-
tions on the Lincoln Center Plaza (weather permitting), it em-
braces nudity with the moralistic fervor of John Brown. The theatre
has lively antecedents in the circus; dedicated ones in the medieval
players who set up their Punch-and-Judy carts in the marketplaces
and (as Adam and Eve and poor, old drunken Noah) stripped to
the glory of God and demonstrated the divorce of nakedness from
innocence. Of course nobody knows exactly what they did until the
time came around when somebody thought to arrange the "improvisations" into word patterns and commit them to paper and posterity.

From your letter, dear Miss Worthington, I detect an impulse to
set out for "New York, where the action lies," and where there are
workshops and basements and attics in which you and your like-
minded friends can scramble around together in dedication, sometimes generating creative fire. I wish I could become less aware of
the enabling power behind all this, the television commercials which

you count on doing, giving you each day your daily non-bleached-flour-unfattened-wheat-germ-grade-AAA-creamery-butter bread. It's really all right, I would suppose, if you can digest it. Why do I mistrust it? Perhaps I have a hangover realization that it was these daily-bread gentlemen who wrung the neck of the radio and TV industry back in those blacklist days. Also perhaps I am just a snob, and cannot rid myself of the belief that Lorenzo de Medici (one of the least admirable characters in history) was a more effective patron of the arts than most budget directors of big commercial advertising.

But I wish you didn't have to make this bargain for your life. I wish you'd go out to somewhere like Tiffin, Ohio, to a new repertory company. Yes, I know the drawbacks to that also—an audience that doesn't want to see what you want to do; the inevitable subsidy, a lot of it probably coming from the same ultimate sources as your television sponsorships. Also, of course, your agent will oppose you. There was a time when the theatre could operate without agents; it was small enough for managers to know who the actors were. Not any more. Your agent will want you to go where the money lies. (I once wrote to mine: "It is very uphill work, being your client.") There are few who will care more about your turning yourself into an actress. Agents must bear a very heavy responsibility for deflecting young talent like yours in the wrong direction for the sake of the quick return, and starving the young theatres—especially those outside New York—of the personnel they need and must have. Find, if you can, the Exceptional Agent.

Equity, too, must accept some responsibility for the poor quality of many of the "LORT" theatres—that is, the professional repertory companies outside New York, since it has refused to allow the importation of non-American actors trained in the classic tradition, who can serve as exemplars of it, even if they are not themselves star names. It is much easier for Stratford, Ontario, to recruit a good company than it is for Stratford, Connecticut. One is free, the other isn't. The best performances in Connecticut usually come from a few of the older, trained generation; an occasional American-to-be Englishman, and Canadian importations. You will not see very much there from which you can learn the particular skills you need. British Equity will be equally culpable if it cuts off the new ideas and techniques which demand the American actors who evolved them, bringing new blood to an old culture. The economic benefits are short-term; the theatre philosophy narrowing and destructive.

I wish I could discern for you a career, a continuing, life career, amid all the available liveliness. You can't, you know, prance about in Dionysiac improvisations when you get to be forty—fifty—sixty. Nor will you then discover that you are suddenly able to play the great plays where there are great parts for you (not so many for you, as a woman, poor Miss Worthington; far more for your brother). To learn how to act this sort of thing takes time, purpose, practice, assiduity. Actors of your generation are far better physically trained than we were; they are marvelously athletic and gymnastic—as they should be. The "Method," American-style, now in decline, has left a valuable psychological legacy in its search for truth.

What no one seems to know how to teach or to learn is the power and proper use of language, the only lasting essence of enduring theatre. Peter Brook, for the Royal Shakespeare Company, has recently done a *Midsummer Night's Dream* which was just about as unorthodox, as acrobatic, as "far-out" as you could get; but it was also spoken with veracity, penetration and beauty. For this reason it became a great and memorable production, one of the Ibsen sort "for ever swinging free on beauty's vine," for ever alive in memory. If your generation can accomplish things like that, your mother's prohibition about going on the stage becomes ridiculous.

Do not think, however, that all this about classical acting and classical training has no application to the interpretation of modern plays. Last season on Broadway John Gielgud and Ralph Richardson, both in their sixties, garnered all the acting laurels that were around—they had already scooped up the London ones. They were not athletic at all. They hardly moved; but their art was compared to great music, great painting, moving and timeless. The play was not by Shakespeare; it was a contemporary piece about two old men in an insane asylum. But the training behind their achievement was the training of classic actors. Their means of communication was the voice and the words.

You young actors nowadays are having more fun than we used to have, "doing your own thing." But, you see, I don't believe the theatre *is* doing your own thing; on the contrary, it is doing someone else's thing. An actor—and, even more, a director—is a medium, an interpreter, a channel of communication. The last person who matters is himself. He is something through which people can see other people. There is an old saying to the effect that you never grow up until your mirrors turn into windows. Neither the actor nor, God save us! the director, should be holding up mirrors for his own pleasure. They should be making other things visible.

This demands first, of course, the visionary and daring spirit, the probing mind, the heart wide open and receiving—aware of the poet's deepest spring of feeling and of every audience nerve. Second, it demands the instrument—the voice, the voice; a most beautiful instrument, capable of as much music and of a far wider and more subtle intellectual range than any brass or reed or string, more flexible in speech than in song, more persuasive and compelling.

The words—the word made flesh—this is what the theatre is for. If I have seemed in this book to underrate the playwright because so much of my directorial career has lain—as Bernard Shaw remarked —with dead ones, that is merely happpenstance. I do not undervalue the words that are put on paper by Williams and Miller and Albee and Pinter and Beckett and other younger still crescent lights. They are the heart of the matter, the only thing which will survive and record and tell the future the message of our time. You, dear Miss Worthington, should you become an actress, will be there to bring the words alive.

Barbarians have swept down through the ages on all civilizations, wielding fire and sword and saying "Ugh—Ugh," in tones of terrible ferocity. They destroyed cities and monuments and works of art and miracles of engineering; but they knew that in order to conquer they had to destroy language; and that was much harder. Occasionally they did it, but not often. Language is the hardest thing of all to annihilate from without. But it can be destroyed from within, and there is a host of barbarians in our midst busily destroying it. I cannot hope to make it clear to my local telephone company that it simply must not announce, as it did in my local paper today, that there is to be a "power outage" tomorrow. But you, the theatre people, will be the guardians of language. You must speak it; otherwise, why should any dramatist bother to write it?

And you haven't, most of you, the ghost of a notion as to how. Did you ever hear Charles Laughton's readings? or see him in the last act of *Major Barbara?* No, you are too young. He was rough, uncouth, unmusical; but how he charged the words with gunpowder! Have you listened to the finesse of Gielgud's silk-screen speaking? the hair-line gradations of pitch and tempo that precisely communicate his sensitive comprehension?

In London, a little while ago, I turned on the television casually, not knowing the program, and, as I walked away, was suddenly transfixed by a great cry of agony—the words, wholly familiar, yet never, ever heard before:

> *A heavy weight of hours has chained and bow'd*
> *One too, like thee—tameless, and swift, and proud . . .*
>
> > *. . . Be thou, Spirit fierce,*
> > *My spirit! Be thou me, impetuous one!*
>
> *Drive my dead thoughts over the universe,*
> *Like wither'd leaves, to quicken a new birth!*
> *And, by the incantation of this verse,*
>
> *Scatter, as from an unextinguish'd hearth*
> *Ashes and sparks, my words among mankind!*

And then came a soaring paean that lifted me like wings:

> *Be through my lips to unawaken'd earth*
>
> *The trumpet of a prophecy! O wind,*
> *If Winter comes, can Spring be far behind?*

I hadn't turned round, I couldn't have moved; but I did then, knowing, of course, what I should see—an old lady of eighty-eight with an ivory face and blazing eyes sitting in front of a microphone —Sybil Thorndike: a great champion of humanity, a woman who had known both triumph and agony, who was probably, even at that moment, "chained and bow'd" by the pain that seldom left her; and moreover an actress who even now, in her ninetieth year, does vocal exercises every morning.

Perhaps, dear Miss Worthington, you will never be able to sweep people clear off their feet with Shelley and his Western Wind, lines so overquoted and reluctantly studied that every schoolboy skips past them as a flaccid cliché. That will depend on what you become as a person, as well as an actress. But if you decide for the theatre, you must know that it can be done, *if* you learn to honor the word, to penetrate the image, to make it alive. If you think, for instance, that *Othello* is relevant to our time, you are right; but if you suppose that Shakespeare knew anything about the social and economic problems of black Americans in the Nineteen-Seventies, or had any direct comments to make on them, if you try to force the play to be about the ghetto, you will make nonsense of it and yourself. Shakespeare is relevant because his people live and know the essence of suffering and express it.

Do you remember Othello's lines in the last scene, when he is groping for some terms of torture commensurate with the crime he finds he has committed?

> *Blow me about in winds! roast me in sulphur!*
> *Wash me in steep-down gulfs of liquid fire!*

Images—impossible images of agony . . . ? No. We have invented and used napalm. We have dropped an atom bomb on Hiroshima. We have translated them into literal fact. We have preserved their relevance.

You cannot do the great plays without a profound imagination and understanding, going far beyond political convictions, however sincerely felt and held. Recently the Yale Drama School Company did a production of Ibsen's *When We Dead Awaken*—a most laudable undertaking, since it is a play which no professional theatre in the country will touch. But the results seem to have been meaningless to most people. Why? Because the author was a poet in his seventies who had explored the heights and depths of human experience and emerged as a very difficult old man, twelve feet tall, whose work demands directors and actors who, along with an unremitting excitement about the human condition, are also the masters of trained, disciplined and perfected instruments. The first can be found among "amateur" actors on all levels; the second is rare indeed.

A budding soprano knows perfectly well that she must learn to take a pianissimo high C; a ballet dancer that he must execute an entrechat-six; a sculptor must handle a chisel so delicately that he can shave away the merest filigree-flake of stone. An actor must know that his disciplines are just as demanding, if he is to take an audience with him on his journeys into the far countries of the human spirit.

But. Yes, but. To reach this perfection he must have the opportunity to work at it—to practice—to do it—and to do it complete with audience (let us not forget this totally essential factor)—constantly, unrestingly, unrustingly. Anything else may be fun—therapy

—a release—even a social service of considerable value and significance; but not and never a great art.

And where is he to do this? How? To whom? Where is he to live? How does he pay for the supermarket bills, the rent, his children's education? I don't know. That, of course, is the reason why Mrs. Worthington does not want to put her daughter on the stage. That is the problem you have to face.

I was luckier. I have been able to do what I wanted to do, what I also thought of as "service," to devote my life to doing it as well as I knew how, to enjoy it—and to earn my living; a rare and quite staggering gift of fortune—or of God. I cannot wish you better than that. Perhaps you may never feel that you have reached the height Ibsen described—"to live in memory . . . to rest in people's minds free of the mildew and rust of age." Such a thing is not often granted. But if you can travel even my sort of road, if you can make yourself a skilled artisan and an average artist, proud of your craft, and willing to use it for affirmation and not just for vanity, go ahead. Say "yes" now, and "thank you" at the end. Good luck.

MARGARET WEBSTER

Gay Head, Massachusetts
December 1971

Index

A NOTE ON THE TYPE

The text of this book was set in Garamond, a modern rendering of the type first cut in the sixteenth century by Claude Garamond (1510–1561). He was a pupil of Geoffroy Tory and is believed to have based his letters on the Venetian models, although he introduced a number of important differences, and it is to him we owe the type which we know as Old Style. He gave to his letters a certain elegance and a feeling of movement which won for their creator an immediate reputation and the patronage of the French King Francis I.

This book was composed, printed, and bound by Kingsport Press, Inc., Kingsport, Tennessee.